Changing Tracks

CHANGING TRACKS

PREDATORS AND POLITICS IN
MT. McKINLEY NATIONAL PARK

TIMOTHY RAWSON

University of Alaska Press
Fairbanks

Library of Congress Cataloging-in-Publication Data

Rawson, Timothy.
      Changing tracks : predators and politics in Mt. McKinley National Park / Timothy Rawson.
         p. cm.
      Originally presented as the author's thesis (M.A.)--University of Alaska, Fairbanks.
      Includes bibliographical references (p.).
      ISBN 1-889963-52-6 (alk. paper) -- ISBN 1-889963-17-8 (pbk. : alk. paper)
       1. Wolves--Alaska--Denali National Park and Preserve--History. 2. Wildlife management-
      -Government policy--Alaska--Denali National Park and Preserve--History.
      I. Title

QL737.C22 R39 2001
333.95'9773'097983--dc21   2001027190

© 2001 by the University of Alaska Press
All rights reserved. First printing.
International Standard Book Number: cloth, 1-889963-52-6
                                      paper, 1-889963-17-8
Library of Congress Catalog Number: 2001027190

Printed in the United States of America by Thomson-Shore, Inc.
This publication was printed on acid-free paper that meets the minimum requirements for
the American National Standard for Information Science—Permanence of Paper for Printed
Library Materials ANSI Z39.48-1984.

Publication coordination and production by Pamela Odom, University of Alaska Press.
Cover design by Dixon Jones, IMPACT/Graphics, Rasmuson Library, University of Alaska
Fairbanks.
Text design by Deirdre Helfferich, University of Alaska Press.
The text of this book was set in Adobe Garamond. The display font, used in the chapter
titles and running heads, is Skia, from Apple Computer, Inc.

Cover and title page: The cover is adapted from photographs courtesy of the Adolph Murie
Collection, Alaska and Polar Regions Archives, Rasmuson Library, University of Alaska
Fairbanks, reprinted by permission. The title page is also courtesy of the Adolph Murie
Collection, Alaska and Polar Regions Archives, Rasmuson Library, University of Alaska
Fairbanks, reprinted by permission.

For my mother

Contents

Illustrations

Acknowledgements

Many thanks to the people at the libraries and archives used in researching this book. Gretchen Lake and her staff provided consistently patient assistance at the Alaska and Polar Regions Department, Rasmuson Library, University of Alaska Fairbanks. In Juneau, Dean Dawson and Al Minnick guided me through the pertinent holdings of the Alaska State Archives. I was fortunate to receive a research grant from the American Heritage Center at the University of Wyoming, where Rick Ewig and Lori Olson proved good hosts. Robert Bates, esteemed mountaineer and author, forwarded my query on Belmore Browne to the Dartmouth College Library, where Philip Crononwelt, curator of manuscripts, made sure I received photocopies of relevant materials from the Browne Collection. I found materials at the National Archives with the kind help of R. Bruce Parham, assistant director of the Alaska Regions office in Anchorage, and the staff at the National Archives in Washington, D.C.

The National Park Service provided support and assistance as I researched this question of its background. At the Regional Office in Anchorage, Sandra Anderson, senior historian, provided initial enthusiasm for this project, and Frank Norris, regional historian, graciously read initial drafts and gave me valuable responses. Jennifer Wolk and Cindy Alvidre-Lattin aided me in finding obscure files and materials at Denali National Park and Preserve headquarters.

Louise Murie MacLeod was very gracious in consenting to be interviewed, and Jan Murie has consistently offered support.

I originally wrote this as my M.A. thesis at the University of Alaska Fairbanks. Thanks go to my graduate advisory committee: Karen Erickson, Colin Read, and especially to my friend and mentor Terrence Cole, who urged me to be ambitious. Judith Kleinfeld, director of the Northern Studies Progam, contributed her staunch support; Stephen MacLean, professor in the Biology/ Wildlife Department, provided a keen ecologist's perspective and many helpful comments.

I also appreciate the faith and effort shown by staff of the University of Alaska Press, and comments of the three reviewers. During my studies at the University of Oregon, Richard Maxwell Brown and Jeffrey Ostler encouraged me to continue with this project in the midst of other academic obligations. Jim Ducker, editor of *Alaska History*, assisted with finding photographs; a large part of this book's chapter eight appeared earlier in that journal, and is reprinted here with permission.

Friends provided lodging and hospitality during my travels: Katherine Bellows, Freddy Lafarga, Stephanie Kessler, and Jim and Char Mansfield. Gary Goldstein offered consistent moral support, and Paul Dry helped in more ways than he knows. Bruce Hampton's expertise and friendship has made this project a pleasure.

Most important, I could not have completed this project without the support of my wife, Alison Cojocar.

To all, many thanks.

Chronology of the McKinley Park Wolf-Sheep Controversy

1917   Congress establishes Mount McKinley National Park as a "game refuge," particularly because of its Dall sheep.

1927–30   First federally organized predator control effort is undertaken in Alaska. National Park Service declines involvement, but rangers continue to shoot park wolves when possible.

1929–32   Winter conditions are severe for two consecutive years; observed sheep mortality and suspected population crash.

1931   Camp Fire Club of America officially queries Park Service about sheep deaths and policy toward wolves.

1935   New Park Service Director Arno Cammerer halts wolf killing as part of "protect all native fauna" policy.

1936   Under pressure, Park Service reverses course and rangers resume killing park wolves.

1939–41   Adolph Murie conducts his research at McKinley Park.

1944   Government Printing Office publishes Murie's *The Wolves of Mount McKinley*; park wildlife largely ignored during the war years.

1945 Territorial Legislature requests federal funds for aerial wolf hunts in park. Adolph Murie returns to survey park wildlife. He finds sheep numbers down, and recommends killing ten to fifteen wolves.

1946 Congressional hearings on legislation to mandate park wolf control.

1948 Bipartisan fact-finding team visits park and recommends unlimited wolf control, which Park Service accepts. Congress appropriates $104,000 for federal predator control in Alaska.

1952 Sheep population shows signs of increase; wolf numbers stable to declining.

1954 Wolf killing in park officially ceases.

Changing Tracks

Introduction

An entire generation of Americans has grown up with an unprecedented regard for wolves. In the human mind, wolves have always been more than just another animal; they have served as potent symbols, and our appropriations of their image have spanned the gamut of emotions, from fear and loathing to totemization. Our fascination with wolves reflects our fascination with the wild, in all its ambiguities. Although most people have never seen a wild wolf, reproductions of wolves stare at us through the whole range of visual media: computer screen savers, greeting cards and calendars, limited edition porcelain plates, T-shirts, and objects in the toniest art galleries. Authors have also found wolves to be a rich subject; since 1978, with the publication of Barry Holstun Lopez's critically acclaimed *Of Wolves and Men*, no less than thirty adult nonfiction books for the general reading public have appeared, most after 1990.[1]

So why another book on wolves—why this book?

My interest in this topic was sparked by the furor that erupted in 1992–93 over a proposed wolf management scheme in Alaska. A statewide commission of citizens, biologists, and state wildlife managers had derived a plan that included curbing wolf numbers in several game management areas. Not coincidentally, these were popular hunting areas for residents of Fairbanks and Anchorage where caribou and moose populations had declined. Opposition to the plan emerged quickly and loudly, particularly

Mt. McKinley.
Adolph Murie Collection, temp box 13. Courtesy Alaska and Polar Regions Archives, Rasmuson Library, University of Alaska Fairbanks.

from non-Alaskans, and various interest groups urged a tourist boycott, threatening a major sector of the state's economy. This caused me to wonder when, exactly, had wolves become contentious? For most of our country's history, there was agreement about wolves: they had no place in proximity to humans. When had Americans begun arguing about the fate of wolves? And why? I soon realized the answer lay in Alaska, in what became known as the "wolf-sheep controversy" in Mount McKinley National Park. (In 1980 the park was enlarged and renamed Denali National Park and Preserve. To avoid confusion with period sources, I have used its earlier name.)[2] My investigation became a master's thesis at the University of Alaska Fairbanks and continued to become this study.

At its surface, the wolf-sheep controversy seemed a struggle in defining the purpose of wildlife management in national parks. Were parks to be a type of open-air zoo with assemblages of visible animals deemed gratifying to the expectations of visitors, or were they to be places where all the animals native to the area could live with minimal human interference? A recent examination of this by Park Service historian Richard Sellars, *Preserving Nature in the National Parks: A History* (1997) provides an excellent overview of this question, and makes a good companion to my focused work on national park history. Until the 1930s, the large predators in parks—wolves, coyotes, cougars—had been managed by elimination. A handful of men in the National Park Service proposed that wolves should be protected, a bold and heretical stance they justified by asserting that predators were part of a presumptive "balance of nature" and that the Park Service's ideal should be to preserve that balance. By the time this argument gained momentum wolves were found only in Alaska's Katmai and McKinley national parks, and only McKinley had the right combination of factors—name recognition, purpose as a park, concerned individuals and groups, relative ease of access, and visitation—to make it the scene for the nation's first encounter with protection rather than persecution of wolves. But to do so required that the Park Service change tracks. It is to the agency's credit that its changes, however halting, preceded those of the broader society.

Beneath the surface, the controversy in the 1930s and 40s emerged from a clash between negative attitudes toward wolves rooted in long-standing traditions and economic rationales, and modern ideas emerging from scientific models of nature. The wolf celebrated by so many in the final quarter of this century is a recent invention, dependent on time, place, and culture. Because wolf predation affects so few people's livelihoods, it allows others to find new virtues in wolves. Scientific theories based on ecological principles helped define the wolf anew, and this too is a tale of the twentieth century. Overlying these attitudinal changes was the Park Service's wavering direction in defining park resource management policies. National parks became places to experiment with the balance of nature, and the Park Service became the agency to experiment with making predators palatable to a skeptical public. The wolf-sheep controversy helped pave the way for the recent rehabilitation of the wolf's reputation across much of American society, as well as for the current reintroduction of wolves into former ranges.

Another reason for this book is that the story of wolves and people in Mt. McKinley National Park has not been previously told in full, and should

Dall sheep in McKinley National Park.
Adolph Murie Collection, temp box 13. Courtesy Alaska and Polar Regions Archives, Rasmuson Library, University of Alaska Fairbanks

the reader be interested in animals, Alaska, or national parks, it is an intrinsically interesting story. I have taken more of a narrative than an interpretive approach. There are profound intellectual issues contained within this tale—such things as cultural definitions and boundaries of nature, psychological theories on human relations with other species, and ecological questions about predator-prey interactions—which are but briefly included; the footnotes will direct readers toward relevant scholarship. The wolf-sheep controversy has been recognized by other scholars, but is typically told in a brief fashion. The sheep population of McKinley Park suffered a sharp decline in the 1930s, and some people blamed wolves. To protect its animal assets, the National Park Service dispatched one of its biologists, Adolph Murie, to study the situation in 1939. He completed the first research-based study of wolf ecology, which demonstrated that wolves fed on feeble and diseased prey. Although some people disagreed, the Park Service stood firm in its desire to protect wolves and sheep. The animals lived happily ever after, and wolves became interesting. While Murie's study is central to the story, there is much interest before and after.

This book, then, is an expansion of the brief accounts that exist.[3] The wolf-sheep controversy did not end until 1954, when the Park Service finally ceased killing wolves in McKinley Park. Its beginnings are less definite. It could start with the Park Service predator policies in the 1930s, or with the creation of McKinley Park in 1917, or with the scientific definition of the northern white mountain sheep in the 1870s. But these are timid jumps backward, and I think we need to retreat to the beginnings of livestock domestication to find the roots of the wolf-sheep controversy. This is the starting point in chapter one, which moves on quickly through discussions of wolves, sportsmen, and the establishment of McKinley Park.

The second and third chapters develop a number of background issues necessary for understanding the controversy. Chapter two examines predator policy within two diverging federal agencies, the Bureau of Biological Survey and the National Park Service. These agencies had cooperated in killing undesired park animals, but in the 1920s scientists began proposing alternate views on the role of wildlife in parks. This included recognition of possible benefits of predators, a cause championed by a particular dissenting group within the Park Service. Chapter three establishes the Alaska context for the controversy, examining the relationships between residents and animals, particularly during the 1930s, and explores why Alaskans found any protective feelings toward wolves in McKinley Park unfathomable.

The wolf-sheep controversy takes shape in chapter four, as increased sheep mortality attracts the attention of an East Coast sportsmen's group, the Camp Fire Club of America. Its answer was simple and customary—kill wolves—but it ran up against a new park policy counter to this approach. This was the nub of the conflict over park wildlife management. Alaskans also thought the territory needed fewer wolves, and certainly none in a game refuge. The Park Service retracted its protection of McKinley Park's wolves, but also invoked scientific management in the form of biologist Adolph Murie. Chapter five details his career and predator studies through his two-year effort in McKinley Park.

The Second World War interrupted the controversy and the wolf studies, but also laid the grounds for the argument's resumption. Chapter six discusses Adolph Murie's return to the park in 1945, where he found that more wolf killing was in order, but not for wholly scientific reasons. The Camp Fire Club tried another tactic by attempting to resolve the question legislatively, the focus of chapter seven. The Park Service deflected this, but still needed to take action. Chapter eight details the visit of a bipartisan team invited by the Park Service to make management recommendations. This ended in apparent victory for the Camp Fire Club, as in 1948 the Park Service director ordered that wolves would be killed indefinitely. The controversy ends with the cessation of wolf control in 1954, and the reasons for this.

The ninth chapter summarizes the meaning of the wolf-sheep controversy in conservation history, the limitations of science in park management, and the deceptive usefulness of the balance of nature. The narrative continues in the aftermath of the controversy and what it meant for subsequent changes in attitudes toward wolves and wolf management controversies.

Differences of opinion and conflicts over wolf management are still very much alive in Alaska, though the conflicts now include wolves outside Alaska's national parks. The recent reintroduction of wolves in Idaho and Yellowstone culminated years of contention, with continued vigorous opposition. As before in Alaska, the ecological issues have held less importance than public perception. Reams of scientific research and expanded knowledge of predator-prey interactions have not altered the fundamental questions: how do we value animals, and how shall we coexist? The wolf-sheep controversy in McKinley Park was the first national argument over wolves and marked a turning point in our attitude toward them.

Notes

1   In chronological order: Barry Holstun Lopez, *Of Wolves and Men* (New York: Charles Scribner's Sons, 1978); Durward Allen, *Wolves of Minong: Their Vital Role in a Wild Community* (Boston: Houghton Mifflin Co., 1979); R. D. Lawrence, *Secret Go the Wolves* (New York: Holt, Rinehart, and Winston, 1980); Erik Zimen, *The Wolf: A Species in Danger,* translated by Eric Mosbacher (New York: Delacorte Press, 1981; Munich: Meyster Verlag GmbH, 1978); David E. Brown, ed., *The Wolf in the Southwest: The Making of an Endangered Species* (Tucson: University of Arizona Press, 1983); Roger Peters, *The Dance of the Wolves* (New York: McGraw-

Hill, 1985); R. D. Lawrence, *In Praise of Wolves* (New York: Henry Holt, 1986); Candace Savage, *Wolves* (San Francisco: Sierra Club Books, 1988); James C. Burbank, *Vanishing Lobo: The Mexican Wolf and the Southwest* (Boulder: Johnson Books, 1990); L. David Mech, *The Way of the Wolf* (Stillwater, MN: Voyageur Press, 1991); Rick Bass, *The Ninemile Wolves* (Livingston, MT: Clark City Press, 1992); L. David Mech, *Wolves of the High Arctic* (Stillwater, MN: Voyageur Press, 1992); Jim Brandenburg, *Brother Wolf* (Minocqua, WI: NorthWord Press, 1993); Steve Grooms, *The Return of the Wolf* (Minocqua, WI: NorthWord Press, 1993); Rick McIntyre, *A Society of Wolves: National Parks and the Battle Over the Wolf* (Stillwater, Minn.: Voyageur Press, 1993); John A. Murray, ed., *Out Among the Wolves: Contemporary Writings on the Wolf* (Anchorage: Alaska Northwest Books, 1993); Richard P. Thiel, *The Timber Wolf in Wisconsin: The Death and Life of a Majestic Predator* (Madison: University of Wisconsin Press, 1993); Erwin A. Bauer, *Wild Dogs: The Wolves, Coyotes, and Foxes of North America* (San Francisco: Chronicle Books, 1994); Robert H. Busch, ed., *Wolf Songs: The Classic Collection of Writing about Wolves* (San Francisco: Sierra Club Books, 1994); Mike Link and Kate Crowley, *Following the Pack: The World of Wolf Research* (Stillwater, MN: Voyageur Press, 1994); Robert H. Busch, *The Wolf Almanac: A Celebration of Wolves and Their World* (New York: Lyons & Burford, 1995); Hank Fischer, *Wolf Wars: The Remarkable Inside Story of the Restoration of Wolves to Yellowstone.* (Helena, MT: Falcon Press, 1995); Rick McIntyre, ed., *War Against the Wolf: America's Campaign to Exterminate the Wolf* (Stillwater, Minnesota: Voyageur Press, 1995); Rolf O. Peterson, *The Wolves of Isle Royale: A Broken Balance* (Minocqua, WI: Willow Creek Press, 1995); Peter Steinhart, *The Company of Wolves* (New York: Alfred A. Knopf, 1995); Art Wolfe, *In the Presence of Wolves* (New York: Crown, 1995); Jay Robert Elhard, *Wolf Tourist: One Summer in the West* (Logan, UT: Utah State University Press, 1996); Ken L. Jenkins, *Wolf Reflections* (Merrillville, IN: ICS Books, 1996); Michael K. Phillips and Douglas H. Smith, *The Wolves of Yellowstone* (Stillwater, MN: Voyageur Press, 1996); Bruce Hampton, *The Great American Wolf* (New York: Henry Holt, 1997); R. D. Lawrence, *Trail of the Wolf* (Buffalo, NY: Firefly Books, 1997); Thomas McNamee, *The Return of the Wolf to Yellowstone* (New York: Henry Holt, 1997); L. David Mech, *The Arctic Wolf: Ten Years with the Pack* (Stillwater, MN: Voyageur Press, 1997, rev. ed.).

2   Denali—"Great One"—is a traditional Alaska Native name for the mountain and is preferred by Alaskans. In 1896 Republican gold prospectors fired with election-year enthusiasm attached William McKinley's name. Mount McKinley remains the official name of the peak. Attempts to change the name to Denali have been thwarted by the intransigence of Ohio's congressmen unwilling to diminish the memory of a president from their state.

3   Some of the sources that include reference to the wolf-sheep controversy include: James B. Trefethen, *Crusade for Wildlife: Highlights in Conservation Progress* (Harrisburg, PA: Stackpole, 1961), 300-2; Durward L. Allen, *Our Wildlife Legacy*, rev. ed. (New York: Funk & Wagnalls, 1962), 242-45; William E. Brown, A *History*

of the Denali—Mt. McKinley Region, Alaska (Washington, D.C.: GPO, National Park Service, 1991), 196-200; R. Gerald Wright, *Wildlife Research and Management in the National Parks* (Urbana: University of Illinois Press, 1992), 65-66; John A. Murray, ed., *Out Among the Wolves: Contemporary Writings on the Wolf* (Anchorage: Alaska Northwest Books, 1993), 213, 231; Peter Steinhart, *The Company of Wolves* (New York: Alfred A. Knopf, 1995), 56-57; Rick McIntyre, *A Society of Wolves: National Parks and the Battle Over the Wolf* (Stillwater, MN: Voyageur Press, rev. ed., 1996) 12-13, 90; Bruce Hampton, *The Great American Wolf* (New York: Henry Holt, 1997), 154-59; Richard West Sellars, *Preserving Nature in the National Parks: A History* (New Haven: Yale University Press, 1997), 158-60.

Unless a refuge is set aside…
—Belmore Browne

1

Sheep, Sportsmen, and Mount McKinley National Park

Relations between people and wolves go back to the dawn of human consciousness, but the dynamic has undergone three significant shifts. The first occurred approximately twelve thousand years ago when people domesticated willing wolves, producing dogs. The second began several thousand years later when people domesticated sheep and goats, followed by the other livestock animals. The third shift occurred in this century, as people no longer dependent on livestock redefined our perceptions of wolves. This book concerns this latter change and understanding its origins and implications requires examining some prior history. It might seem odd to begin a book on wild animals in a national park by discussing domestic mammals, but the definition of wild animals was a result of domesticating others. Once people began keeping livestock, predators became a threat to property; wolves became fierce and feared, while attitudes toward the ancestors of livestock became increasingly protective. America's first wolf controversy did not emerge because thoughtless men sought to extirpate the wolves of Mount McKinley National Park: they sought to safeguard wild sheep from mortal threats that included predators, but in so doing encountered the harbingers of the third shift in our regard for wolves.

Globally, members of the family Canidae—dingo, jackal, fox, coyote, African wild dogs, and wolf—were second only to humans as successful large mammals, if success is measured by adaptability and dispersal. Include dogs, and they are our equal. Dogs began as wolves; behaviors are similar, and chromosomal studies have confirmed the linkage. Coyotes, too, are interfertile with them, blurring species differentiation and genetic history. The wolf, *Canis lupus*, is an animal of the Northern Hemisphere. Its various subspecies once were found from the Arctic Ocean coasts to the deserts of Arabia and subcontinent of India. Its ecological niche, or role, is to prey upon other large mammals. Wolves will eat carrion if available, making them susceptible to poisoning; they will drive other animals, such as grizzly bears, away from food sources; they will eat virtually anything that moves, from flightless ducks taken from their nests to domestic dogs. They may eat each other, if one is wounded, trapped, or dying, especially if from a different pack; but their physical and social structures have evolved for the pursuit, capture, and digestion of large prey. The most important prey species are caribou, moose, elk, deer, mountain sheep, beaver, and in the absence of those, hares and rabbits. To be successful— to live long and breed often—a predator must gain more calories from its prey than it expends pursuing it, which means that wolves will kill the most readily available individual of a prey population. A modern misconception concerning wolves is that they prey only on the sick, diseased, inferior, young or old animals. While these may be the easiest animals to catch, and thus constitute the bulk of the kills, wolves are capable of killing healthy adults of any prey species, though hardly with the effectiveness of legend.[1]

Wolves have roamed the Northern Hemisphere far longer than humans; the genus *Canis* was evident during the Pliocene epoch five million years ago. They are part of the Holarctic fauna, the assemblage of northern animals that spread across Eurasia and North America during the millennia of Ice Ages and shifting continental connections. Early humans moving north into Eurasia met wolves about 1.5 million years ago at the start of the Pleistocene epoch, the last period of great continental glaciation, a time in which the climate favored the evolution of large herbivores in the steppes and grasslands. This environment precluded the omnivory possible in the tropics; to survive, humans had to hunt, just like wolves, and compete for similar prey. In a provocative line of thought, some scholars argue that early hominids became modern humans precisely because of this contact with wolves in a cold climate. This argument rejects that our social evolution is best understood by examining primate behavior, instead pointing toward the similarities between wolves and early hunters. Wolves live in small social groups that recognize hierarchy, cooperate in hunting and raising young, and roam a recognized territory from a fixed home site; they communicate with one another through behavioral rituals and vocalizations, and strategize hunting opportunities. Did watching these social predators help humans learn more than hunting tactics? That might strain our credulity, but regardless, the history of wolves and humans is an intimate one.[2]

Wolves no doubt watched the first humans arriving in North America, and during the next few millennia the two species developed shared dominance at the top of the food chain. The Pleistocene landscape hosted numerous and diverse large mammals, and as ocean levels fell and rose with the surge and retreat of continental glaciers, these mammals dispersed to adjacent land masses. North America's connection to Eurasia came via the wind-swept grasslands of the Beringian steppe, a broad plain that appeared during periods of glacial advance. Horses and camels made their way west, while from Eurasia came beaver, caribou, bison, sheep and wolves, among others. Beringia included what is now interior Alaska, a cold but not forbidding place that had dry summers and light winter snowfalls, because the six hundred-mile-long Alaska Range blocked the moisture-laden weather systems that swept up from the south. While glaciers buried southcentral Alaska, grasslands to the north supported mammoths, steppe bison, ground sloths, camels, and horses, who in turn fed the carnivores: saber-toothed cats, short-faced bears, and the dire wolf. Almost all of these Pleistocene megafauna were larger than their extant related species. Biologist Valerius Geist wondered if these large predators inhibited the dispersal of humans into North America. Geist observed the correlation between the period of megafaunal extinction that began about 20,000 B.P. (before the present) and the subsequent spread of humans across the continent. Perhaps the big bears and dire wolves had to die off before people could expand their range from the coastal fringes. The reasons for the extinctions certainly include climatic changes as the final Ice Age ended, and hunting by humans may have had a significant impact. Regardless, the consequences for people and wolves were the same: the land warmed, the largest mammals died out, leaving the familiar forms of today—moose, caribou, bison, bighorn sheep—which people and wolves could hunt effectively.[3]

The end of the Ice Age brought about the first shift in relations between people and wolves, as dogs made their appearance in the archaeological record. The process of domestication occurred with wolves because of shared attributes of sociability and hierarchy, which is why other canids did not succeed as domesticates. We can assume that taming various wild animals occurred with some frequency, a common practice among people the world over, and one generally ascribed to women and children. Tamed animals are captured when young; domestication occurs as humans begin controlling the feeding and breeding of the animal, particularly for certain traits. In wolves, those traits included the willingness to respond to humans and cooperate in the hunt. Not all tamed wolves would have accepted this, and those that did lived to pass on their traits to offspring. Domestication produced morphological changes; in dogs, these appeared first in the skull and dentition, and later in overall size and shape. Selected behavioral and physical traits represented a process known as neoteny, the arrested development and retention of juvenile characteristics. Evidence of dogs appears in Eurasia in many places and in sites dated from twelve to ten thousand years ago. Why this occurred is unknown, though common explanations invoke wolf domestication as part of the adaptive processes of hunter-gatherers to the post-Ice Age environment. Presumably the groups of migrants from Siberia to North America brought dogs with them. Dogs provided companionship, complementary hunting skills, protective reactions, meat and pelts, and haulage of goods. While this has long been viewed as the first human triumph over the animal world that eventually led toward civilization, a coevolutionary perspective urges consideration that wolves selected humans as a survival strategy as much as we selected them. The dog, *Canis lupus familiaris*, is but the juvenile wolf in our household.[4]

The introduction of livestock produced the second shift in relations with wolves, for humans began producing animals much easier to kill than other prey. Sheep and goats, related taxonomically in the tribe Caprini, followed the dog as the next domesticates, but of a considerably different kind; rather than protecting, they needed protection from unplanned mortality in order to provide the consistent availability of food that was one of domestication's great virtues. Exactly how livestock domestication occurred remains speculative, but it is likely that incipient domestication of cereal plants preceded that of grazing animals; perhaps the need to protect crops from wild grazers led to more frequent control over the movements of the animals, who could then be persuaded to remain in the vicinity by gleaning the harvested fields. But why sheep and goats? Hardiness and a willingness to eat a variety of plants helped. Temperament counted for much, as did their social system based on submissiveness to single herd leaders. The world's various deer, gazelles, and antelopes differed in both respects and were never domesticated. Contingency mattered, too, for apparently the right combination of climate, sufficient human population, declining stocks of hunted animals, early agriculture, and an acceptable ancestral sheep, *Ovis orientalis*, and goat, *Capra aegagrus*, occurred only once in the world's history. With the addition of livestock to human life, appreciation for the dog increased as it showed a willingness to defend stock from predators, and any regard for the wolf as a fellow hunter decreased.[5]

As the pastoral economy developed and grew dominant in southwest Asia by 7,000 B.P., the presence of livestock changed just about every part of the lifestyle that had been the lot of humanity for hundreds of generations. Livestock provided incalculable and, presumably, necessary advantages as increasing human populations depleted stocks of wild herbivores. Meat on the hoof needed no curing or storage, animal manure fertilized crops, harvested seeds fed people while inedible stalks fed livestock, and the milk, skins, wool, bones, and horns were readily available for use. Cattle and then horses provided new possibilities for traction and haulage, including a use for the axle and wheel. People began to experiment with new ways of landscape manipulation— fire being an ancient technique—to enhance their food sources, both plant and animal. Changes in social systems resulted from sedentarism: physical territories connected with village grazing herds gained increasing definition as property, while individual social status accrued less from wisdom or ability in the hunt and more to the size of one's flocks. Stratification within communities inevitably resulted, yet with stratification came social organization and the specialization of skills leading toward civilization. Society still valued bravery, but it became increasingly exhibited against one's neighbors rather than against large and dangerous animals.

This was the context in which the Old Testament was recorded, and the Bible offers reminders about how attitudes toward sheep and wolves developed in the Judeo-Christian heritage. Abel, the second son of Eve and Adam, was a keeper of sheep, whose offerings pleased God and aroused the enmity of brother Cain, the tiller of the earth (Genesis 4). Materially, abundant livestock were evidence of God's favor to His faithful. When Job's faith had been tested and found sufficient, God returned first to Job his flocks, beginning with fourteen thousand sheep, and then "also seven sons and three daughters" (Job 42:12–13). Symbolically, sheep became a metaphor for the relationship to God. The Psalmist gave praise from "we thy people and sheep of thy pasture" (Psalms 79:13), and for the prophet Isaiah the Israelites "like sheep have gone astray" (Isaiah 53:6). The life of Jesus resolved this metaphorical relationship, coming both for our sakes to be sacrificed as the Lamb of God (John 1:29, 36) and acting on our behalf as the Good Shepherd (John 10). The wolf appears far less frequently in the Bible than the sheep but carries similar symbolic potency. Unfaithful leaders of the Israelites were "in the midst of her [Israel] like wolves tearing the prey" (Ezekiel 22:27). Jesus warned his disciples that heathens were like wolves, who would not spare the flock after His departure (Matthew 10:16, Acts 20:29). Most famously, Isaiah foretold that the Messiah must come so that paradise could again be found on earth, where the "wolf also shall dwell with the lamb" (11:6).

The Western religious tradition, which emerged from the pastoral economies of the Middle East, had profound consequences for our attitudes toward animals. Protecting livestock from predation remained important for agricultural economies for centuries, but more than a matter of utility, it became thoroughly imbued with moral overtones. Although the creation story in Genesis did not mention predation, Isaiah's paradisaical vision implied that wild animals became so due to original sin, thus becoming evil incarnate. The Medieval mind associated wolves with the Devil, who dwelt in the wilderness, and the Christian duty was to eliminate both to ensure the safety of livestock and humans. The Puritans departed English shores already cleaned of wolves and perceived themselves spiritually challenged by a New World full of wolves and their counterparts, Native Americans, who the Reverend Increase Mather called "ravening wolves, who lye in wait to shed blood." The son of another minister remarked, "After the redskins the great terror of our lives...was the wolves.... The noise of their howling was enough to curdle the blood of the stoutest... God made them to be hated." The howling wilderness of the American colonies would, in the span of ten generations, be replaced by the placid sounds of livestock herds numerous beyond the imagination of any Judean patriarch.[6]

The second shift of wolf-human relations did not begin in North America until the Spanish introduced their livestock to Mexico, as the Native Americans did not domesticate the sheep of the western regions (or any other mammal except the dog). These American *Ovis* came from the evolutionary center of Old World sheep in central Asia, where various species intergrade into the Siberian mountain sheep that look much like their cousins in Alaska. Sheep, like wolves, are endemic to the Northern Hemisphere; in his 1964 book, James Clark of the American Museum of Natural History described their distribution as "The Great Arc of the Wild Sheep," the genus linking the deserts of southwest Asia with the deserts of North America via the high latitudes of Beringia. Sheep were relative latecomers to the faunal assemblage of North America. Most likely different genetic stocks migrated at different times and over generations moved south along the mountain ranges as glacial conditions permitted; the sheep in Alaska may represent the latest member of the genus. Archaeological evidence from the deserts indicates that humans ate sheep at least 10,000 years ago, and sheep are the most numerous animal depicted in prehistoric rock art.[7]

Westerners had virtually no understanding of mountain sheep until the nineteenth century. Europeans considered the wild mouflon of Corsica and Sicily to be the ancestors of domestic sheep, logically enough, although these sheep are now thought to be feral stocks of the original domesticates. Marco Polo returned from his thirteenth-century travels with reports of great wild sheep living in the ranges of central Asia. These seemed as fanciful as the dragons he described, and not until the 1830s did a British Army officer return with a set of the magnificent horns of *Ovis ammon poli*. Only slightly more was known about sheep in North America. In 1702 Franciscan missionaries in Baja California provided the first good descriptions of borrego cimarrón, the desert bighorn. In 1804 the Royal Society of London provided its imprimatur after examining a specimen shipped back by a North West Fur Company trapper. Honoring its geographical origin, the British labeled the sheep *Ovis canadensis*. Simultaneously, as they worked their way up the Missouri River, Lewis and Clark's expedition encountered bighorns; like everyone else, they commented on the superior gastronomic quality of wild mutton. These sheep were part of a population estimated at two million, but in the following decades sheep numbers declined drastically; like Indians, the sheep died by bullet, loss of habitat, and introduced diseases. The final type of American sheep gained an identity after the purchase of Alaska in 1867. William Dall, a versatile scientist in federal employ, described the thin-horned, white-fleeced sheep of the North, recognizing its similarity to Siberian sheep. Hides and horns of this new animal came back to the National Museum via Edward Nelson, who began his distinguished career working in Alaska for the U.S. Army Signal Corps. Nelson named the sheep *Ovis montana dalli*, subsequently shortened to *O. dalli*. The area in between the Rockies and Yukon Territory also had sheep who appeared intermediary in form, but by the end of the century, the North American sheep had been named and placed in general terms.[8]

This process held greater import than, say, figuring out the distribution of squirrel species, for at the same time as Americans learned about their continent's wild sheep, there emerged a new notion of the hunter, the sportsman. The fox-hunting social aristocrats of the middle and southern American colonies sustained sport hunting's European roots. For different reasons, the Puritans and those who needed meat disdained the sporting practice.[9] Yet before and after the Civil War, writers in northern cities began promoting a sportsmen's code with several constituent parts: a distinction between wildlife harvest for commercial purposes and that for personal recreational fulfillment; the assumption that regulations could help the sustainability of wildlife populations; the need for behavioral mandates, including self-denial and fair practices, which identified one as a gentleman. Anglo upper and middle classes promulgated the code of conservation, endowing it with social and racial prejudices. Sportsmen recognized that hunting was part of the American tradition, yet knew that practices had to change under the pressures of population, settlement, and technology. Thomas Dunlap asserts that this new style of hunting led the way toward preserving wildlife, though only certain species found defenders. Sportsmen organized politically and socially to start the modern conservation movement, although, as historian John Reiger asserts, this has received less recognition than it should. Sport hunters considered the activity important in demonstrating manhood and the virtues that had conquered a continent, virtues thought to be threatened by modernization. Demonstrating these was presumably good for one's character, and undeniably for one's social status, as prestige accrued by pursuing animals more exotic and difficult to obtain than deer or moose. Out west, high in the hills, lived a new game species for American hunters.[10]

Human hunters have always ascribed traits to their prey with reference to themselves, and doing this reflects self-perception. The mountain sheep became, along with bears, the apotheosis of the hunter's skill and bravery. However, unlike bears, sheep represent no threat to humans; in the absence of hunting, sheep are quite friendly, as Valerius Geist discovered during his research in British Columbia.[11] Yet that did not prevent hunters from building an image of sheep hunting that enhanced themselves. A Denver businessman, J. A. McGuire, a veteran of many hunts for grizzlies and bighorns, considered the latter the more dangerous object because of the rugged alpine terrain of the sheep's haunts. That exemplar of his times, Theodore Roosevelt, thought sheep hunting tested "the manliest qualities of a hunter." The hunter needed "great skill and caution…steady head, sound lungs, and trained muscles." While the successful hunter could thus claim those personal attributes, the trophy on the wall also proclaimed to others a social rank, exemplified in the comment of writer Owen Wister:

> The tame sheep is hopelessly bourgeois; but this mountain aristocrat, the frequenter of clean snow and steep rocks and silence, has, even beyond the big bull elk, that same secure,

unconscious air of being not only well bred, but high bred, not only game but fine game, which we still in the twentieth century meet sometimes among men and women.[12]

The exoticism of wild sheep enhanced their value for upper-crust sportsmen, their ability to pursue sheep an example of the "conspicuous consumption" assailed by social critic Thorstein Veblen. But the sheep also held psychosexual implications connected to masculinity. From ancient times the domestic ram was a symbol of virility; the Egyptians often depicted the carnal form of the sun god Amon-Ra as a ram. The large curving horns highlighted the distinction between the sexes, serving to intimidate less endowed rams and displaying vigor for receptive females.[13] In the bighorn sheep, horns allow thunderous assertions of male dominance. To slay a wild ram in a visit to an environment entirely inhospitable to humans indicated one's own vigor. Men made the bighorn sheep into the most desirable North American game trophy because they thought it reflected their own virtues as men at a time when Darwinism supposedly buttressed competitive urges, personal aggressiveness, and social inequalities.

This combined, then, with the long history of humans and domestic sheep to produce distinctive feelings toward the wild sheep. Over the centuries the wildness had been bred out of sheep, making them pliant, dumb, and dependent on the shepherd. The shepherd kept the flock, largely ewes and lambs, safe from harm, most famously from wolves. Transferring this protective obligation from the fold to the field was no great stretch for sportsmen, especially when it seemed so thoroughly imbued with Christian symbolism. That Alaska's Dall sheep were white powerfully added to their symbolic appeal, white representing purity and chastity. Hunting rams was no contradiction; they were, after all, the standard sacrificial offering to the God of the Old Testament. Yet it was important that humans do the killing, not wolves. Western ranchers and miners had already done too much sheep killing; California banned sheep hunting in 1873, Arizona and New Mexico in 1912, and Nevada in 1917. But up north, in Alaska Territory, still lived the mysterious Dall sheep, threatened by unruly men and unholy wolves.

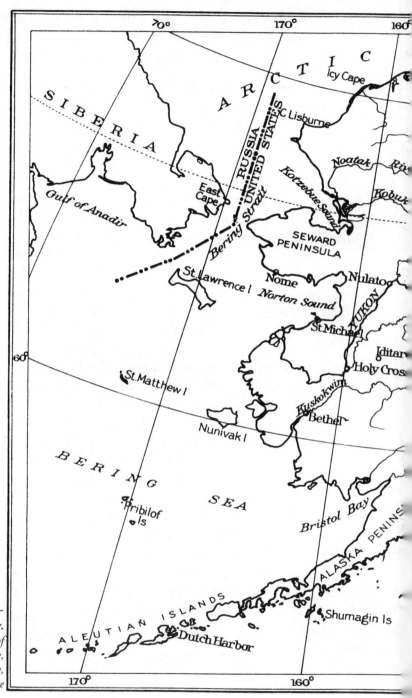

Alaska, mid-
twentieth century.
*Map courtesy of
National Park Service,
Alaska Regional Office,
Anchorage*

39602

The discovery of gold in the Yukon River drainage during the 1890s brought an influx of Europeans and Americans to interior Alaska. Their travel routes avoided the Alaska Range, seeking ingress from the Bering Sea up the Yukon River, or up the coast from Seattle and Vancouver through the fjords and passes that led into the headwaters of the Yukon in Canadian territory. The town of Fairbanks sprang up near the Tanana River in 1903 as a result of nearby gold deposits. Lone prospectors and military surveyors seeking transportation routes and more gold explored the rivers flowing down the north slopes of the Alaska Range. While they found few mineral resources, they did find the area's animals. Americans pushing westward ahead of settlement had long been impressed by the abundance of wildlife. In Alaska, Henry Allen's expedition up the Copper River in 1885, or J. C. Castner's 1898 wanderings in the upper Tanana Valley belied that history, finding the North to be a hungry land. However, experiences of the initial groups traveling the northern slopes of the Alaska Range in the Mount McKinley region were a revival of those enjoyed by explorers in the American West. On assignment with the U.S. Geological Survey, Alfred Hulse Brooks led the first group to traverse these slopes. In 1902 they debarked with their pack horses on the muddy shores of Cook Inlet. Their route ascended the valleys of the Susitna and Skwentna rivers, crossed the Alaska Range, and then headed northeast along the mountains through the broad tundra meadows to the Nenana River, which they took north to the Tanana and the Yukon rivers. The arduous travel through the swamps and forests south of the Alaska Range contrasted with the ease of travel on the drier northern slopes, and they commented that game animals there "were unusually plentiful…. The party was never without fresh meat."[14]

The following year federal Judge James Wickersham and four others attempted the first ascent of Mount McKinley, approaching from Fairbanks after ice left the rivers. Although the formidable defenses of McKinley's north wall—later named after the judge—prevented any significant altitude gain, Wickersham wrote that the "beautiful, rolling grass-lands and moss covered hills" made the area a "hunter's paradise." The year 1903 saw another attempt on Mount McKinley, the first by Frederick Cook. His party repeated the southern approach of the Brooks expedition and became the first to circumnavigate the McKinley massif. As they trekked northeast along the easy hills after failing to climb the mountain, Cook wrote, "Here along the northern slope of the McKinley ground, we crossed the best game country in America."[15]

Reports of the wild sheep of the McKinley area drew Charles Sheldon northward, a man who would turn his obsession with sheep into the establishment of Alaska's first national park. Born in Vermont in 1867, Sheldon was virtually the archetype of his era's sportsmen: family wealth, a boyhood spent fishing and hunting, an enthusiastic amateur naturalist, educated at prep school and Yale, by temperament intellectual yet with the muscular athleticism considered ideal in the complete man. Business contacts led to a position managing the construction of a railroad in Chihuahua, Mexico, where he worked from 1898 to 1902. This offered him a chance to hunt big game, and the desert bighorns captured his interest as he explored the mountain ranges of the Sonora Desert. Shares in the area's richest silver mine allowed Sheldon to retire in 1903, when he was only thirty-five. Seeking to combine science with adventure, he became acquainted with the government's leading naturalists, C. Hart Merriam and Edward Nelson of the U.S. Biological Survey, who were happy to use Sheldon's interest in the rest of the continent's wild sheep. He took several trips between 1904 and 1906 to the Canadian Rockies, the Coast Ranges, Vancouver Island, and distant ranges of Yukon Territory, as well as later forays back into the Sonoran country. Sheldon had little in common with the typical guided hunter and earned commendation the hard way, with a combination of physical prowess, enthusiasm, skills, observational powers, and writing abilities. An excerpt from his 1905 upper Yukon trip is significant on several symbolic levels, and gives an indication of the deep emotional meaning Sheldon found in the sheep.

> Sitting on the rock, I rested and smoked my pipe. Three hard-earned trophies were before me. Under such circumstances, among mountain-crests, when the pulse bounds and the whole being is exhilarated by the vigorous exercise of a dangerous climb and the sustained excitement of the stalk, are attuned to the highest pitch of appreciation of the Alpine panorama, there is no state of exaltation more sublime than that immediately following the climax of a day's successful hunt for the noble mountain ram.[16]

Sheldon hunted for personal reasons, certainly, enjoying the challenges of weather and terrain, the geometries of stalking, and the satisfaction of the well-placed bullet. But he combined these with commendable scientific motives in an era when studying an animal often necessitated shooting it. Zoological societies sponsored many of his trips, particularly the American Museum of Natural History, whose scientists needed hides and bones to study and specimens to display. Vertebrate biology in the early 1900s was not behaviorally or ecologically oriented, but largely taxonomic: the classification of animals by morphological comparisons. Valuable as Sheldon's field notes were, scientists wanted tangible pieces of animals to examine. The national pride of the Gilded Age affected naturalists as well as politicians, and museum directors sought to build their collections of animals from the globe's most distant locales. Although Sheldon loved the activity of hunting, he was far more than a trophy hunter, combining his hunting skills with the aims of science. A gifted writer, he faithfully recorded his observations by candlelight each evening, demonstrating an eye for the variety and minutiae of the natural world as well as the game animals he so patiently stalked. None other than George Bird Grinnell called him "our most famous big-game hunter," significant praise coming from hunting and conservation's most respected authority.[17]

Sheldon first visited the McKinley area in the summer of 1906. In Fairbanks he engaged the services of two packers, including the well-regarded Harry Karstens, who had come north with the gold rush. The men traveled by small boats to the gold mining area of Kantishna, and pushed on with pack horses to the base of Mount McKinley. Alone, Sheldon climbed slopes near the Peters Glacier to 8,900 feet, discovering remnants of both Wickersham's and Cook's expeditions, and sat spellbound as avalanches roared down the mountain's flanks. In search of sheep, the party moved northeast along the natural fault line that separates the high glaciated mountains from the Outer Ranges, a lower belt of treeless hills that gave way to the northward lowland forests. Along their way they shot caribou for camp meat and bears for specimens, and found the sheep that would make the area world famous. As autumn storms turned the hills white, they left the area and Sheldon returned south. His interest had been piqued; recognizing how little was really known of the sheep, he vowed to "return and devote a year to their study."[18]

Harry Karstens again accompanied Sheldon on his return to the sheep ranges. In August 1907 they built a small cabin on the Toklat River, caching provisions and firewood for the winter. While still collecting museum specimens, Sheldon attempted to learn the habits of the sheep and caribou and wrote detailed field notes on mammals and birds of the area. His writings reveal a man in the tradition of Thoreau and Muir. He described the "wild sublimity of the mountains…the haunting mystery and isolation of the deep recesses of the unknown wilderness and…happiness so intense that not even the imagination of a poetic genius could adequately express it." On January 12, 1908, he wrote in his journal thoughts of making this area a national park and game preserve, anticipating the "enjoyment and inspiration visitors will receive." This represented a continuation of ideas discussed with Karstens the previous year, about the "beauties of the country and of the variety of the game and wouldn't it make an ideal park and game preserve…. We would talk over the possible boundaries of a park and preserve which we laid out practically the same as the present park boundaries." After a winter and summer of adventure and hunting, Sheldon was "leaving forever this region…leaving the joys I have tried to describe," but his sorrow was mitigated by his commitment to seeing this area turned into a game preserve.[19]

Charles Sheldon returned from Alaska to New York City in August 1908, the national park idea gestating in his mind. To turn the idea into reality, Sheldon needed allies, men of influence, power, prestige, and similar commitment. He had all of those in his fellow members of the Boone and Crockett Club, where he was chairman of the Game Committee.

The Boone and Crockett Club had its origins in 1887, when 29-year-old Theodore Roosevelt, fresh back from his adventures out west, proposed the formation of an exclusive organization of gentlemen hunters. Hunting clubs had existed in eastern states for decades, but these served largely fraternal and expedient ends. Membership confirmed the desirability of fellow nimrods for their socializing and ensured access to private lands for their shooting. Roosevelt wanted to change such private interests into public ones, and formed an organization of like-minded men who worked politically to promulgate ideas of fair play and legislative protection of animals. The club limited its membership to one hundred regular members, and one of the criteria was that a member had killed at least one species of big game in "fair chase" (later increased to three species). The club's goals were to "promote manly sport with the rifle," to promote exploration, game preservation, natural history knowledge, and to exchange information among members. It was a homogenous group dominated by New Yorkers who were gentlemen of the monied class, educated, and well traveled. The membership was a who's who of political and economic influence.[20]

The Boone and Crockett Club became the first group to address national conservation topics effectively. Even before the McKinley region became an issue, the club had addressed Alaskan concerns, actively supporting congressional protective game bills that passed in 1902 and 1908. Sportsmen had fresh memories of the depletion of western game herds; acting with foresight in the Alaska Territory could prevent a recurrence. Much to the dismay of resident Alaskans, the club successfully established the precedent for federal control of Alaska's game. After Sheldon's address to the annual dinner on January 26, 1909, Boone and Crockett club members enthusiastically endorsed his proposal for a McKinley game reserve, although they decided to wait until the upcoming presidential election before bringing a proposal to Congress.[21]

In the interim, the Camp Fire Club of America, another New York conservation group, included the creation of a national park in the McKinley area on its agenda. When founded in 1897, the club's charter members included wildlife author Ernest Thompson Seton and Boy Scouts of America founder Dan Beard; the club also enrolled Gifford Pinchot, Zane Grey, and Theodore Roosevelt. Many of the Camp Fire Club members were avid trophy hunters, like their Boone and Crockett counterparts. But closer to home, the club provided a way for men to escape from the city to a two-hundred-acre estate in nearby Chappaqua, where members could build weekend retreat cottages. Biannual campouts drew upwards of one hundred men who engaged in shooting and camping skills competitions, all for the sake of bragging rights and medals. As one member said, "We would seriously play...." Members also took conservation seriously, and the club's bylaws emphasized working for the preservation of forests and wildlife for future generations. The club maintained a local profile until the formation of its conservation committee in 1909, when it began to address national issues. The group had already worked with the Boone and Crockett Club on related matters, such as the 1912 migratory bird legislation. But the Camp Fire Club's mission to save the game of Mount McKinley developed independently of the Boone and Crockett Club's, though in a similar fashion due to the experience and insistence of one of its members, Belmore Browne.[22]

Browne's experiences in Alaska spanned his lifetime, with a boyhood family steamer cruise in 1889 in the Panhandle, climbing expeditions on Mount

McKinley, and advising the National Park Service on its wolf problems after World War II. He established a national reputation as a landscape and wildlife painter, with the North inspiring much of his work. Like Sheldon, he first trekked through Alaska's mountains as a specimen hunter for the American Museum of Natural History in 1902 and 1903, gaining wilderness skills and an interest in Mount McKinley.[23]

Browne's first two expeditions to McKinley involved controversy. Frederick Cook recruited Browne for an expedition in 1906, mostly for Browne's hunting and bush skills. After initially admitting defeat and returning to Cook Inlet, Cook left most of the party, including Browne, and returned to the peak's southeast flanks. Upon descent, Cook claimed victory on the continent's highest peak. Although Browne was skeptical, the country's geographers and mountaineers accepted Cook's triumph. Another skeptical expedition member whom Cook had left behind shared doubts with Browne: Dr. Herschel Parker, a physics professor at Columbia University with mountaineering experience in the Canadian Rockies. Their doubts gained strength in the autumn of 1909 as both Cook and Robert Peary claimed to have reached the North Pole. Peary's claim held up; Cook's did not, which motivated Browne and Parker to reexamine his McKinley ascent. In 1910 they returned to Alaska to retrace Cook's alleged route. They did not climb the peak, but brought back convincing photographic evidence that revealed Cook's hoax.[24]

The success of the next three attempts on Mount McKinley, though only the last attained the summit, was due in part to the game animals in what would become the national park. Browne's 1906 and 1910 trips started near where Anchorage now stands. Packing supplies through the forests and swamps south of the Alaska Range was a taxing ordeal. A separate expedition in 1910 found the key to McKinley's summit, and it lay in the game country. Unimpressed by the failure of non-Alaska city folks to climb the mountain, four Alaska prospectors approached from Fairbanks by dog team in the spring, stopping in the foothills to hunt fresh meat to accompany their flour and beans. They claimed the ascent, but soon it became apparent that the Sourdough Expedition had climbed the lower north summit—a remarkable achievement, at 19,470 feet the highest point attained on the continent, but the main peak remained untrodden. In 1912 Browne teamed up with Herschel Parker and Merl LaVoy for a summit attempt. They left their steamship in Seward and mushed dogs north on the mail trail, packing little food. Instead of assaulting the mountain's southern defenses, they crossed the range at Anderson Pass into game country on the north side, where they too loaded up with fresh meat before ascending the Sourdough's route up the Muldrow Glacier. In one of the great disappointments in mountaineering history, abrupt, vicious storms twice beat them back from within several hundred yards of the summit. The mountain was finally climbed the following year by a party of four led by Episcopalian Archdeacon Hudson Stuck, who followed the same route and ate the same diet of caribou and sheep. Much of the team's strength, savvy, and meat was a result of including Sheldon's friend Harry Karstens on the team. The key ridge leading from the Muldrow Glacier to the upper reaches of the peak was later named Karsten's Ridge, with the granite prominence at its head named Browne's Tower.[25]

Belmore Browne's involvement with McKinley was by no means over. Following the 1912 expedition he returned to the states, married, and pursued his writing and painting careers. At some point on his return from Alaska in 1912, he met with Secretary of the Interior Franklin K. Lane to discuss making McKinley a national park, but the political situation precluded such an idea. Browne and his colleagues of the Camp Fire Club waited for an appropriate opening.[26]

Railroads had played an important role in helping establish and make accessible previous national parks in the American West.[27] A railroad provided the impetus for the creation of Mount McKinley National Park, though less for reasons of tourist accessibility than fears of the railroad's impact on the area's game populations. Alaska had gained territorial status through passage of an Organic Act in 1912, which included the creation of a territorial legislature, as well as the directive to build a railroad to Alaska's interior to spur development of the area's coal and gold resources. Among several alternatives, the route from Seward to Fairbanks was chosen, leading past the McKinley area via the Nenana River canyon, one of the few breaks in the rampart of the Alaska Range. In 1914 President Wilson signed the Alaska Railroad Act, putting the federal government in the place of private companies in the building and financing of the line. Construction crews began laying track, and contractors faced the problem of feeding workers in a region that lacked agriculture. Crews of hunters supplied the railroad camps with meat, thereby threatening the game resources that had already absorbed the demands of thousands of gold-seekers and the growing populace of Fairbanks.[28]

Commercial meat hunting in the North had started with the Klondike gold rush in 1898, as 30,000 stampeders intent on the diggings flooded into the Yukon valley and hunting as an ancillary service industry became an economic necessity. The gold rush to Fairbanks began in 1903, and by 1905

Dall sheep rams killed by gold miners near Eagle, Alaska, 1904.
Clarence Andrews Collection, Division of Speical Collections and University Archives, University of Oregon Library System

the town had eight thousand people at the end of a tenuous supply line from Seattle. Miners testified to a federal subcommittee about the absence of fresh meat except for wild game in the interior, and freight rates brought the price of a fifty-pound sack of flour to $10.[29] Caribou, the most widely distributed game animals, were the "staples of the interior," selling for as little as $.15 per pound in Fairbanks. Moose brought a similar price, while sheep meat fetched $.40 per pound.[30] Entrepreneurs tried to supply domestic meat: Jack Dalton drove several herds of stock from tidewater on Lynn Canal over the mountains to Fort Selkirk, where they were loaded onto scows and floated down the Yukon River. In 1906, two such herds arrived in Fairbanks, comprising 400 sheep, 80 cattle, and 10 hogs. While consumers were willing to pay higher prices for this meat, it failed to curtail the sale of wild game. The local Tanana

Valley Railroad, constructed in 1905 to supply the gold camps near Fairbanks, provided a precursor of what was feared on a larger scale with the Alaska Railroad: in November 1907 alone, one hunter shipped almost six thousand pounds of caribou on the Tanana rails.[31]

The nineteenth-century sportsmen had identified market hunting as an unjustifiable assault on the nation's game and wildfowl, deplorable for its effects on animal populations and for its taint of unmannerliness. From the sportsman's viewpoint, the market hunter was "disgusting...selfish...unmanly...heartless," a "disagreeable character that a well-bred sportsman is likely to be thrown into contact with."[32] The rural market hunter, however, placed value on efficiency, on supplying urban market demands, and perceived the imposition of class discrimination on the historically egalitarian access to game. The sportsmen of the Boone and Crockett Club and the Camp Fire Club decried market hunting and sought restrictive legislation wherever it threatened game or bird populations. Conservationists still held vivid memories of the passenger pigeon's demise and the "holocaust of the Great Plains" involving the bison. Few could fail to be moved by Belmore Browne's description of Alaska's white sheep, where "a young ram, shot through the neck, turns end for end and falls, and an old ewe, paunched by the same soft-nosed messenger, staggers slowly downhill. The slaughter is on...but a few frantic forms survive...."[33] The threat to McKinley's game herds caused by the proximity of the Alaska Railroad's tracks spurred the park proponents into action.

Following a formal endorsement by the Boone and Crockett Club in September 1915, Charles Sheldon wrote to Alaska's congressional delegate, James Wickersham, inquiring about the latter's views on the creation of a park. Wickersham did not wish to inhibit mineral exploration and development in the Alaska Range, but Sheldon convinced him that some mining activity could be compatible in a park and that the game resource deserved protection. Shortly afterwards, Belmore Browne, on behalf of the Camp Fire Club, traveled to Washington to propose park legislation and found to his surprise that others had preceded him. The groups quickly joined forces, and on April 16, 1916, Delegate Wickersham and Senator Pittman of Nevada introduced identical bills to create a park.[34]

The Senate Committee on Territories held a hearing on May 5, 1916, with William Greeley and Belmore Browne representing the Camp Fire Club, Charles Sheldon speaking for the Boone and Crockett Club, and James Wickersham present on behalf of Alaska. As with previous attempts to convince senators to create national parks, proponents carefully noted that the area had few usable resources: it was unsuitable for agriculture, would not attract homesteaders, had few mineral resources, and no timber. Economic arguments highlighted the potential attraction to tourists: Greeley noted that with completion of the Alaska Railroad the area would be accessible in three weeks from New York. Sheldon then said that since the government was spending thirty million dollars to build the railroad, it should seek to "exploit everything that will be of value near that railroad." More important, they also considered a park vital to the preservation of the game herds. The rationale was more than esthetic, as the park would supposedly create a sanctuary for breeding so there would be excess animals to replenish adjacent areas for hunters. Belmore Browne said the area was so productive that it was "beaten flat by the herds of big game." The senators often raised the issue of the scenic value of the glacier-clad mountains, but the overarching theme of the arguments concerned game animals. The proposed park boundaries barely touched Mount McKinley itself, but included the Outer Ranges where the caribou "gave one the impression of being on a cattle range in the West," while excluding the gold diggings of Kantishna. Wickersham stated that Alaskans were in favor of the park as long as prospectors could still hunt for their needs. He was successful in obtaining language in the bill protecting that right. Browne included in the testimony a written plea that put the matter in unmistakable terms:

> Slowly but surely the white man's civilization is closing in, and already sled loads of dead animals from the McKinley region have reached the Fairbanks market. Unless a refuge is set aside in which the animals that remain can breed and rear their young unmolested, they will soon 'follow the buffalo.'[35]

The park bill failed to pass in that Congress, due to a procedural delay in the House. Further efforts on the bill's behalf were evident as the congressmen returned to session in 1917. They were presented with a copy of a *National Geographic* article by Stephen R. Capps of the U.S. Geological Survey, in which he outlined the "last chance for the people of the United States to preserve, untouched by civilization, a great primeval park in its natural beauty."[36] Capps again raised the fear of commercial hunting. He cited several hunters who said that 1,500 to 2,000 sheep were taken from the area for the Fairbanks market each winter. A National Parks Conference held for the benefit of legislators helped sway votes, and with virtually no opposition the legislation passed on

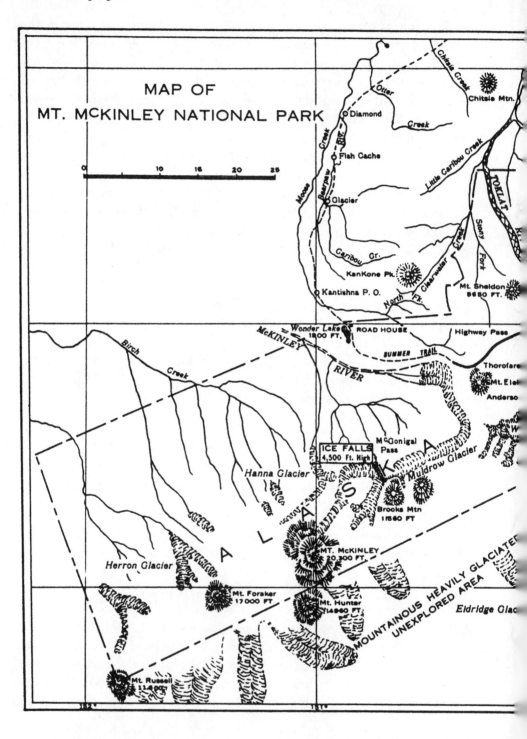

MAP OF
MT. McKINLEY NATIONAL PARK

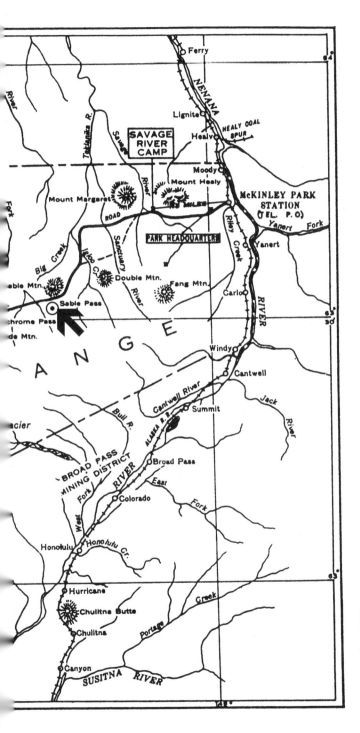

Map of Mount McKinley
National Park, from a 1937
pamphlet. An arrow points to
the site of the East Fork cabin.
*Courtesy of the National Park
Service, Denali National Park and
Preserve*

February 19. President Wilson signed it into law, reserving 2,200 square miles as Mount McKinley National Park.

Little changed in the McKinley area, though, since Congress had not appropriated any funds for personnel to protect the park. The territorial game wardens, ostensibly in charge of enforcement of game laws, were notoriously lax in their duties. The warden in Fairbanks was reportedly "perfectly helpless.... Everyone knows that he never made an arrest and never will.... Whenever I went away on a trip he promptly went on a drunk."[37] A visiting Easterner described hunter's cabins surrounded by heaps of "old antlers of sheep and caribou, while the ground for several hundred yards around was well carpeted with discarded skins of the same animals."[38] The Boone and Crockett Club and the Camp Fire Club both submitted resolutions in 1919 urging an appropriation for the park, but war debts were cited as the delay in funding. The actions of the sportsmen's groups finally came to fruition in 1921, with an eight thousand dollar appropriation. At the urging of Charles Sheldon, repaying debts to his faithful packer, Director Stephen Mather appointed Harry Karstens as the first park superintendent.[39]

Shortly after Karstens began his duties he hosted two brothers, Olaus and Adolph Murie, who would be central figures in the ensuing wolf-sheep controversy. They were products of a tough Midwestern childhood that was particularly hard on their parents. Marie Frimanslund Murie and Joachim D. Murie came from Norway in the great wave of late nineteenth-century Scandinavian immigration and settled in the fertile valley of the Red River near Moorhead, Minnesota. In 1889 Marie gave birth to Olaus, and later another son, Martin. When Olaus was only six, father Joachim died. At some point the widow apparently remarried a relative of her late husband, for her third son, Adolph, also carried the Murie surname. After Adolph's birth on September 6, 1899, tragedy again struck Marie, as her second husband died only six weeks later. Olaus and Martin grew up quickly in a family lacking an adult male income. They offset the privation of the household with the fruits of their fishing, hunting, and trapping forays along the river, while Marie worked as a laundress. As he grew under his brothers' tutelage, Adolph also contributed to the family income. He peddled milk to neighbors and worked in a truck garden. The boys enjoyed not only the nearby wilds of the Red

The young woodsman: Adolph Murie with a cabin he helped build near Moorhead, Minnesota, 1921.
Adolph Murie Collection, temp box 13. Courtesy Alaska and Polar Regions Archives, Rasmuson Library, University of Alaska Fairbanks

River, but the books of America's most popular writer of the natural world, Ernest Thompson Seton, which likely fired their imaginations beyond the confines of the farm-flanked river sloughs. Mrs. Murie did not have much leisure, nor did she enjoy a husband's companionship in her later years, but her sons matured with passable Norwegian language skills, a strong work ethic, boundless intellectual curiosity, and the determination to retain a boyhood spirit of adventure in their professional work.[40]

Adolph initially learned his outdoor skills from his older brothers and spent his adolescence reading Olaus' letters from afar, as Olaus began to fashion a career of studying animals in the wilds. He began postsecondary education at nearby Fargo College; when his zoology teacher moved to Oregon's Pacific University, Olaus followed, and received his biology degree in 1912. He then spent a year working for the Oregon State Game Commission. In 1914 he went north to Hudson Bay as a specimen collector for an expedition sponsored by Pittsburgh's Carnegie Museum, and convinced his bosses to let him stay the winter: "here was a way of life I had only read about, and I was in it!"[41] From a boyhood interest in art, Olaus refined his skills and regarded his pencils and paints as essential parts of his field kit, allowing him to quickly capture a scene without having to rely upon a camera. Two years later he went to Labrador, and by the time Adolph graduated from high school Olaus was as skilled in the north country as any American biologist. This yielded Olaus' next assignment. In 1920 the U.S. Biological Survey sent him to Alaska Territory to study the migration of the caribou herds—critical as a food supply for both Whites and Natives. Olaus had persuaded his boss, Edward W. Nelson, to provide him with assistance in the form of his brother Martin, but on May 4,

Claer and Adolph Murie with their mother at home in Moorhead, Minnesota, 1922.
Adolph Murie Collection, temp box 13. Courtesy Alaska and Polar Regions Archives, Rasmuson Library, University of Alaska Fairbanks

1922, Martin suddenly died of tuberculosis. By this time Adolph was enrolled in Fargo College, where he played basketball on the varsity team. During the war he had served a short stint in the U.S. Army; the discharge papers showed his character as "excellent," but in marksmanship, "unqualified." Olaus, who had "always been more than a big brother to me," invited Adolph to come north in Martin's place. Nelson's letter of commission to Adolph indicated that he should record "continuous observations of the birds and mammals" of the McKinley Park region as well as becoming thoroughly familiar with caribou. Adolph took a steamer to Seward in the fall of 1922, at last able to join Olaus for adventure in a far-away place.[42]

Less than a generation old, the gold-mining town of Fairbanks was the largest settlement in mainland Alaska. The Murie brothers settled into one of the small cabins that composed the residential part of town and prepared for their assignment, a fifteen-hundred mile tour of interior Alaska by dog team. While waiting for the rivers to freeze and snowpack to deepen, the men bought and packed supplies and trained with their dogs. Adolph applied himself during the lengthening nights by learning to type, but there were nearby distractions only a block away in the Thomas-Gillette household. Olaus had become acquainted with the daughter Margaret Thomas the previous year, and that fall the rugged young men were frequent guests of Margaret and her ten-year-old half-sister Louise. The half-brothers had met their future half-sister wives.[43]

The primary purpose of their trip was to study the interior caribou herds and the status of fur-bearing animal populations. Of no economic significance, but to satisfy his curiosity, Edward Nelson directed the Muries to shoot sheep specimens in the Brooks Range for comparison with those in McKinley Park. Their route made a broad clockwise loop from Fairbanks: west down the Tanana and Yukon rivers, then north into the Koyukuk River country; after penetrating the Brooks Range, they would return by following the Chandalar River east and south to the Yukon River, then catch the mail trails through the mining district back to Fairbanks before spring greenup. They left on November 24, with the rivers frozen and enough snow for the sleds. Olaus was an old hand at these matters; Adolph got an education in a hurry, from untangling teams of fighting dogs, to judging routes through forests, over tundra, and across overflow ice, to living and functioning in the subarctic gloom of winter in temperatures that rarely saw the top side of zero and plunged as low as minus sixty-eight. The people, too, were part of the education: nights spent with sourdoughs in lonely cabins, being asked by Indian girls to dance at evening affairs at the trader's stores, and learning Eskimo ways through weeks spent traveling with a

**Adolph Murie (left) and Ranger Gus Berman, Savage River, McKinley Park,
July 17, 1923.**
*Adolph Murie Collection, temp box 13. Courtesy Alaska and Polar Regions Archives, Rasmuson Library,
University of Alaska Fairbanks*

family from Allakaket. Adolph's quick learning pleased Olaus: "I was realizing
what a good outdoorsman my young brother was, and on this trip to the
Kobuk I was amazed at how easily he took to snowshoes."[44] After five months
of hard travel, the Muries arrived back in Fairbanks by sledging at night on a
quickly disappearing snowpack.

Compared with that trip, their ensuing labors on behalf of the Biological
Survey seemed like a vacation. They spent the summer and autumn of 1923
with Harry Karstens in Mount McKinley National Park, which Adolph
described as "just like being in heaven."[45] The Biological Survey's Edward Nelson
had ordered them to capture some caribou bulls from the park, since he felt
they were bigger than those in other parts of Alaska and represented the pinnacle
of the species. An economic rationale stood behind this, as the caribou were to
be transported down river to the west coast for crossbreeding with reindeer

herds. Reindeer had been brought to Alaska in the 1890s as food and a potential economic base for the coastal Eskimos. On the upper Savage River, on a known migration route, the Muries built brush drive fences based on Athabaskan designs to funnel the caribou toward a corral. In the end their labors went for naught; they eventually managed to capture five caribou which ended up at the Biological Survey's experimental reindeer farm near Fairbanks, but none went to the coast.[46]

Adolph also started recording encounters with the park's wolves and Dall sheep into his field journals. He had at least one occasion to hunt sheep. President Warren Harding visited Alaska in July 1923 to help celebrate the completion of the Alaska Railroad from Seward to Fairbanks, and scheduled a stop in the six-year-old national park. Harry Karstens passed along to the Muries a request from Harding's retinue for a meal of Dall sheep, considered the prime fare of Alaska's game animals. Harding's train was due the following day, and the Muries located, shot, dressed, and packed a sheep twenty miles to the rail siding, only to discover that Harding's train had stopped only briefly and departed two hours earlier; apparently he was suffering from an illness. In telling this story later, Adolph expressed some embarrassment for having shot a sheep within the national park, but "things were a little bit looser at that time than they are today."[47] At least when Harding died from an embolism in San Francisco only two weeks later, it could not be blamed on wild sheep meat.

Notes

1   On the canids, see Jennifer W. Sheldon, *Wild Dogs: The Natural History of the Nondomestic Canidae* (San Diego: Academic Press, 1992), and M. W. Fox, ed., *The Wild Canids: Their Systematics, Behavioral Ecology, and Evolution* (New York: Van Nostrand Reinhold, 1975).

The best single source on the wolf is L. David Mech, *The Wolf: The Ecology and Behavior of an Endangered Species*, 3rd ed. (Minneapolis: University of Minnesota Press, 1984). The literature on the wolf is extensive and best documented in Erich Klinghammer, Monty Sloan, and De Wayne R. Klein, *Wolf Literature References: Scientific and General Books and Articles Listed Alphabetically by Author* (Battle Ground, IN: North American Wildlife Park Foundation, Inc., 1990); this group provides addenda at two year intervals.

2   See the essays in Roberta L. Hall and Henry S. Sharp, eds., *Wolf and Man: Evolution in Parallel* (New York: Academic Press, 1978). Bruce Hampton provides an expanded summary of this in the second chapter of *The Great American Wolf* (New York: Henry

Holt, 1997). This hypothesis dates back to a British psychologist, Carveth Read, who expounded on it in the *Origin of Man and of His Superstitions* (Cambridge: Cambridge University Press, 1920).

3 An introduction to Alaska's landforms and ice age life is in *Interior Alaska: A Journey Through Time,* Robert M. Thorson et al., (Anchorage: Alaska Geographic Society, 1986). On Pleistocene issues, see Valerius Geist, "Did Large Predators Keep Humans Out of North America?" in *The Walking Larder: Patterns of Domestication, Pastoralism, and Predation,* ed. J. Clutton-Brock, 282–94 (London: Unwin Hyman, 1989); Marc Stevenson, "Dire Wolf Systematics and Behavior," in Hall and Sharp, *Wolf and Man,* 179–96; Paul S. Martin and Richard G. Klein, eds., *Quaternary Extinctions: A Prehistoric Revolution* (Tucson: University of Arizona Press, 1984).

4 Juliet Clutton-Brock's *Domesticated Animals From Early Times* (Austin: University of Texas Press, 1981) provides a good introduction to the process. Hans-Peter Uerpmann suggests that the dog "niche" became more valuable to humans as the Eurasian steppe became forested, due to the utility of the dogs' scenting for prey; in "Animal Domestication—Accident or Intention?" in *The Origins and Spread of Agriculture and Pastoralism in Eurasia,* ed. David R. Harris, 227–37 (Washington, D.C.: Smithsonian Institution Press, 1996), 230. Early American evidence is summarized in the first chapter of Marion Schwartz, *A History of Dogs in the Early Americas* (New Haven: Yale University Press, 1997). The coevolutionary argument is presented in Stephen Budiansky, *The Covenant of the Wild: Why Animals Chose Domestication* (New York: William Morrow, 1992).

5 See chapters four and five in Clutton-Brock, *Domesticated Animals*; Hans-Peter Uerpmann, "Animal Exploitation and the Phasing of the Transition from the Paleolithic to the Neolithic," in *The Walking Larder*, 91–96; Hans-Peter Uerpmann, "Animal Domestication"; Tony Legge, "The Beginning of Caprine Domestication in Southwest Asia," in *Origins and Spread of Agriculture*, 238–62.

People in China and Southwest Asia domesticated the pig at about the same time, some 9000 B.P., followed much later by the cow and horse. Biologist Jared Diamond presents a stimulating analysis of domestication—particularly why so few animals became that, and what domesticates did for the course of world history—in *Guns, Germs, and Steel: The Fates of Human Societies* (New York: W. W. Norton & Co., 1997), 157–75.

6 Letter from Samuel Smith to son Ichabod, 1 January 1699, in *The History of Ancient Wethersfield, Connecticut,* Vol. 1, ed. Henry R. Stiles (New York: Grafton Press, 1904), 154–55. Mather quoted in Peter Carroll, *Puritanism and the Wilderness* (New York: Columbia University Press, 1969), 208–9. Barry Lopez's intriguing book is unequaled for a treatment of attitudes toward wolves; *Of Wolves and Men* (New York: Charles Scribner's Sons, 1978). See also Beryl Rowland, *Animals with Human Faces: A Guide to Animal Symbolism* (Knoxville: University of Tennessee Press, 1973), 161–67.

7 The complex natural history of the Asian sheep is summarized in George B. Schaller, *Mountain Monarchs: Wild Sheep and Goats of the Himalaya* (Chicago: University of

Chicago Press, 1977). James Clark's *The Great Arc of the Wild Sheep* (Norman: University of Oklahoma Press, 1964) is dated insofar as evolutionary history is concerned, but contains a fascinating account of his nine-month sheep collecting trip in 1926, where by foot and beast his party became the first westerners to travel overland from Bombay to Beijing. On Native American rock art, see Campbell Grant, "The Desert Bighorn and Aboriginal Man," in *The Desert Bighorn: Its Life History, Ecology, and Management*, eds. Gale Monson and Lowell Sumner, 7–39 (Tucson: University of Arizona Press, 1980).

8   Clark, *Great Arc*, 49, 62–3; William Wishart, "Bighorn Sheep," in *Big Game of North America: Ecology and Management* (Harrisburg, PA: Stackpole, 1980), 161; Durward Allen, *Our Wildlife Legacy*, rev. ed. (New York: Funk & Wagnalls Co., 1962), 240. On Dall, see Morgan Sherwood, *Exploration of Alaska, 1865–1900* (New Haven: Yale University Press, 1965), 36–56.

Consensus recognizes two American sheep species, likely representing different stocks of migrants and populations isolated during the ice age. *O. canadensis* has five to seven subspecies, depending on who is counting, including the desert bighorns. *O. dalli dalli* is the Alaska sheep, while *O. dalli stonei* is the sheep of northern British Columbia.

9   Hans Huth, *Nature and the Americans: Three Centuries of Changing Attitudes*, 2nd ed. (Lincoln: University of Nebraska Press, 1990), 54–6.

10   Thomas R. Dunlap, *Saving America's Wildlife* (Princeton: Princeton University Press, 1988), 8–16. See also John F. Reiger, *American Sportsmen and the Origin of Conservation*, 2nd ed. (Norman: University of Oklahoma Press, 1986), and Roderick Nash, *Wilderness and the American Mind*, 2nd ed. (New Haven: Yale University Press, 1973), for good discussions of these evolving attitudes in the nineteenth century. Dunlap questions Reiger's argument and evidence in "Sport Hunting and Conservation, 1880–1920," *Environmental Review* 12 (Spring 1988): 51–60.

11   See Valerius Geist, *Mountain Sheep: A Study in Behavior and Evolution* (Chicago: University of Chicago Press, 1971), and the more personal *Mountain Sheep and Man in the Northern Wilds* (Ithaca: Cornell University Press, 1975).

12   J. A. McGuire, *In the Alaska-Yukon Gamelands* (Cincinnati: Stewart Kidd Co., 1921), 92; Theodore Roosevelt, *The Wilderness Hunter* (New York: G. P. Putnam's Sons, 1893), 126; Owen Wister, "The Mountain Sheep: His Ways," in *Musk-Ox, Bison, Sheep and Goat*, eds. Caspar Whitney, George Bird Grinnell, and Owen Wister (New York: Macmillan, 1904), 183.

13   Rowland, *Animals with Human Faces*, 135. I am indebted in this section to the provocative thoughts in former wildlife biologist David E. Brown's essay, "Rambo: The Desert Bighorn Sheep as a Masculine Totem," in *The Desert Bighorn*," 188–200.

The attractiveness of wild sheep appears undiminished. A Montana game warden noted that bighorns were the most poached animal in the Yellowstone area; Henry J. Fabich, "Poaching for Profit," in *Proceedings of the 60th Annual Conference of the Western Association of Fish and Wildlife Agencies*, July 13–17, 1980, Kalispell, MT, 184.

14   Alfred H. Brooks, *An Exploration to Mount McKinley, America's Highest Mountain* (Washington, D.C.: GPO, 1904), 460.

15   James Wickersham, *Old Yukon: Tales, Trails, Trials* (Washington, D.C.: Washington Law Book Co., 1938), 275. The broad Wickersham Wall, dominating the view of McKinley from Wonder Lake in the national park, rises 14,000 feet in an unbroken forty degree slope, one of the largest mountain walls in the world. It is infrequently ascended. Frederick Cook, "Round Mount McKinley," *Bulletin of the American Geographical Society* 36 (1904), 326.

16   Charles Sheldon, *The Wilderness of the Upper Yukon* (New York: Charles Scribner's Sons, 1911), 214–15. Such was Sheldon's style, with no evidence of self-parody. Lest the reader be tempted to conclude that hunting substituted for personal inadequacies, Sheldon married in 1909 and fathered four children before his death in 1928. Son William will appear later in this narrative.

      A fine short biography of Sheldon is in the "Introduction" of *The Wilderness of the Southwest: Charles Sheldon's Quest for Desert Bighorn Sheep and Adventures with the Havasupai and Seri Indians*, eds. Neil B. Carmony and David E. Brown (Salt Lake City: University of Utah Press, 1993).

17   Grinnell's quote from the "Introduction" of Charles Sheldon, *The Wilderness of Denali* (New York: Charles Scribner's Sons, 1930), which was posthumously edited from his field journals by the prominent biologists C. Hart Merriam and Edward W. Nelson. Grinnell had ridden with Custer, spoke several Plains Indian tongues, witnessed the bison's demise, and returned to New York to edit the influential magazine *Forest and Stream*; see Reiger, *American Sportsmen and the Origin of Conservation*.

18   Sheldon, *Wilderness of Denali*, 13–16, 103. See also a brief and entertaining biography of Karstens by his protégé and later superintendent of McKinley Park: Grant H. Pearson, *The Seventy Mile Kid* (Los Altos, CA: By the author, 1957).

19   Sheldon, *Wilderness of Denali*, 261, 272, 385; quoted in William Brown, *A History of the Denali-Mt. McKinley Region, Alaska* (Washington, D.C.: GPO, National Park Service, 1991), 85. The National Park Service would later name a peak near the cabin Mount Sheldon.

20   See Madison Grant, "Brief History of the Boone and Crockett Club," in *Hunting at High Altitudes*, George Bird Grinnell, ed. (New York: Harper & Bros., 1913): 435–91.

21   An expanded authorized history is in James B. Trefethen, *Crusade for Wildlife: Highlights in Conservation Progress* (Harrisburg, Pennsylvania: Stackpole Co., and the Boone and Crockett Club, 1961). This was revised as *An American Crusade for Wildlife* (New York: Winchester Press, and the Boone and Crockett Club, 1975). The former contains more material on Alaska, especially the role of the club in the early Alaska game laws of 1902, 1908, and 1925, and in its involvement with McKinley Park. On federal laws and Alaskans, see Trefethen, *Crusade for Wildlife*, 128–44, and Morgan Sherwood, *Big Game in Alaska: A History of Wildlife and People* (New Haven: Yale University Press, 1981).

22   George Reiger, "Golden Oldies," *Field & Stream*, October 1993, 18–20. The 1912 Weeks-MacLean Law eliminated spring hunting seasons and allowed the secretary of agriculture to impose closed seasons on particular bird species; see Trefethen, *Crusade for Wildlife*, 168–71. James C. Clark, *Good Hunting: Fifty Years of Collecting and Preparing Habitat Groups for the American Museum* (Norman: University of Oklahoma, 1966), 126, describes the campouts. As a professional taxidermist and hunter, Clark claims to have derived the "scoring system" for horns and antlers subsequently adopted by the Boone and Crockett Club that became synonymous with trophy definition; see p. 154.

23   Biographic information is from Michael S. Kennedy, "Belmore Browne and Alaska," *Alaska Journal*, Spring 1973, 96–104, and Robert H. Bates, *Mountain Man: The Story of Belmore Browne* (Clinton, NJ: Amwell Press, 1988). The latter focuses mostly on Browne's earlier years in Alaska and on his subsequent painting career.

24   Cook's account of the climb is in *To the Top of the Continent* (New York: Doubleday, 1908). A plethora of writings exist on Cook and Peary; arguably the best analysis of the McKinley hoax is by Bradford Washburn, Adams Carter, and Ann Carter, "Dr. Cook and Mount McKinley," *American Alpine Club Journal* (1958): 1–30.

      Cook still has defenders who insist he could have reached McKinley's summit and that he was subsequently defamed in this and the polar controversy. Additional evidence is presented in a recent reprint of *To the Top of the Continent* (Mukilteo, WA: AlpenBooks, for the Frederick A. Cook Society, 1996).

25   Browne described his three McKinley expeditions in *The Conquest of Mount McKinley* (New York: G. P. Putnam's Sons, 1913). The fascinating story of the audacious prospectors can be found in Terrence Cole, ed., *The Sourdough Expedition* (Anchorage: Alaska Northwest Publishing, 1985). A comprehensive work on all the early McKinley climbs is Terris Moore, *Mount McKinley: The Pioneer Climbs* (Fairbanks: University of Alaska Press, 1967). The first ascent tale is in Hudson Stuck, *The Ascent of Denali (Mount McKinley), A Narrative of the First Complete Ascent of the Highest Peak in North America* (New York: Charles Scribner's Sons, 1914; reprinted as *The Ascent of Denali* [Seattle: The Mountaineers, 1977]).

26   Bates' biography handsomely reproduces a collection of Browne's paintings and reprints of popular magazine articles. Browne wrote three adventure books directed at boys, based on his experiences and stories collected in Alaska, all published by G.P. Putnam's Sons: *The Quest of the Golden Valley: A Story of Adventure on the Yukon* (1916), *The White Blanket: The Story of an Alaskan Winter* (1917), and *The Frozen Barrier: A Story of Adventure on the Coast of the Behring Sea* (1921).

27   See Alfred Runte, *Trains of Discovery: Western Railroads and the National Parks* (Flagstaff, AZ: Northland Press, 1984).

28   Theodore Catton's, *Inhabited Wilderness: Indians, Eskimos, and National Parks in Alaska* (Albuquerque: University of New Mexico Press, 1997), offers an interesting analysis on the creation of McKinley Park, sportsmen, and national park history.

29   Congress, Senate, Subcommittee of Committee on Territories, *Hearings on Conditions in Alaska*, 58th Cong., 2nd sess., 22 July 1903.

30   From Adolph Murie's diary, 17 December 1940, from a conversation with a former market hunter; A. Murie Collection, Box "Field Notes on Wolves," Alaska and Polar Regions Department, Rasmuson Library, University of Alaska Fairbanks (hereafter UAF).

31   Audrey Loftus, "Tom Gibson Meat Hunter," *The Alaska Sportsman*, August 1967, 20–21. This is a three part article on the trade, with the first installment in the June 1967 issue.

32   Quoted in James Tober, *Who Owns the Wildlife? The Political Economy of Conservation in Nineteenth-Century America* (Westport, CT: Greenwood Press, 1981), 46, 53. For the market hunter's perspective, see David and Jim Kimball, *The Market Hunter* (Minneapolis: Dillon Press, 1969), with reminisces from Chesapeake Bay and Minnesota. The latest interpretive treatment of market hunting is found in Louis S. Warren, *The Hunter's Game: Poachers and Conservationists in Twentieth-Century America* (New Haven: Yale University Press, 1997).

33   From an article by Belmore Browne, "Where the White Sheep Roam," *Outing* (May 1912); reprinted and quoted from Bates, *Mountain Man*, 243–257.

34   See Madison Grant, "The Establishment of Mt. McKinley National Park," in *Hunting and Conservation: The Book of the Boone and Crockett Club*, George Bird Grinnell, ed. (New Haven: Yale University Press, 1925), 438–45; Brown, *History of Denali*, 75–98; Catton, *Inhabited Wilderness*, chapter four.

35   The preceding material from Congress, Senate, Committee on Territories, *Hearing on the Establishment of Mount McKinley National Park*, 64th Cong., 2nd sess., 5 May 1916.

36   Stephen Capps, "A Game Country Without Rival in America," *National Geographic*, January 1917, 69–84. Given the longevity of the phrase "last chance" in arguments for the preservation of land areas in Alaska, it is amusing to speculate that this may have been its public origin.

37   Olaus J. Murie, assistant biologist and fur warden, to E.W. Nelson, chief of the U.S. Biological Survey, 26 October 1921; MS 51, Box 4, Folder 1, Alaska State Historical Library (hereafter ASHL).

38   William N. Beach, *In the Shadow of Mt. McKinley* (New York: Derrydale Press, 1931), 211.

39   Sheldon to George B. Grinnell, 5 March 1917; Stephen Mather to Sheldon, 27 January 1921, Sheldon Collection, Box 2, UAF. See also Brown, *History of Denali*, 135–37.

40   Biographic information is compiled from several sources: Olaus J. Murie, *Journeys to the Far North* (Palo Alto: American West Publishing, 1973), 246–49; James M. Glover, "Thinking Like a Wolverine: The Ecological Evolution of Olaus Murie," *Environmental Review* 13 (Fall/Winter 1989): 29–45; Peggy Simson Curry, "Portrait of a Naturalist," *The Living Wilderness*, Summer-Fall 1963, 15–21; Gregory D. Kendrick, "An

Environmental Spokesman: Olaus J. Murie and a Democratic Defense of Wilderness," *Annals of Wyoming* 50 (Fall 1978): 213–302. Also a posthumously-written seven-page biography of Adolph by his wife, which mentions an adopted sister, Claer; Louise Murie MacLeod, "Adolph Muric, 1899–1974," from the Denali National Park and Preserve Library (hereafter DENA).

41 O. Murie, *Journeys to the Far North*, 40; also James M. Glover, "Sweet Days of a Naturalist: Olaus Murie in Alaska, 1920–26," *Forest & Conservation History* 36 (July 1992): 132–40.

42 Glover, "Sweet Days of a Naturalist," 134; Adolph's discharge papers in A. Murie Collection, Box 2, Folder "Biographical Material," American Heritage Center, University of Wyoming (hereafter AHC); Adolph Murie, *A Naturalist in Alaska* (New York: Devin-Adair Company, 1961), 4; E. W. Nelson to A. Murie, 18 Aug 1922, MS 51, Box 4, Folder 5, ASHL.

43 A. Murie Collection, Box 11, Folder "Notes 1921–22," UAF. His typing practice shows up on the backsides of his journal pages. Margaret E. Murie, *Two in the Far North* (New York: Alfred A. Knopf, 1957; reprint, Edmonds, WA: Alaska Northwest Publishing Company, 1978), 77–79 (page references are to reprint edition). Margaret was born in 1902 in Seattle. She and her mother moved to Fairbanks in 1911 to join her stepfather, the new assistant U. S. attorney for Alaska's Fourth Judicial District. His name apparently was Gillette, since this was Louise's maiden name. Born in Fairbanks in 1912, Louise held a position of local prestige as one of the "Native Sons and Daughters of the Golden North."

44 O. Murie, *Journeys in the Far North*, 137; he provides a chapter on this winter trip, from which this paragraph is derived. Adolph provides a shorter version of this trip in the first chapter of *A Naturalist in Alaska* (New York: Devin-Adair Company, 1961).

45 Adolph Murie, interview by Herbert Evison, 19 October 1962, transcript, Adolph Murie Collection, Western History Department, Denver Public Library.

46 Brown, *History of Denali*, 160.

47 Louise Murie MacLeod, "Adolph Murie, 1899–1974"; A. Murie interview by Evison, 4. William Brown records that a week earlier Olaus had provided sheep meat for a large party sponsored by the *Brooklyn Daily Eagle* newspaper; in *History of Denali*, 156.

N.P.S. is the only bureau that can.
　　—*Harold C. Bryant*

2

The National Park Service and Wildlife Management

In 1932 the director of the National Park Service, Horace Albright, received a letter from Paul Redington, director of the Bureau of Biological Survey, the federal agency responsible for coordinating predator control projects on public lands. Redington's wolf hunters had been operating in Alaska for several years, but had not yet turned their attention to wolves in McKinley Park. In his letter, Redington repeated an offer previously made: "If you desire any help in regard to any special predatory animal problem in the Park, I wish you would let us know. We might be able to…aid in the control of the wolves and other animals that are destroying the beneficial wildlife of the Park." The letter circulated among Albright's administrators. One of them, Harold C. Bryant, assistant director of research and education, scrawled a reaction in the margin which signified a shift in park wildlife management: "Why designate game in a national park as any more beneficial than predators. Think we need to take a broad view on this, N. P. S. is the only bureau that can."[1]

This letter serves as a useful point of departure for discussing numerous issues pertinent to what became the wolf-sheep controversy. The controversy took shape in 1935, when the Park Service decided to include McKinley's wolves in a wildlife policy that protected all park animals, including predators. It became a conflict because such a policy represented a change from previous practices. Bryant correctly assessed his agency's potential for creating a distinctive wildlife policy, but doing so proved difficult. He received opposition from

Should predators have a place in national parks? The debate begins within the National Park Service. Harold Child Bryant's handwritten message on the letter to Horace Albright reads: "Why designate game in a national park as any more beneficial than predators. Think we need to take a broad view on this, N.P.S. is the only bureau that can. H.C.B." Albright's response to Bryant: "I think that since coyotes are not native to Alaska they should be removed just like the elk from Yosemite, only the predators we must kill—Horace."

National Archives, Washington D.C., RG79, Entry 7, File 719, Box 1415 many within the Park Service, as well as from other federal agencies. Foremost of these was the Biological Survey, which formalized the general cultural antipathy toward wolves, but also helped spark significant questions within the scientific community on the ecological role of predators and the appropriateness of their wholescale destruction. This questioning by his fellow biologists supported Harold Bryant, who played an important role in reshaping Park Service wildlife policies. That brief letter from Redington to Albright, one small piece of historical evidence, thus contains a number of issues concerning parks and animals that would be tested by the wolves and wild sheep of McKinley Park.

Although the federal government had not assumed responsibility for predator control until the twentieth century, Americans had long organized to eliminate hazards to their livestock. Habitat alteration, coordinated village hunts, and the individual pursuit of bounty payments eliminated wolves from settled areas by the American Revolution. Wolf killing was as much a part of settlement as clearing trees and tilling soil, and was virtually a community obligation. Traps, pits, poisons, and organized hunts accompanied the westward expansion. Group hunting proved more efficient than individual efforts, and wolfing could help knit together communities of settlers on the frontier's edge. A series of "Wolf Meetings" in 1843 united Oregon settlers against the wolf as well as against British sovereignty. Individual efforts were enhanced by the appearance of crystalline strychnine in the mid-1800s, a lightweight, easily used tool against the wolves. On the Great Plains, professional wolfers followed the buffalo herds, killing some and burying strychnine in the carcasses, and then collecting and selling the pelts from the wolves attracted by the scent of freshly killed meat.[2]

Mass production of the steel trap in the mid-nineteenth century provided a practical tool for wolf control, and served as a symbol of the progress of industrial civilization. Traps had for centuries been hand forged slowly and laboriously. A trapper and trap-making blacksmith named Sewell Newhouse joined the utopian religious Oneida community of upstate New York in 1848, and his talents combined with others to create a mass production system. A group of Oneida machinists enlarged the blacksmith's shop into a factory by bringing in water power and stamping presses; production rose rapidly, from

25,945 traps in 1857 to 275,532 traps in 1864, and Oneida, under the market name of Newhouse traps (and the later Victor line), dominated the North American market.[3] Eight trap sizes covered the range of animals from rats to bears; the No. 4, with a 6 $1/_2$ inch jaw, became the standard wolf trap. Market competition led Oneida to publish *The Trapper's Guide*, a series ostensibly written by their company figurehead, Sewell Newhouse. These books blended tall tales, how-to trapping information, and a sales pitch for Newhouse traps. The company viewed itself as playing a vital role in history, for the trap, along with the axe and plow, "forms the prow with which iron-clad civilization is pushing back barbaric solitude; causing the bear and beaver to give place to the wheat-field, the library, and the piano." Newhouse traps would spread civilization around the world: the caption to the drawing of the forty-two pound Great Bear Trap trumpeted that:

> [I]t ought to go wherever ferocious animals exclude man from
> the soil. India…needs it to exterminate the Tiger. Africa needs
> it in her long battle with the Lion. South America needs it for
> grappling with the Jaguar and the Boa Constrictor. There is
> not an animal living that can defy it…."[4]

With demands from the Great Plains wolfers for a more effective tool, in 1895 Oneida enlisted the help of noted naturalist and nature writer Ernest Thompson Seton to help design and market an enlarged trap with toothed jaws for western wolves. The No. 4 $1/_2$ Newhouse trap became the standard tool used by ranchers and professional trappers alike.[5]

Once the bison were slaughtered, becoming almost extinct before anyone realized what had happened, their niche as primary grassland herbivore and prey for wolves and coyotes was filled by domestic livestock. The combination of empty range and railroad links to urban markets provided new opportunities in livestock raising, changed methods, and led to the involvement of the federal government in predator control. The age-old practices of stock management— fencing, supervision by herdsmen, dogs to repel wolves—fell into disuse in the free-ranging late 1800s, yet stock owners could still make money. Nevertheless, economic motives and centuries of habituated attitudes led to extensive campaigns against predators; ranchers organized private bounty funds, and encouraged territorial and state legislatures to do the same. Since stockmen were virtually the only taxpayers in the newly settled areas, their legislative demands could not be ignored. The bounty system was a popular political tool, serving to disperse cash to rural voters, but it was ultimately ineffective in eliminating wolves. Professional bounty hunters could obtain a modest living by killing wolves and coyotes, yet they were concerned less with protecting livestock herds than with roaming to where the predators were numerous, and hence profitable. They realized that if they were too thorough, their livelihood would disappear. Stockmen and local governments attempted and failed to organize a unified bounty system in the western states in 1899. Growing disillusionment with bounties led them to request federal predator control efforts.[6]

The agency that assumed responsibility for predator control began in 1886 as the Division of Economic Ornithology and Mammalogy within the Department of Agriculture. Its first director, C. Hart Merriam, came from a background in ornithology and justified the creation of a new agency on the premise that bird research would be beneficial to the nation's farmers.[7] While Congress intended the division to engage in applied research of economic value, Merriam's primary interest turned to the biogeography of North American mammals. He directed his field collectors to obtain specimens systematically for creating species distribution maps, and he conducted research on the food habits of birds and mammals through analysis of stomach contents.[8] The vast numbers of specimens flowing into Washington, D.C., from field agents allowed an expansion in the distinction and naming of species and subspecies—one way to achieve fame in biologic circles. Merriam held controversial theories on speciation: in modern parlance, he was a "splitter," naming new species on arcane skeletal differences.[9] His longtime friend and amateur naturalist Theodore Roosevelt, among others, objected to Merriam's "excessive multiplication of species based upon trivial points of difference." Appreciating his friend's vanity, Merriam promptly discovered a new species of elk in Washington's Olympic Peninsula, *Cervus roosevelti* Merriam, which flattered Roosevelt for a short time.[10] Merriam's division published extensively and widely on all mammals and birds, providing a valuable foundation of information for twentieth century biologists.

At the turn of the century the agency expanded its activities. These included wildlife surveys in Alaska, Canada, and Mexico, as well as enforcement responsibilities under the Lacey Act of 1900, which forbade the interstate commerce of game meat. In 1905, Congress upgraded and renamed the division the Bureau of Biological Survey, still within the Department of Agriculture. Increasing scrutiny followed, as bureaucrats questioned Merriam's scientists on the usefulness of their basic research to the needs of agriculture.[11] In addition to research on biogeography and food habits, the survey conducted disease investigations in wild animals, fur resources development, rodent control, and the protection of animals that were "not only valuable but delight the nature lovers and attract sportsmen to their haunts in proper season."[12]

Additional duties came with increasing evidence of the ineffectiveness of bounty incentives at eliminating predator populations in the western states, although wolves had been severely reduced.[13] The ranching industry wanted federal action on the problem, since most of the grazing lands were in the public domain.[14] Merriam had already publicly criticized state bounty programs on raptors and questioned the negative opinions popularly held toward "chicken hawks" and their kind. He took an aggressive stance towards western predators to appease the ranching industry and convince Congress of his agency's value.[15] In 1905 Merriam loaned veteran field biologist and brother-in-law Vernon Bailey to the Forest Service to investigate the wolf problem on government forest lands. After finding "enormous losses" of both livestock and game animals, Bailey wrote a pamphlet, *Wolves in Relation to Stock, Game and the National Forest Reserves,* to "put in the hands of every hunter, trapper, forest ranger, and ranchman directions for trapping, poisoning, and hunting wolves and finding the dens of young."[16] Forest rangers received traps and instructions for their use, and became the first government predator control agents. In 1907 they took 1,800 wolves and 23,000 coyotes from western forest reserves.[17] Bailey's pamphlet received widespread publicity in a short *National Geographic* article, which noted that Biological Survey men were working out the best methods for killing wolves in order to reduce stock losses and the destruction of game in forest reserves and national parks.[18] This "fierce warfare" was considered virtuous in 1907, and served to keep the Biological Survey in business, although detrimental to its broader scientific programs.

Merriam resigned as head of the Biological Survey in 1910, and his successor, Henry Henshaw, continued the direction toward national predator control.[19] Sportsmen's groups and the livestock industry recognized the success of forest rangers in diminishing predator populations. Their pressure on Congress resulted in the authorization of the Biological Survey to exert direct efforts in "experiments and demonstration in destroying wolves, prairie dogs, and other animals injurious to agriculture and animal husbandry," with a 1915 appropriation of $125,000.[20] Biological Survey agents organized western areas into control districts and supplied advice, traps, poison, and hunters. Newhouse traps became the major tool. In 1911 the Oneida Company developed a new double-spring wolf trap, the No. 44, for government use, and after 1916 the Biological Survey was Oneida's largest single customer. In 1925 the No. 44 sold for $15.62 per dozen, and Oneida shipped them to the federal government and western states in "carload lots."[21]

Henshaw's replacement in 1916, Edward Nelson, had joined the Biological Survey in 1890 following his ground-breaking ethnological studies of Alaska Eskimos between 1877 and 1881, and subsequent biologic field investigations.[22] World War I increased demand for beef and wool, justifying further predator control efforts.[23] In 1917 Nelson reported that 175 to 300 "expert hunter and trappers" worked for the benefit of both livestock and game populations. He confidently stated, "There is little question that in five years we can destroy most of the gray wolves and greatly reduce the numbers of other predatory animals."[24] The development and distribution of poisons for predators and rodents was an important advance in animal control; in 1923 1.7 million poisoned baits were used in this "fine art."[25] Economic concerns dominated the survey's work through the 1920s, with little emphasis on basic research. In 1923 it received $24,000 for biological studies and $502,240 for economic research projects, the bulk of the latter going toward animal control.[26] From 1915 to 1928 federal hunters killed 366,981 coyotes and 6,958 wolves, and even more died unwitnessed and unrecovered from poisons.[27] In light of the effectiveness of federal control and declining populations of wolves, as well as the continuous fraud perpetrated in attempts to claim bounties, most western states withdrew their bounty programs. Stockmen continued to offer private incentives on the few remaining wolves, many of which gained national notoriety through the popular press.[28]

The legislation enabling predator control encouraged Biological Survey agents to assist private trappers, as well as spending time themselves in the field in pursuit of predators on the public domain. More extensive cooperative predator control projects followed, involving stockmen's groups, states, and other federal agencies, including the Forest Service, the Office of Indian Affairs, and the National Park Service.[29] Effective lobbying in Washington, D.C., by western interests resulted in a 1928 proposal by the Department of Agriculture for a ten-year program of expanded cooperative predator control projects. Conservation groups and naturalists opposed this, fearing that survey actions would result in the final extinction of predators, although the survey claimed it merely sought control, not eradication.[30] Nevertheless, by 1929 the survey's historian concluded that "the end of the wolf is in sight."[31]

The federal government first came to Alaska's aid against the wolf in 1923, when Stanley Ligon, the "most expert hunter" of the Biological Survey, came to the islands of southeastern Alaska to determine if control could be accomplished as in the western states. (In one of the ironies of history and nomenclature, the wolf subspecies of the area would be named *C. lupus ligoni*.) He managed to trap and poison enough wolves to be optimistic, and the 1924 annual report of Alaska's governor looked forward to the day when further federal funds would be applied to the territory's situation.[32]

Funds became available three years later, and federal wolf control moved to mainland Alaska in 1927. That summer representatives of four government offices signed a cooperative agreement to enhance the efforts of private bounty hunters. The territorial legislature provided $10,000 and the Alaska Game Commission offered information collected by its fur wardens. The Forest Service loaned a ranger boat in southeast Alaska, while the Biological Survey contributed an additional $2,000 and a wolf trapper, R. K. Stewart. His background included predator work in the western states; his Alaska mission was to study the wolf and coyote situation first, then derive a control plan for the territory, followed by demonstrations of trapping techniques to residents. Stewart spent two years on an initial survey, traveling widely and talking with hunters, wardens, traders, and trappers, noting with a touch of conceit that many traveled considerable distances at their own expense for "personal contact with the leader."[33] Alaskans welcomed free traps and scents; they were less enthusiastic about a reduction in bounty money. Part of the territorial contribution to this project came from cutting the biennial bounty appropriation from $15 to $10 for wolves and coyotes alike.[34] In effect, this reduced private incentive for the sake of a one-man operation, a ludicrous proposition in the vastness of Alaska. Governor George Parks, while approving the cooperative effort, pleaded for further federal assistance for a "comprehensive program," and suggested that a funding level three times greater would allow for effective action "while there is still time to destroy these animals."[35]

In August 1928 Stewart's boss, Paul Redington, chief of the Biological Survey, joined him for two days in McKinley Park, and the men surveyed the situation with Superintendent Harry Karstens. Redington had just spent some memorable days in Fairbanks helping fight a fire burning just north of the university campus, near the Biological Survey's reindeer station; a falling spruce had left him with bad bruises. He assumed that wolves were a problem in the park, and the reports he received confirmed this: among others, the president of the Boy Scouts of America, present as a tourist, assured Redington that sheep and caribou were imperiled. Stewart had spent time in the Savage River drainage and did not find game populations threatened, but did note a more immediate problem: due to wolves, the park sheep were "becoming wild and not to be so easily approached for observation by visitors." Redington's own observations belied any sense of crisis. He reported seeing two hundred sheep only seven miles into the park, and Karstens generously estimated the park's sheep population at fifty thousand.[36] But Redington's mind was set. He subsequently sought to enlist the cooperation of the National Park Service in the control effort by writing to Acting Director Arthur Demaray, informing him of the "bad condition of affairs," that the wolves had scattered the Dall sheep so that it was "more and more difficult for tourists to observe them." He suggested using Park Service financial support to aid in the "eradication of predatory animals." Demaray offered the services of a ranger patrol in the park, but little else. Governor Parks put the matter more bluntly to Demaray the following summer, describing the cooperation between the territory and the Biological Survey, their $20,000 budget, the "encroachment" of wolves and coyotes on the park, and the inability to protect the park's game animals unless financial cooperation was available. Demaray again had nothing to offer.[37] With or without the Park Service, R. K. Stewart completed his surveys, the 1929 territorial legislature appropriated $30,000 for the predator control project over the next biennium, and Stewart decided to go after the predators in earnest.

Stewart hired trappers to work in the Talkeetna Mountains, and chose for himself the town of Chitina as a base of operations. He had two reasons for this: Chitina's rail access to the port of Cordova, and its proximity to the supposed coyote migration route from Canada through the nearby White River drainage. In July 1929 Stewart hired two bachelors to assist him directly: forty-five-year-old C. L. Gelsinger and Ed Steen, a twenty-six-year-old ex-Marine. Outfitted with locally purchased camp gear and over $500 worth of groceries shipped from the Shwabacher Brothers merchants in Seattle—everything from matches and candles to seedless raisins and evaporated eggs—the men set out for the field. They traveled the Kotsina, Kluwesna, and Kuskulana rivers, with a trip north to the Nabesna River, trapping and visiting the Athabascan villages to offer trapping instruction. Stewart wrote a brief progress report to Governor Parks in November in which he noted that private trappers were harvesting coyotes in increasing numbers after his "coaching," and emphasized that salaried hunters would not be as effective as the cooperative method between his team and private trappers. The response of the trappers led him to state optimistically that "the problem may be worked out well and that we may confidently look for a practical solution of this rather serious matter."[38]

Six months later, however, Stewart found himself relieved of his duties. Discontent surfaced first from Ed Steen, whom Stewart had fired in December. Understandably resentful, Steen sat down on Christmas Day to write an explanatory letter to Harry Watson, Governor Parks' secretary. Steen cast doubt on Stewart's trapping ability, noting that during their six months of field work they had trapped only two coyotes, one fox, two bears, and several lynx. Steen predicted the following season of trapping would yield little, and felt the entire predator menace existed only on paper. In regard to sheep, he blamed people, not wolves, for declining numbers. In contrast with Stewart's reports, Steen claimed that Stewart was in hot water with the private trappers because of the reduction in bounty money, costing him "confidence and cooperation." In Steen's eyes, Stewart's chief asset was an ability to "compose an elaborate and convincing report." He closed the letter with a veiled threat to expose the predator control operation to the press.[39] Steen also wrote a second letter that day, informing his colleague Gelsinger of his dismissal by Stewart.

It turned out that Gelsinger had handed in his own resignation on December 26. On his way back home, Gelsinger stopped in the village of Copper Center and awkwardly used the typewriter at John McCrary's store to compose a letter to Steen.

> I am taking care of the store here to day and Ed sure appreciate having all I want to eat onc more and as soon as i get out i am going to have a medical board examine as to sanity for there must be something seriously rong with a fellow to go back there where we went and go through what we went through for what we got out of it.... if what I went through is training a man to trap I am a siwash and dont know it.... Ed if you took his typewriter away from him he would be like a men without arms or legs and half a head and helpless but also harmless to the Territory which would be a good thing for the people here. we dont kneed him here...is about as mutch

use to us here as six tails would be to a dog.... I took the trouble to show him the facts and figures where the whole system was a huge joke on the Territory...it would not only be a waste of my time but a waste of Territory funds to continue farther under the present system.[40]

Along with Steen's letter, Gelsinger's found its way to the governor's office in late February, and by May Stewart had been reassigned with the Biological Survey to duties outside Alaska. Stewart *was* good at composing relentlessly optimistic reports, whatever his trapping ability, and seemed convinced that his project had merit. Discontent from his men had two further sources. The salary disparity was large; Steen and Gelsinger each earned $471 for their half-year effort, while Stewart was receiving annual compensation of $3,600. And the men disliked the intended cooperation with Alaska Natives. Steen called them "diseased and insect infested," and the training situations were likely strained, with one party full of assumed superiority and the other quite underwhelmed by the expertise of the professionals. Nevertheless, the predator control project by this time had its own momentum, and continued without this unhappy trio.[41]

Harlan Gubser assumed leadership of the project—and Stewart's salary—amid growing controversy over wolf control. Gubser had been one of those hired by Stewart to work in the Talkeetna Mountains in the winter of 1929–30, and he had been no more successful than Stewart at finding wolves and coyotes. Private trappers continued to criticize the reduction in bounty money and claimed it reduced their incentive to target the elusive wolves. Warden Sam White of the Alaska Game Commission found this argument "absurd"; he criticized trappers for operating solely with "mercinary" *[sic]* motives rather than a "sense of loyalty" toward the "campaign on the predatory animals." Trappers in the Interior complained they were running out of ammunition for defense against the packs, and that wolves were eating everything including lynx and fox.[42] From the western part of the state came dire reports about wolf predation on the reindeer herds, and in the summer of 1930, Gubser made a trip to the reindeer areas.

Gubser's initial report to Governor Parks confirmed localized depredations, but also observed that owners ignored good herding techniques, and many reindeer were lost due to the scattering of the animals. Since the region was so large, Gubser recommended against employing salaried hunters, but instead proposed working with Natives to increase trapping productivity. A hunter began control duties in September in the lower Yukon River area, and Gubser assisted with setting up the base camp by backpacking supplies sixty miles through a "continuous downpour." This may have contributed to his comment that year to Edward Nelson that even if large numbers of predators were taken, it would not justify the expense of "operations of this character in remote sections."[43]

Nevertheless, Gubser's report on activities through 1930 cast the program in a positive light, noting that while one man could hardly halt depredations in the entire reindeer country, the Native trappers had been receptive to his demonstrations and gifts of scent baits. Overall, he claimed an increase of eighty-eight percent in wolves taken in the four years following the inception of the control program, although this could have followed from the concurrent increase of residents and wolves even without the trapping demonstrations. Although Gubser claimed success at his mission, he warned of the predators "waiting like a smouldering fire" for favorable conditions to increase their activities. In May 1931, however, Governor Parks offered office space and clerical help for Gubser's work, but declined to contribute further funds to the cooperative project. He had been advised by H. W. Terhune, the executive officer of the Alaska Game Commission, that the reports of wolf depredations by the reindeer supervisors had "no real foundation," based on the field reports of Terhune's wardens. Parks expressed regrets that this "very necessary work" should end, but realistically concluded it would be up to local people to halt the depredations.[44] The cooperative project officially ended when Gubser transferred all of the equipment—traps, sleds, tents, pots, and pans—to the Alaska Game Commission. Yet the plea for wolf control would continue from western Alaska, and Harlan Gubser would soon be back on the reindeer ranges.

Paul Redington's 1932 letter to the Park Service's Horace Albright was only the latest in a series of offers to assist in killing McKinley Park's wolves. The Park Service had not participated in this first federal control project in the territory, probably because no sense of crisis existed then, and no public constituency demanded control in the park. Yet precedent aplenty existed for such action, for wolves had been eliminated from all other national parks. But there was Harold Bryant writing in the margin that the National Park Service was the only agency that could take a different view toward predators. Significant changes in park wildlife management had occurred, ones that caused the service to be the first government agency to propose protecting wolves rather than killing them.

The underlying ideals for a national park system took several decades to evolve, although several patterns can be discerned in the late nineteenth century. While Yellowstone is celebrated as our first national park, having been withheld from private development in 1872, the precedent had been set eight years earlier in a Congressional act placing the Yosemite Valley under the management of the California governor for public recreation. Yellowstone began and remained under federal control, however, and became the paradigm of an American national park: large size, located in the West, seemingly unsuited for agriculture or industry, and containing curiosities of geology and topography that conformed to a scenic ideal of monumentalism.[45] Lacking a clear mandate or an administrative structure in Washington, D.C., to coordinate these new land areas, the early parks were primarily the creations of activist individuals with particularly local interests, rather than the products of national policy. While in later years national parks would be viewed as a democratic American reaction to the closed and guarded European hunting preserves—author Wallace Stegner called the nation's parks "absolutely American, absolutely democratic"—there were few people other than the wealthy who were involved in the creation of the parks or in their use, since parks were far away and accessible only by train travel. Ultimately, the creation of a federal administrative unit for national parks came from a need to define their role in the spectrum of public lands.[46]

Proposals to create a park management bureau began in 1900, but little effective action ensued for a number of years.[47] Chief opponent to the creation of a Park Service had been Gifford Pinchot, Theodore Roosevelt's chief forester and ideologue for utilitarian conservation. Pinchot opposed mere preservation of lands, especially for recreational purposes, believing that scientific development for commercial purposes was the best use of lands and resources, and he sought to place the national parks within the jurisdiction of the Forest Service and Department of Agriculture. Pinchot went out of office after the election of President Taft, clearing the way for legislation in 1910 to create a Park Service. This remained blocked for several years by a combination of Pinchot-trained Forest Service men and western congressmen, until Interior Secretary Lane enlisted wealthy California businessman Steven Mather for the parks campaign in 1915. A mountain-climbing Sierra Club member, Mather brilliantly used his business contacts, the popular media, and his flair for promotional trips to unify preservation-minded groups in the cause of esthetic conservation. This proved important, for it would allow the Park Service an independence that gave rise to distinctive philosophies and policies. President Wilson signed a National Park Service Act on August 25, 1916, unifying the existing twelve national parks and nineteen national monuments under the Department of the Interior, with Mather becoming the first service director, a post he held until 1929.[48]

The early national parks owed their existence to scenic features rather than protection of wildlife. Yellowstone was created to highlight its geysers and canyons and secondarily its fauna. Its enabling legislation prohibited only wanton destruction of wildlife, while allowing hunting, trapping, and fishing for park residents or visitors. Nearby sawmills in 1877, for example, requested 20,000 pounds of meat for their workers, and the hills of Yellowstone were obvious destinations of the market hunters. George Bird Grinnell, through his *Forest and Stream* magazine, had since the late 1870s urged the protection of Yellowstone's animals, particularly the bison, which had been hunted almost to extinction. He articulated the benefits of creating a game sanctuary that would allow the surplus animals, breeding undisturbed in the park, to spill out into the adjacent areas that had been depleted by hunters, an idea that brought sportsmen into the ranks of park supporters.[49] Birds and mammals received a measure of protection with the passage of legislation in 1883 that banned killing them.

Aside from such champions as Grinnell, fauna in parks other than Yellowstone were secondary to the scenery and only eventually gained importance. Director Mather regarded parks as being primarily for tourists, and he had little sense of a wildlife ideal until late in his administration. Mather and his assistant, Horace Albright, had been given charge of a park system that had accumulated rather than being systematically planned, and their quest for appropriations from Congress necessitated clear goals for the Park Service. This resulted in a set of principles published in a 1918 letter from Interior Secretary Lane to Mather, which established the ambiguous language of the parks being maintained "in absolutely unimpaired form for the use of future generations," yet preserved for the "use, observation, health, and pleasure of the people." The only animals mentioned in these park principles were cattle, which were permitted to graze in all parks except Yellowstone.[50] Albright capitalized on the public appeal of visible wildlife after becoming the

Caribou with Mount McKinley in background.
Adolph Murie Collection, temp box 13. Courtesy Alaska and Polar Regions Archives, Rasmuson Library, University of Alaska Fairbanks.

superintendent at Yellowstone. He established a small display of caged animals and nightly bear feedings at hotel garbage dumps, complete with bleachers for tourists. For Park Service administrators, the lesson was clear: grand scenery was good, but big animals walking around in front of the scenery was even better.

Predators did not receive protection in national parks. Organized efforts to eliminate wolves, coyotes, and mountain lions had occurred since the 1890s in Yellowstone; later, rangers assigned to predator control added bobcats, foxes, minks, weasels, otters, and fishers to the list of undesirable park animals. Following the creation of the National Park Service in 1916, Director Stephen Mather understood the need to cultivate a public image for the parks and realized that public support—particularly from the sportsmen's groups, who were essential to retain as local allies—would follow from a policy that protected game animals and minimized predators. The Bureau of Biological Survey was conveniently poised to assist in clearing parks of predators. Yellowstone's wolves did not last long: the last ones killed were two pups in 1926, making a total of 136 in the previous twelve years, and wolves were sighted only occasionally in subsequent years.[51]

Similar patterns of predator control prevailed in other national parks. A trapping and poisoning campaign in Glacier National Park in the 1920s almost eliminated its wolves, although occasional sightings continued. The same decade saw the elimination of wolves from Crater Lake, Death Valley, Grand Teton, Mount Rainier, Olympic, Rocky Mountain, Sequoia, Yosemite, and Grand Canyon parks, despite Director Mather's 1926 statement that "it is contrary to the policy of the Service to exterminate any species native to a park area."[52] Such campaigns had less to do with Park Service administration malevolence than with ignorance of the functioning of biological systems and the need to follow dominant public attitudes—and hence continue congressional appropriations. Predator control was firmly in the tradition of utilitarian conservation: wolves, coyotes, and pumas had no economic value, while livestock and hunting ranges adjacent to national parks did.[53]

Two situations involving game animals showed the inadequacy of simply creating refuges. For tourists wishing to observe game animals, Yellowstone's managers deserved commendation. In the absence of hunting and the diminution of predators, the elk, bison, and antelope had multiplied into a spectacle available nowhere else. However, park boundaries had not been drawn with regard to its animals. Their ancestral winter ranges were blocked by ranches, whose owners expected the government to keep game out of their hayfields. This forced game animals to utilize inferior winter ranges where they soon degraded the limited forage. Attempts to cull elk populations by shipping them away for transplant into nearby national forests was costly and insufficient to stop the growing population.[54] Harsh winters in 1916–17 and 1919–20 caused the death of thousands of elk (an estimated 14,000 in the latter), yet public opinion would not tolerate liberalized hunting regulations, preferring instead to support feeding programs, which perpetuated high herd numbers.[55] The Park Service was caught in the conventional dichotomy between game and vermin, and the sanctuary of Yellowstone looked more and more like a trap for its grazing animals.

A further jolt to prevailing game management models occurred in Arizona. In 1906 President Roosevelt created a national game preserve to protect the deer herd, estimated at four thousand, in part of the Kaibab National Forest adjacent to Grand Canyon National Park. Reduced domestic grazing combined with predator control by forest rangers followed, and by 1924 the deer multiplied to about 100,000. Sixty percent of them died during the following two winters. Range denudation had been reported by 1918, but recommendations to expand sport hunting had been ignored, while predator control continued. Ever the promoter, Park Service Director Stephen Mather opposed culling the herd because they were a tourist attraction adjacent to his national park. Public sentiment opposed bullets as a control measure, despite unequivocal evidence of damage to flora the deer needed for survival. A too-late effort by government hunters to kill excess deer in 1928 met with opposition from sportsmen, animal lovers, and Arizona's governor and game wardens. While subsequent wildlife biologists have questioned the validity of the simplified story of predator-prey relations on the Kaibab Plateau, the drama of the wolfless forest littered with starving deer provided game wardens with "the greatest lesson of their lives" in animal mismanagement.[56]

The evidence was plain: game animals could multiply excessively in the absence of checks on their numbers. One alternative was to manage game like livestock. The Boone and Crockett Club, in its recommendations to the Park Service, considered this common sense.[57] This approach would solve the forage problems and maintain herds for tourist pleasure, but it seemed to violate a tenet of national park philosophy and that of the game refuge; plenty of people had let it be known they would not stand for the rational killing of the friendly herbivorous park animals. Another alternative was available, one that included predators and invoked a presumptive balance of nature with the parks as places to preserve it. This emerged from the scientific community, and particularly, for the Park Service, from a zoologist in California, Joseph Grinnell.

Grinnell is a seminal figure in American vertebrate biology, because of his prolific research and leadership of the West Coast's finest zoological museum.[58] His legacy for most Americans is tangible, if invisible to all but scholars, in the national parks and their wildlife management. Historian Alfred Runte called him "the biological conscience of the National Park Service." Grinnell profoundly shaped park philosophy and his ideas persist, particularly those regarding predators.[59] Born in 1877 in Indian Territory of Quaker parents, Grinnell's predeliction toward natural history showed early. A self-described "bird-fiend," by age eighteen he catalogued his first avian collection, taken from the Pasadena area where his family had settled, and he had established his reputation as a field ornithologist by the time he entered Stanford for graduate work in 1900.[60] A private benefactor endowed the Museum of Vertebrate Zoology at the University of California, and Grinnell became its first director in 1908, a post he held until his death in 1939. While questions of species distributions and the habits of birds dominated his research, he publicly championed numerous conservation causes, none more fervently than on behalf of national parks and their appreciation by an educated public.

Areas that then or later became California's national parks—Yosemite, Death Valley, Lassen, Sequoia—were well known to Grinnell from his field forays. Even though national parks had been founded for scenery's sake rather than to preserve animal habitat, scientists used parks as natural laboratories for taxonomic work in classifying species and for testing theories of population dynamics. Before Congress established the Park Service, Grinnell recognized an important value of parks to scientists: "they furnish samples of the earth as it was before the advent of the white man." He recommended the "rigid exclusion" of domestic animals from parks, and minimal numbers of roads, buildings, and other human modifications. What Grinnell and his students sought to retain would become a central concept of wildlife management in national parks, the notion that "from the plant and animal life of the parks, their original balance should be maintained."[61] For these biologists, the parks represented an unprecedented opportunity to preserve not just scenery, but the balance of nature itself.

The development of this concept involved changes in the roles of both God and humans. That the world had been shaped by gods for the good of humans was a cosmological view that extended from ancient times to the mid-1800s.[62] This view had remained unchallenged by the leading natural historians of eighteenth-century Europe, but in the nineteenth century Charles Lyell's 1830 *Principles of Geology* and Charles Darwin's 1859 *Origin of Species* cast doubt on the idea of an orderly world divinely created for humans.[63] In 1864 American George Perkins Marsh published *Man and Nature,* a book that would presage much of the conservation movement in this country. Marsh argued that human activity largely determined the health of the landscape, and that cumulative human activities usually resulted in large-scale degradation of the earth, to the eventual detriment of society:

> But man is everywhere a disturbing agent. Wherever he plants
> his foot, the harmonies of nature are turned to discords. The

proportions and accommodations which insured the stability
of existing arrangements are overthrown.[64]

The second edition of his book contained the plea that would be echoed
by Joseph Grinnell, as Marsh urged the protection of large primitive areas as
sanctuaries for animals and study areas for students of natural history.[65]

Predators benefited from a view of the natural world that considered it
balanced in the absence of humans, and from the development of the study of
ecology. The originator of the word *oecologie*, Ernst Haeckel, described it in
1866 as "the science of the relations of living organisms to the external world."[66]
Theories which sought order and predictability in the natural world needed to
account for all components of the native fauna, forcing acknowledgment of
some sort of beneficial role for predators. Grinnell reserved his place in the
history of ecological ideas by contributing the durable concept of the niche—
an animal's role— in a 1917 paper.[67] Recognition of the niche concept included
predators, and Grinnell published one of the earliest pleas for predator
protection. In this he articulated a scarcely recognized purpose of national
parks as areas where even "predaceous animals should be left unmolested and
allowed to retain their primitive relation to the rest of the fauna."[68]

Evolution allowed a new sense of the value of predators, since they and
their prey had developed together over time. This notion provided a more
sophisticated rationale for allowing predators to coexist, and it carried profound
implications for prey management. Competition within and between species
was a central tenet of Darwin's thought, given its enduring—if misleading—
summation in Herbert Spencer's phrase "survival of the fittest," which defined
endless struggle in positive terms for the health of species. Henry Fairfield
Osborn, of the American Museum of Natural History, addressing the fittest
members of American society at the elite Boone and Crockett Club, presented
the conventional Victorian view: "You have all read your Darwin carefully
enough to know that neither camels, horses, nor deer, would have evolved as
they did except for the stimulus given to their limb and speed development by
the contemporaneous evolution of their enemies in the dog family."[69] The
idea occurred to Olaus Murie, traveling through interior Alaska's forests and
mountains: "I have a theory that a certain amount of preying on caribou by
wolves is beneficial to the herd, that the best animals survive and the vigor of
the herd is maintained."[70] Charles Adams, who received one of the country's
first Ph.D. degrees in ecology, thought it desirable that predators kill "the

weaklings among the game in our parks and forests."[71] The concept found an advocate in England, as the eminent ecologist Charles Elton included it in the first edition of his *Animal Ecology*.[72] While maintaining the fitness of prey through predation made intuitive sense to biologists, its general acceptance lay far in the future.

Despite the early glimmerings of attitudinal change toward predators among animal ecologists, these changes were hardly diffused in the cultural context. In early twentieth century America, the wolf still preyed on the sheep, cattle, and imaginations of the populace. Although most Americans had never seen a wolf, they read magazine and newspaper stories about government trappers pursuing the Custer Wolf or Old Three Toes. Such stories were not limited to the pages of sportsmen's magazines, but also appeared in the *Ladies Home Journal, Literary Digest, Popular Mechanics*, and the *New York Times*.[73] Influential nature writers such as Theodore Roosevelt, John Burroughs, and William Hornaday drew public attention to diminishing animal populations and promoted appreciation and protection for mammals and birds. Predators, however, received no sympathy. Wolves were dangerous and noxious animals, "the beast of waste and desolation," and provided manly sport for Roosevelt and his ilk.[74] Burroughs, perhaps the most popular nature writer in America, brought anthropomorphized song-bird stories to readers, and in his idealized world "the fewer of these [predators] there are, the better for the useful and beautiful game."[75] William Hornaday, a hunter turned animal protector who became director of the New York Zoological Society in 1896, published widely in defense of animals. His 1913 book, *Our Vanishing Wild Life*, took aim at hunters, immigrants, African-Americans, fashion-conscious women, ranchers, and the lower social strata in general for causing the demise of the continent's fauna. Hornaday's concern for animals never included the large carnivores, however. He described the wolf as "sanguine, crafty, dangerous and cruel..., the most degenerate and unmoral species on earth." Hornaday's 1920 congressional proposal for stronger game laws in Alaska included "regulations to provide for the wholesale killing of wolves, by poison or otherwise."[76] Another enormously popular nature writer provided an alternate perception of wolves. Ernest Thompson Seton, who had once trapped wolves in New Mexico, did not diminish the carnivorous realities of wolves in his writings and paintings. However, he differed from his literary peers in describing wolf characters with attractive traits: emotional, courageous, dignified, monogamous, a justifiable part of a natural world. Nevertheless, Seton's greatest triumph as a wolf trapper occurred when he killed Lobo, King of the

Currumpaw, by using his mate's carcass to lure the old hunter, and his account by that name became a bestseller. For all of Seton's self-identification and affection for the wolf, his paintings—*La Poursuite*, *The Black Wolf of Currumpaw*, *The Triumph of the Wolves*—emphasized their wildness and ferocity. He did not portray wolves as the kind of animal people wanted living in a civilized land.[77]

We take for granted that we will see, in our national parks, something that looks like nature as it was meant to be, regardless of how that notion crumbles under scrutiny. If that seems self-evident today, it was by no means guaranteed to become part of national park philosophy. Joseph Grinnell's ideas powerfully shaped the emergence of wildlife management in parks through his close involvement with Yosemite, his connections with Berkeley alumni Stephen Mather and Horace Albright, and his students who became Park Service employees. Grinnell's intellectual legacy also extended through the wolf-sheep controversy of McKinley Park.

One person well-poised to further Grinnell's ideas was Harold Bryant, the "HCB" of the marginal comment on the Redington-to-Albright letter. Bryant earned his doctoral degree in zoology from the University of California Berkeley in 1910—his dissertation supervised by Grinnell. Following graduation he worked for the California Fish and Game Commission and in his spare time volunteered to give evening lectures and nature walks to visitors at Tahoe and Yosemite parks. Grinnell had pressed the new Park Service to expand activities to encourage park visitors to understand the natural history of their surroundings, to be able to interpret, rather than just view, what lay before their eyes. Director Stephen Mather approved this approach after seeing the popularity of these early efforts led by Grinnell's students. In 1920–21 Mather authorized a formal summer program of interpretive activities in Yosemite, along with establishment of a park museum, under Harold Bryant's guidance.[78] In 1920 Horace Albright hired the Park Service's first year-round naturalist in Yellowstone. During the next four years most of the western parks designated staff naturalists, yet California remained the center of park naturalist training. In 1925 the Park Service created its Educational Division, headquartered at the Yosemite Field School at the University of California Berkeley.[79] This center coordinated educational and training activities for park

Harold Bryant, Assistant Director, National Park Service.
A. E. Demaray Collection, American Heritage Center, University of Wyoming

personnel, and provided a close connection to Grinnell's Museum of Vertebrate Zoology. That year Director Mather indicated his support for this branch of the service with a firm directive to park superintendents on the importance of the Educational Division, yet within the hard-bitten ranger ranks the naturalists were regarded as "posy pickers" and "Sunday supplement scientists." Rangers in the expansive early park years spent their time in trail and road construction, poaching patrols, fire fighting, and predator hunting. They found it easy to disdain the interpreters—whose ranks included women—who provided less rugged services to the park clientele. With its success assured by public popularity, the Educational Division found a need to educate within Park Service ranks, to confirm that nature guiding consisted of "matters for manly interest."[80]

The Yosemite Field School's success and the need to coordinate such activities within the Park Service led to the creation of the Branch of Research and Education. In 1930 Harold Bryant left his Berkeley home for Washington, D.C., to assume this administrative duty as assistant director. He had responsibility for the Park Service's general educational policy, publication of scientific and historical literature, public relations, and wildlife matters. Horace Albright left Yellowstone and became Park Service director the same year, and while he recognized the importance of wildlife in the parks, his major interest and legacy to the service was in historic preservation. During his tenure the service added battlefields and monuments previously managed by the military. This left Bryant as the primary administrator with academic training and interest in wildlife, at a time when the Park Service began using science, rather than sentiment, to address animal management.[81]

Another Berkeley graduate with an interest in park wildlife exerted a profound impact on the acceptance of predators in national parks. George Wright took a degree in forestry, but also studied under Joseph Grinnell for a minor in vertebrate zoology. In 1926, while still a student, he took a trip to Mount McKinley National Park with Grinnell's assistant, Joseph Dixon, to survey the park's animals. Following this, Wright joined the Park Service as a naturalist in Yosemite. Independently wealthy and far thinking, he proposed an ambitious, multiyear project to Bryant and Albright: a national survey of park fauna. With their blessing and his own money, Wright hired Dixon and another Yosemite employee, Ben Thompson, a Stanford graduate. In 1929 the trio set out on a two-year national park tour.[82]

Their travels resulted in prescient, thoughtful analyses of the status of park animals and in recommendations that would resound for decades in park policy.[83] Their first two publications provided the Park Service with a philosophic foundation for policy, firmly based on preservation of all native fauna managed through science-based methods. *A Preliminary Survey of Faunal Relations in National Parks* appeared in 1933, followed a year later by *Wildlife Management in the National Parks*.[84] The authors urged that human modification of parks be minimized, and that intervention be primarily for the sake of maintaining or restoring the primitive condition existing at the time of Euroamerican settlement. They repeatedly discussed the preservation of wilderness at a time when, with New Deal monies, the parks expanded their roads, campgrounds, and accommodations for tourists:

> Our national parks are a great philosophical venture in which
> we are attempting to pry open for ourselves the intricate and
> delicately balanced system of wilderness values....[85]

These biologists offered policy suggestions that addressed the issue of predators:

> That the rare predators shall be considered special charges of
> the national parks in proportion that they are persecuted
> everywhere else.
>   That no native predator shall be destroyed on account of its
> normal utilization of any other park animal, excepting if that
> animal is in immediate danger of extermination, and then only
> if the predator is not itself a vanishing form.

They recognized the significance of McKinley Park's wolf population, and urged that "every effort should be made to save it." Wright and his partners predicted that fifty years hence "we shall still be wrestling with the problems of joint occupation of parks by men and mammals," yet their inclusion of all animals in the natural balance of parks became the still-existing policy. Historian Richard Sellars regards Wright and company's work as "the threshold to a new era" in the Park Service.[86]

After the New Deal initiatives of 1933 the Park Service expanded in several ways, including the creation of a Wildlife Division within Harold Bryant's Research and Education branch. Young George Wright became director of the new division, headquartered at Berkeley. He died in a car accident in 1936, cutting short a brilliant career. His successor as chief of the Wildlife Division was Carl Russell, also a Berkeley graduate in zoology who maintained the connection with Joseph Grinnell. Within the space of a few years, science became the method by which animal problems would be solved, rather than depending on the variously-trained ranger corps, which represented a victory for Bryant's struggle to find respect for nature study within the Park Service ranks.[87]

Harold Bryant, along with many others in the Wildlife Division, held memberships in the professional organizations of animal biologists, which formed important allies for the Park Service. These groups had opposed indiscriminate predator control from an early date. The Ecological Society of America, organized in 1915, comprised a broad variety of plant and animal scientists mostly connected with the growing body of academicians across the

United States, and it held representation on the Council on National Parks, Forests, and Wildlife during the late 1920s.[88] The more vocal opponent to predator control was the American Society of Mammalogists, an organization which since its inception in 1919 held academicians among its members, as well as game managers of the Park Service and Biological Survey, which allowed competing federal organizations to dispute within the context of a professional group.

The Biological Survey's vigorous predator control in the 1920s provoked dissension within the mammalogist's society, aired out at a symposium on predatory mammals during the society's 1924 annual meeting. Joseph Dixon and Lee Dice presented papers on the scientific value of predators, and Charles Adams pleaded for management policies based on science rather than the "vicious propaganda" that accompanied policies made by public opinion. National parks, according to Adams, should be "without question…our main sanctuaries for predacious animals," and he invoked the disturbance of the primitive balance of nature caused by White settlement of the continent.[89] E. A. Goldman presented the Biological Survey's response: predators in national parks were untenable because they would eat the game in the park and then spread to adjacent settled areas in search of livestock, and Goldman concluded that predators "no longer have a place in our advancing civilization." Unswayed, the society passed a resolution condemning the "nationwide campaign for the destruction of predatory animals."[90]

Other organizations voiced their defense of predators in 1929. The New York Zoological Society (William Hornaday having resigned three years earlier) resolved that the Park Service suspend destruction of predators, and the Boone and Crockett Club resolved that predators be accepted as natural and desirable components of parks.[91] Joseph Grinnell's Cooper Ornithological Club, the Audubon Societies, and numerous other groups added their voices for predator protection.[92] Despite these, the political power of the western livestock industry remained undiluted, and western congressmen sponsored legislation in 1929 for an expanded ten-year campaign by the Biological Survey against predators.[93]

As before, the American Society of Mammalogists responded with a predator symposium, held during their annual meeting in May 1930. Charles Adams emphasized that five years had passed since the mammalogists called for research to precede "wholesale destruction and extermination," yet the survey spent its money on trappers and poison, not science. With predators still hunted in national parks, Adams asked, "But we are probably the richest nation on earth, and what would be the cost of maintaining one hundred mountain lions in North America? Would it stagger American civilization?" A. Brazier Howell concluded the session by labeling the Biological Survey "not our federal wildlife warden, but the guardian of the sheep men and other powerful interests."[94] Another resolution passed condemning indiscriminate poisoning of predators, yet the following year the Biological Survey received its enlarged appropriation from Congress. The year was 1931, and as the Great Depression deepened, the opinions of several hundred scientists were not going to halt efforts to support the livestock industry and preserve jobs in rural America.[95]

The National Park Service, however, appeared to be more receptive to the scientists. Joseph Grinnell spoke to a park superintendent's conference in 1928 on the value of predators in natural systems and they voted to suspend the use of steel traps, followed by Horace Albright's ban on the use of poisons in 1930.[96] After the mammalogists' 1930 symposium, Albright produced a policy statement for predators, published in the *Journal of Mammalogy*. He affirmed that all animals had a place in parks, both for the pleasure of visitors and as subjects for scientists. "Predatory animals are to be considered an integral part of the wild life protected within national parks, and no widespread campaigns of destruction are to be countenanced."[97]

But Horace Albright was no friend of park predators; he had overseen the elimination of wolves in Yellowstone during his superintendency in the 1920s. Writing in 1929 on "Our National Parks as Wild Life Sanctuaries," he described the threat posed to McKinley's sheep by wolves, who were "rapidly increasing in northern Alaska, following the reindeer south, and overrunning Mt. McKinley Park." Predators needed controlling to enhance the "species of animals desirable for public observation and enjoyment."[98] Albright visited McKinley Park in 1931, hosted by Superintendent Harry Liek, a protégé from Yellowstone days; Albright had made sure Liek became the park's second superintendent in 1928. A coterie of congressmen accompanied Albright to inspect the road and hotel construction as well as take a backcountry trip by horse, yet his activities were abruptly curtailed by an attack of appendicitis; a doctor in Fairbanks removed the offending organ.[99] But Albright had had enough time to assess the game situation, and learned that sheep populations seemed healthy. In his annual report, Albright noted that park rangers were "watching this situation carefully and control measures will be taken as necessary."[100] Liek had plenty of experience with predators from his Yellowstone days; in fact, out on a winter coyote patrol, he had received a taste of his own medicine when a fellow ranger mistakenly put strychnine rather than baking powder in the flapjack batter. Liek continued unquestioned predator control at McKinley Park, making "determined efforts to stamp out the predatory animals." Albright seemed conditioned to concur; he supported Liek by authorizing McKinley's rangers to "kill wolves on sight," yet at the same time did not regard the wolves to be a threat to the sheep population. Orthodoxy ran deep, apparently.[101]

Although Albright did not take Paul Redington's offer to help kill those wolves, he clearly did not share Harold Bryant's notion that sheep were no more beneficial than wolves. Considerable sheep mortality occurred in 1932, in a winter when ice-crusting on the snow weakened the sheep. Harry Liek blamed the sheep losses on wolves and coyotes and urged their eradication.[102] In response to Liek's views, Bryant argued:

> The National Park Service needs to champion the idea that there is interrelation between living forms, and that the best attitude is to believe that they each have a function and that the chain of interrelation is easily broken by man's interference. With that view, instead of emphasizing the protection of one species as against another, *we should cherish and protect all forms of life.* Any move to destroy wolves in McKinley will have to be made over my *continued* protest.[103]

Albright responded one month later in a memorandum to the wildlife staff. He felt it absolutely necessary that wolves be controlled. Given the vast size of Alaska, wolves could never be eliminated, and there was no reason to make the park a wolf preserve. On the basis of his visit, Albright felt "the sheep constitute about the only interesting thing for the tourist to see in this park when the mountain is enveloped in clouds, as it often is." Bryant reacted vigorously and succinctly six days later. "I stand firm on my protest against control of wolves in Alaska. My argument is based on a broad biological viewpoint rather than on the limited one of wishing to display sheep to the public." The following day, Albright again turned to the wildlife staff for advice. "Why should we take any chances on having our magnificent display of sheep lost to the public?" While criticism might be received from scientists, "if we lose those marvelous bands of sheep we are going to be criticized by the public at large, and rightly so."[104]

Albright and Bryant were not even arguing the same issue. Albright had been with the Park Service from its inception and had played a central role in educating and enthralling Americans about national parks. To ensure the success of the parks, they needed visitors who would become park supporters, and Albright excelled at park promotion. His concerns over animals focused on their availability for public viewing. Yellowstone's fame resulted from its thermal features and game herds; McKinley's fame rested on a mountain rarely seen and its game herds, especially the sheep which could be seen nowhere else by tourists. Harold Bryant's background and professional affiliations were in science. He desired to "keep mammalogists and ecologists with us rather than against us."[105] He too encouraged public use of the parks, yet he wanted visitors to reach an understanding of natural processes, not merely view a sanitized version of nature.

The letter from Redington to Albright contained yet another strand of park wildlife policy worth mentioning. Underneath Bryant's comment is a response from Albright: "I think that since coyotes are not native to Alaska they should be removed just like elk from Yosemite, only the predators we must kill." More will be said on the recent dispersal of coyotes to Alaska. They seemed problematic to the Park Service because of the idea that parks preserved "natural" conditions as they were at a point generally defined as when White settlement occurred. Unnatural species included feral domestics, such as burros or boars, and few disagreed that the Park Service should eliminate them. More problematic were animals such as transplanted elk and mountain goats, as well as the various trouts planted in park waters. These were undeniably attractive to tourists, but became difficult to reconcile with park policies and remain some of the most controversial management problems.[106]

Horace Albright left the Park Service in 1933, and Bryant saw his stance on McKinley's wolves adopted by the next director, Arno Cammerer. He halted wolf killing in 1935, telling Superintendent Liek, "Do not be concerned over the cry that wolves are about to sweep the country.... Should the reports of an unusual abundance of wolves be correct, then it is to be assumed that game is abundant too." Cammerer instructed Liek to answer local criticism of wolf protection by offering the example of Yellowstone, where starving elk lacked wolves and cougar.[107] Comparing McKinley to Yellowstone failed to satisfy Park Service critics, and a protective stance toward wolves provoked stiff opposition. In Alaska, relations among predators, prey, and humans were wound much tighter than in the states.

Notes

1   Redington to Albright, 15 March 1932, RG 79, Entry 7, File 719, Box 1415, National Archives (hereafter NA).

2   Two books chronicled the American history of wolves and people prior to the recent increase in the literature: Stanley P. Young and Edward A. Goldman, *The Wolves of North America* (Washington, D.C.: The American Wildlife Institute, 1944), and Stanley P. Young, *The Wolf in North American History* (Caldwell, Idaho: Caxton Printers, 1946). Bruce Hampton's *The Great American Wolf* (New York: Henry Holt, 1997) is the best broad historical update to these; see also the documentary collection of Rick McIntyre, ed., *War Against the Wolf: America's Campaign to Exterminate the Wolf* (Stillwater, MN: Voyageur Press, 1995).

3   Richard Gerstell, *The Steel Trap in North America* (Harrisburg, PA: Stackpole, 1985), 177. The history of the Oneida company forms the core of this book.

4   Sewell Newhouse, *The Trapper's Guide,* 6th ed. (New York: Oakley, Mason & Co., 1874), 212, 215.

5   Gerstell, *The Steel Trap,* 192.

6   Young, *Wolves of North America,* 380–81. See the comments on bounties in Durward L. Allen, *Our Wildlife Legacy,* rev. ed. (New York: Funk & Wagnalls, 1962), 266–76, and L. David Mech, *The Wolf: The Ecology and Behavior of an Endangered Species* (Garden City, NY: Natural History Press, 1970), 332–33.

7   See Keir B. Sterling, *Last of the Naturalists: The Career of C. Hart Merriam* (New York: Arno Press, 1977), and "Builders of the U.S. Biological Survey, 1885–1930," *Journal of Forest History* 33 (October 1989): 180–87.

8   Sterling, *Last of the Naturalists,* 66–67; Paul G. Redington, "The United States Bureau of Biological Survey," *The Scientific Monthly* 37 (October 1933): 293.

9   For example, Merriam wrote a 1918 monograph on brown and grizzly bears in which he listed 86 species in North America; *A Review of the Grizzly and Big Brown Bears of North America,* North American Fauna No. 41, (Washington, D.C.: GPO, 1918). As taxonomy evolved, biologists tended to minimize species differences and converge previously differentiated animals. We now recognize only three bears: black, brown/grizzly, and polar.

10   Sterling, *Last of the Naturalists,* 173, 178–79. Sterling deals at length with the intellectual questions of the speciation controversy. Citing the need to protect his namesakes, Roosevelt created Mount Olympus National Monument in 1909.

11   Jenks Cameron, *The Bureau of Biological Survey: Its History, Activities, and Organization* (Washington, D.C.: GPO, 1929; reprint New York: Arno Press), 37 (page numbers are to reprint edition); Donald C. Swain, *Federal Conservation Policy 1921–1933* (Berkeley: University of California Press, 1963), 32; A. Hunter Dupree, *Science in the Federal Government: A History of Policies and Activities to 1940* (New York: Harper & Row, 1957), 253.

12   Redington, "Biological Survey," 292.

13   Stanley Young estimated bounty payments, in their various forms, of $100 million prior to WW II. He also noted that in no other country in the world had so many laws been passed against an animal, yet the wolf's demise was caused more by habitat alteration following human settlement than by bounty hunting; *Wolves of North America*, 338–39.

14   Robert H. Connery, *Governmental Problems in Wildlife Conservation* (New York: Columbia Univ. Press, 1935; reprint New York: AMS Press, 1968), 85 (page numbers are to reprint edition); Nathaniel P. Reed and Dennis Drabelle, *The United States Fish and Wildlife Service* (Boulder, Colorado: Westview Press, 1984), 75.

15   Sterling, *Last of the Naturalists,* 79–80, 258. Merriam is likely unique in his gustatory appreciation for some predators. Vernon Bailey, a protégé and highly effective field agent who married sister Florence Merriam in 1899, wrote back to family while on a Grand Canyon trip with his boss: "Merriam killed a big wild cat last night + we have had it cooked for breakfast + dinner.... Skunks and cats are his favorite meat + he is especially fond of Eagle." Ibid., 115.

16   Vernon Bailey, *Wolves in Relation to Stock, Game, and the National Forest Reserves* (Washington, D.C.: GPO, Department of Agriculture, 1907), 5.

17   Cameron, *Bureau of Biological Survey*, 46; David E. Brown, ed. *The Wolf in the Southwest: The Making of an Endangered Species* (Tucson: University of Arizona Press, 1983), 48.

18   "Wolves," *National Geographic*, February 1907, 145–47. Merriam had served on the founding committee of the National Geographic Society in 1888, and quite possibly used the magazine as his ally in the public opinion stakes.

19   For years Merriam had struggled in his work with a government salary of $3,500. He had accompanied the lavish scientific excursion to Alaska organized by millionaire Edward Harriman in 1899, subsequently editing the official summary of that trip; see *Alaska: The Harriman Expedition, 1899* (New York: Dover Publications, 1986, originally Doubleday, 1901). Upon Merriam's retirement, Charles Sheldon and Theodore Roosevelt convinced Harriman's widow to endow him with a lifetime salary and research funds of $17,000 annually for independent research; Sterling, *Last of the Naturalists,* 281. Among Merriam's later works was the posthumous editing of Charles Sheldon's diaries into *The Wilderness of Denali*.

20   Cameron, *Bureau of Biological Survey,* 47.

21   Gerstell, *The Steel Trap,* 198, 203, 214, 297.

22   Nelson's contributions to ethnology are summarized in Margaret Lantis, "Edward William Nelson," *Anthropological Papers of the University of Alaska* 3 (December 1954), 5–15. He also collected animal and bird specimens during his Alaska years and is credited with the formal discovery of *Ovis dalli*, the white mountain sheep of Alaska which subsequently attracted Sheldon to the McKinley region.

23   Brown, ed., *The Wolf in the Southwest,* 57.

24 Quoted in Trefethen, *American Crusade for Wildlife,* 165.

25 Cameron, *Bureau of Biological Survey,* 52.

26 Swain, *Federal Conservation Policy,* 40.

27 Cameron, *Bureau of Biological Survey,* 315.

28 Lopez, *Of Wolves and Men,* 191–93.

29 Cameron, *Bureau of Biological Survey,* 60.

30 Swain, *Federal Conservation Policy,* 44; Thomas R. Dunlap, "Values for Varmints: Predator Control and Environmental Ideas, 1920–1939," *Pacific Historical Review* 53 (May 1984): 141–61.

31 Cameron, *Bureau of Biological Survey,* 51.

32 Alaska Governor's *Annual Report,* 1923, 50; Governor's *Annual Report,* 1924, 33. Curiously, Stanley Ligon was rookie Forest Service ranger Aldo Leopold's supervisor in New Mexico, responsible for wolf control there; see James C. Burbank, *Vanishing Lobo: The Mexican Wolf and the Southwest* (Boulder, CO: Johnson Books, 1990), 100–7.

33 Following information taken from Stewart's "Report to the Governor of Alaska on Cooperative Predatory Animal Investigations and Control in the Territory, March 1, 1929," File 639.9, St3r, ASHL.

34 Territorial appropriation for bounties were $30,000 in 1927–28 and $25,000 in 1929–30, rising to $40,000 in 1931–32 with a $15 bounty for both wolf and coyote; see Donald E. McNight, "The History of Predator Control in Alaska," internal report for the Alaska Department of Fish and Game, 1970.

35 Governor's *Annual Report,* 1928, 10; Governor's *Annual Report,* 1929, 12.

36 Redington personal diary, August 4–8, Paul Goodwin Redington Collection, Box 2, American Heritage Center, University of Wyoming (hereafter AHC). That predators would increase the wariness of game animals to the detriment of tourists, and thus damage the purpose of a park designated as a 'game refuge,' found strange echoes years later in Glacier Bay National Park, where the hunting of seals by Tlingit Indians upset tourists desirous of proximity to the flighty seals; see Theodore Catton, *Inhabited Wilderness: Indians, Eskimos and National Parks in Alaska* (Albuquerque: University of New Mexico Press, 1997), 72.

37 Redington to Demaray, 19 November 1928; Parks quoted in "Résumé of Principal Correspondence on Sheep-Wolf Relations at Mount McKinley National Park"; Redington to Demaray, 7 June 1929; Demaray to Redington, 20 June 1929; all RG 79, Entry 7, File 715, Box 1415, NA.

38 Grocery invoice, 7 June 1929; Stewart to Parks, 2 November 1929, RG 101, Box 303, ASA.

39 Steen to Watson, 25 December 1929, RG 101, Box 303, ASA.

40 Gelsinger to Steen, 13 January 1930, RG 101, Box 303, ASA. The apparent errors in my transcription are those of the original.

41   Stewart, "Fiscal Summary Report," November 1931; Steen to Watson, 25 December 1929, RG 101, Box 303, ASA.

42   White to H.W. Terhune, 29 January 1930, RG 101, Box 303, ASA; *Fairbanks Daily News-Miner*, "Wolves Depleting Fur Bearers Thru Interior District," 8 February 1930.

43   Gubser to Parks, 6 July 1930; Gubser, "Report to the Governor of Alaska on Cooperative Predatory Animal Investigations and Control in Alaska, 1 March 1931"; Gubser to Nelson, n.d. 1930; all RG 101, Box 318, ASA.

44   Gubser, "Report to the Governor of Alaska on Cooperative Predatory Animal Investigations and Control in Alaska, 1 March 1931"; telegram from Redington to Parks, 4 May 1931; both RG 101, Box 318, ASA. Terhune to Parks, n.d.; Mark A. Winkler to Terhune, 25 April 1930, RG 101, Box 303, File 25, Folder 4, ASA. Parks to Redington, 5 April 1932, RG 101, Box 333, Folder 4, ASA.

45   This principle, along with that of park withdrawals being approved by Congress only if the lands were considered to be essentially worthless, forms the backbone of Alfred Runte's *National Parks: The American Experience,* 2nd ed. (Lincoln: Univ. of Nebraska Press, 1987). Additional views are available in "The National Parks: A Forum on the 'Worthless Lands' Thesis," *Journal of Forest History* 27 (July 1983): 130–45. See too Richard Sellars, *Preserving Nature in the National Parks: A History* (New Haven: Yale University Press, 1997), chapter two.

46   Stegner quoted in John C. Freemuth, *Islands Under Siege: National Parks and the Politics of External Threats* (Lawrence: University of Kansas Press, 1991), vi. Further works on the National Park Service include Jenks Cameron, *The National Park Service: Its History, Activities, and Organization* (Washington, D.C.: GPO, 1922; reprint, New York: AMS Press, 1974); John Ise, *Our National Park Policy: A Critical History* (Baltimore: Johns Hopkins Press, 1961); William Everhart, *The National Park Service* (Boulder, CO: Westview Press, 1983); Ronald A. Foresta, *America's National Parks and Their Keepers* (Washington, D.C.: Resources for the Future, 1984).

47   A detailed account of the creation of the National Park Service is Donald C. Swain, "The Passage of the National Park Service Act of 1916," *Wisconsin Magazine of History* 50 (Autumn 1966): 4–17. Other accounts are in previously noted works, as well as Horace Albright, *The Birth of the National Park Service: The Founding Years, 1913–33* (Salt Lake City: Howe Brothers, 1985), and Donald C. Swain, *Wilderness Defender: Horace M. Albright and Conservation* (Chicago: University of Chicago Press, 1970).

48   See Robert Shankland, *Steve Mather of the National Parks,* 2nd ed. (New York: Alfred A. Knopf, 1970).

49   John Reiger, *American Sportsmen and the Origin of Conservation,* 2nd ed. (Norman, OK: University of Oklahoma Press, 1986), 99–104. Conventional histories of U.S. conservation invoke the early names of Thoreau, Marsh, Muir, Pinchot, and Roosevelt; Reiger's work argues for recognition of the hunting and fishing fraternity's inspiration for much of conservation's success. Grinnell is the central figure of Reiger's book, written in part to provide recognition for a previously-ignored figure in American conservation.

50   The full text of the 1918 principles can be found in Ise, *National Park Policy*, 194–95. Ise, like most authors, thought that Mather probably wrote the letter, but Albright claims authorship in his autobiography, *Birth of the National Park Service*, 69–73.

51   John Weaver, *The Wolves of Yellowstone: History, Ecology, and Status* (National Park Service, Natural Resources Report No. 14, 1978), 11; Victor H. Cahalane, "The Evolution of Predator Control Policy in the National Parks," *Journal of Wildlife Management* 3 (July 1939): 234–35.

52   Cahalane, "Evolution of Predator Control," 235. Also see the lavishly-illustrated book by Rick McIntyre, *A Society of Wolves: National Parks and the Battle Over the Wolf*, rev. ed. (Stillwater, MN: Voyageur Press, 1996).

53   See Sellars, *Preserving Nature*, 71–75.

54   Aubrey Haines, *The Yellowstone Story: A History of Our First National Park*, Vol. 2 (Colorado Associated University Press, 1977), 79.

55   The National Parks Association, founded in 1919 to champion park causes, found its first public challenge in Yellowstone's elk situation, and considered its defeat of hunting proposals to be a victory; see John Miles, "Charting the Course," *National Parks*, November-December 1993, 40.

56   Quote by Arizona Game Warden K. C. Kartchner, in Barry C. Park, "Problems From Creation of Refuges for Big Game," in *Transactions of the Eighth North American Wildlife Conference* (Washington, D.C.: Wildlife Management Institute, 1943), 342.

     The story of the Kaibab deer and the 'lessons' learned from it are part of the canon of American wildlife tales. The standard account is John P. Russo, *The Kaibab Deer Herd: Its History, Problems, and Management* (Phoenix: Arizona Game and Fish Department, Wildlife Bulletin No. 7, 1964). Graeme Caughley revealed the flaws of the simple predator-prey story in "Eruption of Ungulate Populations, with Emphasis on Himalayan Thar in New Zealand," *Ecology* 51 (Winter 1970): 53–72. Thomas R. Dunlap sketches the effect of the simplified lessons of the Kaibab story on first and second generation game managers in "That Kaibab Myth," *Journal of Forest History* 32 (April 1988): 60–68.

57   From a policy statement adopted by the club in 1923; reproduced in *Hunting and Conservation*, eds. George Bird Grinnell and Charles Sheldon (New York: Arno Press, 1970), Appendix A.

58   The ecologist G. Evelyn Hutchinson stated "Joseph Grinnell was perhaps the greatest student of North American birds and mammals whom the continent has yet produced"; quoted in Steven G. Herman, *The Naturalist's Field Journal: A Manual of Instruction Based on a System Established by Joseph Grinnell* (Vermillion, SD: Buteo Books, 1986), 3. Herman's book describes one of Grinnell's legacies, a standard field notation system still taught in American universities.

59   Alfred Runte, "Joseph Grinnell and Yosemite: Rediscovering the Legacy of a California Conservationist," in *Yosemite and Sequoia: A Century of California National Parks*, eds. Richard J. Orsi, Alfred Runte, and Marlene Smith-Baranzini (Berkeley: University of

California Press, 1993), 92. Further explication of Grinnell is in Runte, *Yosemite: The Embattled Wilderness* (Lincoln: University of Nebraska Press, 1990).

60   His widow, Hilda Wood Grinnell, contributed a biography to the journal Joseph had long edited, which describes well his vigorous and prolific scholarly life; see "Joseph Grinnell: 1877–1939," *The Condor* 42 (January-February 1940): 3–34. Grinnell's second bird collection came from Alaska, on a youthful eighteen-month adventure with friends to the gold rush on the Bering Sea. They did not find much gold, but upon return he published *Birds of the Kotzebue Sound Region*, Pacific Coast Avifauna No. 1 (Santa Clara: Cooper Ornithological Club, 1900). The "bird-fiend" is from this, page 3.

61   Joseph Grinnell and Tracey Storer, "Animal Life as an Asset of National Parks," *Science* 44 (15 September 1916): 377, 379, 377.

62   See Frank N. Egerton, "Changing Concepts in the Balance of Nature," *The Quarterly Review of Biology* 48 (June 1973), 322–50, and Clarence J. Glacken, *Traces on the Rhodian Shore: Nature and Culture in Western Thought from Ancient Times to the End of the Eighteenth Century* (Berkeley: University of California Press, 1967).

63   Donald Worster's *Nature's Economy: A History of Ecological Ideas* (Cambridge: Cambridge University Press, 1977) provides good access to these intellectual questions.

64   George Perkins Marsh, *Man and Nature* (Cambridge: Harvard University Press, centenary edition 1965), 36.

65   Paul Brooks, *Speaking for Nature: How Literary Naturalists from Henry Thoreau to Rachel Carson Have Shaped America* (Boston: Houghton Mifflin Co., 1980), 93. For Marsh's role in the development of ecology, see Frank N. Egerton, "Ecological Studies and Observations Before 1900," in *History of American Ecology*, ed. Frank N. Egerton (New York: Arno Press, 1977).

66   Quoted in Worster, *Nature's Economy*, 192.

67   Joseph Grinnell, "The Niche-Relationships of the California Thrasher," *The Auk* 34 (1917): 427–33. Despite the importance of Grinnell's contributions to biology, the niche was his only significant contribution to ecology, according to Thomas Dunlap. Grinnell even opposed ecological studies by his students under his direction, preferring they stay in taxonomy or distribution studies; *Saving America's Wildlife* (Princeton: Princeton University Press, 1988), 54.

68   Grinnell and Storer, "Animal Life as an Asset of National Parks," 378.

69   Henry Fairfield Osborn, "Preservation of the Wild Animals of North America," in George Bird Grinnell, ed., *American Big Game in its Haunts* (New York: Forest and Stream Publishing, 1904), 354.

70   O. Murie to E. W. Nelson, 18 July 1923, MS 51, Box 4, Folder 5, ASHL.

71   Charles Adams, "The Conservation of Predatory Animals," *Journal of Mammalogy* 6 (February 1925): 92.

72   Charles Elton, *Animal Ecology* (London: Sidgwick & Jackson, Ltd., 1927), 115, 119. While Grinnell proposed the niche concept, Elton was responsible for its subsequent development.

73   See Lopez, *Of Wolves and Men*, 193; historian Lisa Mighetto provides a useful chapter, "Working Out the Beast," in *Wild Animals and American Environmental Ethics* (Tucson: University of Arizona Press, 1991). Also useful is the bibliography of "Popular Articles on the Gray Wolf" in Erich Klinghammer, Monty Sloan, and De Wayne R. Klein, *Wolf Literature References: Scientific and General Books and Articles Listed Alphabetically by Author* (Battle Ground, Indiana: North American Wildlife Park Foundation, Inc., 1990).

74   Mighetto, *Wild Animals*, 79.

75   Quoted in Brooks, *Speaking for Nature*, 126; Dunlap, *Saving America's Wildlife*, 27.

76   William T. Hornaday, *Our Vanishing Wild Life; Its Extermination and Preservation* (New York: New York Zoological Society, 1913); Hornaday, *The Minds and Manners of Wild Animals* (New York: Charles Scribner's Sons, 1927), 17, 223; Hornaday, A *New Game Act for Alaska for the Better Protection and More Rational Utilization of Alaska's Game Animals* (New York Zoological Park: Permanent Wildlife Protection Fund, Bulletin No. 6, 15 February 1920), 30.

77   Lisa Mighetto champions Seton in beginning the rehabilitation of the wolf's reputation; see "Wolves I Have Known: Naturalist Ernest Thompson Seton in the Arctic," *Alaska Journal*, Winter 1985, 55–59. Thomas R. Dunlap regards Seton's sympathies as "limited"; see "Values for Varmints," 145. In another article Dunlap notes that humans were often cast as intruders into a balanced natural world; "The Realistic Animal Story: Ernest Thompson Seton, Charles Roberts, and Darwinism," *Forest & Conservation History* 36 (April 1992): 60. See too Betty Keller's *Black Wolf: The Life of Ernest Thompson Seton* (Vancouver: Douglas & McIntyre, 1984), and Ralph H. Lutts, *The Nature Fakers: Wildlife, Science, & Sentiment* (Golden, CO: Fulcrum Publishing, 1990).

78   Runte, *Yosemite*, 114–16; Harold C. Bryant and Wallace W. Atwood, Jr., *Research and Education in the National Parks* (Washington, D.C.: GPO, National Park Service, 1932): 47–48; Harold Bryant, "Nature Lore for Park Visitors," *American Forests* 35 (August 1929): 501; Ann and Myron Sutton, "The Man From Yosemite," *National Parks*, July-September 1954, 102–5, 131–32, 140.

79   See C. Frank Brockman, "Park Naturalists and the Evolution of National Park Service Interpretation Through World War II," *Journal of Forest History* 22 (January 1978): 24–43.

80   Quoted in Polly Welts Kaufman, *National Parks and the Woman's Voice: A History* (Albuquerque: University of New Mexico Press, 1996), 87. Although women comprised a significant percentage of students at the Yosemite Field School, Bryant and others actively discouraged the hiring of women as naturalists in the parks; see also Kaufman, "Challenging Tradition: Pioneer Women Naturalists in the National Park Service," *Forest and Conservation History* 34 (January 1990): 4–16.

81   See Thomas R. Dunlap, "Wildlife, Science, and the National Parks, 1920–1940" *Pacific Historical Review* 59 (May 1990): 187–202.

82   Biographic information on Wright from Harold Bryant, "George M. Wright, 1904–1936," *Bird-Lore*, March-April 1936, 137; Harold Bryant, "Obituary Notices: George

Melendez Wright," *Journal of Mammalogy* 17 (May 1936): 191–92. Alston Chase provides a lively account of the formation of the Wildlife Division in *Playing God in Yellowstone: The Destruction of America's First National Park* (New York: Harcourt Brace Jovanovich, 1987), 233–39; see also Wright, *Wildlife Research*, 14–16. Richard Sellars emphasizes that wildlife research was the only major program in the park service to be started by private funds, and might not have happened for many years had not Wright taken the initiative; *Preserving Nature*, 94.

83   Committees appointed in the 1960s to investigate faunal conditions in national parks found themselves repeating the recommendations of these surveys conducted thirty years earlier. See F. Fraser Darling and Noel D. Eichhorn, *Man & Nature in the National Parks: Reflections on Policy* (Washington, D.C.: The Conservation Foundation, 2nd ed., 1969).

84   George M. Wright, Joseph S. Dixon, and Ben H. Thompson, *Fauna of the National Parks of the United States: A Preliminary Survey of Faunal Relations in National Parks*; Fauna Series No. 1 (Washington, D.C.: GPO, National Park Service, 1933); George M. Wright and Ben H. Thompson, *Fauna of the National Parks of the United States: Wildlife Management in the National Parks*; Fauna Series No. 2 (Washington, D.C.: GPO, National Park Service, 1934).

85   Wright, *Wildlife Management*, 55.

86   Wright, *Preliminary Survey*, 147, 148; Wright, *Wildlife Management*, 15, 25; Sellars, *Preserving Nature*, 98.

87   Dunlap, "Wildlife, Science, and the National Parks," 193–95.

88   For a summary history of this group, see Robert L. Burgess, "The Ecological Society of America," in *History of American Ecology*, ed. Frank N. Egerton (New York: Arno Press, 1977).

89   A summary of the meeting appeared in "Sixth Annual Meeting of the American Society of Mammalogists," *Journal of Mammalogy* 5 (August 1924): 218–21. The interest in this issue may be surmised by the subsequent publication in the *Journal of Mammalogy* 6 (February 1925) of the major papers presented at this meeting. Charles Adams, "The Conservation of Predatory Mammals," *Journal of Mammalogy* 6 (February 1925): 93, 90, 84. See also Hampton's account in *The Great American Wolf*, 139–46, and Dunlap, *Saving America's Wildlife*, 50–61.

90   E. A. Goldman, "The Predatory Mammal Problem and the Balance of Nature," *Journal of Mammalogy* 6 (February 1925): 33; "Sixth Annual Meeting of the American Society of Mammalogists," *Journal of Mammalogy* 5 (August 1924): 218.

91   Reported in "Comment and News," *Journal of Mammalogy* 10 (February 1929): 95.

92   Numerous articles against poisoning appeared in the Audubon Societies' journal, such as "Wild Life in National Parks," *Bird-Lore*, January-February 1931, 100–1; "Poisoning Campaigns," *Bird-Lore*, May-June 1932, 235–39. The local societies melded into the National Audubon Society in 1940, and *Bird-Lore* changed to *Audubon* in 1941.

93 Cahalane, "Evolution of Predator Control," 235; Swain, *Federal Conservation Policy,* 44; Congressional bills were S. 3483 (Sen. Norbeck, South Dakota) and H.R. 9599 (Rep. Leavitt, Montana).

94 Charles C. Adams, "Rational Predatory Animal Control," *Journal of Mammalogy* 11 (August 1930): 354, 357; A. Brazier Howell, "At the Cross-Roads," *Journal of Mammalogy* 11 (August 1930): 388.

95 Two historians that have examined this controversy over predator control disagree as to its significance. Donald Worster devotes a chapter, "The Values of a Varmint" in *Nature's Economy*, concluding that a changing attitude toward predators lies at the "very center" of the broad ecological consciousness of modern times, and that predator defenders used moral arguments to buttress their stance. Thomas Dunlap argues that a scientific rationale using the balance of nature ideal, although not yet proven, underlain the ecologists' defense of predation, rather than a moral view; "Values for Varmints."

96 Cahalane, "Evolution of Predator Control," 232, 235.

97 Horace Albright, "The National Park Service's Policy on Predatory Animals," *Journal of Mammalogy* 12 (May 1931): 185–86.

98 Horace Albright, "Our National Parks as Wild Life Sanctuaries," *American Forests* 35 (August 1929): 536.

99 Swain, *Wilderness Defender*, 196–97; Albright, *Birth of the NPS*, 262–64. The congressmen, including members of the House Subcommittee on Interior Department Appropriations, were impressed enough to approve adding 300,000 acres near Wonder Lake to the park lands.

100 Department of the Interior, *Annual Report of the Director of the National Park Service to the Secretary of the Interior,* 1931, 64; Albright's visit is described in William E. Brown, *A History of the Denali-Mt. McKinley Region, Alaska* (Washington, D.C.: Government Printing Office, National Park Service, 1991), Chapter 8.

101 Haines, *The Yellowstone Story*, 313. See "Report of Supt. Harry J. Liek," in Department of the Interior, *Annual Report of Director of the National Park Service to the Secretary of the Interior* (1930). Authorization to shoot wolves recounted in a letter, Albright to W.B. Bell (of the Biological Survey), 16 November 1931, RG 719, Entry 7, File 719, Box 1415, NA.

102 Superintendent's "Annual Report," 1932, DENA.

103 Bryant to Albright, 17 December 1932, RG 79, Entry 7, File 719, Box 1415, NA; emphasis in original.

104 Albright to staff, 17 January 1933; Bryant to Albright, 23 January 1933; Albright to staff, 24 January 1933; all RG 79, Entry 7, File 719, Box 1415, NA.

105 Bryant to Albright, 17 December 1932, RG 79, Entry 7, File 719, Box 1415, NA.

106 See Wright, *Wildlife Research*, 91–110, and Sellars, *Preserving Nature*, 78, 258–61.

107 Cammerer to Liek, 25 February 1935, RG 79, Entry 7, File 719, Box 1415, NA. Bryant went on to serve as superintendent of Grand Canyon National Park until 1954.

There must first be a lot of wolf killing done.
—*Frank Dufresne*

3

Animals and Alaskans

Alaska is a poor place for farming or ranching, and the primary food product of the land is still wild meat, fowl, and fish. Annual consumption of wild foods by Alaskans totals more than forty million pounds. Personal consumption varies depending on place of residence, cash flow, and preference. According to the state Division of Subsistence, per capita harvest by urbanites in Anchorage and Fairbanks equals ten to twenty pounds per person annually, while many bush villagers average over five hundred pounds of wild protein.[1] Subsistence foods remain an important part of the state's economy and personal larders, while also providing sport for many. Wild foods were even more important earlier in the century. With game meat vital to the diet and the rituals of hunting firmly embedded in the regional culture, the dynamics of prey populations directly affected human attitudes toward wolves, and thus the politics of animals in Mount McKinley National Park.

These days, when needing answers to questions of animal population ecology, modern wildlife biologists can take advantage of tools that would seem to maximize the accuracy of their conclusions: airplanes and helicopters allow scientists to soar like ravens, pharmacologic tricks make animals go to sleep and then wake up, and radio collars allow distant surveillance. Even today, though, seemingly straightforward questions about animals are answered with large degrees of uncertainty. Questions of animal populations are fundamental to decisions of management policy: how many caribou can be taken by hunters this year? How many wolves represent a threat to game populations? How many sheep are in McKinley Park? The wildlife ecology of large mammals was poorly understood in the early twentieth century, and management decisions were subject to both insufficient data and political vicissitudes. Attempting to answer such questions for the decades preceding aerial and electronic sensing is highly speculative, involving the credibility of eyewitness sources, cultural biases, political motives, forest fire histories, and variations of climate, abundance, and scarcity that affect animal populations in northern latitudes.[2] Yet a survey of wildlife estimates for the early decades of this century is worthwhile. Even if the people responsible for making guesses about animal populations were inaccurate, their estimates represent what Alaskans thought was happening to the game. Understanding responses toward the National Park Service's wildlife management policies necessarily includes these perceptions of game populations. The perceived trends all helped further hostility toward wolves.

The largest land mammal in Alaska played the smallest role in the early controversy over wolves. Moose, *Alces alces gigas*, were relative newcomers to Alaska, following the spread of their preferred woody browse plants north as the Ice Age glaciers melted. Yet in Alaska they became the largest moose in the world, surpassing the other subspecies of North America and Europe, weighing upwards of one thousand pounds. Moose live singly or in cow-calf groups, although travel on winter routes can temporarily concentrate groups. They cope well with northern winters, their long legs elevating them above the snowpack and their upright forage—preferably willows—usually accessible. But too much snow, or too little browse, can produce winter mortality. Death also comes from wolves, who take advantage of pack numbers and weakened moose to minimize the damage moose can inflict in combat. In McKinley Park moose numbered in the hundreds. Market hunters may have depressed their numbers, for moose were considered scarce in 1922–23, yet by the late 1920s their numbers increased in the park and elsewhere.[3] Crusted snow in the spring of 1932 led to difficulties and deaths. Park rangers reported that the ice crust caused bleeding and damage to moose legs. Nevertheless, Joseph Dixon's survey of park fauna in 1932 found the moose population to be healthy.[4] Moose were an important prey for people and wolves, yet wolf predation provoked less outcry than it did with other game species. Perhaps the homely moose in the willows attracted fewer human defenders than did other species. And perhaps the expansion of its range into western and northern Alaska, and increasing availability to hunters, minimized concern on its behalf.[5] In the years since statehood, though, with increasing numbers of Alaskan hunters, fluctuations in moose populations have inevitably triggered appeals for wolf control.

Dall sheep *(Ovis dalli)* live in Alaska's mountains from the Brooks Range to the Chugach Range and eastward into Canada, but McKinley Park is one of the few places a tourist can readily observe them in their natural habitat. Living in bands in the unglaciated mountains that flank the ice-covered peaks, sheep eat mostly grasses and sedges, as well as lichens, moss, willows, and various forbs. Seasonal variation in ranges is common, the winter spent on windblown ridges where underlying vegetation is available, with wider dispersal to areas of good forage during summer months. Their defense against predation consists of visual acuity and maneuverability in steep, rocky terrain that defeats the running ability of wolves.

The McKinley Park area is virtually the only location where observers estimated and recorded sheep numbers in the early 1900s. This resulted from its proximity to Fairbanks, the ease with which sheep could be seen on the natural travel corridor through the park, where its road now runs, and the interest accorded sheep by hunters and park personnel. Market hunters, active until about 1921, found the sheep abundant enough to make harvest and transport to Fairbanks profitable, but they do not seem to have posed a threat to the overall population. Charles Sheldon and early park rangers recorded healthy sheep populations through 1928, with estimates of five, ten, and even twenty-five thousand.[6] Heavy snows in April 1929, a month when the sheep's fat reserves and forage were at their minimum, resulted in a large die-off. Rangers reported an even greater kill during the winter of 1931–32, as rain followed record-setting snows in February, forming an ice crust that prevented efficient feeding. The sheep population dropped to an estimated 1,500 in the summer of 1932 and continued declining until 1945. The sheep herds were the primary reason for the park's creation, so when reports filtered back to the east coast about declining numbers, the Park Service began to receive inquiries as to the status of the sheep and the steps taken by park rangers to protect the remaining survivors. Indignation followed when the Park Service indicated that predator control would not be one of the measures used to rebuild sheep populations.

The caribou of the North have long been likened to the bison of the plains, with their vast numbers darkening distant hillsides, unpredictable migration patterns, ceaseless movement across the open lands, and ability to supply human hunters with food and skins for clothing and shelter. They have lived in the north country for over a million years; two subspecies live in Alaska,

Grant's caribou *(Rangifer tarandus granti)* of the Alaska Peninsula, and Stone's caribou *(R. t. stonei)*, which range across the mainland, excluding southeast Alaska. They eat a larger variety of foods than any other member of the deer family. Common edibles are the ground and tree lichens, as well as grasses, sedges, and browse in season. Gregarious animals, caribou are typically found in aggregations of ten to several hundred individuals, with larger gatherings in the spring and fall when herds migrate between their calving and wintering grounds. Their reproductive rate is fairly slow, and calf mortality by wolves and grizzly bears can be high. Herd behavior and fleetness defend caribou against wolves, but observers have found that wolves can bring down caribou in at least half their attempts.[7]

Alaska herds are named and associated with geographic areas: the Nelchina herd, the Porcupine, the McKinley, and others. Home ranges, hundreds of square miles in size, have been more useful for nomenclatural convenience than respected by the caribou. One of the problems faced by researchers constructing herd histories is knowing whether the absence of caribou in a particular place and time is because the animals have died or because the herd has changed ranges. Researchers generally agree that broad herd movements allow forage to grow and renew overall range health. They disagree on the phenomenon of large-scale herd shifts and on the reasons for population variability.

The McKinley Park caribou form one of the smaller recognized herds, and this herd's position in the center of Alaska has allowed it contact and influence from surrounding areas. American observers in 1866–67 considered caribou abundant in the Norton Sound area, but by the 1890s the coastal tundra was virtually devoid of caribou. Wildlife biologist Ronald Skoog speculates there may have been a population shift to the east and north in the 1880s, thus adding to the herds in the Yukon/Tanana drainages. Part of his evidence is that at the time reports indicated increasing numbers of caribou in the McKinley region, with estimates of up to 30,000 by the 1920s.[8] While the home ranges of McKinley Park's moose and sheep are small enough to be contained by the park's boundaries, the caribou—and the wolves—have moved fluidly across the straight lines drawn to protect them. Wide variance in summer and winter ranges have been reported for the McKinley caribou herd, from Lake Minchumina to Broad Pass and northwards to the Tanana River, thus resulting in varying population estimates for the park's caribou. Surveys in the 1940s indicated a declining herd. One explanation supposed a large-scale migration toward the western coast, but evidence is slim for that.[9]

The importance for the park was that caribou numbers fell at a politically volatile time.

Alaskans counted on caribou as staple food, and the history of the Fortymile herd of east-central Alaska is relevant because of its proximity to McKinley Park and pre-WW II Alaska's population centers. Olaus Murie, an eyewitness to the fall migration in 1920, estimated the Fortymile herd at five hundred thousand animals, and he considered an estimate of one million to be well within reason, though probably generous.[10] This herd, crucial for feeding gold rush miners along the Yukon River and its tributaries, apparently maintained a large population through the 1920s, yet by the end of that decade caribou numbers seemed to be dwindling. The last large herd seen on the Steese Highway, northwest of Fairbanks, was in 1934. Residents of Eagle reported caribou scarce since the mid-1930s. A large herd crossed the Yukon River in 1938 and was then seen no more in the previous ranges.[11] The population low, in the early 1940s, was estimated at ten to twenty thousand animals, a precipitous change from Murie's half million.

People offered a number of explanations for the caribou's decline. Some blamed the Natives, newly armed with repeating rifles and thought to lack the "sportsman's code" that ostensibly controlled White hunter's excesses. Others blamed White hunters. Alaska's game laws allowed prospectors to shoot game as needed for human or dog food. Alaska residents blamed visiting trophy hunters. Wolf predation was a popular explanation shared by everyone. More recent theories focus on population shifts to other ranges, and the effects of fires and logging on the wooded winter habitat needed by caribou. Ronald Skoog dispenses with hunting theories by noting that Eskimos along the Bering Sea did not have enough rifles and ammunition to affect caribou numbers seriously, and the herds had deserted the coast well before 1900. With the Fortymile herd, he estimates a human harvest of thirty-five thousand annually in the 1930s, and concludes this level of hunting was insufficient to affect a herd of half a million. Skoog also notes that caribou numbers across Alaska increased at the height of gold-mining operations, from 1897–1930, rather than decreasing, as would have been the case if hunting were an important factor. His explanation for caribou population changes revolves around "centers of habitation," from which herds disperse into less optimal ranges when population densities exceed a certain point. Not all scientists agree with Skoog, and given the variability of the animal and its changing environment, we are unlikely to know what really caused previous patterns.[12] What is important for this study is how the declining caribou herds of the 1930s and 1940s

Winter meat: Soldiers from Fort Egbert with caribou from the Fortymile herd, 1897.
Clarence Andrews Collection, Division of Special Collections and University Archives, University of Oregon Library System

affected Alaskans' attitudes toward wolves, for few understood why the National Park Service would protect wolves when game animals were in decline. And the issue was not just game animals, for Alaska was thought to be on the verge of developing its own livestock industry.

Olaus Murie was a biologist, not a stockman, and his bias toward the wild over the domestic was plain when he wrote, "The caribou's greatest menace is not the wolf, nor the hunter, but man's economic developments, principally the reindeer." To a stockman's mind, reindeer were the answer to Alaska's need for economic diversification. Senator Thomas Kendrick of Wyoming, who had gone west as the transition was made from bison to cattle, recognized "the strongest kind of a parallel between this particular venture [Alaska's reindeer industry] and the old range cattle days." An entrepreneurial reindeer owner, Carl Lomen, regarded the animal as "among the earliest and best friends man has ever had." Frank Dufresne, a fur warden who became the executive director of the Alaska Game Commission, predicted, "If there is any hope of making a stock country out of interior Alaska, there must first be a lot of wolf killing done."[13] Olaus Murie feared genetic dilution of the caribou, but overly so. Kendrick and Lomen saw their pastoral dreams foundered by poor range management and racial politics. Dufresne saw interior Alaska fail to become a stock country, but not for lack of killing wolves for the sake of reindeer herds.

The reindeer has been intimately associated for centuries with Old World humans from Norway to Chukotka. Scholars do not agree as to exactly when or where humans made the shift from only hunting reindeer to domesticating them.[14] The reindeer has only recently become part of the New World landscape. In response to White observers' perception that the Eskimos of northwest Alaska faced imminent starvation, Dr. Sheldon Jackson, a Presbyterian churchman, had imported 1,280 reindeer from Siberia and Norway between 1892–1902. He also arranged for Siberian and Lapp herders to instruct the Eskimos in the care of this new animal.[15] Jackson and others expected them to use the reindeer for food, clothing, and as a way to achieve financial self-determination and an entrance into the ways of the western world. Natives were already suffering cultural disintegration, however, from contact with commercial whaling crews, and were affected by the diminution of coastal caribou herds during the preceding several decades. Using the starvation threat, Jackson convinced churches and the federal government to finance the initial importation of the reindeer. Within a few years no further mention was made of imminent starvation, and Jackson sought the development of a domestic food industry for the territory, a change hastened in 1899 by the Nome gold rush and the resultant need for meat.[16] The reindeer range eventually spread from the Alaska Peninsula to the Arctic coast and inland to the edge of the spruce forest, with the industry centered on the Seward Peninsula.

Once the presumed Eskimo starvation was averted, there was little plan for the reindeer's future. They were initially government property, with loans of one hundred animals made to the Lapp herders and interested Eskimos, to be repaid in five years with the increase belonging to the herder. Harvests were local affairs for local food needs. The situation changed in 1914, however, as a Norwegian-American family, the Lomens of Nome, received permission from the government to buy a herd. Reindeer numbers had increased spectacularly. The Lomens wanted to create a reindeer meat export industry to stateside markets, and to this end they sought outside investment, built corrals and abattoirs, and purchased refrigerator ships. They also employed almost six hundred Eskimos as herders and laborers. The Lomens thought they were providing a valuable service to Alaska and its Natives. Despite the harvest of enough animals to ship 257,000 pounds of meat in 1920, the reindeer herds continued to increase, as did controversy over the direction of the industry.[17]

Lomen & Company was a complex operation that few understood and many envied. Father Gudbrand Lomen, appointed federal judge for the Nome district in 1921, had four sons. All had roles in the business, which included commercial stores and lighterage companies, and sons Ralph and Alfred gained election to the territorial legislature. As the Lomens built their reindeer industry, they began to attract criticism.[18] Objections to a White-owned, profit-making industry in what was envisioned as an Eskimo improvement project found sympathetic ears in Washington, D.C., culminating in the 1937 Alaska Reindeer Act, which granted all future reindeer ownership to Natives. Testimony given by Carl Lomen to Senator Kendrick's 1931 Committee on Reindeer revealed Lomen's bewilderment at being accused of perfidy in his business:

> The original policy of the Government to create interest through apprenticeship of the Eskimos in the reindeer industry has completely broken down and been abandoned. The Eskimo has lost personal interest in the reindeer....They [Eskimo] have failed to mark their herds and have kept only desultory records....Demoralization became chaos....The White herds have received proper care and enjoyed their natural increases.[19]

Regardless of the quality of herding, reindeer numbers increased rapidly. The government's reindeer experts assumed a range capacity of up to four million animals, so no concern emerged as the estimated population surpassed a half million.[20] With continuing growth, though, people wondered about range deterioration. Near the coast the reindeer and caribou feed primarily on ground-covering lichens and, because of their slow growth, a grazed-out range needs up to twenty-five years to recover. The obvious way to reduce the impact of excess reindeer on their feeding grounds was through slaughter and export, but the harvests—stunted by weak market demand and difficult supply logistics—proved insufficient to check overpopulation.[21] The herd population reached an estimated maximum of 614,000 in 1932 before abruptly declining. This reduction occurred almost twice as fast as the buildup. By 1950, only 25,000 reindeer remained.[22] The ecologic catastrophe contained within those

Reindeer herd in corral made of ice blocks, Wainwright, 1924.
Clarence Andrews Collection, Division of Special Collections and University Archives, University of Oregon Library System

fifty years was explained by a variety of factors, including predation, but also contained a clash of human as well as animal ecology.

Much as reformers expected the Lakota and Cheyenne to become farmers and ranchers on their reservations in the American West, they expected Eskimos to follow the examples of the Lapp herders and become tied to the reindeer herds. Reindeer husbandry in the Old World included the practice of "close herding," in which the reindeer herders literally lived and moved with the animals. Successfully practiced over centuries, close herding encouraged the rotation of ranges, positive ownership claims, and defense from predators.[23] America's western livestock industry followed a different "loose" pattern, with open ranges and large numbers of livestock cared for by relatively few people, a model which seemed appropriate for Alaska's tundra. Some Native reindeer owners did try close herding initially, but then abandoned it in the late 1920s because of an inability to sell their animals, opportunities for wage labor, and continued reindeer multiplication despite neglect. More important, perhaps, were cultural reasons. Most Eskimos were reluctant to abandon their seacoast lifestyle dominated by the annual cycles of marine mammal subsistence hunting and substantiated through generations of habits and myths. Besides, it was easy to shoot a few reindeer whenever desired without spending one's days following the herds. White culture could not grasp how a subsistence lifestyle was preferable to getting rich by accumulating a large herd of livestock, and much disparagement of the Eskimos resulted as the reindeer populations plummeted, even though by this time Whites owned most of the herds.

The Bureau of Biological Survey played a major role in Alaska's reindeer industry as part of its emphasis on economic mammalogy. Edward Nelson, chief of the survey, visited the reindeer ranges in 1920, and established a laboratory at Unalakleet. Research projects examined forage and range management, carrying capacities, and disease and parasite protection.[24] Survey personnel also experimented with stock improvement by crossbreeding reindeer with caribou, which included the Murie brothers' attempts to capture bulls from McKinley Park in 1923. *Rangifer tarandus* includes both caribou and reindeer, but the caribou are longer-legged and rangier than the imported reindeer. Eventually bulls were secured and transported to Nunivak Island for breeding with reindeer, with promising crossbred bulls then placed in the mainland reindeer herds.

Some people thought the interbreeding to be a threat to Alaska's wild caribou. Nelson had stated privately that there was "no justification" for bringing reindeer inland to caribou country. This did not prevent William Lopp, supervisor for the Bureau of Education, from sending a herd to the Broad Pass area near McKinley Park, where he had seen potential grazing grounds near the Alaska Railroad and its markets.[25] In October 1921, starting from Goodnews Bay in southwest Alaska, six herders escorted 1,162 reindeer. They traveled through the winter and calving season along the northern flanks of the Alaska Range, through the park, then south on the Nenana River to Broad Pass, arriving in August 1922. While some railroad shipments of reindeer carcasses went to market, the herd was gone by 1928, a victim of poor herding practices, predation by wolves, and intermingling with migrating caribou herds.

While Olaus Murie helped with improving breeding efforts, he opposed the mingling of reindeer with Alaska's wild caribou, which were "a splendid type…coming near at least to being the largest on the continent." Concern over the genetic diminution of caribou reflected Murie's understanding of the role of the caribou as an important wild food source for Alaska residents. Another concern was for the genetic purity of caribou that migrated through nearby Mount McKinley National Park, as the Park Service recognized its role in preserving examples of native flora and fauna "unimpaired." Observers reported reindeer and suspected reindeer-caribou crossbreeds in the park in 1926, and park rangers had standing orders to shoot them.[26] Adolph Murie thought it "fortunate" that the Broad Pass reindeer were exterminated. Another proposal to drive reindeer through the park to Broad Pass surfaced in 1928, a result of conversations between the Alaska Railroad's director and the Lomen brothers, who brought their proposal to Washington, D.C., for discussion with federal agencies.[27] This idea failed, as both Biological Survey Director Paul Redington and Park Service Director Horace Albright registered strong disapproval, fearing reindeer would cause genetic damage and undesirable hybrids among the caribou.[28] Albright echoed previous suggestions to segregate the reindeer and caribou herds, an unlikely prospect in the varied Alaska terrain with animals capable of long migrations.[29] Other Park Service naturalists opposed the proximity of reindeer to McKinley's caribou. The American Society of Mammalogists went a step further. In a resolution they urged that "reindeer not under complete control of herders" be killed rather than letting them run with McKinley Park caribou.[30] Such fears reflected the contemporary understanding of genetics and natural selection, and a fundamental preference for the wild over the tame by Park Service personnel.[31]

The scientific and aesthetic appreciation of the wild fauna by biologists and Park Service personnel reflected the distinction between preservationists and those with more utilitarian views toward conservation, such as the people responsible for game management in the territory. While appreciating the fine wild vigor of caribou was easy for anyone who had watched their great herds roam across the landscape, transferring that feeling to predators placed the aesthetes in a very small minority. Frank Dufresne of the Alaska Game Commission echoed the majority opinion: the wolf was the "master killer of all wildlife," the "villain in Alaska's pageant of wildlife," and the "worst natural enemy" of the sheep, moose, caribou, and reindeer.[32] The population status of Alaska's large prey animals, combined with Alaska's attempt to develop a livestock industry, provided ample justification for wolf control efforts.

While biologists made early estimates of Alaska's big game populations more by reckoning than quantifiable evidence, people were concerned enough over the number of meat animals to attempt keeping track of them. For predator populations, little can be said with any degree of certainty except the number claimed for bounty. Available evidence indicates that wolves in interior Alaska were relatively low in number during the first quarter century, and increased thereafter. A Biological Survey agent, who followed the gold rush trail from tidewater to White Pass and down the Yukon River to St. Michael in 1900, wrote, "The country along the Yukon is not well suited for wolves and they are seldom seen there." A follow-up survey in the Yukon-Tanana area by the same biologist in 1903 produced a similar conclusion: "wolves are seldom reported, except in limited numbers in winter."[33] Belmore Browne, who spent months afield in various locations during five hunting trips between 1902 and 1910, saw only one wolf. Charles Sheldon, in over a year on the flanks of the Alaska Range in what would become Mount McKinley National Park, rarely mentioned wolves, and only once saw tracks in the area. He also reported that the tracks of a wolf in the Kantishna area occasioned comment from the residents. A market hunter pursuing sheep in 1915–16 in the McKinley area did not see any wolves.[34] The annual reports filed by Alaska's governors contain no mention of wolves in mainland Alaska until 1919. A deputy fur warden in 1920 reported that wolves were seen "only rarely by trappers from the valleys of the Yukon and Kuskokwim."[35] Olaus Murie was sent to Alaska initially as a fur warden for the Biological Survey in 1920, with explicit instructions to "be sure and get all the information you can concerning the predatory animals and their relations to game." During a year's travel throughout interior Alaska, including the McKinley area, he made no comment on wolf predation in his reports and saw only one wolf in 1921. During the 1,500-mile trip with Adolph up through the Brooks Range in 1922–23, they saw not even a wolf track.[36]

The situation seems to have changed in the mid-1920s, however. The governor reported in 1919 that "wolves are commencing to appear in unprecedented numbers and are becoming a great menace to game." After a six-year absence, wolves again appeared in the 1926 governor's report, "increasing in spite of the bounty...doing much damage to fur and game."[37] From 1926, a predator update would become an annual report feature.

Following their winter inspection in 1923 Olaus Murie received reports that wolves were "rather plentiful in some sections now," and that poison had been requested by local men for the wolves, an idea that did not meet with his approval. In another report some years later, he noted that "wolves were never alarmingly numerous, although more recently they have been seen in greater numbers."[38] A long-time Alaskan trapper, Oscar Vogel, recalled that wolves were scarce in the 1920s, but "by the early '30s they had arrived in force." From 1925, wolves were reported as increasingly common in McKinley Park and throughout interior Alaska.[39]

Obviously predator populations are related to prey. Whatever natural cycles may have existed among animal populations in Alaska were undoubtedly altered by the importation of reindeer. Unlike bison, which had been replaced in their habitat by cattle, reindeer had augmented the total prey population in western Alaska, since caribou were still roaming in large herds. The irresistible question then concerns wolves: was their population trend of the 1920s related to the soaring reindeer numbers, which were easy prey and not receiving the benefit of close herding? Biologists A. Starker Leopold and F. Fraser Darling flirted with the notion in a 1952 report, writing of "the wolves fattening and increasing on the thousands of strays."[40] Did an increased wolf population spread eastwards into the interior?

The slim available evidence does not support this hypothesis. The earliest report of western Alaska wolf numbers came from Edward Nelson, who spent 1877 to 1881 in the region prior to becoming head of the Biological Survey. He had seen numerous wolf skins at the trading post in St. Michael and established that wolves followed the caribou herds during their large-scale wanderings. Yet these caribou are supposed to have shifted to the interior in the 1880s, leaving the reindeer ranges relatively predator-free.[41] A 1922 Department of Agriculture bulletin said that depredations along the coast were not extensive and few wolves were present; a 1926 bulletin does not even mention wolves.[42] Carl Lomen wrote of the wolf, "that great scourge of the North," appearing on the reindeer ranges in the 1920s. Other sources indicate that wolves moved into the western ranges in the 1930s, when reindeer predation became noticeable.[43] The importation of reindeer to Broad Pass was followed several years later by increased wolf sightings in McKinley Park. Questions of causality in population ecology are rarely answered with high degrees of certainty, and the evidence available for this question permits only provocative speculation. Regardless of what really happened, the evidence points to increased wolf populations in the 1930s.

While increasing reindeer numbers may have been a factor in increasing wolf numbers, did the increase in wolves cause the collapse of the reindeer herds in the 1930s? Despite having as little proof to answer this question as the previous one, wolves offered the most convenient and popular explanation, since blaming wolves cast nó doubt on the ability or desire of Natives to care for their herds. It allowed for sympathetic appeals to the territorial legislature for bounty appropriations, and convinced the federal government to supply predator control agents. A survey in 1948 of Natives and Whites in the reindeer areas found that both listed wolves as the leading cause of decline of the herds.[44] Although Leopold and Darling were willing to speculate that wolves increased because of reindeer, their conclusion concerning reindeer decline was definite: overgrazing of the range, not wolves, caused the population crash.[45] Regardless of range problems, protection of reindeer from wolf depredations would justify control efforts for years.

To add further complications to predator-prey relations, an unwelcome southerner, the coyote, dispersed into mainland Alaska. Not native to the North, *Canis latrans* is thought to have been kept distinct from the wolf since the Pleistocene by geographic, behavioral, and ecologic boundaries, despite their interfertility. While pack structure sometimes occurs, coyotes are less socially organized than wolves. Control attempts by humans seem to play a factor in pack organization, as livestock ranges are usually populated by breeding pairs, while in protected areas—such as national parks—a greater degree of social bonding occurs. Originally found on the plains and prairies, coyotes are opportunistic in diet, less able to bring down large prey animals and more dependent on rodents, scavenging, and plant materials. Domestic sheep are easy prey, and coyotes became the primary target of informal and government predator control once wolves were eliminated. Despite control efforts, the adaptability of the coyote and its willingness to live in proximity with humans has allowed it to spread into areas cleared of forest cover by agriculture and the opening of predator niches caused by the elimination of wolves. By the 1850s coyotes had spread east into Illinois and Michigan, and west to the Pacific Northwest. By 1925, they were found in New England, the Hudson Bay region, and the Florida peninsula. Coyotes currently live from the Arctic coasts of Alaska to Nova Scotia and as far south as Panama.[46]

Reasons for the spread of coyotes to Alaska are speculative, as various explanations have been offered with little evidence. A connection seems to exist between the sudden influx of humans to the North following the 1896 discovery of gold in Yukon Territory and the northward expansion of the coyote.

An 1829 account placed the boreal maximum of the coyote as northern Alberta and Saskatchewan, but coyotes were killed near Whitehorse in 1907 and in the Pelly district (Yukon) by 1912.[47] Lacking, however, is evidence of whether this range extension was a gradual dispersal or, as is more colorfully assumed, that coyote populations moved north suddenly, drawn by the trail of dead horses and garbage left by prospectors rushing north overland from Telegraph Creek and the Cassiar District of British Columbia.[48] Frank Dufresne, executive officer of the Alaska Game Commission from 1935 to 1944, supplied inconsistent reports: he wrote variously of the first coyotes appearing in southeastern Alaska at the turn of the century, of their first Alaska appearance in 1925, and of their spread through half of Alaska's land area between 1913 and 1938.[49] Another account had coyotes entering interior Alaska from the south by following the construction camps of the Alaska Railroad, a theory that fails to explain the genesis of coyotes in southcentral Alaska.[50] Their first mention in the governors' annual reports occurred in 1916. The 1919 report postulated another route of immigration, from Canada via the White River into the Chisana and Nizina River valleys, where coyotes were reportedly harrying sheep and caribou. A trapper from the Kenai Peninsula, writing to the Alaska Game Commission, reported the arrival of coyotes in 1928.[51] In the Mount McKinley area, Charles Sheldon's keen eye failed to see any coyotes in 1907–08, but they were present in 1926, and by 1932 coyotes had increased in the park to become a "serious competitor" with native carnivores, the wolf, wolverine, and fox.[52] The 1931 governor's report described a "heavy infestation" of wolves and coyotes with substantial losses of game in the McKinley region, and noted that coyotes had spread westward as far as Stony River on the Kuskokwim River and Marshall on the lower Yukon River.[53]

Scientists and trappers alike viewed with alarm the spread of the coyote. Reports came back from Alaska of coyotes killing foxes, a valuable fur resource; of coyotes diminishing the populations of other carnivorous furbearers, such as marten and lynx, by competing for the smaller mammals and birds that formed their common prey; of coyotes killing the prized mountain sheep; and of the threat to nesting waterfowl posed by this new four-legged "archpredator."[54] Known examples of the introduction of foreign species to North America carried unpleasant lessons—the English starling, the Norway rat—and the popular classification of coyotes as vermin put them in the same category. The coyote added ample justification for bounty appropriations and federal predator control projects in Alaska.

These population trends of Alaska's large animals are approximate, summarized from historical references rather than from techniques available to modern wildlife biologists. No accurate counts existed prior to the widespread use of airplanes in Alaska's game management following WW II. Olaus Murie, arguably as able a field biologist as any in the 1920s, estimated two million caribou in Alaska, but also estimated the Fortymile herd to range from one half million to a million, a variation of one hundred percent. In an important sense, though, the accuracy of population estimates was moot: what really mattered were perceptions, what Alaskans thought was happening to the numbers of predators and prey.

These perceptions brought the wolf into prominent disrepute in the 1930s. The numbers of Dall sheep in McKinley Park, the animal so prized by sportsmen and the reason for the park's creation, experienced a sharp decline well after the cessation of market hunting. The caribou herds of interior Alaska, important as a food source for residents of Alaska's largest town, Fairbanks, and others in the Yukon River drainage, dwindled markedly for no apparent reason. The reindeer, an animal predicted to have significant economic benefit to the territory, died by the hundreds of thousands after showing decades of promising increase. At the same time, wolf populations rebounded and the newly arrived coyote appeared to be everywhere. For Alaskans who counted on game as a food resource, the increased predator numbers in the 1930s represented a threat that had to be countered. Settlers expected a repeat of the familiar chronology of North American frontier development, which included elimination of wolves. The abundance of wolves and coyotes represented a symbolic failure of the progress of civilization in Alaska. By the 1930s the wolf problem had been solved in the contiguous states by federal control programs (with the exception of the Great Lakes area), leaving only Alaskans still confronting this wilderness denizen.

Subsequent advances in wildlife science allow us to recognize the factors that led to some of these changes in animal populations. Climatic pressures and diseases curbed the excessive population of Dall sheep. Habitat alteration by humans and hunting with increasingly effective weapons helped curb caribou numbers. The herds also changed what humans regarded as traditional ranges, leaving hunters wondering where the caribou had gone. Overgrazing of available range caused starvation in the reindeer herds. Coyotes found abundant prey and a predator niche between foxes and wolves. The wolf increase is still a mystery. But these explanations arose only in retrospect. Game management was a young science in the 1930s, and the basic facts of predation seemed sufficient cause to blame declining prey populations on coyotes and wolves.

Politically, these trends combined in a potent brew. While no one could control the weather conditions, or the frequency and extent of wildfires, or caribou dispersal, or the growth rate of lichens, people could hunt predators.

If the history of predators in the western states had been repeated in Alaska, the National Park Service now would be seeking to reintroduce the wolf to its lands. A familiar sequence started in Alaska, with wolf shooting by White settlers a matter of course, followed by a government bounty system that did not seem to curb predator numbers, a livestock industry which suffered depredations, and finally the arrival of the formal organization, expertise, and tools of the Biological Survey hunters. No one seriously expected to eliminate wolves from Alaska, with its vast size, amount of forest cover, and sparse human population, but the government experts were fully confident of their ability to eliminate the wolves from the areas of White settlement, preserve the herds of caribou and moose for human use, and protect the reindeer industry.

Alaska Natives held no particular antipathy toward the wolf, regarding it with a measure of respect as another hunter and as a source of useful fur. Trapping methods predated European contact. Georg Wilhelm Stellar, the naturalist aboard the Bering/Chirikov expedition of 1740, found a wooden torsion trap washed up on the beach of the posthumously named Bering Island, where the expedition foundered on its way back to Russia.[55] These traps, using the power of twisted sinew to drive a spike into the animal's head, remained in use even after the introduction of metal traps in Alaska. Iñupiaq Eskimos softened a pointed strip of whalebone, bent it into an *S* shape, concealed the bone inside a piece of blubber, and let it freeze; the bone would straighten out inside the wolf's stomach and eventually kill the animal. Yupik Eskimos used pit traps with camouflaged tops insufficient to hold the wolf's weight.[56] Another type of Native trap was described in an 1829 report as a box made of slabs of ice, into which the wolf was lured by a bait and killed by a triggered deadweight slab.[57] Ingenious as these methods were, they posed no threat to wolf populations.

Wolf pelts had market value, but not enough to convince White settlers to view them as a resource and manage wolves for sustained fur harvest; Alaskans soon offered bounty payments to encourage their destruction. Offering bounties was an ancient practice, first recorded in Plutarch's *Lives*, in which a male wolf was worth five drachmas, or the price of an ox. Bounties on wolves in England dated back to the thirteenth-century reign of Henry III. Wolves disappeared from the English landscape by the end of the sixteenth century, from habitat changes, state and landowner organized hunts, and bounty incentives, though they lingered in the wilds of Scotland until 1743.[58] English settlers in the New World brought livestock and soon turned to bounties as a tactic against the plentiful wolves. The Massachusetts Bay Colony passed the first American bounty law in 1630, followed by the Grand Assembly of Jamestown in 1632, with all colonies eventually following suit. Bounty payments consisted of cash, grain, or powder and shot; contributions to the bounty fund came from livestock owners. Indians were brought into the new market for wolf heads and made eligible for the receipt of bounties, although their reward sometimes fell short of that given to settlers. Fraudulent bounty claims were present even in Puritan New England, and Connecticut found it necessary to pass laws against the submittal of wolves killed outside the colony's boundaries and against raiding another's traps or pits in order to claim the bounty on caught wolves. Everywhere that settlers took livestock, bounty legislation soon followed, supplemented by private bounty funds offered by stockmen's organizations. Fraud persisted, as did a reluctance by professional "wolfers" to be too effective, as their livelihood depended on the continued existence of wolves and coyotes.[59] Even though the bounty system had, by the turn of the century, proven a costly failure in the western states, Alaskans enthusiastically adopted bounties on unwanted animals. The 2nd Territorial Legislature in 1915 appropriated twenty thousand dollars in order to pay a ten-dollar bounty on wolves, the act specifically to "preserve the food supply of Alaska." The legislature raised the bounty to fifteen dollars in 1917, twenty dollars in 1935, thirty dollars in 1945, and fifty dollars in 1949, where it remained. A further indication of changing wolf and coyote populations in Alaska may be gained from bounty records: the territory paid bounty on 467 wolves in 1921–22, and on about 1,300 wolves and coyotes in 1925–26.[60]

Alaskans created bounties for other animals as well. They placed bald eagles on the list in 1917, assuming that eagles ate live salmon and preyed on commercially raised fur foxes. The national symbol, dead, brought fifty cents. Although the birds were protected in the states since 1940, territorial residents legally killed eagles until 1953, when federal legislation finally overturned the territorial legislature bounty on them. Alaskans killed between 93,000 and 103,000 eagles and received $164,000 for them. Governor Ernest Gruening, appointed in 1940, opposed the eagle bounty from the beginning of his tenure. His arguments to the legislature cited scientists as well as the deleterious effect on public opinion created by the eagle bounty, such as a 1949 *Denver Post* article: "The Alaska Legislature, hoping to become the 49th state under the wings of the eagle, nevertheless voted Wednesday to place a bounty on eagles."[61] The territorial legislature consistently passed eagle bounty appropriations with near unanimity, indicating the fiscal popularity of this activity in Alaska's narrow economy. The salmon industry promoted and partially funded eagle persecution, and the industry also started bounty appropriations for hair seals (1927) and Dolly Varden char (1933). Salmon packers convinced people that eagles, seals, and char damaged potential fisheries profits, and the public popularity of bounties easily convinced legislators that helping the salmon industry meant helping Alaskans. The fishing industry could not be ignored either: in 1931 and 1932 it accounted for eighty-one percent of the territory's revenues, and in 1933 added $15,000 to the char bounty fund, doubling the government's contribution.[62] Storekeepers in Bristol Bay villages accepted dried char tails as legal tender, and over one million tails, worth two and a half cents each, were brought for payment to the Bureau of Fisheries in 1938.[63] The legislature dropped the char bounty in 1941 because of rampant fraud, with many thousands of rainbow trout, steelhead, and grayling tails submitted for payment. One observer reported spending a day with a gill-netter who caught seven hundred rainbow trout, lopped off their tails, and threw the bodies overboard, which yielded $10 for his efforts.[64] Coyotes were added to the official bounty list in 1929, and wolverines in 1953. Governor Gruening had proposed eliminating all bounties during the war years, calling them an "expensive and short-sighted territorial delusion," but they persisted.[65] Alaska spent almost three million dollars cumulative in bounties prior to statehood in 1959, with wolves, coyotes, and seals accounting for ninety percent of the payments.

Obtaining cash has always been a problem in rural Alaska. Bounty hunting significantly shaped attitudes toward animals and had economic and social impacts. Numerous arguments in favor of bounties noted that Alaska Natives would be the principal recipients. This held particular importance before the late 1940s, when increased federal aid monies began to flow to Natives.[66] Bounties offered new ways of using animals. Olaus Murie reported seeing Natives raiding eagle nests for chicks and then raising them for bounty payment. While furbearing animals had long been the sole significant income for many Natives, bounties allowed wolves to serve as a source of money. At least one village began broadcasting poison baits in 1926 specifically because of the

bounty incentive.[67] A White trader in the Copper River Valley, John McCrary, commented, "There has been no Wolves or Cyotes Dug out or Shot Since the Bounty Money run out Natives refuse to hunt them if the money is not in Sight There fore we Will have More Wolves and Cyotes Next season" *[sic]*.[68] Some Native groups changed their hunting patterns from winter—when wolf fur was at its best—to spring, since finding a litter of pups in a den was far more lucrative.[69] Pups paid full value: one miner near Fairbanks found a litter of thirteen and proudly posed for a picture, the pups worth twenty dollars each. Another claimant with tiny pup hides and attached front leg bones (required for a bounty claim) made some calculations with the wildlife agent and concluded the bones were worth forty times their weight in gold.[70] Trapping was the most popular method of obtaining wolves, as good shooting opportunities were usually spontaneous rather than calculated. Following World War I, the Oneida company developed a special trap for the Alaskan market, the double long spring, 8 ½ inch toothed-jaw No. 114. Magazine advertisements urged trappers to "Cash in!" and "Be sure of your share of the bounty."[71] Game wardens distributed No. 114s at Seattle cost, $32.28/dozen, to "bona fide trappers who will use them exclusively for predatory animal work," as well as free of charge to Natives in the reindeer areas.[72] The financial incentive for wolf trapping included the price paid for the pelt, which was as high as fifty-five dollars in the 1930s, but more typically stayed

Advertisement from *The Alaska Sportsman*, January 1937

in the twenty-dollar range.[73] Alaska's bounty system was lucrative enough to entice both Whites and Natives to smuggle wolf and coyote pelts from the adjacent Yukon Territory, where bounty payments had been halted between 1933 and 1946. To curb these, Alaska game wardens conducted joint patrols with their Canadian counterparts, confiscating pelts and contraband strychnine.[74]

The Great Depression only exacerbated rural Alaska's cash flow problem, and many Alaskans headed to the forests, coasts, and hills in search of predators. Articles in *The Alaska Sportsman* magazine lauded the bounty hunter life and implied that an adequate income could be obtained from the pursuit, at least in southeast Alaska. "Adventurous Life" and "The Life that Never Knows Harness" are typical of the genre: "My ambition had been to find an isolated spot where I could make a living without working for someone else"; "I like to fish and hunt—particularly to hunt for these highwaymen of the sea and air and forests." The magazine offered regular how-to articles on wolf trapping and claiming bounties, as well as placing bounty animals in the same economic resource category as salmon fishing, mink farming, prospecting, and logging.[75] These, of course, were not the occupations of gentlemen, and the decade deepened the resentment toward nonresident trophy hunters. One man in Kodiak, lobbying for a bounty on brown bears, growled, "'Put a bounty on 'em and give us fellers a chance."[76] Appropriations for wolf and coyote bounties rose from a low of $7,000 in the 1921–22 biennium to $165,000 by the 1937–38 biennium, a not insignificant amount of money spread over a population of 70,000.[77] Summary numbers for wolf and coyote pelts shipped from Alaska indicate change during the decade.

Wolf and coyote pelts shipped from Alaska, 1931-1940.

	1931	1932	1933	1934	1935	1936	1937	1938	1939	1940
Wolf	63	58	87	57	42	4	30	40	5	44
Coyote	6	16	99	39	97	98	330	355	507	80

These numbers suggest several possibilities: increased availability of wolves and coyotes, increased pursuit by humans, or both. The numbers claimed for bounty are unavailable for these years, but since these were pelts, the chance of increased bounty fraud does not pertain.[78] Nor does an increase in resident population, although some otherwise unemployed people no doubt headed north. Outside, in the dusty states of the 1930s, the images of the forests and waterways in Alaska, where a straight-shooting man could go where he pleased, answer to no boss, and hunt varmints all day, must have been powerfully appealing and enhanced the mystique of the country's Last Frontier.

The New Deal did not benefit the territory as much as it did the states, but Alaskans welcomed any federal assistance. The Civilian Conservation Corps (CCC) not only built public works, such as recreation cabins in national forests and buildings at McKinley Park, but also participated in predator control. It probably looked good on paper, but unemployed loggers or fishermen posed little threat to the wolf population. The government offered only thirty dollars per month exclusive of board and clothes for predator control workers, and had trouble retaining good men. Nor were all the jobs as romantic as articles in *The Alaska Sportsman* depicted wolf hunting. For thirty dollars a month, someone had to take the malodorous job of manning the CCC-constructed scent-bait building. Scent-baits, composed of both "natural" and "fetid" materials, were distributed free to trappers, and the caretaker had to keep the fire stoked in the building to "hasten the aging of the scent."[79] Discontent surfaced when CCC men in the Kotzebue area found they could not retain proceeds from the sale of wolf and coyote pelts. In southeast Alaska, proposals called for up to fifty CCC men for predator control, the rationale being that posting them to various islands would remove them from relief rolls and competition with town residents. No doubt these men had little effect on wolf populations; their supervisors, veteran trappers on annual salaries of $2,500, took the majority of wolves in these make-work efforts.[80]

Changes in the fur industry during the 1930s cast an economic pall over rural Alaska, fostering sentiment against any possible competitor for furbearers. During the late 1920s, Americans had average annual fur expenditures of $4.40 per $1,000 of disposable personal income, which fell to $2.60 from 1930–34.[81] Fur shipments in 1929 provided Alaskans with $4.5 million in revenue, yet this fell by more than half with the onset of the depression and only slowly recovered by the decade's end. From 1929 to 1930 red and white fox revenues fell from $1,777,081 to $263,696. By 1932, a trapper received only $17.18 for a white fox pelt, which three years earlier brought $60.25 (average values). In a two-year period revenues from beaver declined from $850,512 to $9,520— the decline enhanced by a closed season in 1930 to allow replenishment of beaver stocks. The total value of mink fell from $500,000 to $200,000 in one year, and other furbearers declined to pre-WW I values. While financial inducements for wolves and coyotes included both bounty collection (raised in 1935 from $15 to $20) and sale of furs, the average price for wolf pelts decreased from $41.55 to $8, and coyotes dropped from $20.50 to $4.11. Little wonder, then, that strong arguments existed for increased bounties on predators through years of financial hardship for trappers. While wolves did not prey heavily on furbearing animals, except for beaver, the coyote did, and popular sources linked the decline in fur to the increase in predators.

The decade heightened the differences between the animals deemed economically useful to Alaskans and those considered harmful. Bounties provided a public service where opportunities were limited. Few politicians in Juneau could fail to be moved by a plea from the director of an orphanage in Seward to increase bounties so that his young men could "take advantage of this opportunity to earn a livelihood and at the same time help the salmon and game birds and aminals [sic]."[82] Although wolves and coyotes provided cash, their supposed effect on more valuable furbearers and depredation on declining game animal populations outweighed their utility. In hard times, people sought scapegoats and targets for their frustration. The proposal by the National Park Service to protect its wolves on behalf of an intangible ecological ideal was an alien concept, unappreciated and disliked by Alaskans. They were joined across space and social class by the sportsmen of the Camp Fire Club of America.

Notes

1   "Alaskans' Per Capita Harvest of Wild Foods," *Alaska Fish & Game*, November-December 1989, 14–15. A broader look at this is R. J. Wolfe and R. J. Walker, "Subsistence Economies in Alaska: Productivity, Geography, and Development Impacts," *Arctic Anthropology* 2 (1987): 56–81.

2   A brief and interesting attempt to verify the conventional wisdom concerning the "recent" spread of moose in Alaska by using the records of early European explorers and Indian linguistic evidence was done by Harold J. Lutz, *History of the Early Occurrence of Moose on the Kenai Peninsula and in Other Sections of Alaska* (Juneau: Alaska Forest Research Center, U.S. Department of Agriculture, 1960).

3   Adolph Murie, *The Wolves of Mount McKinley;* Fauna Series No. 5 (Washington, D.C.: GPO, National Park Service, 1944; reprint, Seattle: Univ. of Washington Press, 1985), 184 (page numbers are to reprint edition); Morgan Sherwood, *Big Game in Alaska: A History of Wildlife and People* (New Haven: Yale University Press, 1981), 82.

4   Joseph Dixon, *Fauna of the National Parks of the United States: Birds and Mammals of Mount McKinley National Park, Alaska*; Fauna Series No. 3 (Washington, D.C.: GPO, National Park Service, 1938), 198.

5   Recognition of global warming is nothing new, and biologists suggested it as a cause for the moose's expansion in 1953; A. Starker Leopold and F. Fraser Darling, *Wildlife in Alaska: An Ecological Reconnaissance* (New York: The Conservation Foundation and Ronald Press, 1953), 87.

6   A. Murie, *Wolves of Mount McKinley*, 64–65; his was the first systematic collection of references on animal populations in the park. See also Gordon C. Haber, "Socio-Ecological Dynamics of Wolves and Prey in a Subarctic Ecosystem" (Ph.D. dissertation, University of British Columbia, 1977), which provides historical population summaries up until the 1970s; for pre-WW II information, Haber depends heavily on Murie's work.

7   A. T. Bergerud, "Caribou," in *Big Game of North America: Ecology and Management*, ed. John L. Schmidt and Douglas L. Gilbert (Harrisburg, PA: Stackpole Books, for the Wildlife Management Institute, 1978), 85–86.

8   Olaus Murie, *Alaska-Yukon Caribou* (Washington, D.C.: GPO, Bureau of Biological Survey, 1935), 60; Ronald Skoog, "Ecology of the Caribou in Alaska," (Ph.D. dissertation, University of California Berkeley, 1968), 233–35. This work quite ably summarizes historical references to caribou numbers in reconstructing past cycles, as does Haber's caribou history summary in "Socio-ecological Dynamics," 161–69.

9   A. Murie, *Wolves of Mount McKinley*, 146–48; Skoog, "Ecology of the Caribou," 236.

10   O. Murie, *Alaska-Yukon Caribou*, 6.

11   These are from a variety of primary sources summarized by Ronald O. Skoog, "Range, Movements, Population, and Food Habits of the Steese-Fortymile Caribou Herd," (M.S. thesis, University of Alaska, 1956), 57.

12   Skoog, "Ecology of the Caribou," 245, 332, 356–57; Skoog, "Steese-Fortymile Caribou," 60. Of course, if the Fortymile herd was much less than Murie's estimate, the combined effects of hunting, predation, low recruitment, and loss of winter range to fire damage could have caused the herd's decline. For an opinion which upholds predation by wolves and humans together as the cause of caribou declines, see Arthur T. Bergerud, "Decline of Caribou in North America Following Settlement," *Journal of Wildlife Management* 38 (October 1974): 757–70.

13   O. Murie, *Alaska-Yukon Caribou*, 7; Kendrick, Department of the Interior, *Hearings Before the Reindeer Committee in Washington, D.C.*, February-March 1931, 2; Carl Lomen, *Fifty Years in Alaska* (New York: David McKay Co., 1954), 28; Dufresne, from a 1926 report, a fragment of which was in the A. Murie Collection, Box "Field Notes on Wolves," Folder "Wolves 4/28/40–7/31/41," UAF.

14   The term "domesticating" is ambiguous when applied to reindeer, as reindeer-dependent people adapted their lifeway to the animal more than they changed the reindeer to fit human needs. Scholars recognize an alternative mode of production, transhumance, to describe the reindeer herding lifeway. For an analysis of hunting patterns, see Ernest

S. Burch, Jr., "The Caribou/Wild Reindeer as a Human Resource," *American Antiquity* (July 1972):339–68.

15 James and Catherine Brickey, "Reindeer, Cattle of the Arctic," *Alaska Journal*, Winter 1975, 16. Another useful summary is Margaret Lantis, "The Reindeer Industry of Alaska," *Arctic* 3 (April 1950): 27–44. The most comprehensive history of Alaska's reindeer industry is Richard Olav Stern's "'I Used to Have Lots of Reindeers'—The Ethnohistory and Cultural Ecology of Reindeer Herding in Northwest Alaska" (Ph.D. dissertation, State University of New York at Binghamton, 1980). Also useful is Stern's *A Selected Annotated Bibliography of Sources on Reindeer Herding in Alaska*, Occasional Papers on Northern Life, No. 2. (Fairbanks: Institute of Arctic Biology, University of Alaska Fairbanks, n.d.). For a brief account of reindeer history with photos, see Alice Postell, *Where Did the Reindeer Come From? Alaska Experience, the First Fifty Years* (Portland, OR: Amaknak Press, 1990).

16 Whether Sheldon Jackson accurately understood the Native's situation is a matter of contention. Observers were shocked at what they saw, but then the dietary fulfillment of hunting/gathering people varied seasonally and with the status of prey animal populations. Dorothy Jean Ray, in her chapter "The Eskimos and Domesticated Reindeer," in *The Eskimos of Bering Strait, 1650–1898* (Seattle: University of Washington Press, 1975), concluded that Jackson did not fully understand the situation and the Natives did not need a new food source. Ernest S. Burch, Jr., in "The Caribou/Wild Reindeer," 356–57, notes the importance of the decline of the coastal caribou herds in the last half of the nineteenth century, a trend that began to reverse about 1905. Likely pertinent, too, is the evidence provided by Burch of what he calls the "Great Famine" of 1880–83 in the area just north of where Jackson brought the reindeer. The famine, in conjunction with the absence of caribou, resulted in widespread relocation of groups searching for consistent sustenance; see *The Iñupiaq Eskimo Nations of Northwest Alaska* (Fairbanks: University of Alaska Press, 1998).

17 Brickey, "Reindeer," 18.

18 See Lomen, *Fifty Years in Alaska*, for his family's side of the story.

19 *Hearings Before the Reindeer Committee in Washington, D.C.*, 20 February 1931, 73.

20 Lawrence J. Palmer, *Raising Reindeer in Alaska* (Washington, D.C.: GPO, Department of Agriculture, 1934), 5.

21 Leopold and Darling, *Wildlife in Alaska*, 70; Lomen, *Fifty Years in Alaska*, 72–73. See also Bob Callan, "The Lomens of Nome," *Alaska Life*, March 1946, 8–10, 35–37.

22 Herd numbers from Skoog, *Ecology of the Caribou*, 340. Skoog cites his sources in his tabulation of reindeer numbers; others estimate an even greater maximum number.

23 A Sámi herder described this reaction: "When the wolf pack howled nearby, the whole herd would press together near the kota (the conical Sámi tent) and its fire in order to gain some protection." From Pekka Aikio, "The Changing Role of Reindeer in the Life of the Sámi," in *The Walking Larder: Patterns of Domestication, Pastoralism, and*

Predation, ed. Juliet Clutton-Brock, 169–84 (London: Unwin Hyman, 1989), 171. For a good recent summary of world reindeer, see Hugh Beach, "Comparative Systems of Reindeer Herding," in *The World of Pastoralism: Herding Systems in Comparative Perspective*, eds. John G. Galaty and Douglas L. Johnson, 255–98 (New York: The Guilford Press, 1990).

24   L. J. Palmer, *Progress of Reindeer Grazing Investigations in Alaska*, Department Bulletin No. 1423 (Washington, D.C.: GPO, Department of Agriculture, 1927), 3.

25   Nelson to O. Murie, 15 April 1921, MS 51, Box 4, Folder 1, ASHL; Jack R. Luick, "The Cantwell Reindeer Industry 1921–1928," *Alaska Journal*, Spring 1973, 108; subsequent summary from this.

26   O. Murie, *Alaska-Yukon Caribou*, 7; Dixon, *Birds and Mammals of Mount McKinley*, 209.

27   A. Murie, *Wolves of Mount McKinley*, 163; William H. Wilson, "Railroad and Reindeer," *Alaska Journal*, Winter 1980, 56–61.

28   *Hearings Before the Reindeer Committee*, 9 March 1931, 29; Redington's stance in a letter from Arno Cammerer to Horace Albright, 11 May 1929, RG 79, Entry 7, File 719, Box 1415, NA.

29   L. J. Palmer recommended this in 1926, recognizing the "great intrinsic value" of caribou, in *Raising Reindeer*, 5.

30   George M. Wright, Joseph S. Dixon, and Ben H. Thompson, *Fauna of the National Parks of the United States: A Preliminary Survey of Faunal Relations in National Parks*; Fauna Series No. 1 (Washington, D.C.: GPO, National Park Service, 1933), 50; "General Notes," *Journal of Mammalogy* 16 (August 1935): 239; Adolph Murie was, at this time, chairman of the Committee of Economic Mammalogy of the Society.

31   Ronald Skoog concluded that reindeer had no deleterious effects evident today on wild caribou, arguing that physical characteristics of reindeer would have been genetically recessive when crossed with caribou, and that had these characteristics— shorter legs, size, pelage color—been truly inferior, they would have been selected out of the reindeer populations in favor of more fit animals; *Ecology of the Caribou*, 342.

32   Frank Dufresne, *Alaska's Animals and Fishes* (New York: A.S. Barnes, 1946), 80, 83.

33   Wilfred H. Osgood, *Results of a Biological Reconnaissance of the Yukon River Region*, North American Fauna No. 19 (Washington, D.C.: GPO, Division of Biological Survey, 1900), 40; *Biological Investigations in Alaska and Yukon Territory*, North American Fauna No. 30 (Washington, D.C.: GPO, Bureau of Biological Survey, 1909), 28.

34   Belmore Browne, "In the Caribou Country," *Outing*, June 1910, in Bates, *Mountain Man*, 237; Sheldon, *Wilderness of Denali*, 315, 299; A. Murie, *Wolves of Mount McKinley*, 65.

35   Lee R. Dice, "Notes on the Mammals of Interior Alaska," *Journal of Mammalogy* 2 (February 1921): 21.

36   Nelson to O. Murie, 3 Dec. 1920, MS 51, Box 4, Folder 1, ASHL; copies of Murie's reports are in this box; A. Murie, *Wolves of Mount McKinley*, 13–14.

37   Department of the Interior, *Annual Report of the Governor of Alaska on the Alaska Game Laws*, 1919; reprint in RG 126, Entry 1, File 9-1-33, Box 304, NA; *Annual Report of the Governor of Alaska to the Secretary of the Interior*, 1926, 63 (hereafter Governor's *Annual Report*).

38   O. Murie to Nelson, draft "Report on Game and Fur Animals," 18 July 1923, MS 51, Box 4, Folder 5, ASHL; O. Murie, *Alaska-Yukon Caribou*, 8.

39   Oscar Vogel, "My Years with the Wolves," *Alaska*, May 1972, 11; A. Murie, *Wolves of Mount McKinley*, 15, 65.

40   Leopold and Darling, *Wildlife in Alaska*, 62.

41   A. Murie, *Wolves of Mount McKinley*, 12–13. Murie concluded from Nelson's comments that wolves were plentiful in Alaska, which seems a rather large extrapolation. Skoog summarizes historical references to caribou movements in "Ecology of the Caribou," 216–359.

42   Seymour Hadwen and L. J. Palmer, *Reindeer in Alaska*, Bulletin No. 1089 (Washington, D.C.: GPO, Department of Agriculture, 1922), 52; L. J. Palmer, *Progress of Reindeer Grazing*.

43   Lomen, *Fifty Years in Alaska*, 284; Skoog, "Ecology of the Caribou," 333.

44   Alaska's newspapers were full of stories concerning reindeer killing by wolves, many of which will be cited later in this study. A 1942 history blamed the increase in wolves for the decrease in reindeer; see Brian Roberts, "The Reindeer Industry in Alaska," *Polar Record* 3 (January 1942): 569; Lantis, "The Reindeer Industry," 36.

45   Leopold and Darling, *Wildlife in Alaska*, 74; they noted the population cycle of reindeer on islands lacking wolves in the Bering Sea.

46   On coyotes, see J. Frank Dobie, *The Voice of the Coyote* (Boston: Little, Brown and Co., 1949); Stanley Paul Young and Hartley H. T. Jackson, *The Clever Coyote* (Harrisburg, PA: Stackpole, 1951); M. W. Fox, ed., *The Wild Canids: Their Systematics, Behavioral Ecology, and Evolution* (New York: Van Nostrand Reinhold, 1975); Marc Bekoff, ed., *Coyotes: Biology, Behavior, and Management* (New York: Academic Press, 1978); Jennifer W. Sheldon, *Wild Dogs: The Natural History of the Nondomestic Canidae* (San Diego: Academic Press, 1992).

      Changing faunal distribution patterns still occur: puma (cougar) tracks and sightings near Aklavik, Yukon Territory, in 1993–94 may indicate a northward spread of this carnivore; *Fairbanks Daily News-Miner*, "Migration of Cougar Draws 'Wow,'" 7 February 1994.

47   Young and Jackson, *The Clever Coyote*, 44–66.

48   Dobie, *Voice of the Coyote*, 41–42; Gier, "Ecology and Behavior," 248; the dead horse theory appears frequently in the popular literature on the coyote.

49   Dufresne, *Alaska's Animals and Fishes*, 84; Dufresne to Ernest Gruening, 14 January 1943, RG 101, Box 470, ASA; *Annual Report of the Alaska Game Commission to the Secretary of Agriculture*, July 1938 to June 1939 (hereafter AGC Annual Report).

50   Dixon, *Birds and Mammals of Mount McKinley*, 163.

51   Governor's *Annual Report*, 1916, 63; Governor's *Annual Report*, 1919, 62; AGC *Annual Report*, 1928.

52   Dixon, *Birds and Mammals of Mount McKinley*, 163–64; first reported by Dixon in "General Notes: A Coyote from Mount McKinley, Alaska," *Journal of Mammalogy* 9 (February 1928): 64.

53   Governor's *Annual Report*, 1931, 84–85.

54   E. A. Goldman, "The Coyote—Archpredator," *Journal of Mammalogy* 11 (August 1930): 328–29. Goldman was with the Biological Survey.

55   Richard Gerstell, *The Steel Trap in North America* (Harrisburg, PA: Stackpole, 1985), 23.

56   Edward W. Nelson, *The Eskimo About Bering Strait* (Washington, D.C.: GPO, 1899; reprint, Washington D.C.: Smithsonian Institution Press, 1983), 121–23 (page numbers are to reprint edition).

57   Stanley Paul Young and Edward A. Goldman, *The Wolves of North America* (Washington, D.C.: The American Wildlife Institute, 1944), 297. This may be one of the stories Young accepted uncritically.

58   Young, *Wolves of North America*, 339; Erik Zimen, *The Wolf: A Species in Danger*, translated by Eric Mosbacher (New York: Delacorte Press, 1981; Munich: Meyster Verlag GmbH, 1978), 310.

59   Rick McIntyre's documents in *War Against the Wolf: America's Campaign to Exterminate the Wolf* (Stillwater, MN: Voyageur Press, 1995) make good reading on these issues.

60   Alaska Legislature, *An Act to Preserve the Food Supply of Alaska, Placing a Bounty on Certain Wild Animals and Providing for the Payment of Same*, 2nd sess., 1915, S.B. 11. Donald E. McNight, "The History of Predator Control in Alaska," internal report, Alaska Department of Fish and Game, 1970. McNight's report lists 1,467 wolves bountied in 1925–26; subsequent details on animals bountied and payments are taken from this nine-page summary unless otherwise indicated. An earlier report from a Biological Survey predator agent lists 1,111 wolves and coyotes for those years; Harlan H. Gubser, "Report to the Governor of Alaska on Cooperative Predatory Animal Investigations and Control in Alaska," 1 March 1931, RG 101, Box 470, ASA.

61   Gruening to Speaker of the House, 21 March 1949, RG 101, Box 470, ASA.

62   "Message of Gov. George Parks to the Eleventh Session of the Alaska Territorial Legislature," n.d., RG 101, Box 349, ASA; Gov. John Troy to Hans Seversen, Iliamna, 28 June 1933, RG 101, Box 349, ASA.

63   Editor's response to letter, *The Alaska Sportsman*, June 1939, 4; "From Ketchikan to Barrow," *The Alaska Sportsman*, November 1938, 19.

64   Russell Annabel, "Flying in for the Big Ones," *Field and Stream*, January 1942, 16–18, 57, 68–69. An article apologizing for the "occasional" rainbow trout taken for bounty is Joseph Lester, "Come and Get 'Em," *The Alaska Sportsman*, April 1940, 8–9, 24–25.

65 Ernest Gruening, *Many Battles: The Autobiography of Ernest Gruening* (New York: Liveright, 1973), 318.

66 Robert F. Scott, "Wildlife in the Economy of Alaska Natives," in *Transactions of the Sixteenth North American Wildlife Conference* (Washington, D.C.: Wildlife Management Institute, 1951): 514. A game warden calculated in 1954 that bounty payments in the village of Anaktuvuk Pass amounted to $44.40/person; Ray Tremblay, *Trails of an Alaskan Game Warden* (Anchorage: Alaska Northwest Publishing Company, 1985), 130. Also Leopold and Darling, *Wildlife in Alaska*, 44.

67 O. Murie to Otto Geist, 4 December 1936, Otto Geist Collection, Box 16, Folder "Murie, Olaus, '34–'36," UAF; Sidney Huntington, "Koyukuk and Yukon Valley Wildlife, Yesterday and Today," *Alaska*, January 1985, 62. The Alaska Game Commission outlawed use of poison in the 1930s because of its indiscriminate harvest of other furbearing animals.

68 Alaska Game Commission, *Annual Report of the Executive Officer to the Alaska Game Commission*, 1938, 84; hereafter Exec. Officer's Annual Report to AGC.

69 Robert O. Stephenson and Robert T. Ahgook, "The Eskimo Hunter's View of Wolf Ecology and Behavior," in *The Wild Canids: Their Systematics, Behavioral Ecology, and Evolution*, ed. M.W. Fox (New York: Van Nostrand Reinhold, 1975), 287.

70 "From Ketchikan to Barrow," *The Alaska Sportsman*, October 1940, 21; "From Ketchikan to Barrow," *The Alaska Sportsman*, September 1942, 17.

71 Gerstell, *The Steel Trap*, 200; Oneida ads were common in *The Alaska Sportsman* in the 1930s and 1940s.

72 Memorandum to wardens from Clarence Rhode, Alaska Game Commission, 6 May 1931; Harlan Gubser, "Report of Predatory Animal Control, Alaska District, 1 July 1937 to 31 December 1937"; both in RG 101, Box 475, ASA.

73 C.R. Snow, "The Trap Line," *The Alaska Sportsman*, December 1935, 20.

74 Bernard L. Smith, "The Status and Management of the Wolf in the Yukon Territory," in *Wolves in Canada and Alaska*, Ludwig N. Carbyn, ed. (Edmonton: Canadian Wildlife Service Report Series Number 45, 1983), 48. Wildlife Agent Sam White gained renown for his pioneering use of aircraft in game management. His month-long aerial patrol with an RCMP constable allowed the speedy prosecution of violators in either Eagle or Dawson, saving "a considerable sum which would have gone toward illegal bounty claims." From White, "Report of Cooperative Boundary Patrol, March 9 to April 7, 1939," RG 101, Box 474, ASA.

75 From *The Alaska Sportsman*, see Harold Snyder, "Adventurous Life," October 1940; D.L. Sancrant, "The Life that Never Knows Harness," May 1941; Elmer Perkins, "Bounty Hunter," May 1938; William Putvin, "Wolves, Eagles, and Seals," January 1940; C. R. Snow, "The Trap Line," December 1935; Frank North, "Wilderness Opportunities," July 1940.

76 From a report by warden Hosea Garber to the Alaska Game Commission, 25 August 1939; copy in A. Murie Collection, Box "Reports, Journals, Articles," UAF.

77   McNight, "History of Predator Control", 4. Alaska's 1939 census showed a population of 72,524, from George W. Rogers and Richard A. Cooley, *Alaska's Population and Economy* (College, Alaska: University of Alaska, 1963), Table P-3.

78   Pelt numbers from a report filed by Frank Dufresne, executive officer of the Alaska Game Commission to the territorial legislature, 2 January 1940, RG 101, Box 470, ASA. McNight's "History of Predator Control" shows number of wolves and coyotes bountied prior to 1929 and after 1945.

79   Harlan Gubser, "Report of Predatory Animal Control, Alaska District, 1 July 1937 to 31 December 1937"; D. Wood, Jr., "Report of Predatory Animal Control, Alaska District, 1 January 1938 to 31 March 1938"; both in RG 101, Box 475, ASA.

80   "A Plan for Special Wolf Control Work in Southeastern Alaska under Federal Emergency Relief Administration Funds," n.d., RG 101, Box 475, ASA; Albert Schueneman, "I Match Wits With Wolves," *The Alaska Sportsman* , April 1941, 18.

81   Victor R. Fuch, *The Economics of the Fur Trade Industry* (New York: Columbia Studies in the Social Sciences #593, Columbia University Press, 1957), 75; following data on furs from the Exec. Officer's *Annual Report* to AGC, 1938, UAF.

82   Charles T. Hatten to Gov. Troy, 22 May 1933, RG 101, Box 349, ASA.

Protest Made Against Protection of
Outlaw Animals
  —Fairbanks Daily News-Miner

4

The Opposition to the
National Park Service

Sportsmen regarded Alaska as one of the world's great destinations for hunting big game, whether for the largest bears and moose or the wandering caribou and lordly Dall sheep. But such prizes came with a price. Before WW II, only those with several months and at least five thousand dollars to spend made the journey to Alaska. A safari in Africa could be less expensive for East Coast sportsmen than a trip to the territory.[1] The relative democratization of hunting trips to Alaska occurred after the war with the advent of commercial air service. This did not make a trip inexpensive, but more hunters could take a trip to Alaska because air travel reduced the amount of time a man spent away from work. But decades before this, men like Charles Sheldon and Belmore Browne created Alaska's reputation. They brought knowledge of the Dall sheep and caribou to their social peers, ensuring that McKinley Park's game became a matter of concern for many wealthy and politically well connected men outside Alaska. Browne and the sportsmen of the Camp Fire Club's Conservation Committee became the chief opponents to any Park Service policy to protect wolves. But to accuse them of unthinking hatred toward wolves ignores their own sense of obligation to preserve the sheep.

The Camp Fire Club had played a major role in the creation of McKinley Park and continued its involvement with the territory and park. The club helped Territorial Governor Thomas Riggs work toward improved game laws in 1920, and supported legislation in subsequent years to curb the then-legal

113

taking of game in the park by miners, a practice officially banned in 1928.[2] The following year the club published suggestions for national park standards which fit quite well with prevailing Park Service philosophy. Toward wildlife, the club recommended, "That each park area shall be a sanctuary for the scientific care, study, and preservation of all wild plant and animal life within its limits, to the end that no species shall become extinct."[3] The club wrote these standards with the same words and phrasing used by the Park Service, but the club's interpretation of these differed increasingly as the service matured. The sportsmen had either an unclear understanding of the implications of the statement, or were unwilling to entertain alternatives to the prevailing good animal/bad animal dichotomy. The Camp Fire Club had worked to establish McKinley Park specifically as a game sanctuary, and as the wolf-sheep controversy developed it became apparent that "preservation of all wild plant and animal life" did not include wolves, nor did science have any effect on the club's stance. The decline of McKinley Park's sheep prompted a crisis state, with demands for immediate action and implicit faith in human intervention. Concern for the sheep caused the club to change from Park Service ally to a skeptical interest group, with enough clout to cause reactions at the highest levels.

One of its members, William Beach of New York, led the early attack on the Park Service. An 1892 graduate of Yale, he retired in 1926 from a career as a cement company executive, and, married but childless, spent the next quarter-century pursuing his hunting passion.[4] Beach made a total of sixteen hunting trips to Alaska, making him a recognized figure in the territory. He was also known by Park Service officials. While he had the blessing of Director Horace Albright, who regarded him as a friend of the service, Harold Bryant compiled an uncomplimentary 'Beach File' to share with equally skeptical colleagues.[5] Charles Sheldon had earned his reputation by dint of the skills he worked hard to develop, and his hunting style. Beach represented another kind of sportsman, one who liked the shooting found on Scottish game preserves where gamekeepers rigorously suppressed predators, hosts guaranteed plentiful shooting, and only gentlemen had access. He first traveled to Alaska in 1921 and returned the following year to again visit McKinley Park, which he called "a veritable game paradise." As if in a dream world of a sportsman's making, he wrote with wonderment of traveling through the park surrounded by various herds of sheep all visible at the same time, concluding that "this was the greatest ram pasture in the North, in fact the whole world."[6] Beach itched to shoot the wolves he saw in the park. He wrote, without a trace of irony, "I realize there are many so-called conservationists who would prefer to have the sheep, caribou, moose, and deer killed off by wolves…than to have them hunted and killed by man."[7]

No doubt Beach's guides and packers appreciated him as a client, but he was hardly an heir to Charles Sheldon's reputation. He lacked skill, for one thing, as well as self-discipline, and made no attempt to conceal it. In his collection of published hunting tales, *In the Shadow of Mt. McKinley*, Beach recounted instances of emptying his rifle magazine against far distant animals, wounding and maiming game with unconscionably poor shooting to stagger off or be tracked down by his guides for dispatch—and these not as a rookie hunter, but an experienced one.[8] Beach's ethical standards were as crooked as his aim. Prior to his first trip to McKinley Park he wrote to Edward Nelson of the Biological Survey requesting a special permit to hunt in the park, seeking to override the park managers. Beach reasoned that since it was a game sanctuary, there must be a surplus of animals. Nelson peremptorily denied the request. Newly appointed park superintendent Harry Karstens wrote back to Nelson that Beach's party "were very much put out that they were not allowed to kill game in the park." In a telling comment, Karstens went on to warn Nelson that Beach and his friends intended to recommend to their political contacts that the park be "opened to hunters of their class," as if it was an estate for the gentry.[9] Karstens rightly noted this would be ill-received by Alaskans, who already resented the way federal game laws allowed visiting sportsmen the right to shoot large numbers of animals, including specimens of all ages and sexes, as long as the hunters carried 'collecting' permits from the stateside natural history museums—whose directors invariably enjoyed memberships in the sportsmen's clubs. Nevertheless, Beach shot at least one sheep in the park on his 1922 trip, afterwards sending new Mauser rifles to Karstens for helping assist his trip and to a witness—a game warden, no less—for keeping the poaching quiet. Unfortunately, his bragging back home in New York City brought this violation to light. In his defense, Beach claimed that his party needed meat, and that park rules allowed such hunting. This latter was true, but Beach's claim crumbled when Karstens produced notes showing that Beach's party had left park headquarters with eight pack horses and enough supplies to last five months. Beach proposed an out-of-court cash settlement to the Park Service, but the government's legal counsel rejected this. Eventually Beach pled guilty in a Fairbanks courtroom and received a nominal ten dollar fine.[10]

While Beach's authority on game was self-bestowed, and his early history with McKinley Park hardly made him credible, his criticism of the Park Service carried the implied backing of the Camp Fire Club.

Social factors and pragmatic realities forced the Park Service to respond to the criticism of such an organization. From its inception the service sought allies among politicians and business leaders. Legislators needed grooming, as they created parks and appropriated funds. Businessmen, particularly those involved with providing the infrastructure for tourism, wanted friends in the Park Service. Sportsmen's groups proudly proclaimed their role in the creation of national parks and provided associate memberships to service leaders. Numerous linkages intertwined club members, politicians, and civil servants. These met the community of scientists through the museum directors, who disbursed research funds, helped direct wildlife policies, and depended on wealthy sportsmen to provide the skins, bones, antlers, and horns of the world's fauna for public display. A membership list of the Boone and Crockett Club from the late 1940s illustrates these linkages: Park Service directors Horace Albright and Newton Drury held associate memberships, as did Director Ira Gabrielson of the Fish and Wildlife Service; the American Museum had four full and five associate members, with further associate members representing the Field Museum of Chicago, the Smithsonian, and Philadelphia's Academy of Natural Sciences.[11] Settings such as the Cosmos Club in Washington, D.C., provided the after-hours brotherhood that enhanced connections. These days we call it networking; then, it was less for personal gain than a necessary way for Park Service officials to maintain allies for a new government institution with new ideals. Bilateral benefits accrued in a symbiosis that has always pervaded relations between government and business organizations.

Yet the sportsmen's groups did not always agree on issues. The Boone and Crockett Club was the most exclusive, with its lineage from Teddy Roosevelt, limit of one hundred members, and stringent requirements for membership. The Camp Fire Club was less exclusive, appealing to a more middling urban class, yet some members also enjoyed Boone and Crockett membership. In 1929 the Boone and Crockett Club detailed a committee to examine the issue of predators in national parks, and from that study came unequivocal conclusions supporting the Park Service's trend toward preceding policy decisions with research. The club passed a resolution at its 1929 annual meeting recommending that parks protect all their native fauna, and opposed "drawing a line between game animals and those of predatory habits, to the detriment of the latter."[12] As events unfolded in Alaska, the club did not join in the campaign against McKinley Park's wolves, though not for lack of effort to enlist it by the Camp Fire Club.

William Beach and fellow Camp Fire Club members raised questions concerning the park's Dall sheep population even before the big winter die-off of 1931–32. The park did not allow sport hunting within its boundaries, and the game animals were expected to reproduce quickly in the sanctuary. Excess animals would then provide a continual supply of new game to adjacent areas, ensuring continued good hunting; this was, after all, the long-standing rationale used to enlist hunter support for national parks. Yet spillover did not seem to be working, at least in Alaska. In 1931, after a disappointing sheep hunting trip just east of the park in the White River area, Beach wrote to Governor Parks requesting information on sheep numbers and their protection from predation. Parks tried to allay Beach's concern by noting that Alaska still had large caribou herds, despite wolves.[13] At Beach's urging William Greeley, chairman of the Camp Fire Club's Game Conservation Committee, questioned Horace Albright in 1931 about the sheep. Greeley cited vague reports of one thousand sheep killed by wolves in the McKinley area and wondered about the Park Service's response, adding that his committee did not share "the views of those sentimentalists who would rather let the mountain sheep be wiped out by depredators than to destroy any of the depredators." Superintendent Harry Liek foresaw little reason for concern and downplayed, for the time, the supposed sheep decline.[14]

The next upsurge in Camp Fire Club activism occurred in 1937. Beach returned to the McKinley area that year, this time with a collecting permit from the Smithsonian Institution, which wanted moose and caribou specimens for an exhibit. Upon his return, Beach wrote Park Service director Arno Cammerer about the decreased numbers of Dall sheep in the park. Apparently everyone assumed the sheep population of the 1920s represented the norm. Now the sheep were fewer in number, and Beach laid the blame on wolves. He predicted the demise of all the park's game animals in ten years unless the wolves were killed. Assistant Director Arthur Demaray responded: "Since this Service is interested in preserving all forms of wildlife in their natural relationship, we are obliged to find out first what the ecological status of some mammalian predators is in the park." Beach preferred the opinions of his hunting guides and told Demaray, "I am very sorry to hear that the Park Service is so partial to the retention of wolves."[15]

Dissatisfied with the service's response, Beach submitted a five-page report to the club's Conservation Committee, which Greeley forwarded on to

Cammerer. Beach was "terribly shocked" at the low numbers of sheep, and recommended the Camp Fire Club petition the Park Service to destroy its wolves and save the prey species. The park, he argued, should function as a protected breeding ground for game rather than for wolves, which have "run all over the other sections of the Alaska Range." The club's purpose was not to see the wolf exterminated, according to Greeley, but the preservation of the game herds as they had been in the early days of the park. Beach gave his opinions greater publicity by articles in the February and May 1938 issues of *The Backlog*, the Camp Fire Club's bulletin. He outlined the differences he perceived in the park's game between his trips in the 1920s and his return in 1937, and castigated Park Service management for its failure to protect the sheep. He concluded the February article with a call to action: "Are we going to stand aside and permit a huge wolf and coyote breeding-ground to continue?"[16]

Beach's five-page report provoked a quick response from Arthur Demaray, who wired a priority telegram to Harry Liek at McKinley Park requesting the latest animal census data before writing a response. With this information, Demaray told Beach that his 1937 trip in the park had been ill-timed to see game, with the sheep scattered in the high crags and the caribou summering outside the park, and calmly affirmed the ideal that all native fauna would be preserved.[17] While Beach's strenuous arguments rested on the impressions received during hunting trips spanning twelve years, Demaray's response came from access to the best sources available, his rangers that lived in McKinley Park year-round. The annual animal censuses filed by Liek outlined a different picture than that drawn by William Beach.[18]

Annual animal census, 1935 to 1938.

	1935	1936	1937	1938
Caribou	15,000	25,000	20,000	18,212
Sheep	3,000	3,000	3,000	3,793
Wolf	50	75	75	77

Harry Liek wrote a response to Beach, noting that his rangers had seen few wolves in the park that winter, and that during the previous summer almost all visitors to the park had been pleased with the number of game animals seen. Demaray had confidence in the balance of nature as expressed in the

Dall sheep ewes and lambs in valley, vulnerable to wolf predation.
Adolph Murie Collection, temp box 13. Courtesy Alaska and Polar Regions Archives, Rasmuson Library, University of Alaska Fairbanks

Park Service's wildlife management philosophy, assuring Beach that "if sheep, wolves, and caribou have lived together for many thousands of years without one exterminating the other then, other things being equal, there seems to be no reason why they cannot now." Demaray recognized McKinley Park's national significance because of its extant wolves, and he accurately forecast that future generations would actively seek places to "see and hear a timber wolf in its native state."[19]

The wolf-sheep issue strained relations between the Park Service and the Camp Fire Club, but did not produce unseemly personal hostilities. Officials from both groups, when in Washington, D.C., or New York, paid cordial office visits and shared discussions over drinks in their respective clubs. In February 1939 Carl Russell, chief of the Park Service's Wildlife Division, traveled to New York to attend the Committee on Conservation's monthly meeting. He explained the Park Service's policies and thoughts on the wolf-sheep situation, but upon questioning, admitted that no plan yet existed to ensure the health of the sheep population. In attendance was another potentially influential club member: Ray P. Holland, editor of *Field & Stream* magazine, published in New York City. After the meeting a skeptical Holland wrote to Park Service Director Cammerer, "I don't know a great deal about mountain sheep, and my knowledge of wolves is far from extensive. But it does seem to me that the Park Service should do a little wolf killing and do it right away." He had avoided using the magazine to comment editorially on the McKinley Park situation, despite pressure to "tear into the Park Service" for lack of action against the wolves. He requested a frank statement, but Cammerer successfully convinced Holland to keep the issue out of the magazine—at least temporarily.[20]

Camp Fire Club members felt a sense of ownership toward Mount McKinley National Park, and reports of declining sheep numbers provoked questions that went to the heart of park philosophy. To answer these concerns, Park Service administrators had an evolving philosophy toward the protection of all native fauna, but little research-based information. Apart from Joseph Dixon's visits to the park in 1926 and 1932, they had the animal census reports from Harry Liek and his rangers, but these were educated guesses. They did know, however, that sheep numbers had declined markedly over the decade. The Camp Fire Club expected vigorous action to protect the sheep, an expectation also held by Alaska residents.

Alaska's development mirrored the American West's in many ways: few people, exploitable natural resources, and social attitudes molded by three centuries of frontier history. Alaskans needed pragmatic skills and gumption to make a living in the developing territory. Fishing, trapping, gold mining, and lumbering dominated local industry. Unlike the West, ranching was a minimal part of the economy, with the exception of the reindeer ranges. Alaskans ate wild meat, and game animal numbers fluctuated mysteriously and unpredictably, providing reason to minimize causes of mortality. Ensuring a stable and

Lone ram in terrain safe from wolf predation.
Adolph Murie Collection, temp box 13. Courtesy Alaska and Polar Regions Archives, Rasmuson Library, University of Alaska Fairbanks

continuing meat supply seemed sufficient reason to minimize wolf numbers, in addition to the unquestioned history of the country's wolf extirpation. Esthetic and scientific reasons for predator protection did not fill the stew pot. A biologist once told long-time trapper Oscar Vogel that wolves had an equal right to the game as did humans, to which he replied, "No, they don't. I pay taxes."[21] Few Alaskans understood why federal money went toward a purported sanctuary for wolves right in the middle of the territory when everyone else sought to eliminate wolves. Pressure on the Park Service by Alaskans came from all sides and with broader justification than the sportsmen's concern for the park's Dall sheep.

The Alaska Game Commission provided the administrative jurisdiction in the territory for sport fish, bird, fur, and game resources. Established in

1925 by congressional action, the five-member commission reported to the director of the Biological Survey (which evolved into the Fish and Wildlife Service in 1939), under the Department of Agriculture. The commission's officers and wardens oversaw the establishment and enforcement of hunting, trapping, and fishing regulations. Like their peers in state game and fish organizations, the Alaska Game Commission sought to maximize human harvest of animal populations without long-term depletion. Lacking a corps of biologists to monitor animal populations, the commission solicited animal population information from residents, using these and the impressions of its wardens to make rules on hunting and trapping seasons and bag limits. These reports provide a great deal of anecdotal evidence about the increasing numbers of predators during the 1930s. Alarmed by this upsurge and by the previous year's withdrawal of federal predator assistance, in its 1932 meeting the commission passed a resolution calling upon the federal government to assist with bounty payments and supply more hunters.[22] At the same time, the commission outlawed the use of poisons in predator control, in order to protect the indiscriminate killing of furbearing animals attracted to poisoned baits. Not everyone thought that was smart. A trapper living near Lake Minchumina responded, "The wolves are going to take the country. This thing of taking all the poison away from everybody isn't working and never was [sic]."[23]

Just southeast of that lake and its trapper lay McKinley Park, and wolf policies there received the scrutiny of the game commission at its 1935 meeting, especially after hearing of the order from Park Service director Cammerer to cease wolf killings in the park. Commissioners voted to contact Superintendent Liek to determine his current control efforts and level of diligence in pursuing wolves; if unsatisfied, they would protest through the Biological Survey. The game commission recognized the variety of factors that affected faunal numbers in the 1930s—improved rifles, new roads for access—but an increasing wolf population provided a traditional, popular, and nonhuman excuse.[24] The commission wanted predators minimized, an attitude consistent with other states and with Alaskans; the Park Service held the anomalous position, a stance utterly lacking popular support.

Despite the commissioners' consistent attitude toward wolves, many in Alaska perceived the game commission, whose members received appointments from Washington, D.C., rather than election by residents, to be further evidence of the federal government's unnecessary and restrictive powers over Alaska's resources. This attitude persisted despite the members of the game commission being respected Alaskans, and their willingness to consider—indeed, their dependence on—public participation in creating wildlife regulations. Antifederal sentiment often found a voice through the territorial legislature, whose members firmly believed in local control of fish and game. The legislature in 1933 and 1935 passed joint memorials to Washington, D.C., which condemned the game commission as "oppressive and repugnant," accused the game commission of favoring commercial fur trappers over subsistence trappers, and requested that all control of game and fur resources be vested in the legislature.[25]

Alaskans had ambivalent attitudes toward the National Park Service. A destination such as McKinley Park provided both regional pride and tourist dollars, yet many viewed the service as another unnecessary federal imposition. A proposal to add a bear reserve on Admiralty Island to Alaska's trio of national parks—McKinley, Katmai, and Glacier Bay—provoked the legislature in 1939 to state that Alaskans did not want it and that parks were not in the best interest of the territory, as settlers had been "persecuted and harassed" by park officials.[26]

The Park Service's changing attitudes toward predators particularly galled legislators. A 1933 joint memorial to the U.S. Congress pointed out that wolves and coyotes continued to increase despite the territory's expenditure of $130,000 in bounties during preceding years. Legislators bewailed the government's abandonment of its predator control through the Biological Survey. To solve this, the memorial requested matching federal bounty monies and federal action against predatory animals in McKinley Park, the symbol of federal management folly. Six years later the legislature unanimously repeated the memorial with even stronger language, accusing all three national parks in Alaska of "incubating" predators and requesting "an aggressive program under competent superintendence" to minimize wolves.[27] Such ambivalence toward the federal government, welcoming some agencies and efforts while opposing others, typified Alaska's dependent relations then, and ever since.

Alaska's governors also figured into the political stew over wolves. Territorial governors did not win elections, but were appointed by the president and reported to the secretary of the interior. Yet the governors responded to their constituency and seemed quite willing to address Alaskan concerns over wolf issues. Complaints and responses followed a predictable pattern. For example, in January 1931 a sourdough named Charles Trundy, from Kantishna, the mining district adjacent to McKinley Park, wrote to the game commission about the protected park wolves spreading out into the adjacent country and killing caribou by the "hundreds." Trundy had spent time as a sheep hunter for the railroad camps, but had no trouble justifying that activity.

> The game cranks and the partly informed conservationist they made an awful holler about his [the market hunter's] waste of Game and predicted the extermination of the sheep and caribou heards [sic], yet these same people have very little to say about the wolves and brown bear that kill many times more than these hunters (most of whom were Prospectors selling this meat for Grubstake) would kill.[28]

Another Kantishna resident wrote the game commission about McKinley's wolves "being farmed by Park Commission in McKinley Park for tourist consumption." Both letters ended up on the desk of Governor George Parks, who subsequently sent them to Park Service headquarters with a query as to the service's stance. Acting Director Arno Cammerer wrote back to the governor with what became the standard response: "We are trying hard to take a sensible view relative to predatory animal control and we have given instruction to our superintendents to gather statistics and information helpful in determining this policy." Cammerer sent to Superintendent Liek a copy of Trundy's letter, Horace Albright's just-published predator policy outlining a protective stance, and instructions to gather information in order to keep the governor informed.[29]

Anthony Dimond, Alaska's congressional delegate, also challenged Park Service policy on behalf of his constituents. Calling to Director Cammerer's attention the 1939 antipark memorial of the territorial legislature, Dimond wrote:

> It is useless for the people of Alaska residing anywhere within one hundred miles from the Park to try to protect themselves against the depredations of wolves if they are permitted to increase and be free of molestation within the boundaries of the Park.... Measures should be taken at once by the Park authorities to have the wolves in the Park killed off so far as possible.... [T]here are bound to be plenty of wolves in Alaska until it attains a population which would entitle it to statehood.[30]

In response, Assistant Director Arthur Demaray pointed out that wolves had been subject to control in the park and invoked the service's philosophy toward nature's wisdom: "Survival of the fittest produces good game just as artificial selection produces good domestic stock." He assured Dimond of the value of research and thought that since wolves could be taken for bounty in all of Alaska but McKinley Park, the situation represented a "balance which is fair to all interests concerned." Nevertheless, Dimond continued to decry the Park Service's wolf sanctuaries:

> It seems useless for the Territory to continue its control of predatory animals or to pay bounties for their destruction when [the national parks] serve as uncontrolled breeding grounds for the same predatory animals.... It will not do to say as has been said in the past that Nature will take care of the balance.[31]

The equanimity of the Park Service response failed to appease Alaskans.

Antiwolf sentiment gained a significant media voice in 1935 with the founding of *The Alaska Sportsman*, a magazine which historian Morgan Sherwood called the "single most important private, institutional influence in the history of game animals and people in the Territory."[32] Emory Tobin founded and edited the magazine until 1958. He had worked as a newspaperman for the *Boston Ledger*—supervised by Ernest Gruening, before his government service—and in 1920 had moved to Ketchikan with his father, a stampeder to the Koyukuk District.[33] The magazine's contents reflected a dual audience. Tobin recognized the allure of Alaska to nonresidents and used the magazine to promote Alaska to potential settlers, writing in the inaugural issue that it was a magazine "by Alaskans for everyone," to give a "true idea of the country." The editorial column "Main Trails and Bypaths" repeatedly extolled the virtues of Alaska's natural resources and its people. Feature articles provided instruction on the territory's geography and gee-whiz lessons on the size of Alaska potatoes and bears. For local residents, the *Sportsman* published how-to articles on trapping, making pemmican, salmon fishing, and the like. Another theme for residents concerned "advising intelligent conservation" of animal resources. The magazine served as the mouthpiece for the Alaska Sportsmen's Association, formed under the motto "Help keep Alaska the Sportsman's Paradise. Protect and propagate wild life."[34]

Finding "ways and means for wolf extermination" formed a "major objective" of the Sportsmen's Association, and *The Alaska Sportsman* lost no

From an article in the first issue of *The Alaska Sportsman*, January 1935. The caption
with the photo reads: "The wolves' fangs account for countless thousands of harmless
denizens of the woods each year. A dead wolf is a good wolf."

time in furthering that cause. Its first issue in January 1935 contained an article on wolves that established a model for many more to follow: wolves were on the increase, they threatened game and killed for sport, and the successful wolf hunter needed bravery, skill, and luck. Besides providing adventurous reading, articles prominently depicted wolves as a problem for the territory to solve as the states had done. The February issue urged higher bounties on "those gangsters of the wilds," in order to provide sufficient incentive for trapping wolves. The cover of the following issue showed a snarling coyote caught in a trap, and the editorial averred that an increased bounty—from fifteen to twenty-five dollars—was a matter of "vital interest and importance" to Alaskans. Another article in the March issue detailed how to collect the bounty on wolves. First-person wolf hunting articles became a magazine staple. In "I Stalk Villains of Wildlife," the author went after "carnivorous menaces…I chalk up mentally the twenty bucks his head will bring, as I send him a leaden missile that mushrooms when it rips into the vital spot, and send the snarling creature to the ground.… [A]ll I did to that fellow was to put a lead 'period' at the end of his murderous career." By 1939 *The Alaska Sportsman* had a circulation of thirty thousand. It provided a consistent platform for information and sentiment to help Alaskans eliminate wolves.[35]

The repeated charges of McKinley Park serving as a sanctuary for wolves had little basis in practice, although this seemed to go unrecognized by opponents of its wolves. The Park Service did not participate in the previously described cooperative predator control program of 1927–31, but park rangers did kill coyotes and wolves. From the earliest reports of the spread of coyotes into interior Alaska, the Park Service regarded these so-called brush wolves as unwelcome intruders. In 1932 George Wright called them a "difficult and insidious problem." To protect McKinley's native carnivores, he urged that "every step should be taken against this encroachment as an exotic and an alien."[36] Joseph Dixon concurred in a letter to Horace Albright, who instructed Harry Liek to encourage his rangers to kill any coyote found eating anything larger than a rodent. For reasons unknown, though not for lack of coyotes, rangers killed only four of them between 1930–34. They had better success with wolves, killing twenty-three in the same period, before being instructed to cease control by Director Cammerer in 1935.[37]

Cammerer's order to quit killing wolves followed similar instructions to Yellowstone rangers to quit killing coyotes. This resulted from the evolving Park Service philosophy toward hands-off management with trust in natural processes. The evidence available to Cammerer for McKinley Park seemed to justify his order. Harry Liek's 1934 annual report to the director did not mention wolves or depredations, and said the previous winter had inflicted minimal damage to animal populations. Liek made the first ever aerial animal census in 1934 with game warden Sam White, who pioneered the use of aircraft in wildlife work. They estimated a sheep population of three thousand, and did not regard that number as evidence of a crisis. Liek submitted consistently similar reports to the Alaska Game Commission. In February 1936 Liek had taken a 248-mile park survey and saw no wolves or signs of wolves. His comments seemed to justify ceasing wolf control: "I found no evidence where the wolves are increasing within the Park boundary." In that report he also notified the game commission of his far-distant superior's order to halt wolf killing within the park.[38]

As far as Alaskans were concerned, the Park Service's protective stance toward wolves contradicted the evidence all around them. Of the recommendations concerning predators received and printed by the Alaska Game Commission in 1936, Harry Liek's 'no wolves here' letter stood alone. From all around the territory—Hoonah, Stony River, Noatak, Chulitna, McCarthy—observers reported increasing wolf numbers and depredation of game. Newspaper headlines in the spring of 1936 painted a gloomy picture: "Wolves Increasing Here Say Mushers"; "Wolves Kill 500 Reindeer Near Barrow"; "Reindeer Are Devastated By Wolf Bands"; "Wolves Run In Big Packs Along Kobuk."[39] The territory even advertised in stateside papers for people to hunt wolves in Alaska.[40] The well-known McKinley Park sheep received attention from Fairbanksans, who began to notice and comment that McKinley's sheep seemed less numerous. A visitor to the park in 1936 saw three sheep supposedly killed by wolves and "was surprised that the government protects wolves from hunters." The game commission considered declining sheep numbers to be due "almost entirely to depredations of coyotes and wolves," a conclusion supported by the Biological Survey.[41] Concerned that wolf predation on reindeer herds was "imperiling Native food supplies," Governor John Troy requested federal assistance from Interior Secretary Ickes. In May Congress approved Troy's request with an appropriation for a predator hunter. In Idaho later that summer, Harlan Gubser packed his bags and set out for Kotzebue to "wage war on predatory brutes," four years after his first employment with the cooperative predator program.[42]

In spring 1936, local sentiment against predators received organized support with the formation of the Tanana Valley Sportsmen's Association, based in Fairbanks. When twenty men created the association on April 3, their discussion focused on the introduction of new species of fish and game—elk, pheasant, Scandinavian grouse, rainbow and lake trout—to interior environs. Seventy people attended the following week's meeting, and the increased numbers of wolves and coyotes came up for discussion. Sam White, the pilot wildlife agent, introduced a new concept in predator control which had far-reaching effects: "he had conceived the idea of fighting wolves by shooting at them from airplanes with automatic shotguns." The sportsmen's association opposed "the Park rule that nothing may be killed there," for its members were convinced that wolves and coyotes were responsible for the decreased game numbers within the park and were spreading into surrounding areas.[43] A sensational editorial in the *Fairbanks Daily News-Miner* lauded the aerial hunting concept and urged Uncle Sam's assistance: "If Alaska is to preserve her game and fur animals she—with aid of the federal government—must wake up and carry relentless warfare into the ranks of the enemy—not tomorrow but today—not at some convenient season but in this hour of emergency." Consternation erupted as Fairbanksans learned of the Park Service's new wolf policy, which was reflected in bold headlines: "Sportsmen Take Aggressive Steps on Wolves and Coyotes; Protest Made Against Protection of Outlaw Animals in McK. Park."[44]

Such local sentiment could do nothing but strain relations between residents and park employees. National Park Service leaders had long understood the need to encourage favorable opinions. Steven Mather and Horace Albright had encouraged park superintendents and rangers to become involved with nearby communities and help spread the national park philosophy. Harry Liek, upon arrival at McKinley Park in 1929, had to replace an authentic sourdough, Harry Karstens, as superintendent of a park few Alaskans visited. In 1931, Liek admitted to Albright that he had made little progress in swaying public opinion. To get some attention for himself and his park, he and ranger Grant Pearson joined Minneapolis lawyer Alfred Lindley and ski instructor Erling Strom to make the second ascent of Mount McKinley. The stunt worked, and Liek found himself accepted by Alaskans and active in many capacities outside the park.[45]

But public relations suffered over the wolf issue, resulting in greater efforts to counter negative publicity. Park Service representatives became fixtures at the Fairbanks Winter Carnival and Anchorage Fur Rendezvous, where they judged dog races, cooking contests, and beauty pageants. Park rangers also showed wildlife films and gave lectures to groups at schools, hospitals, chambers of commerce, and Alaska Railroad employees. Harry Liek cultivated local leaders in Fairbanks and Anchorage and dutifully recorded public contacts in his monthly reports. For example, a trip to Fairbanks in March 1936 provided Liek an opportunity to talk with the mayor, governor of Yukon Territory, postmaster, newspaper editor, district judge, and presidents of the Chamber of Commerce and First National Bank. Although Alaskans disagreed with wolf protection in the park, they understood that policies came from Washington, D.C., not from their neighbors at the park. But even those distant officials recognized the fractures emerging in Alaska, taking pains to minimize them. Rangers sent eleven pictures of wolf-killed animals in McKinley Park to Park Service headquarters, where administrators buried them in files and sent word back not to distribute them: "it would seem advisable to take every precaution against their being broadcast indiscriminately, or placed in the hands of persons who might use them as propaganda against the wolf."[46]

Fairbanksans also viewed wolves as a threat to a new source of revenue, tourist dollars. Although McKinley Park was the least visited of all national parks, even during the Great Depression enough wealthy travelers visited the park—as many as 1,500 annually—to impress residents eager to receive them.[47] Each summertime steamer from Seattle and train from Seward received newspaper coverage indicating the number of tourists aboard and persons of note. Then as now, McKinley Park dominated the venue for tourists venturing inland from Alaska's coast, and local residents were justifiably proud of their backyard attraction. In 1936 park visitation increased by sixty-four percent over the preceding year, to the delight of the hoteliers and merchants of Fairbanks.[48] During their park visit, tourists wanted to see the famed sheep and caribou, objects of interest in the largely treeless landscape. Horace Albright had correctly noted on his 1931 visit that Mt. McKinley itself lay hidden behind clouds more than half the summer days. Alaskans took a dim view of any factor which threatened to diminish the visitor's experience. If wolves held down game numbers, then clearly wolves had to go.

Two important officials visited in 1936, and their reactions belied the crisis trumpeted by residents concerned about the wolf threat. Ernest Gruening, then with the federal Office of the Territories, toured Alaska on behalf of the Department of the Interior (he would be appointed governor in 1940). Gruening gave the keynote speech at the University of Alaska's commencement ceremony and toured the park, where he was "thrilled" by the wildlife display. Assistant Parks Director Arthur Demaray also arrived in June in the middle of a month-long itinerary in the territory. He traveled the park road only one day, June 24, but announced "In no other park have I seen so many fine specimens of wild animal life." Demaray delighted a Fairbanks audience by announcing passage of a federal appropriations bill providing $100,000 for extending the park road to Wonder Lake to increase accessibility.[49]

As he met with local and state leaders during his June visit, Demaray encountered first-hand the depth of public opinion against the Park Service's protective wolf policy. Simultaneously, reports from the park changed. While in February Harry Liek had not regarded wolves as a problem, his July 1936 report offered a different view. Wolves were becoming a "menace to the sheep...more numerous and...so bold they will come right into a camp in broad daylight." A later report in 1936 also laid the blame for declining numbers of sheep to the "steady increase the past two years" in wolf numbers, and Liek recommended continued control efforts.[50]

In August, back in Washington, D.C., Demaray reversed the tenuous wolf protection policy and gave permission to "kill a moderate number." The Park Service realized it had critics on both sides of the issue: killing wolves would "probably answer local critics who believe the wolf population should be reduced," yet to allay potential criticism from animal biologists, it would be done under the guise of research by saving wolf stomachs and contents for dietary analysis. Demaray cautioned Liek to "pay great attention to details as the value of the results and freedom from criticism of conservation organizations will depend largely upon you and your staff." Ever conscious of this, Harold Bryant made a marginal notation on the copy of this memorandum circulated among the staff: "Hope you go slow on this! Mammalogists will protest mightily at *any control*." The headline in the *Daily News-Miner* read "Rangers Now Allowed Kill Park Wolves."[51]

Notes

1   Russell Annabel, *Hunting and Fishing in Alaska* (New York: Alfred A. Knopf, 1948), 5. The price of a hunting trip has only doubled in sixty years; the Alaska Department of Fish and Game figures a brown bear hunt on Kodiak Island costs an American visitor $9,545 (average). About seven thousand nonresident hunters now visit Alaska annually; from National Research Council, *Wolves, Bears, and Their Prey in Alaska: Biological and Social Challenges in Wildlife Management* (Washington, D.C.: National Academy Press, 1997), 155.

2   Governor's *Annual Report*, 1920, 47; Daniel Beard (Park Service Wildlife Division), "A Brief Summary of Camp Fire Club Activities Relative to Mount McKinley National

Park," n.d., probably 1939, RG 79, Entry 7, File 719, Box 1415, NA. See William E. Brown, *A History of the Denali-Mt. McKinley Region, Alaska* (Washington, D.C.: GPO, National Park Service, 1991), 146–49, and Theodore Catton, *Inhabited Wilderness: Indians, Eskimos, and National Parks in Alaska* (Albuquerque: University of New Mexico Press, 1997), chapters four and five on the issue of legal hunting by miners in the early park.

3   Camp Fire Club, "National Park Standards, as Defined by the Camp Fire Club of America," *American Forests* 35 (August 1929): 476.

4   "William Beach," obituary, *New York Times*, 6 May 1955.

5   'Beach File' compiled by Harold Bryant about this "self-styled conservationist"; copy sent to Harry Liek, 29 July 1938, RG 79, Entry 7, File 715, Box 1414, NA.

6   William Beach, *In the Shadow of Mt. McKinley* (New York: Derrydale Press, 1931), 288, 39; Beach, "Game Marches On," *The Backlog*, February 1938, 3. *The Backlog* was the bulletin of the Camp Fire Club.

7   Beach, *Shadow*, 285–86.

8   Beach, *Shadow*, 83, 85, 183. In all fairness, other contemporary sportsmen wrote of similarly poor shooting on hunts.

9   'Beach File,' Bryant to Liek, 29 July 1938, RG 79, Entry 7, File 715, Box 1414, NA.

10 Other versions of this in Brown, *History of Denali*, 156–57, and Catton, *Inhabited Wilderness*, 123. Catton writes that the cash settlement was accepted and Beach escaped the embarassment of court, but the 'Beach File' indicates otherwise.

11 Membership list not dated, but latest date of any member's inclusion is 1947; RG 79, Entry 7, File 719, Box 1415, NA.

12 Quoted in James B. Trefethen, *Crusade for Wildlife: Highlights in Conservation Progress* (Harrisburg, PA: Stackpole, and the Boone and Crockett Club, 1961), 299.

13 Beach to Parks, 10 November 1931; Parks to Beach, 21 November 1931; Harlan Gubser to Parks, 21 November 1931; all RG 101, Box 333, Folder 4, ASA.

14 Beach sent a summary report to the Game Commission; see Exec. Officer's *Annual Report* to AGC, 1932; Greeley to Albright, 17 July 1931, RG 79, Entry 7, File 719, Box 1415, NA. Following his resignation from the Park Service, Albright became a member of the Camp Fire Club on Greeley's invitation; see Donald C. Swain, *Wilderness Defender: Horace M. Albright and Conservation* (Chicago: University of Chicago Press, 1970), 255.

15 Beach to Cammerer, 11 October 1937; Demaray to Beach, 15 October 1937; Beach to Demaray, 10 November 1937; all RG 79, Entry 7, File 715, Box 1414, NA.

16 Beach to Camp Fire Club Conservation Committee, 1 November 1937; Greeley to Cammerer, 16 November 1937; Greeley to Cammerer, 8 December 1937; Beach to Demaray, 7 December 1937; all RG 79, Entry 7, File 719, Box 1415, NA; Beach, "Game Marches On," 4.

17   Demaray to Liek, telegram, 19 November 1937; Demaray to Beach, 24 November 1937; both RG 79, Entry 7, File 715, Box 1414, NA.

18   "McKinley Park Animal Reports," 1935–38, RG 79, Entry 7, File 710–715, Box 1414, NA. The apparent precision of the 1938 figures reflects early attempts at aerial surveying.

19   Liek to Beach, 17 February 1938, RG 79, Entry 7, File 715, Box 1414, NA; Demaray to Beach, 30 October 1937, RG 79, Entry 7, File 719, Box 1415, NA.

20   Albright to Cammerer, February 1939; Holland to Cammerer, 7 February 1939; Holland to Demaray, 20 February 1939; Holland to Cammerer, 17 March 1939; all RG 79, Entry 7, File 719, Box 1415, NA.

21   Oscar H. Vogel, "My Years with the Wolves," *Alaska*, May 1972, 57.

22   "Minutes of the Annual Meeting of the Alaska Game Commission," 1932, 29–30; AGC *Annual Report*, 1932–33, UAF.

23   Exec. Officer's *Annual Report to AGC*, 1934, 64, UAF.

24   "Minutes of the Annual Meeting of the Alaska Game Commission," 1935, 8; Exec. Officer's *Annual Report to AGC*, 1936, 82, UAF. For more on the Alaska Game Commission perspective, see Frank Dufresne, "What of Tomorrow?" *The Alaska Sportsman*, April 1937, 9; Dufresne, "The Game and Fur Belong to All the People," *The Alaska Sportsman*, April 1944, 16–18, 21.

25   Alaska Legislature, *Senate Joint Memorial No. 8*, 11th Legislature, 1933; *House Joint Memorial No. 7*, 13th Legislature, 1935; *Daily News-Miner*, "Senate Favors Game Control By Alaskan," 2 February 1935.

26   Alaska Legislature, *Senate Joint Memorial No. 16*, 14th Legislature, 1939. On Alaskan ambivalence, see Frank Norris, "A Lone Voice in the Wilderness: The National Park Service in Alaska, 1917–1969," *Environmental History* 1 (October 1996): 66–76.

27   Alaska Legislature, *House Joint Memorial No. 10*, 11th Legislature, 1933; *Committee Substitute for Senate Joint Memorial No. 2*, 14th Legislature, 1939.

28   Trundy to Alaska Game Commission, 12 January 1931, RG 79, Entry 7, File 719, Box 1415, NA.

29   Terhune to Parks 8 April 1931, Cammerer to Parks, 2 June 1931, RG 101, Box 318, ASA; Cammerer to Liek, 17 July 1931, RG 79, Entry 7, File 719, Box 1415, NA. Kantishna area residents may have been particularly hostile to the park service at this time, as in 1928 park regulations changed to prohibit their subsistence hunting within park boundaries.

30   Dimond to Demaray, 20 February 1935, RG 79, Entry 7, File 719, Box 1415, NA.

31   Demaray to Dimond, 21 February 1935; Dimond to Cammerer, 14 April 1937; Dimond to Cammerer, 6 March 39; all RG 79, Entry 7, File 719, Box 1415, NA.

32   Morgan Sherwood, *Big Game in Alaska: A History of Wildlife and People* (New Haven: Yale University Press, 1981), 57.

33 The magazine's history, and biographic information on Tobin, is found in Ethel Dassow, "The Voice of the Last Frontier," *Alaska*, October 1984, 15–21, 85–89, 92–93. Ms. Dassow began her long employment with the magazine during WW II and became assistant editor, rewriting manuscripts to give a balance between good grammar and colloquial expression.

34 "Main Trails and Bypaths," *The Alaska Sportsman*, January 1935, 4; "The Alaska Sportsmen's Association," *The Alaska Sportsman*, January 1935, 20.

35 From *The Alaska Sportsman*: F. W. Gabler, "The Wolf Pack," January 1935, 16, 17; "Main Trails and Bypaths," February 1935, 4; "The Alaska Sportsmen's Association," February 1935, 15; "Main Trails and Bypaths," March 1935, 5; C. R. Snow, "The Trap Line," March 1935, 20; R. W. Irwin, "I Stalk Villains of Wildlife," March 1943, 14, 16.

36 Wright, et. al., *Fauna of the National Parks*, 47–8. Recent research indicates that these fears may have been justified, as some coyote experts think that man's persecution of the coyote in this century has resulted in animals "larger, smarter, more adaptable, faster, and more cunning"; see H. T. Gier, "Ecology and Behavior of the Coyote *(Canis latrans)*," in *The Wild Canids: Their Systematics, Behavioral Ecology, and Evolution*, ed. M. W. Fox (New York: Van Nostrand Reinhold, 1975), 261.

37 Dixon to Albright, 27 October 1932; Albright to Liek, 14 November 1932; Liek to Cammerer, 18 January 1935; all RG 79, Entry 7, File 715, Box 1415, NA.

38 Superintendent's "Annual Report," 1934, 1935, RG 79, Entry 7, Box 1405, NA; Liek to Alaska Game Commission, n.d., in AGC *Annual Report*, 1936, UAF; see also Dave Hall, "Sam O. White: The First Flying Game Warden," *Alaska*, May 1986, 14–17, 59–62.

39 *Daily News-Miner*, "Wolves Increasing Here Say Mushers," 27 February 1936; "Wolves Kill 500 Reindeer Near Barrow," 26 March 1936; "Reindeer Are Devastated By Wolf Bands," 31 March 1936; "Wolves Run In Big Packs Along Kobuk," 2 April 1936.

40 John Mykytya to Governor Troy, 29 June 1936, in response to an ad in Minnesota's *Free Press Prairie Farmer*; RG 101, Box 474, Folder 1, ASA.

41 *Daily News-Miner*, "New Plans Outlined By Tanana Sportsmen At Spirited Meeting," 16 May 36; AGC *Annual Report*, June 1936; AGC *Annual Report*, October 1936; *Annual Report of the Chief of the Bureau of Biological Survey*, 1936.

42 AGC *Annual Report*, 1936; *Daily News-Miner*, "Troy Asks Help From Ickes In Fight on Wolves," 11 February 1936; "Alaska Items Are Carried In Interior Bill," 13 May 1936; "Expert to Wage War On Predatory Brutes," 5 August 1936.

43 *Daily News-Miner*, "Sportsmen Organize With Aim to Bring In New Species," 4 April 1936; "Large And Enthusiastic Gathering Is Held By Fairbanks Sportsmen," 11 April 1936; "Wolves Near Reindeer On Kuskokwim," 30 July 36.

44 *Daily News-Miner*, "Alaska's Warfare on Outlaw Animals," 16 April 1936; "Sportsmen Take Aggressive Steps on Wolves and Coyotes; Protest Made Against Protection of Outlaw Animals in McK. Park," 9 May 1936.

45   Brown, *History of Denali*, 176, 191, 193.

46   See Superintendent's "Monthly Reports," 1936–38, DENA; Lawrence Merriam and E. Lowell Sumner, Jr., to Victor Cahalane, 17 March 1937, RG 79, Entry 7, File 719, Box 1415, NA.

47   Norris, "The National Park Service in Alaska," 70.

48   *Daily News-Miner*, "Tourist Gain By M'Kinley Is 64 Per Cent," 1 October 1936.

49   *Daily News-Miner*, "Director Thrilled By Sight," 20 May 1936; "Park Chief Impressed By McKinley," 2 July 1936; "$100,000 Is Granted To M'Kinley Park," 23 June 36. Demaray's itinerary, Arthur Demaray Collection, Box 29, Folder 1, AHC. For an explication of the park road history and significance, see Gail Evans, "From Myth to Reality: Travel Experiences and Landscape Perceptions in the Shadow of Mount McKinley, Alaska, 1876–1938" (M.A. Thesis, University of California at Santa Barbara, 1987).

50   Superintendent's "Monthly Report," July 1936; Superintendent's "Annual Report," 1936, RG 79, Entry 7, Box 1405 and 1406, NA, resp.

51   Demaray to Liek, 22 August 1936, RG 79, Entry 7, File 719, Box 1415, NA; *Daily News-Miner*, 30 November 1936, "Rangers Now Allowed Kill Park Wolves."

I wish that we had three or four Muries.
—*Victor Cahalane*

5

Wildlife Research
and Adolph Murie

In attempting to change its ways and include predators as legitimate components of park fauna, the National Park Service was trying to do what no other agency had ever done. This decision of a few service employees did not change the opinion of a majority within the agency, however. In fact, a poll would have revealed little sympathy for predators outside the Wildlife Division. Harold Bryant, George Wright, and the others justified their stance by invoking that word "unimpaired" from the service's legislative mandate, but that led to contradictions with other park goals.

More useful was an appeal to science, but the earliest theories of ecologists on predator-prey relations were difficult to reinforce by field observation. The metaphorical question of a balance of nature without mankind's presumably upsetting role continued to influence research. In 1925 Biologist Stephen Forbes published a significant paper based on lake studies in which he posited that predators and prey neatly balanced one another in a "community of interest." An American, Alfred Lotka, and an Italian, Vittorio Volterra, independently derived mathematical equations that made intuitive sense. The Lotka-Volterra logistics equations indicated that a predator population and a prey population would both oscillate over time in a coupled fashion, but even in simple laboratory tests using paramecium this proved difficult to demonstrate. Time scales were important, more so as the animal's size increased. In 1930 the British ecologist Charles Elton proclaimed that the balance of nature did not exist; rather, instability of population numbers resulted from environmental factors. While these fluctuations could be resolved into something that looked like equilibria, the singular 'balance' existed only in the observer's limited understanding. Scientific rationales for predator inclusion in parks would have to be consistent with current theory, but also prove practicable in the public arena.[1]

While the Park Service had clearly committed itself to faunal protection that included predators, this isolated it from the mainstream of public opinion and other government agencies. The evolution in attitude toward predators that started with Joseph Grinnell and the American Society of Mammalogists in the late 1920s continued to spread through the 1930s, providing the Park Service with important allies to help justify its policies. Harold Bryant continued his efforts to rehabilitate predators and found a receptive audience in the Audubon Societies, where he contributed articles to its bulletin, *Bird-Lore,* and gave a speech on the value of predators at their 1936 annual convention.[2] The research on bird predation by a Wisconsin biologist received coverage in *Bird-Lore* as well. Paul Errington studied bobwhite quail for five years and concluded that quality of habitat, rather than predation, curbed quail numbers; furthermore, predator control failed to raise the prey population, supporting the concept that nature worked in balance until man disturbed it.[3]

Another important voice arose in defense of wild fauna during the 1930s, one whose conversion of attitudes toward predators has become one of conservation's most repeated tales. Aldo Leopold, a former Forest Service ranger and later a professor at the University of Wisconsin, became the father of game management during his life. After his death in 1948, his writings joined those of Thoreau and Muir in providing a philosophical foundation for the environmental movement.[4] As a young ranger, Leopold wholeheartedly helped coordinate New Mexico's stockmen and state game wardens with rangers and Biological Survey agents against predators. By his own account, he was "young and full of trigger-itch," providing little evidence of his forthcoming change.[5] In 1925, after the disaster on the Kaibab Plateau and the questioning of predator control by the American Society of Mammalogists, Leopold began to reexamine his views. With predators severely diminished in the southwest, he recognized their possible significance in an ecological system, although still favoring control in certain situations, even in national parks. His ecological views coalesced in *Game Management* (1933), the first book of its kind to appear in the United States and an enduring work still in print. Leopold saw with new clarity the failures of the sportsman's "short-time viewpoint," and the "age-old insistence of the human mind to fix on some visible scapegoat the responsibility for invisible phenomena which they cannot or do not wish to understand." While this represented a step forward in attitudes toward predators, Leopold still wrote from the utilitarian rather than an esthetic or moral stance. He regarded naturalists who wished no predator control to be biologically misguided and willfully oblivious to economic concerns. Leopold shaped his attitudes toward predators by the emerging theories of ecology, and he proved capable of applying them to policy issues faced by wildlife and land managers.[6]

An additional impetus to Leopold's evolution in thought arose from a less tangible concept, the idea of defining wilderness as a land management concept. As early as 1921 he recognized the potential value of undisturbed Forest Service lands for a particular type of recreation, that of the extended trip "through a big stretch of wild country" away from the "hordes of motorists."[7] His proposal bore fruit in the 1924 designation of the Gila Wilderness in New Mexico, the precursor to a much larger system of Forest Service wilderness areas, and in 1935 Leopold joined eight others in creating The Wilderness Society. By promoting wilderness as a place for human fulfillment, Leopold essentially agreed with Theodore Roosevelt and Daniel Beard, who saw wilderness areas preserving opportunities for an imitative experience of the encounter between settlers and the New World. This was a far cry from the Puritan fear of wilderness, and one shared by few who actually tried to make a living on the fringes of civilization, such as many migrants to Alaska, or by people such as Alaska Natives who lived in the landscape without defining a difference between here and there. But defining modern wilderness would prove a necessary step in preserving wolves.

A lengthy visit to Germany and its intensively managed forests brought Leopold a mixture of feelings: admiration for German conservation of game species despite dense human population, and pity for Germany's "bearless, wolfless, eagleless, catless woods," which, to Leopold's mind, was a trade yielding "very little indeed."[8] The following year he journeyed to the mountains of northern Mexico. There he experienced a land affected neither by twentieth-century development nor by resource management, where forests remained healthy and deer abundant, while predators roamed free of "rifle, trap, and poison."[9] Wilderness lacked true wildness in the absence of all its native fauna, and from this time on Leopold urged management schemes that included predators as essential components of healthy lands. Leopold maintained contact with members of the Park Service's Wildlife Division through work on national conservation and game advisory boards, and through the annual meetings of the North American Wildlife Conference. In 1946 when the wolf-sheep controversy moved to the floors of Congress, Leopold actively supported the Park Service.

A 1920 graduate of the University of Wisconsin, Sigurd Olson, experienced a similar change in attitude toward the wolf. Born and raised in northern Wisconsin, Olson began his writing career with newspaper and magazine articles about the canoe country near Lake Superior. A biology instructor and administrator at the junior college in Ely, Minnesota, Olson maintained a guiding business during the summers, traversing the historic water routes of the early French voyageurs. Wolves still roamed the forests and lakes, and Olson's contact with the area's trappers yielded material for two articles in *Sports Afield* magazine. "The Poison Trail" (1930) described with approval this "phase of the warfare between the predatory animal control and the hosts of grey marauders," while the fictional "Papette" (1932) described the bloody life of the wolf pack in the style of Jack London's stories.[10]

When Olson started graduate studies at the University of Illinois, he chose wolves as his thesis topic. Through the 1930s he changed from a hunting and fishing writer to an outspoken advocate for preservation issues, influenced by Leopold and early membership in The Wilderness Society. His academic research, supervised by ecologist Victor Shelford, formed the earliest comprehensive study of the north woods. Olson's previous attitude toward the wolf changed into admiration and respect. Like Leopold, Olson came to appreciate wolves for both their ecological role and symbolic place in wilderness. Olson's master's thesis appeared in the April 1938 *Scientific Monthly*. "A Study in Predatory Relationship with Particular Reference to the Wolf" utilized the lore and knowledge of Olson's trapper and game warden friends to build a case for preserving wolf populations, despite the desire of his informants to see wolves exterminated. Olson concluded that wolves took far fewer game animals than popularly supposed, and that they were a "distinct asset to big game types." The Park Service noticed Olson's work: Harold Bryant wrote a congratulatory letter to Olson and requested five copies, pointing out that "the facts recorded in your article would tend to support our claims that at Mount McKinley evidence is lacking to show that wolves are doing an unusual amount of damage." Olson's work established a precedent for Adolph Murie's more rigorous wolf study, and Olson became a staunch advocate for the Park Service in the McKinley controversy.[11]

Olaus Murie also became a leading figure in the changing appreciation of predators. After his Alaska trips of the 1920s and marriage to Margaret Gillette of Fairbanks, he studied for a year at the University of Michigan, where he organized his notes on caribou into a master's degree thesis. In the spring of 1927 Murie rejoined the Biological Survey, which sent him to Jackson Hole, Wyoming, a locale more similar to Alaska than any other place in the country, with its long winters, scant human population, mountain-studded horizons, and abundance of wildlife. Murie applied his expertise in wild ungulates to a study of the southern Yellowstone elk herd, tracking their annual migration routes, assessing their feeding and quality of range, and identifying leading causes of mortality.[12]

Many people blamed dead elk on predators. Wolves had been eliminated, but coyotes remained plentiful, and Murie turned his attention for several years to coyote research. He needed to assess two factors: causes of elk mortality, and the diet of coyotes. He achieved the first by post-mortem examinations, and the second by examining coyote droppings. He found that elk died of diseases often resulting from good-intentioned supplemental winter feeding, giving a boost to a philosophy toward wildlife management that deferred to a balance of nature. Coyotes, he concluded, liked to feed on elk already dead, but rarely preyed on them, preferring smaller bundles of food such as rodents. Murie's organizational superiors in the Biological Survey did not receive these findings with pleasure. The agency was committed to predator control and minimized the significance of his research findings. He found this disappointing, but the research had confirmed his belief that predation was certainly not harmful and was in all likelihood beneficial to ecosystems.[13] Murie's personal correspondence with his friend, archaeologist Otto Geist at the University of Alaska, reflected his growing positive thinking toward predators.

I do not become irate at the Alaskans who think otherwise. I believe they are sincere and I have much respect for their viewpoints. Most of us felt the same way not so long ago. But some of us have been studying these problems intensively in the last few years and we have had our eyes opened. We find that we can have game and moderate numbers of predatory birds and mammals in the same area.

There is always so much hysteria, as in the case of the starving Eskimo. And so much political propaganda....I realize the whole country is against the animal. Traders will be cussing them. Probably the Eskimo will resent the killing by wolves. I find it necessary to be diplomatic in such cases and quietly gather what data I can. The problem of sincere conservationists is to find places where animals such as the wolf can exist in moderate numbers and prevent their complete extermination.[14]

Reflected as well in this quote is Murie's recognition of the importance of habitat preservation, and he increasingly turned his energies in that direction. By 1937 he had been invited to join the organizers of The Wilderness Society. Preservation work provided an outlet for his convictions, lacking in the orthodox thinking of the Biological Survey. Olaus Murie resigned from his position in 1945 to work with The Wilderness Society, and he and Margaret would go on to become an influential and beloved force in American conservation.

The months spent in Alaska in 1922–24 by the Murie brothers profoundly influenced Adolph's life: he met his future wife in Fairbanks, though marriage was still a decade away; he increased and refined the outdoor skills of his boyhood, becoming familiar with the tools of life and travel in the northern wilderness in the "blessed days" before airplanes, radios, and snow machines.[15] He grew to love the North, its animals, seasons, light, and, in particular, he became familiar with McKinley Park, where he would spend many years of his life. Additionally, for a young man on the cusp of career decisions, he experienced the lifestyle of a biologist in the federal government. Olaus got paid to travel far and wide and do what he liked doing anyway: watching, hunting, drawing, collecting, and classifying animals. Fargo College had closed by the time Adolph returned home, but he enrolled in Moorhead's Concordia College and received his bachelor's degree in 1924. He spent the next year and a half in Montana teaching high school in Hamilton, and he spent two summers as a rookie ranger at Glacier National Park. In 1926 he joined Olaus at the University of Michigan for graduate studies.

Though far from the open skies of the West and wilderness of the North, the University of Michigan had a zoology professor with an appeal for Adolph, a man who combined youthful experiences in the Alaska bush with academic training from one of the country's leading ecologists: Lee Raymond Dice, curator of mammals at Michigan's Museum of Zoology. Dice had become interested in field zoology during studies with Victor Shelford at the University of Chicago, and subsequently worked as a fur warden in Alaska from 1911 to 1913. Upon returning from the North, Dice spent a summer working with one of America's earliest Ph.D.-level ecologists, Charles C. Adams. Dice then enrolled for graduate-level studies at the University of California at Berkeley, where he took his Ph.D. under Joseph Grinnell.[16] By 1925 Dice actively opposed federal predator control and participated in the American Society of Mammalogist's campaigns against it. He made his opposition to a local control program in Michigan known even when having that view placed one in a distinct minority.[17]

As a participant in this academic lineage, the opinions and field techniques that Dice taught Adolph Murie were ones that extended back to Berkeley and Joseph Grinnell. One of Grinnell's enduring legacies was a standard field notation system: a log of the day's events—distances traveled, weather, expenses, and the like—in one notebook, another for site-specific observations, and a third containing observations grouped by species.[18] At the University of Michigan, Murie sharpened his academic skills, absorbed the latest theories of ecology, and began the exacting field studies that would establish his reputation. His dissertation was entitled "The Ecological Relationship of Two Subspecies of *Peromyscus* in the Glacier Park Region, Montana." *Peromyscus maniculatus*, the common deer mouse, was the major research subject of Lee Dice, who used laboratory-reared deer mice for studies in genetics. Once he satisfied his supervisor's research leanings, Murie gravitated toward the study of larger mammals.

Adolph's training and appreciation for the intricacies of the natural world could be seen in his first independent research project. He received his Ph.D. in the spring of 1929. That year the state of Michigan appropriated funds for a comprehensive study of Isle Royale, a 220-square mile uninhabited island in Lake Superior that became a national park in 1940. Murie's attention was soon attracted to the island's dominant animal, the moose, which had migrated from the mainland early in the twentieth century and had multiplied to a population of at least one thousand, placing stress on the island's vegetation. Adolph spent the summer and autumn of 1929 on the island, and returned for the early summer months of 1930. His report on the moose showed his observational skills and avidity of purpose: for example, he described spending an evening in a poplar tree above a mineral lick so he could better observe moose behavior. Murie offered recommendations for moose management with three suggestions for reducing their population that involved human intervention: opening the island for sport hunting, culling moose by paid state hunters, and live trapping and transport to the mainland. Murie preferred a fourth alternative: introducing a wolf or cougar population. No one really knew what effect that might have, since no one had yet studied large predator-large prey interactions. But he thought their addition "would add materially to the animal interests of the island," and held as an ideal that "management should be to give consideration to all life so as to have nature present in good proportions."[19] With this, Adolph joined that small group of biologists, linked through Dice to Grinnell, willing to entertain a new conception of the value of predators, one based not on folk myths or the economics of bounty hunting, but on the ecological integrity of natural systems.

Murie's Isle Royale work helped him obtain an appointment as the assistant curator of mammals at the University of Michigan Museum of Zoology, as well as an invitation to join the museum's trip to British Honduras (now Belize) and Guatemala in early 1931. The group included an ornithologist, geologist, and botanist, with Murie the mammalogist in a collective mission of specimen procurement. Traps, guns, and nets formed Adolph's arsenal, along with the scalpels, borax, cotton, pins, and labels used to preserve the animal skins for transport and filing back at the museum. He employed a local hunter to assist in finding the animals, and experienced some of the problems associated with biological research in the tropics. He found that jaguars ate dogs, that a rifle would be better than their twenty-gauge shotgun for shooting monkeys out of the forest canopy, and that animals killed in traps were quickly eaten by ants. But after five months Adolph had over seven hundred specimens, ranging from bats to manatee bones. He also brought back malaria, which would be a life-long health problem.[20]

Whenever possible, Adolph visited Olaus and Margaret in Jackson Hole, which became the focal point for the whole family. Their mother moved from Minnesota in 1930, pleased to leave the prairies for a landscape more reminiscent of the Norwegian landscape of her childhood. Three generations of Muries took extended summer campouts in the backcountry, where the brothers continued followup studies to Adolph's dissertation on the deer mouse. Meanwhile, romance had blossomed for Adolph. Margaret's family had moved from Fairbanks to Washington's Methow Valley in 1924; three years later Adolph drove Olaus and Margaret there for a visit, where he became reacquainted with then-eighteen-year-old (and "impressionable") Louise. In 1932 Adolph and Louise were married in Jackson, and the newlyweds returned to Ann Arbor.[21]

Adolph Murie collecting specimens in British Honduras (now Belize), 1931.
Adolph Murie Collection, temp box 13. Courtesy Alaska and Polar Regions Archives, Rasmuson Library, University of Alaska Fairbanks

There Adolph addressed his growing interest in predator-prey research with a study on the role of the red fox in the regional ecology at a nearby nature preserve administered by the museum. To obtain his data, Adolph spent a winter following fox tracks (and those of their prey) after snowfalls, noting their movements and hunting patterns. During summer months he roamed the woods and fields collecting and analyzing droppings to determine the fox diet. These were standard methods of zoologists, typical of the descriptive level of field work at the time. His report, *Following Fox Trails*, published in 1936 by the University of Michigan, was a family effort. Lousie typed his notes and Olaus contributed animal sketches, a partnership that continued throughout their lives.[22]

In 1933 the National Park Service created its Wildlife Division, headquartered in Berkeley under the direction of George Wright. Within two years he had recruited twenty-seven biologists whom he called the division's "arms and legs."[23] These included Adolph Murie, who joined the staff in 1934 at a monthly salary of $250, assigned to supervise assistant naturalists and advise on wildlife management at all the western parks. Although based in Omaha, Murie spent little time there. Between September and November 1934 his exhausting itinerary included visits to Glacier, Yellowstone, Grand Teton, Rocky Mountain, Grand Canyon, Zion, Bryce, Crater Lake, Mount Rainier, and Olympic national parks, as well as a stop in Berkeley. The winter months included meetings in Washington, D.C., but Murie preferred the field to the office. He noted that not only did he have to buy a suit for a 1936 conference of national and state park personnel, but "Most of the afternoon was devoted to fish and much loose palaver about little or nothing."[24]

These early years with the Park Service provided a chance for Murie's background and training to integrate with national park ideals, notably those of his colleagues in the Wildlife Division, and he established attitudes and patterns that marked his entire career. Adolph Murie believed that parks were for animals, not people—or at least only the ones who deserved the parks. After an evening spent—presumably incognito—listening to a seasonal ranger naturalist at Glacier National Park, Murie snippily wrote that the naturalist was only hired "to show goats to the tourists at Logan Pass." In Yellowstone, he objected to a golf course development scheme, as well as a proposal to drain a one square mile radius surrounding Old Faithful Lodge to reduce the abundant mosquito population, and thus to reduce the number of complaints received from tourists about sharing their national park with the annoying pests. Superintendent Roger Toll believed "everything possible should be done for the tourist." Murie disagreed with this, and suggested that "the mosquitoes might be a selective agency," keeping out those who did not deserve to be there.[25]

But even if parks were for animals, Murie felt they had to be maintained in a pure state. Tourists, after all, created garbage, and hence the famed garbage dump bears of Yellowstone, which he loathed. Excessive numbers of locusts and crickets plagued Yellowstone in 1935, enough to make the roads slippery for autos, but Murie noticed a benefit of the plague. He followed a bear family one day and realized they were feeding on the plentiful insects, connecting this with reports that the garbage dumps had lately been curiously empty of bears. He approvingly noted "the crickets and grasshoppers must be given due credit for attracting the bears…to desert the garbage pile to live a clean out-of-doors life where bears are bears." In a similar vein he objected to leaving salt blocks for ungulates, as that created "a wild animal with perverted habits."[26]

Adolph consistently registered opposition to development schemes, or any park activities that substituted human actions for natural processes. No less than Olaus or Aldo Leopold, he held a passion for wilderness. In 1935 the Park Service asked for his views on Isle Royale, which was under consideration for park designation. Murie's biases were clear: he opposed visitor developments, including hiking trails, preferring primeval nature; he opposed fire control, preferring natural processes; and he supported the concept of wilderness, "more marvelous (and harder to retain) than the grandiose spectacular features of our outstanding parks."[27] Elaborating further on these feelings in his journal, he wrote:

> Let us leave a few wilderness shrines for those who care not and cannot drink from a beauty which has been changed from a pool of great depth to one shallow, almost dry. Let there be a few outstanding scenes which can be viewed without the attendant chatter of the idly curious.[28]

Murie believed that wilderness in national parks was essential to their role as repositories of biota and biological processes. "Any intrusion, however slight, injects an uncertainty into the natural experiment." His travels through the parks led him to conclude that problems of too many ungulates resulted from the absence of predators and excessive regard for tourists' preference for the visual displays of elk and deer herds. Yet he also showed a sense of pragmatism that he carried throughout his life. In writing about the deer herd of Arizona's Kaibab Plateau, he fully approved of managing the deer at full carrying capacity and culling predators if the deer were threatened. In general, his thoughts on wildlife management mirrored those of Wright, Dixon, and Thompson, whom he admired.[29]

In the spring of 1937 the National Park Service directed Adolph Murie to study the coyotes in Yellowstone, an assignment indicative of the respect he had gained in his three years as a federal biologist. Wolves and cougars had been eliminated from Yellowstone years earlier, leaving the coyote as the largest predator. In 1935, on the recommendation of George Wright, Park Service Director Arno Cammerer decided to halt predator control in national parks. This policy was unpopular with many rangers and superintendents, to say nothing of the disgust of western stockmen. The clamor from voters through Congress to the halls of the Interior Department was loud and clear, but instead of capitulating, Cammerer was able to invoke another evolving park policy, that of basing decisions on scientific research rather than assumptions, traditions, or political pressures: enter Dr. Murie.

Olaus's study in Jackson Hole had already demonstrated that coyotes mostly ate rodents, with little predation on big game animals. Adolph's mission was somewhat different and more broadly conceived. He attempted to explain the ecological function of coyotes, define their role in national parks, and wend his way through the related political cross-currents. He would do this in the flagship park of the national system: as went Yellowstone, so went the rest. As he started his coyote study, Adolph had support for his views from Olaus, his fellow biologists in the Wildlife Division, and his professional peers in the American Society of Mammalogists. Skeptics included western politicians, area residents, most Biological Survey personnel, and the former superintendent of Yellowstone and the retired—but still influential—director of the Park Service, Horace Albright.[30] There were also his colleagues wearing National Park Service uniforms, including the current superintendent of Yellowstone, Edmund Rogers. Citing a purported recent increase in coyote numbers and damage to game, Rogers tried to convince Cammerer that the "policy of protection has been an error." Rogers could not understand why Adolph needed two years on this project and assumed he would "prolong his studies as long as possible because it was a soft job." Murie saw it as "an excellent problem," which somewhat belied the complexity of his task.[31] If he was to rehabilitate the reputation of the coyote, his research would have to be meticulous and his conclusions unassailable.

Adolph's coyote study established new research standards in several ways. He spent a total of fourteen months in the field collecting data, but also conducted historical research on Yellowstone's animals. National parks were supposed to capture slices of primeval America, but the protected areas had been subject to environmental changes from Native Americans and settlers. Changes also had occurred under early park management, before policies, goals, and rationales had been established. Murie went back to the early written accounts of Yellowstone to get a sense of what had once existed, in order to compare the present faunal situation. These accounts included the Lewis and Clark journals, the writings of Maximilian and Nuttall, the fur trapper Osborne Russell, and the reports of the Hayden and Doane surveys in the 1870s. Adolph concluded, on a species to species basis, that Yellowstone's wildlife in 1937 was similar to what had existed one hundred years earlier, with only one broad exception: the absence of large carnivores.[32] Moving from these accounts to park records, Murie compiled a history of predator control in the park. While poisoning campaigns dated to the 1870s, park records from 1904 to 1935 showed a total kill of 121 cougars, 132 wolves, and 4,352 coyotes. His year-round field work expanded on the ecological breadth he first had attempted with the fox study in Michigan, as he sought to describe the relations between coyotes and other animals, including such inobvious ones as ravens and magpies. He watched bison pawing through snow to get at the grasses underneath, while close by stood coyotes, waiting to pounce on any mice or voles disturbed by the bison. He gathered over 5,000 coyote droppings, taking them to Jackson where he painstakingly washed and analyzed their contents; amidst the preponderance of rodent remains were such items as leather gloves, twine, and eight inches of rope. Not content with this, Adolph paid particular attention to prey carcasses, trying to determine their fat content, ages, diseases, and likely cause of mortality, to establish which individuals within the prey species were susceptible to actual predation by coyotes, as opposed to dying from other causes and becoming carrion. He lived outdoors for days at a time, analyzing track patterns, hunting strategies, and ways in which prey animals protected their young. By the time he was finished, no one knew more about coyotes.

Adolph's conclusions were good news for the coyotes. He gathered information from the park's personnel and the public, which ranged from sighting reports to carcasses. From these, and his own observations, he constructed population histories, annual birthing rates, and mortality counts for each of the major prey species, as well as for the coyotes. When combined with the evidence on causes of mortality, the picture was plain: there were too many grazers and browsers for the park vegetation carrying capacity. The elk population was "unquestionably too large," which produced competition for food with the smaller and less numerous game species: deer, antelope, and bighorn sheep. Their populations would all increase if the elk decreased in number. Murie correlated predation by coyotes with the health of the range, since overused range resulted in starving, diseased, and weakened animals. Given this situation, he could hardly conclude that the coyotes were taking too many game animals; the entire park ecosystem would be improved if the coyotes were more effective. In addition to this reasoning, he approved of letting nature run its course as a basis for park philosophy, and finished his report by saying, "the coyote contributes to the interest and variety of [park] fauna."[33]

Adolph Murie recognized that he could educate others during the course of his work and that his research held implications beyond the scientific. Good data on wildlife were essential, but inadequate without impacts on policy that adhered to national park ideals. Of his coyote study, he wrote, "I hope to continue emphasizing problems whose solution will have a bearing on the molding of general conservation thought as well as caring for a local problem."[34] Park Service administrators also recognized the implications of such a volatile topic, and in 1938, as Murie's report began circulating within service offices, numerous people wanted to keep it internal. Yellowstone's chief of operations urged Director Cammerer to delay publishing Murie's study, since it would provoke "unfavorable comment" about the Park Service. The park's superintendent thought the report too biased and wanted to continue coyote control. Horace Albright encouraged an "open war" on the coyote. Others thought that gaining congressional approval for additional parks would suffer if it were known that predators would be sheltered within their boundaries.[35] Despite these, Cammerer maintained his ban on further coyote killing in Yellowstone and approved the publication of Murie's report.

In October 1939 Adolph wrote to family friend Otto Geist in Fairbanks: "Did I tell you the coyote report I made in Yellowstone has gone to the printers after some objections on the part of those whose philosophy it did not agree with?"[36] By this time Adolph was already deep into his next research project. Regardless of those who disagreed with his coyote conclusions, top administrators within the Park Service regarded him highly enough to assign him to investigate the service's next predator headache, the wolves of Mount McKinley National Park. The Yellowstone coyote study proved to be the perfect training exercise for the prolonged controversy over McKinley's wolves.

Arno Cammerer's protective policy toward predators lasted only a year in McKinley Park. Rangers shot wolves occasionally after protection was overturned—fourteen in 1936–38—and Superintendent Harry Liek assigned rangers specifically to springtime predator control, but this did little to satisfy Park Service critics. Administrators, lacking well-researched information on the park's wildlife, realized they had an insufficient body of data to justify their management decisions. The early wildlife surveys by George Wright and Joseph Dixon were mostly descriptive, lists of species with general comments about their status and management. Dixon chastised Park Service officials for downplaying wolf numbers, saying that outside organizations would never trust the service "unless the Park Service shows more willingness to be governed by facts." Dixon encouraged formal study on wolves, since facts would be the only defense against the "sentiment and prejudice amongst the Alaskans." Harry Liek pointed out that "neither I nor anyone can present a comprehensive picture of the wildlife situation here." But at the time, lack of funding precluded any Alaska studies, and in 1937 Yellowstone's coyotes took research priority.[37]

In one of the interesting turns of the wolf-sheep controversy, the Park Service attempted to solve its budget quandary by soliciting funds from the Camp Fire Club. In January 1939 Arno Cammerer wrote a friendly letter to the club's conservation committee chair, William Greeley, in which Cammerer outlined his scheme for a research project. Cammerer indicated that the service would supply a biologist, but a year-long study would cost $4,500. Given the club's interest and many members of "means and intelligence," Cammerer wondered if the Camp Fire Club would be willing to fund the McKinley sheep project. Greeley, who had been a forest ranger under Gifford Pinchot, and later chief forester for presidents Harding and Coolidge, responded tersely to this suggestion. He noted that "uninformed and unintelligent views of certain organizations" held too much sway in the Park Service, that wolves quite clearly presented a menace to the sheep, that wolf control should not be postponed for lack of research, and that "the raising of a fund for investigation is not within the province of this Committee."[38]

Rebuffed but still resolved, Cammerer went ahead and committed funds for a six month research project. A meeting of Park Service officials in California the following month concluded that the service needed to "solve its own wildlife problems and thus avoid pressure for control measures by other agencies." Joseph Dixon, who had made six previous Alaska trips, done prior surveys in McKinley Park, and was a distinguished professor at Berkeley, was the obvious choice for the study. Moreover, the Camp Fire Club approved Dixon's nomination. But Dixon was fifty-five years old. His doctor recommended a short trip and that he "avoid extremes of cold weather and exertion," a fair description of what McKinley Park research would entail. Dixon's credentials notwithstanding, prudence won out and attention shifted to Adolph Murie.[39]

Murie had suggested his participation in a McKinley wolf study as early as 1936, while working at Isle Royale. He recognized the widespread interest such a study would accrue, important for Park Service management as well as conservation and science. After several happy years up north as a young man, Adolph was under "the Alaska spell," according to Louise, and wanted to return following his studies in Michigan.[40] Harold Bryant attempted to get

Murie to Alaska at that time, but the need for the Yellowstone coyote study prevailed. His work there, while it had its detractors, brought him a measure of prominence, enough that in 1938 the director of the Audubon Societies, Richard Pough, recommended Murie to handle the "general hysteria about wolves" in Alaska. He got the job.[41]

In March 1939 Murie eagerly packed his field gear and proceeded on orders from Director Cammerer to Seattle, where he caught a government ferry filled with Civilian Conservation Corps workers. At Seward he boarded the train, arriving at McKinley Park on April 14. Three days later he drove a dog team to a ranger cabin on the Sanctuary River, back in the landscape where he had spent that memorable summer with Olaus sixteen years earlier. During his absence, the pregnant Louise and his daughter Gail, born in 1935, stayed with the rest of the Murie clan in Jackson Hole, where his son Jan was born in July.[42]

Adolph arrived at the park in the midst of a leadership transition. Harry Liek's tenure as superintendent came to a close in May, following reports of gambling, drinking, and a lack of discipline among park supervisory staff.[43] Administrators transferred Liek to Wind Cave National Park in South Dakota and replaced him with Sequoia National Park's naturalist, Frank Been, a graduate of the Park Service's Yosemite Field School. A thin, punctilious man, Been arrived in June 1939, and fit in poorly with the informality of the ranger staff.[44] The self-styled "Cheechako Superintendent" immediately justified his sobriquet by wrecking the park sedan attempting to cross a partially flooded bridge. Further embarrassment followed in Been's first Alaska winter, as he attempted to learn dog mushing. Out for a practice run in December, his lead dog came unhitched and sprinted ahead of the team, only to encounter a wolf in the trail. Been could not stop the sled and the rest of the dogs barreled into the fight. Unsheathing his rifle, Been shot at the wolf and hit his dog Bill instead. The wolf fled, Been fired again and missed, and finally put a mortal round into the wounded dog. Ranger Harold Herning, an old Alaska hand, tracked and killed the wolf the following day.[45]

The change in superintendents likely proved beneficial to Murie's research. While Liek had come from the traditional ranger ranks, Been came from the new "posy-sniffing" branch of park rangers, and brought with him a naturalist's appreciation for research. Adoph approvingly noted that "Been's attitude toward the problem is in accord" with his own. Been recognized that Murie's research could have value on several levels. Within the park staff, "the old school of

Superintendent Frank Been, 1940s.
Courtesy of the National Park Service, Denali National Park and Preserve

rangers has not realized or comprehended the significance of animal observations and recordings." In the broader scope, Been realized the importance of the wolf issue to Alaskans, and understood that "Territorial ramifications" existed. Conclusions destined to influence policies could not be obtained by only a few months of study. Been felt that Alaskans would not accept the study's findings unless it appeared thorough.[46]

As the snowpack melted and springtime greenery returned to the park's valleys and hillsides, Murie delighted in his task. He wrote to Park Service biologist Carl Russell, "You probably have it figured out by now that I have taken my bucket of sourdough and gone prospecting. Indeed, I am prospecting, but the colors I look for are white, and the mother lode is a tooth row, or better four tooth rows. I never before have set out to systematically find skulls of sheep...." He walked an estimated 1,700 miles that summer searching for those skulls, which would be the evidence he needed to understand the sheep population's recent history. Murie understood that his first mission was to

Ram jaw collected by Murie; note the deformity caused by disease.
Adolph Murie Collection, temp box 13. Courtesy Alaska and Polar Regions Archives,
Rasmuson Library, University of Alaska Fairbanks

"determine the need for wolf control" and that "public opinion and various current attitudes must first be considered."[47] After only several months of work, Murie concluded that no crisis existed for the Dall sheep. He wrote—unofficially—that he thought their population would rebound "regardless of any policies adopted for wolf control." Frank Been recognized the policy implications of this, writing in his monthly report that Murie "states that indications point to a favorable report to support the National Park Service policy of protecting all species of native animals."[48]

Murie originally received a seven-month assignment, but efforts to extend this began before that original period ended. The arguments for continued research recognized the basic scientific value of Murie's work, yet also derived from public opinion imperatives: the need to improve relations with the residents of Alaska, allay public apprehension over 'protected' wolves, supply facts to answer critics of service policy, and maintain professional integrity. Administrative changes in Washington, D.C., helped in getting an extension of the wolf study. In July 1939 the Biological Survey had been transferred from the Department of Agriculture to the Interior Department, alongside the Park Service, and then in December the Park Service's Wildlife Division joined the Biological Survey. Murie also gained a good friend as boss, because biologist Victor Cahalane headed the reorganized Wildlife Division. With Murie, Cahalane had studied at Michigan under Lee Dice and had served with the Park Service since 1934. Besides this shared background, the men held memberships in the Society of Mammalogists and The Wilderness Society. Cahalane became a staunch supporter of Murie's research and McKinley Park's wolves.[49] The director of the Park Service, Arno Cammerer, and the chief of the Biological Survey, Ira Gabrielson, had earlier agreed on principles of park wildlife management. These affirmed that "every species shall be left to carry on its struggle for existence unaided," including predators, which would not be killed unless a prey species was threatened with extermination. Frank Been worked hard to convince his superiors to find money for further study by Murie, helped by the joint management principles which stated that investigation would precede any "interference with biotic relationships." Determining whether McKinley's Dall sheep faced extirpation formed the crux of Murie's study, for their status would form the basis of a wolf policy. The Park Service had already placed itself in a vulnerable position by becoming an advocate for predators. Murie's early sense of the wildlife situation gave ample reason for the service to continue his study, as it justified this organizational stance. He wrote to Victor Cahalane, "All the data I have gives strong support to the National Park predatory policies and to the position taken by most biologists. But the report could be worded more strongly if it were based on two years work for the data would of course be more convincing."[50]

Adolph left Alaska in the autumn of 1939, uncertain whether he would return. He arrived in Jackson to find sorrow at the funeral of his mother and joy in meeting his new son. He spent some weeks there organizing field notes before traveling to Washington, D.C., to confer with Park Service officials, who were calling his study "one of the biggest and most critical wildlife jobs ever undertaken by the National Park Service."[51]

While there, Murie received an invitation to present his Alaska findings to the Conservation Committee of the Camp Fire Club. Horace Albright hosted him in New York on April 1, as they met for drinks at the Chemists'

Jan, Louise, and Gail Murie, park headquarters, 1940.
Adolph Murie Collection, temp box 13. Courtesy Alaska and Polar Regions Archives, Rasmuson Library, University of Alaska Fairbanks

Club prior to dinner at the Dartmouth Club—a far cry from Murie's preferred haunts. A friendly spirit prevailed between the two men in their first face-to-face meeting, with Murie emphatic that early Park Service officials need not apologize for good-intentioned policies toward wildlife, and Albright admitting that he had been wrong about Yellowstone's coyotes. Albright introduced Murie to the Camp Fire Club members that evening. Adolph showed pictures and discussed the status of McKinley Park's fauna. The club received him civilly, but he swayed no one in their attitudes toward wolves. He stated that "the wolf controversy is in the nature of a religion with many and therefore can not be won by logic or fact." Albright commended Murie on his "magnificent showing," but the club showed no signs of easing its criticism of the Park Service.[52]

It is likely Murie's study would have continued even if the Camp Fire Club had declared a cease-fire, but perhaps their recalcitrance forced the Park Service's hand. Upon his return to Washington, D.C., Adolph learned that he would be returning to Alaska on a steamer departing Seattle on April 20. Two weeks later Frank Been wrote, "The pleasantest event of the month was the return of Field Biologist Adolph Murie." This time Adolph brought his family, and they spent the next fifteen months in the park.[53]

In many ways the situation in McKinley Park was similar to what Adolph had encountered in Yellowstone: poorly understood faunal interactions needing basic research; perceptions of excessive predation on charismatic game species that were vital to the park's identity; differing opinions on wildlife management within the Park Service between the field staff and distant administrators; and the park's setting in a locale where residents firmly opposed predator protection, yet where trappers patrolled the edges of the park looking to kill predators for bounties. The major differences were that McKinley Park's populations of moose, caribou, and sheep were not excessive and no range degradation was apparent. There was no nearby livestock industry, and coyotes and wolves held different ecological niches. This was a biologist's dream. Adolph had the background, ability, funding, and support to pursue a research problem that lacked precedent and would have national significance. He systematically applied the research strategies he had refined in Yellowstone to this new, but familiar, set of problems. He addressed three major areas: historical records, basic quantifiable data on predator and prey, and wolf behavior.

The few historical records that existed on these animals did not extend very far back. Murie compiled the scattered written evidence to try to sketch known (or suspected) patterns of animal populations over time, including carrying Charles Sheldon's book into the field to compare observations made thirty-two years earlier with his own. He supplemented these by interviewing long-time area residents, especially trappers and hunters. Murie could practically claim his own sourdough status from his months in Alaska in 1922–23, which turned out to add valuable information to his study, more for the absence of wolves than their presence. He speculated that dogs imported during the gold rush years 1897–1905 had spread canine distemper into Alaska's wolf population; the increase in wolf numbers since 1926 was thus a rebound from an artificial low. He postulated an opposite effect for the park's sheep. Estimates of their population in the late 1920s ranged from 10,000 to 25,000, an unsustainable population reduced to more normal levels by the hard winter of 1931–32.[54]

Written records helped form an initial history of the wolves and sheep, but history could also be deduced from the evidence available in such things as the sheep skulls Murie had begun collecting the previous summer. Previous counts of the sheep population were highly subjective; no one had systematically tried to get an accurate count classified by age cohort, and Murie's work represented an important contribution. He eventually collected a total of 829 skulls. From the horns and dentition came clues about the sheep's age, sex, and health at death, which helped answer questions on their diseases and vulnerability to predation. Scat collection and analysis to determine foods eaten was a constant chore, involving untangling droppings with tweezers to identify seeds, plant fibers, hair, and bones. He classified the percentages of various plants comprising the diet of sheep, since understanding the feeding habits would help interpret how winter weather conditions could influence the availability of forage, and thus the sheep's movement patterns. What wolves ate, in many ways, was Murie's central research question. The Park Service had several years of stomach content data from wolves killed in the park, but this information was scant and unsystematic. Wolf droppings provided evidence for the percentage and ages of sheep eaten by wolves.

Murie enlisted park rangers to help collect whatever bones and kills they came across, but most of his information came from solitary efforts using the basic tools of a field biologist in the pre-electronic era. He continued his long hikes, locating fox and bear dens, identifying the hillsides used by herds of Dall sheep ewes and lambs and those used by rams, becoming adept at finding the places where sheep died or had been killed. He sat on hilltops in all weather scanning with field glasses for countless hours, notebook and pencil at hand to record his observations. A personal toughness and, perhaps, a Nordic stoicism went far. Despite the hours spent under relentless attack by Alaska's legendary tundra mosquitoes while recording hundreds of pages of field notes, Adolph made only one comment about the mosquitoes being "mildly bothersome."[55] Nothing lacked significance as he tried to understand the trajectories of relations within and between species and surpass the descriptive research that his predecessors had undertaken. He watched magpies following wolves, waiting for them to make a kill. He followed a flock of foraging snow buntings and realized they fed on the same plant favored by sheep in the winter months. He speculated on the trees killed by porcupines, the porcupines killed by wolves, and the wolves killed by porcupines. Migration patterns of caribou, survival rates of calves and lambs, the lives and deaths of other fauna, the influence of the park road in altering animal habits or making hunting by wolves easier, the competition for carrion between wolves and bears—all of Murie's research was original, meticulous, and done the hard way.

He was working before the introduction of radio telemetry, but he did convince the Park Service to provide him with a film camera. Capturing the lives of wild animals on film was not just a hobby for Adolph, but represented another way to educate the public. He recognized that film could do more than educate. While in Yellowstone, he had suggested to Vic Cahalane that if he had made a film, he would have been able to make his critics "hug the coyote."[56] He had the chance in McKinley Park, and his films became common evening fare for visitors at the park hotel.

One of the most significant contributions of Murie's research was on wolf behavior. No scientist had previously enjoyed the opportunity to observe wolves in a similar fashion. There were not any wolves left in other states, except in the forests of the upper Great Lakes area. In the tundra Murie could enjoy sight lines extending for miles, watching the comings and goings of an entire pack; once he sat for thirty-three straight hours watching a wolf family. Many questions needed answers that scat could not provide: How did the wolves hunt, especially for sheep? What determined pack structures? How many wolves were there? How did they raise their young? He paid special attention to the family life of the wolves, learning to recognize individuals, and many of their stories recorded in his field journal ended up in the final report. His writing lent a personable air to the legendary beast. This, for example: "Just as a laboring husband comes home to the family each evening after working all day, so do the wolves come home each morning after working all night." As a much later wolf researcher put it, Murie's behavioral observations "broke the spell of Little Red Riding Hood."[57]

Adolph himself was a laboring husband and father that summer, with the family living in a cabin on the East Fork River deep in the park. Louise maintained the logistics, ordering monthly food shipments from Anchorage, cooking and baking bread on the wood stove, and tending the two children. Nine-month old Jan needed diapers. According to Louise, Adolph said he carried "water to wash enough diapers to string around the boundaries of McKinley Park." Five-year old Gail had a summer of endless adventure. Louise

Adolph and Gail looking for photo opportunities, 1940.
Adolph Murie Collection, temp box 13 . Courtesy Alaska and Polar Regions Archives, Rasmuson Library, University of Alaska Fairbanks

had kept Gail on a harness during an earlier summer spent with Adolph in Yellowstone, to prevent her wandering off, but in 1940 she was not so restrained. Gail tended Jan, helped her mother with cabin chores and went with her on plant-collecting hikes. In her limited spare time, Louise assembled a thorough collection of the park's flora. Adolph was often gone for days, but Louise was tough and competent. One time a curious grizzly bear poked his nose in the doorway. Telling Gail to stay inside, Louise grabbed the stove poker and vigorously chased the bear away. This incident, along with the presence of wolves in the cabin's vicinity, caused Adolph to write, "when Gail plays outside she must be alert and ready to flee." Adolph often took his daughter with him during evening drives along the park road, eyes scanning the tundra for animal activity under the slanting light of the subarctic summer sun. Newborn caribou were particularly interesting for her, and she watched caribou births and their first faltering steps to their mothers.[58]

In May 1940 Adolph brought home a surprise nestled in his backpack: a week-old wolf puppy, its eyes not yet open. He had found a den site along the East Fork and determined that the female had given birth. Realizing another kind of research possibility, he decided to investigate at close range. Upon his approach the adult wolves only ran off a few hundred yards, watching and howling, while Adolph crawled through the 18- by 21-inch bankside opening. A ten-foot-long tunnel led him to a chamber containing the pups. Using a hooked stick, Murie extracted three of them and kept a female— length $14\,^5/_8$ inches, tail $3\,^5/_8$ inches, ear 1 inch, shoulder height 5 inches. Christened Wags, the wolf pup gained weight quickly on evaporated milk and became a rambunctious play partner for Gail. The Murie family became Wags' pack, and the puppy grew up as tame as the typical Alaska sled dog—not a trick-performing house pet, but a strong dog with a full complement of instincts. When summer ended, the family moved into a cabin at the park headquarters while Adolph continued his research through the winter. At the staff Christmas party, "Santa Claus believers were Dr. Murie's two youngsters."[59]

As he headed into the investigation's final season, determining the need for wolf control rationalized Murie's study, especially regarding sheep. He examined other hazards to sheep—coyotes, lynx, bears, wolverines, and golden eagles—and dismissed them as significant predators. This left the wolf, and Murie analyzed wolf-killed sheep for shared factors which may have increased their availability to the wolves. He also sought other causes of sheep mortality. He concluded that

Gail and Wags, the wolf pup, 1940.
Adolph Murie Collection, temp box 13. Courtesy Alaska and Polar Regions Archives, Rasmuson Library, University of Alaska Fairbanks

environmental conditions such as snowpack and disease caused susceptible sheep to weaken and die. Evidence from sheep skulls showed that wolves preyed primarily on the old, the young, and the sick. This led to the overall conclusion that wolf predation likely provided a benefit to the species by exerting a positive selective effect. Furthermore, Murie regarded the high sheep population of the 1920s as aberrational, and felt that during the 1930s an equilibrium existed between the two species—the balance of nature. This meant that despite ups and downs in the sheep population, they would not be in danger of extirpation by wolves. As a scientist, though, Murie also stated what Park Service critics wanted to hear: "wolves are the chief factor limiting the sheep population."[60] Political pressures had brought him to Alaska. He did not have the luxury of a research project motivated only by curiosity about wolves, but had to answer the Park Service's need to justify a management plan that would satisfy service critics and coincide with service philosophy. He remained convinced that hands-off management was preferable, writing in an unpublished manuscript, "The less control or interference in a given park the more successful we feel that park has been." Murie finished his McKinley work in August 1941, convinced he had accumulated enough data "for solving immediate administrative problems," while leaving those decisions to others. Little did he know the wolf-sheep controversy was by no means over.[61]

While Murie roamed the hills of McKinley Park, watching and recording, efforts continued to improve the Park Service's public image. "Each time the Superintendent leaves the park," wrote Frank Been to his boss, "he runs into criticism of the predator policy at McKinley." Been continued efforts to influence local attitudes positively toward their national park asset, and his superiors regarded local relations "effectively improved" by Been.[62] Been started assigning rangers to accompany park bus tours and provide nightly flora and fauna lectures in the park hotel. Appearances before chambers of commerce and civic organizations became part of Been's annual cycle of activities, and Mrs. Been contributed by speaking at women's groups and schools. These public wildlife lectures included pictures of wolves, providing an opportunity to explain park philosophy concerning predators and curb the prevalent erroneous information about the park. Been also used radio as another publicity tool, and he arranged for two broadcasts directly from the park by Fairbanks station KFAR. In all of these activities, Been encouraged Alaskans to visit their park and adopt it as their own. In addition to lectures, films, and slide shows, Been took less visible public relations steps. While visiting Anchorage, Been saw 'Alaskan wildlife' postcards for sale in Hewitt's Photo Shop, which showed chained bears and caged Dall sheep. He invited Mr. Hewitt to lunch and explained the Park Service role in providing tourists with access to real wildlife. A twenty-three year resident of Alaska, Hewitt had never visited the park. He later received a personal tour by Been and agreed to delete the postcards from his photo shop.[63]

Been also attended the 1940 annual meeting of the Alaska Game Commission, a meeting he regarded as worth "years of experience." This gave Been a chance to combat the "almost complete lack of appreciation for Park Service purposes." Been's presentation on park wildlife policies was well received by the group: one commissioner, a forty-year resident, commented that he had "just found out what the National Park Service is." While the commissioners did not change their attitudes toward predators, Been felt the contact had been important for diminishing direct criticism of park policies by this influential group. In this and other meetings with the public, Been made a point to inform people that park rangers shot wolves when possible, in hopes that this knowledge would modify the "critical attitude toward these predators being completely protected."[64] For the game commission, Been submitted summary information for the previous decade on wolves killed in the park, not only to demonstrate that wolves had not enjoyed complete protection, but also for a visual statement. In its annual report, the game commission published a map of Alaska indicating the location of wolves taken for bounty the previous year. Been offered the park wolf kill data so that "the map of wolves killed will not show the park as a blank. Unfavorable comment may thereby be reduced." The next map published by the game commission showed six wolves taken for bounty within the park.[65]

Adolph Murie, too, contributed to the public relations campaign while he conducted his research. Rangers and other park staff accompanied Murie in his forays through the park, whether on foot or out for an evening drive, and Been commented favorably that Murie was "stimulating and beneficial to park personnel who have gained an improved sense of responsibility for the animals." Rangers readily blamed game kills on wolves, and Murie took these opportunities to broaden their understanding of ecological complexity. Murie also had opportunities for contact with area trappers and miners, and recorded in his diary numerous instances of discussing wolf attitudes and practices with them. He did this with an air of understatement and obliqueness, listening to others respectfully and offering his beliefs as alternatives; years before, he had recorded in his diary thoughts on the efficacy of "more indirect methods" rather than "crusading" on wildlife issues.[66] Prominent visitors during these years often traveled the park road accompanied at their request by Murie, who explained his research and park policies. In Fairbanks, he attended a meeting of the Tanana Valley Sportsman's Association and made a presentation on wolves and game. Victor Cahalane recognized Murie's value to the Park Service, writing to a colleague, "I wish that we had three or four Muries...."[67]

While these efforts improved local public relations, readers of *Field and Stream* in September 1941 found an article that raked the Park Service on its wolf policy. Author Russell Annabel lived in Alaska, making his living guiding and writing for sporting publications. In "Wolves Look Better Dead" Annabel wondered, "why there has never been a campaign to exterminate the wolves in Mt. McKinley National Park." He scoffed at the need to study the park's ecology and blamed officials in Washington, D.C., for holding the park staff in check, citing a "conscientious" unnamed ranger who criticized the "fantastic government policy" that prevented a war on wolves. The article provoked fears among Park Service personnel that *Field and Stream* editor Ray Holland (who had been in attendance at Murie's presentation to the Camp Fire Club in April 1940) was ending his silence on the issue; in fact, Holland retired that year. They wondered who was encouraging polemicists like Annabel, especially after Frank Been received a letter from the author indicating that "the paragraphs dealing with the park were written on assignment." Murie dismissed the article, attributing it to "a man with a facile pen, filled with a bitter hatred," yet called it "hard to combat." Frank Been invited Annabel to revisit the park and he informed the Park Service director that Annabel "has been described by those who know him as 'a blow-hard.'"[68]

One of those who knew Annabel was Lee Swisher, a trapper and occasional park employee, who derided the article in a letter of support to Been. Swisher concluded his letter by saying, "Well, from the way it looks now we will have all we can do to take care of our little yellow brothers across the sea."[69] It was December 8, 1941. The national imagination and effort would be devoted to a far more significant issue than McKinley's wolves. Alaska entered the modern era in an avalanche of defense spending, and McKinley Park became a playground for soldiers. Adolph Murie's research gathered shelf dust, unavailable and unneeded.

Notes

1   A useful work emphasizing Forbes' contributions is Joel B. Hagen, *An Entangled Bank: The Origins of Ecosystem Ecology* (New Brunswick, NJ: Rutgers University Press, 1992). An interesting intellectual history of the tensions between mathematical modelers and field ecologists is Sharon E. Kingsland, *Modeling Nature: Episodes in the History of Population Ecology* (Chicago: University of Chicago Press, 1985). See too Charles Elton, *Animal Ecology* (London: Sidgwick & Jackson, 1927; London: Methuen, 1966), and *Animal Ecology and Evolution* (Oxford: Clarendon Press, 1930).

2   Harold Bryant, "Predators Necessary to Wild Life," *Bird-Lore*, November–December 1936, 448–50; also in the same issue see Leonard Wing, "Predation is Not What it Seems," 401–5.

3   Paul Errington, "Feathered Vs. Human Predators," *Bird-Lore*, March–April 1935, 122. Errington's thoughtful writings for the general public are well worth the reader's time; see *Of Predation and Life* (Ames, IA: Iowa State University Press, 1967), and a collection of shorter essays, many published posthumously, *A Question of Values*, ed. Carolyn Errington (Ames, IA: Iowa State University Press, 1987).

4   A comprehensive biography is Curt Meine, *Aldo Leopold: His Life and Work* (Madison: University of Wisconsin Press, 1988). A more tightly-focused work is Susan Flader, *Thinking Like a Mountain: Aldo Leopold and the Evolution of an Ecological Attitude Toward Deer, Wolves, and Forests* (Lincoln: University of Nebraska Press, 1974). Leopold's best known work is the posthumously published *A Sand County Almanac* (New York: Oxford Univ. Press, 1949; reprint New York: Ballantine Books, 1966).

5   Aldo Leopold, "Thinking Like a Mountain," in *A Sand County Almanac*, 138.

6   Aldo Leopold, *Game Management* (New York: Charles Scribner's Sons, 1933), 246, 212, 230. For Errington's influence on Leopold, see Meine, *Aldo Leopold*, 274–76, 287–88.

7   Aldo Leopold, "The Wilderness and its Place in Forest Recreational Policy," *Journal of Forestry* 19 (November 1921): 720.

8   Aldo Leopold, "Naturshutz in Germany," *Bird-Lore*, March–April 1936, 102; see Meine, *Aldo Leopold*, 358–60, and Flader, *Thinking Like a Mountain*, 139–44 for further details on this trip. Roderick Nash discusses the context from which The Wilderness Society arose in *Wilderness and the American Mind*, 2nd. ed. (New Haven: Yale University Press, 1973), 207–8.

9   Aldo Leopold, "Song of the Gavilan," in *A Sand County Almanac*, 159.

10   Both articles are reprinted in *The Collected Works of Sigurd F. Olson: The Early Writings: 1921–1934*, ed. Mike Link (Stillwater, MN: Voyageur Press, 1988), 121–33, 171–86.

11   *The Collected Works of Sigurd F. Olson: The College Years: 1935–1944*, ed. Mike Link (Stillwater, MN: Voyageur Press, 1990), 21–24, 82–103; Bryant to Olson, 3 June 1938, RG 79, Entry 7, File 719, Box 1415, NA. Olson became the most important

wilderness advocate in the Great Lakes region; his son, Sigurd Jr., became a game biologist for the U.S. Fish and Wildlife Service in Alaska in the 1950s.

12   See Olaus J. Murie, *Journeys to the Far North* (Palo Alto: American West Publishing, 1973) and Margaret E. Murie, *Two in the Far North* (New York: Alfred A. Knopf, 1957). A fine biography is Gregory D. Kendrick, "An Environmental Spokesman: Olaus J. Murie and a Democratic Defense of Wilderness," *Annals of Wyoming* 50 (Fall 1978): 213–302.

13   See Olaus J. Murie, *Food Habits of the Coyote in Jackson Hole, Wyoming* (Washington, D.C.: GPO, Dept. of Agriculture Circular No. 362, 1935), and his personal magnum opus, *The Elk of North America* (Harrisburg, PA: Stackpole Company, 1951).

14   O. Murie to Geist, 18 March 1935; 17 September 1936, Geist Collection, Box 16, UAF. The reference to the starving Eskimo pertains to the common newspaper allegations that wolves were to blame for the demise of the reindeer herds and hence a food supply.

      A fascinating fellow, Geist met Olaus and Margaret in 1924 in Alaska while working as a riverboat engineer. Although without advanced academic training, Geist devoted his life to the archaeology and paleontology of Alaska; his collections formed the nucleus of the University of Alaska museum. See Charles J. Keim, *Aghvook, White Eskimo: Otto Geist and Alaska Archaeology* (Fairbanks: University of Alaska Press, 1969).

15   Adolph Murie, *A Naturalist in Alaska* (New York: Devin Adair Company, 1961), 4.

16   Biographic information on Dice from an extended obituary by Francis C. Evans, "Lee Raymond Dice (1887–1977)," *Journal of Mammalogy* 59 (August 1978): 635–44. His Alaskan experience is summarized in a manuscript, "Interior Alaska in 1911 and 1912: Observations by a Naturalist," copy in Dice Collection, UAF. At the time Shelford was working on a pioneering effort in ecology, attempting to integrate the functions of all the species in a discrete area, which he published as *Animal Communities in Temperate America, as Illustrated in the Chicago Area: A Study in Animal Ecology* (Chicago: University of Chicago Press, 1913).

17   Lee R. Dice, "The Scientific Value of Predatory Mammals," *Journal of Mammalogy* 6 (February 1925): 25–27.

18   See Steven G. Herman, *The Naturalist's Field Journal: A Manual of Instruction Based on a System Established by Joseph Grinnell* (Vermilion, SD: Buteo Books, 1986).

19   Adolph Murie, *The Moose of Isle Royale*, University of Michigan Museum of Zoology, Miscellaneous Publications No. 25 (Ann Arbor: University of Michigan Press, 1934), 24, 42, 43. While biologists and politicians quibbled over management of Isle Royale, Mother Nature solved the problem, as in the 1940s a wolf pack migrated on winter's ice to the island. Its offspring became the most-studied wolves on the continent, and wolves and moose continue to live together on the island; see L. David Mech, *The Wolves of Isle Royale*, Fauna Series No. 7 (Washington, D. C.: GPO, National Park Service, 1966), and Durward L. Allen, *Wolves of Minong: Their Vital Role in a Wild Community* (Boston: Houghton Mifflin Co., 1979). For the rest of the Isle Royale

story, along with an update on worrisome trends in the wolf population, see Rolf O. Peterson, *The Wolves of Isle Royale: A Broken Balance* (Minocqua, WI: Willow Creek Press, 1995).

20 Adolph Murie, *Mammals From Guatemala and British Honduras*, University of Michigan Museum of Zoology Miscellaneous Publications No. 26 (Ann Arbor: University of Michigan Press, 1935); Louise Murie MacLeod interview.

21 Margaret Murie and Olaus J. Murie, *Wapiti Wilderness* (New York: Alfred A. Knopf, 1966), 104–5, 52, 42. While *Two in the Far North* deals with the couple's involvement with Alaska in both their youth and old age, this book lovingly details the years in between spent in Jackson Hole. Also, Olaus J. Murie and Adolph Murie, "Travels of *Peromyscus*," *Journal of Mammalogy* 12 (August 1931): 200–9; "Further Notes on Travels of *Peromyscus*," *Journal of Mammalogy* 13 (February 1932): 78–79; Louise Murie MacLeod interview.

22 Adolph Murie, *Following Fox Trails*, University of Michigan Museum of Zoology Miscellaneous Publications No. 32 (Ann Arbor: University of Michigan Press, 1936); Louise Murie MacLeod interview.

23 George Wright to staff, 27 June 1935, A. Murie Collection, Box 4, Folder "Subject File 1934–1938 ECW assignments," AHC.

24 Ben Thompson to H. C. Bryant, 19 July 1934, A. Murie Collection, Box 4, Folder "Subject File 1934–1938," AHC; Thompson to A. Murie, 1 August 1934, A. Murie Collection, Box 1, Folder "Correspondence 1934–1966, letter re: job transfers," AHC; A. Murie itineraries, Sept.–Nov. 1934, A. Murie Collection, Box 1, Folder "Reports 1934–1936; wildlife reports," AHC; A. Murie diary, 27 January 1936, A. Murie Collection, Box 11, Folder "Olympic Notes 1936," UAF.

25 A. Murie journal, 16 July, 20 August 1935, A. Murie Collection, Box "Field notes on a variety of species," Folder "Field notes—general 7/6/359/17/35," UAF; "Report on Activities . . . August 15 to September 14, 1935," A. Murie Collection, Box 1, Folder "Reports, 1934–1936; Wildlife Reports," AHC.

26 Adolph Murie, "Some Food Habits of the Black Bear," *Journal of Mammalogy* 18 (May 1937): 240; he originally titled this "The Black Bear as an Entomologist," manuscript in A. Murie Collection, Box 14, UAF. A. Murie to Ben Thompson, n. d., but about 1935, A. Murie Collection, Box 4, Folder "Correspondence 1935–1963; memo-salting Yellowstone," AHC.

27 Quoted in John Little, "Adolph Murie and the Wilderness Ideal for Isle Royale National Park," in *The American West: Essays in Honor of W. Eugene Hollon*, ed. Ronald Lora (Toledo, OH: University of Toledo, 1980), 100, 102.

28 A. Murie journal, n. d., A. Murie Collection, Box "Field Notes on a Variety of Species," Folder "Field Notes - General, 10/8/36–7/12/38," UAF.

29 A. Murie to Editor of the *Journal of Forestry*, 18 May 1936, A. Murie Collection, Box 2, Folder "Correspondence 1936–1967," AHC; A. Murie journal, undated, but between

1934 and 1938; A. Murie Collection, Box "Field Notes on a Variety of Species," Folder "Notes on a Management Plan for Grand Canyon National Park," UAF; A. Murie interview by Evison, 7.

30   Writing to Cammerer, Albright stated, "the coyotes are of no possible advantage," and "I find that the impression is quite wide spread that the National Association of Audubon Societies and perhaps other organizations are more interested today in saving the predatory species of birds and mammals than giving reasonable consideration to the species that are regarded as very important by the general public. I hope this is not true of the National Park Service." Albright to director, 18 October 1937, 24 November 1937, A. Murie Collection, Box 4, Folder "Correspondence 1937–1942; Yellowstone Coyote, 1937–1938," AHC.

31   Rogers to Cammerer, 19 February 1937, A. Murie Collection, Box 4, Folder "Correspondence 1937–1942; Yellowstone coyote, 1937–1938," AHC; Rogers quoted in Alston Chase, *Playing God in Yellowstone: The Destruction of America's First National Park* (New York: Harcourt Brace Jovanovich, 1987), 127; A. Murie interview by Evison, 13.

32   His notes on this research are in A. Murie Collection, Box 11, Folder "Historical Notes on Western U. S.," UAF, and summarized in first chapter of Adolph Murie, *Ecology of the Coyote in the Yellowstone*; Fauna Series No. 4 (Washington, D. C.: GPO, National Park Service, 1940), which is the source for the rest of this paragraph.

33   A. Murie, *Ecology of the Coyote*, 57, 86, 102, 115, 148.

34   Memorandum, A. Murie to Cahalane, 15 March 1938, A. Murie Collection, Box 2, Folder "Correspondence 1935–1942," AHC.

35   Albright to Cammerer, 18 October 1937, A. Murie Collection, Box 4, Folder "Correspondence 1937–1942; Yellowstone Coyote, 1937–1938," AHC; Chase, *Playing God in Yellowstone*, 127; Sellars, *Preserving Nature*, 122. R. Gerald Wright notes the influence on the park service's organizational structure of it being modeled on the military; *Wildlife Research and Management in the National Parks* (Urbana: University of Illinois Press, 1992), 5, 11. This likely served to dissuade dissension, and would frustrate Murie through his career.

36   A. Murie to Geist, 16 October 1939, Geist Collection, Box 15, UAF.

37   Superintendent's "Monthly Report," July 1938, DENA; Dixon to director, 10 June 1938; Dixon to Bryant, 28 June 1938; Dixon to director, 16 December 1938; all File 5986, Box 2, DENA; Liek to director, 24 June 1938, RG 79, Entry 7, File 719, Box 1415, NA.

38   Cammerer to Greeley, 31 January 1939; Greeley to Cammerer, 8 February 1939, RG 79, Entry 7, File 715, Box 1414, NA.

39   Dixon to Carl Russell, 24 February 1939, RG 79, Entry 7, File 719, Box 1415, NA.

40   A. Murie to Cahalane, NPS Wildlife Division, 17 August 1936, RG 79, Entry 7, File 719, Box 1415, NA; Louise Murie to Otto Geist, 29 September 1936, Geist Collection, UAF.

41   Pough to Cahalane, 11 March 1938; Bryant to Pough, 21 March 1938; Carl Russell to Cammerer, 7 March 1939; RG 79, Entry 7, File 719, Box 1415, NA; Cahalane to A. Murie, 17 January 1939, A. Murie Collection, Box 5, Folder "McKinley Predator Policies, 1936–1957," AHC.

42   Cammerer to A. Murie, 8 March 1939, RG 79, Entry 7, File 719, Box 1415, NA; Adolph Murie, *The Wolves of Mount McKinley*; Fauna Series No. 5 (Washington, D. C.: GPO, National Park Service, 1944); reprint, Seattle: University of Washington Press, 1985), 1 (page numbers are to reprint edition).

43   Grant Ross to Frank Kittredge, NPS regional director, 4 August 1938; Kittredge to Demaray, 6 August 1938; RG 79, Entry 7, File 207, Box 1405, NA.

44   Grant Pearson, *My Life of High Adventure* (Englewood Cliffs, NJ: Prentice-Hall, 1962), 186–89. Pearson started as a ranger under Harry Karstens and replaced Frank Been as superintendent in 1949. Pearson had a popularity among the men never attained by Been.

45   Superintendent's "Monthly Reports," June, November, December 1939, RG 79, Entry 7, Box 1406, NA; Been to Board of Survey, 8 December 1939, RG 79 Entry 7, File 715, Box 1414, NA.

46   A. Murie to Cahalane, 29 July 1939, A. Murie Collection, Box 5, Folder "McKinley Predator Policies, 1936–1957," AHC; Superintendent's "Monthly Reports," October, December 1939, RG 79, Entry 7, Box 1406, NA.

47   "Annual Report" by A. Murie to Gabrielson, 3 July 1940; "Quarterly Report" by Murie to Cahalane, 6 October 1940, reprints from the Denver Technical Center, National Park Service (hereafter DTC).

48   A. Murie to Russell, 1 June 1939, A. Murie Collection, Box 1, Folder "Correspondence 1933–1974, Adolph, personal-misc.," AHC; A. Murie to Cahalane, 29 July 1939, A. Murie Collection, Box 5, Folder "McKinley Predator Policies, 1936–1957," AHC; Superintendent's "Monthly Report," June 1939, RG 79, Entry 7, Box 1406, NA.

49   Biographical information on Cahalane from Jaques Cattell Press, ed., *American Men and Women of Science*, 12th ed. (New York: R.R. Bowker Co., 1971), 841.

50   Cammerer and Gabrielson to Ickes, 24 November 1939 RG 101, Box 470, ASA. Gabrielson and Cahalane would both visit the park in the summer of 1940. Been to director, 10 January 1940, Entry 7, Box 1406, NA. Superintendent's "Monthly Report," April 1940, Entry 7, Box 1406, NA; A. Murie to Cahalane, 23 December 1939, A. Murie Collection, Box 5, Folder "McKinley Predator Policies, 1936–1957," AHC.

51   Louise MacLeod interview; Carl Russell to Newton Drury, 27 March 1940, RG 79, Entry 7, File 719, Box 1415, NA.

52   A. Murie to Albright, 22 March 1940, Box 2, Folder "Correspondence 1936–1967"; Albright to A. Murie, 27 March 1940, Box 1, Folder "Correspondence 1935–1974; letters re; publications and honors"; A. Murie, personal notes, "Camp Fire Club Meeting, April 1, 1940," Box 2, Folder "Correspondence 1936–1967"; Albright to A. Murie, 2 April 1940, Box 1, Folder "Correspondence 1937–1970, misc. letters"; A.

Murie to Albright, 5 April 1940, Box 2, Folder "Correspondence 1936–1967"; all A. Murie Collection, AHC.

53 A. Murie to Albright, 5 April 1940, A. Murie Collection, Box 2, Folder "Correspondence 1936–1967," AHC; Superintendent's "Monthly Report," April 1940, Box 1406, NA.

54 A. Murie, *Wolves of Mount McKinley*, 14–15, 67. The historical compilations have proven their worth to many subsequent researchers of the larger species of McKinley Park's wildlife; notes for this research in Box "Field Notes on Wolves," A. Murie Collection, UAF. There has been no evidence in support of his distemper theory, despite its theoretical plausibility.

55 A. Murie diary, 16 June 1941, A. Murie Collection, UAF.

56 A. Murie to Cahalane, 29 March 1938, A. Murie Collection, Box 3, Folder "Correspondence 1938–1954, Cahalane," AHC.

57 A. Murie, *Wolves of Mt. McKinley*, 29; Erich Klinghammer, "Introduction," in *The Behavior and Ecology of Wolves: Proceedings of the Symposium on the Behavior and Ecology of Wolves Held in Wilmington, N. C., 23–24 May 1975*, ed. Erich Klinghammer (New York: Garland STPM Press, 1979).

58 There is a photograph of Gail with a caribou calf in Murie, *A Naturalist in Alaska*, 84–85; Louise Murie MacLeod interview; A. Murie to Geist, 2 July 1940, Geist Collection, Box 15, UAF. Louise's research notes are in A. Murie Collection, Box "Research Notes - Botanical," UAF.

59 A. Murie field journal, 15 May 1940, A. Murie Collection, Box 13, Folder "Wolf, April 28, 1940, to August 3, 1941," UAF; A. Murie, *Wolves of Mount McKinley*, 45–50; Superintendent's "Monthly Report," December 1940, DENA.

60 A. Murie, *Wolves of Mount McKinley*, 141–42, 230–31.

61 A. Murie, "Wildlife in McKinley National Park," no date, between 1940–42, A. Murie Collection, Box 7, Folder "Wildlife in McKinley National Park," UAF; "Annual Report" by A. Murie to Gabrielson, 1941; "Quarterly Report," September 1941, reprints from DTC.

Been to director, 10 January 1940; Charles Russell to director, 27 March 1940; RG 79, Entry 7, File 719, Box 1415, NA.

63 See Superintendent's "Monthly Reports" in 1940–41 for specifics of public appearances; *Jessen's Weekly* [Fairbanks], "McKinley Park Is For Alaskans, Says Superintendent Been," 20 February 1942; "McKinley Park A New World," 3 April 1942; Been to director, 5 March 1940, RG 79, Entry 7, File 715, Box 1414, NA.

64 Superintendent's "Annual Report," 1940; Been to director, 29 February 1940, RG 79, Entry 7, Box 1405, 1406, NA; Director to Been, 4 April 1940, RG 79, Entry 7, File 715, Box 1414, NA; Been to director, 13 February 1940, RG 79, Entry 7, File 719, Box 1415, NA.

65   Been to Dufresne, 13 March 1940; Been to director, 6 March 1940, RG 79, Entry 7, File 719, Box 1415, NA; Department of the Interior, *Annual Report of the Alaska Game Commission*, 1940, RG 101, Box 470, ASA.

66   Superintendent's "Annual Report," 1940, 1941, RG 79, Entry 7, Box 1405, NA; "Diary and Field Notes, 1939"; "Personal Diary 1940–41"; "Olympic Notes," 27 January 1936, A. Murie Collection, Box 11, UAF.

67   A. Murie, "Field Notes on Wolves," 7 February 1941, A. Murie Collection, UAF; Murie to Geist, 2 April 1940, Geist Collection, Box 15 UAF; Cahalane to Daniel Beard, 2 May 1941, A. Murie Collection, Box 1, Folder "Correspondence 1935–1951; letters from Cahalane and Drury," AHC.

68   Russell Annabel, "Wolves Look Better Dead," *Field and Stream* , September 1941, 70, 36; Cahalane to Drury, 15 October 1941; Annabel to Been, 20 September 1941; A. Murie to Cahalane, 17 November 1941, A. Murie Collection, Box 5, Folder "Correspondence 1938–1954, Cahalane," AHC; Been to director, 17 September 1941, RG 79, Entry 7, Box 1414, File 715, NA.

69   Swisher to Been, 8 December 1941, RG 79, Entry 7 Box 1407, File 208–06, NA.

*Hadn't something better be thrown
to the wolves?*
     —*Newton Drury*

6

The War Years

Increased federal spending during the Roosevelt administration helped the Park Service expand during the 1930s. The government had recognized the possible benefits that could result from attention to wildlife conservation and used New Deal funds for programs focusing on lands, fish, and fauna as well as to create jobs. The Civilian Conservation Corps (CCC) provided work for thousands of men on conservation projects, such as improving animal habitat, roads, and visitor facilities on federal lands. National parks hosted 118 CCC camps, with enrollees building many of the park system's enduring symbols, such as Glacier Park's Going-to-the-Sun road.[1] The Park Service had the benefit of an advocate at the top, Interior Secretary Harold Ickes, who served from 1933 to 1945. Ickes expanded parks to include historic sites and national seashores; he protected wilderness values and usage patterns in the large western parks.[2] Despite the nation's economic woes, publicity campaigns during the 1930s helped increase park visitation from 3.5 million in 1933 to 16.7 million in 1940, and that year the service received an appropriation of thirty-five million dollars.[3]

This growth came to an abrupt halt in 1941. Wartime priorities caused funding to plummet, and the Park Service received only five million dollars in 1943. Construction halted, maintenance budgets dwindled, and the permanent staff declined by over fifty percent. Harold Bryant's Branch of Research and Education disappeared. Visitation decreased markedly with gas rationing and the general war mobilization, from twenty-one million in 1941 to six million in 1942. In order to make space for military offices, administrative headquarters moved from Washington, D.C., to Chicago, where they remained until 1947. Park Service officials faced years of defending the parks against pressure from businessmen seeking to open protected lands for timber, grazing, and mining resources under the guise of national emergency.

A relatively new Park Service director, Newton Drury, faced these wartime challenges. Born in San Francisco in 1889, Drury attended college with Horace Albright at the University of California. After Drury's 1912 graduation, he taught English and forensics at Berkeley and served in the Balloon Corps during WW I. He began conservation work after the war, serving as executive secretary of the Save-the-Redwoods League, and in 1929 took on additional responsibilities as an officer in the California State Park Commission. Upon Albright's resignation in 1933, an advisory committee unanimously recommended Drury to Secretary Ickes for the post, yet Drury chose to continue his work in California, leading to Arno Cammerer's appointment. When Cammerer, in declining health, asked to be reassigned in 1940, Drury again received an offer, which he accepted in August.[4] While he disliked the world of Washington politics, Drury's preservation philosophies and the support of Ickes kept the parks intact. Military interests wanted park resources, such as the Sitka spruce of Olympic National Park, for airplane construction. Drury deflected these desires by cooperating with the War Department and opening parks to military recreation and training, while trying to keep military activities consistent with essential park values. Drury believed in a caretaker rather than promoter role for the Park Service. With wildlife, he believed in "letting nature take its course insofar as possible," a philosophy that coincided well with his science advisors and advocates of McKinley's wolves.[5]

In Alaska, Frank Been assumed the leadership of a park experiencing its best years ever. A contingent of 211 CCC personnel worked in McKinley Park in 1938, building dog kennels, laying telephone and sewer lines, finishing a ranger station at Wonder Lake, and constructing a park hotel. Secretary Ickes had funded the hotel project through a $350,000 Works Progress Administration appropriation, and during an Alaska inspection tour in 1938 he visited the park to inspect its progress. Although Ickes didn't care for the hotel's design, the two hundred-guest facility opened in June 1939, completing a host of improvements to bring the park out of the cabins-and-snowshoes era.[6]

Superintendent Been departed for active military duty in January 1943 as a captain in the Army's Special Services Division. He reluctantly left the park in the hands of Chief Ranger Grant Pearson, who had joined the staff in 1926. Pearson was cut from the same mold as Harry Karstens—both the product of hardscrabble upbringings, and both embodying the qualities of toughness and congeniality sought in rangers. Grant fulfilled this promise, gaining competence and seniority, as well as accompanying Harry Liek on the 1932 climb of Mt. McKinley. At his request, Pearson had transferred to Yosemite in 1939, just prior to Been's arrival at McKinley, to gain experience in the variety of park problems uncommon in Alaska: large numbers of tourists, illegal livestock grazing, and campground management. After his return to Alaska in 1942, Pearson and Been suffered strained relations; according to Pearson, Been believed him incapable of the superintendent's responsibility.[7] Nevertheless, Pearson ably oversaw the transition of McKinley Park from a tourist facility to Alaska's premier site for military rest and recreation. Six to eight thousand men per month visited the park in 1943, enjoying the scenery, ice skating, hiking, and skiing. Evening recreation included films with footage from Pearson's McKinley climb and Murie's wildlife movies. Hosting soldiers kept the reduced park staff close to headquarters, with minimal attention paid to park wildlife. Pearson quit making monthly wildlife reports for lack of ranger information and an office stenographer.[8]

The war brought massive changes to the territory. Alaska's population in 1939 was 72,524, slightly over half non-Native, with only 500 servicemen. While boosters had long promoted greater settlement, a 1939 proposal by Ickes—the so-called Slattery plan—to resettle up to 50,000 European refugees received near-unanimous criticism in the territory, and failed to pass Congress.[9] Alaska became a theater of war with the Japanese invasion of the Aleutian chain in June 1942. By 1943 152,000 military personnel were in the territory.[10] Native villagers living in log cabins suddenly found themselves surrounded by construction projects as airfields sprouted everywhere. The Alaska Highway brought a welcome transportation link to the states, while in Fairbanks the first "motor toboggan" made its appearance.[11] Anchorage, site of Fort Richardson, began its rise to dominance, and the whole human geography of Alaska changed in several years.

Material shortages caused by the war effort affected the taking of game by Alaskans. New arms and ammunition for sporting purposes became unavailable across the country, as manufacturers devoted their full production to military hardware. A Munitions Assignment Board in Washington, D.C., allocated their products, with civilian usage holding the lowest priority. Given Alaska's distance from production centers, its civilian allocation was even lower. A spokesman for the Assignment Board admitted that little large caliber ammunition was shipped to Alaska, adding "I don't know what they shoot with it up there—grizzly or polar bears, or something of that sort." Alaskans needed to shoot food rather than bears, and by 1943 the lack of ammunition in Native villages became "acute," with only six calibers available in small supplies. Alaska's ammunition needs then superceded even the other western states (where ammo was "needed to keep down predatory animals"), and the following spring seventeen million rounds arrived by steamer from Seattle.[12]

The number of wolf trapping permits declined through the war years, as men left the villages for active duty or construction work rather than running trap lines. Wolves submitted for bounty fell from an average of 625 in 1936–40 to an annual average of 122 over the next three years. Metal shortages forced the Oneida Company to curb trap production, although the Newhouse No. 114, developed specifically for Alaska wolves with the addition of interlocking teeth on the trap's jaws, remained available. The Victor trap company, an Oneida subsidiary, offered a free pamphlet on the care and repair of traps, noting that "Metal's scarce…manpower's scarce…so new traps will be scarce, too!" By 1943 the Alaska Game Commission reported increasing wolf numbers and "much damage" inflicted on game and fur populations. While the game commission could dispatch only eight wildlife agents in all of Alaska to deal with increased numbers of hunters, the U.S. Fish and Wildlife Service put nine predator control agents in the field in 1943, indicative of the importance placed on control at that time.[13]

A national concern arose over the millions of young men in uniform unavailable to pursue accustomed hunting patterns, threatening a surplus of game animals that might damage forage and food crops. At the same time, though, game managers urged continued vigilance in predator control because "every pound of meat saved for human consumption" had significance.[14] Even though Alaskans harvested an estimated 2.5 million pounds of wild animals and birds (dressed weights) in 1942, domestic meats also mattered, and the war forced changes in Alaskan food habits.[15] Meat shipments from Seattle became subject to quotas and were reduced by thirty-five percent from 1941 levels, while government controls kept inflation in check. As the 1943 hunting season approached, Fairbanks grocers and restaurant owners announced "meatless Wednesdays," to reduce imported meat consumption. Adding to the supply problem, caribou did not appear on their customary fall migration route along the Steese Highway northwest of Fairbanks. In McKinley Park the wolves were reportedly "getting thin from lack of food." The snowshoe hare population reached its cyclical high in 1943; in the absence of larger game, newspapers encouraged hunters to harvest hares for winter meat. The university's extension service published a series of articles on wild food preservation and urged people to take to the countryside to harvest berries and mushrooms to augment rationed commercial foods such as dried fruits.[16]

The game situation worsened the following year. Fairbanks hunters harvested only sixteen caribou in the first week of the 1944 season and moose were scarce; the number of hunters in the field, however, was at a record high.[17] Military personnel caused the increase in hunters, since in 1943 Congress had passed a bill allowing soldiers to claim resident hunting licenses after one year in the territory. This followed a well-publicized court case involving the leader of the Alaska Defense Command, Brigadier General Simon Bolivar Buckner. The Alaska Game Commission denied his original request for a resident license, yet Buckner won his case on behalf of the military, and followed this with a detailed General Order to all military personnel to comport themselves with the highest standards of sportsmanship.[18] The game commission's reluctance to offer resident licenses to soldiers followed a general reluctance of Alaskans to allow transient residents the privileges of permanent ones. Emory Tobin in *The Alaskan Sportsman* regarded soldiers with automatic rifles as a "real threat to the game resources of Alaska," and urged "no relaxation of present regulations." The Alaska Game Commission worried about providing "orientation in the rudiments of good sportsmanship" to newcomers. The Game Commission received support from Ira Gabrielson, director of the Fish and Wildlife Service, who regarded Alaska's game as threatened by the "invasion" of new hunters who would be hunting less for food than recreation.[19] Nevertheless, the number of resident hunting licenses issued in Alaska rose by twenty-five percent in 1943, and Fairbanks sportsmen uneasily shared the meager harvest of game with soldiers from nearby Ladd Field. *The Alaska Sportsman* called it "the passing of an era in the progress of The Last Frontier."[20]

Military hunters received the brunt of local blame for poaching and unsportsmanlike conduct, although firm evidence of verifiable incidents is scarce. *The Alaska Sportsman* occasionally printed reports of killings by soldiers, such as whales or moose used for target practice by aerial gunners. The Alaska

Game Commission felt overwhelmed by the inability to monitor numerous violations by soldiers, and warden Sam White resigned in protest over wanton killings by military personnel.[21] A Yukon Territory official said that Americans "fished and killed and left their victims to rot." After the war, an American officer admitted "considerable truth" to reports of shooting safaris by soldiers in the Fairbanks area.[22]

Resentment against military hunters flared in 1943 when General Buckner announced that McKinley Park would be opened for hunting to soldiers on furlough.[23] Acting Superintendent Grant Pearson went directly to local newspapers to ensure negative publicity against this threat to park animals. The *Daily News-Miner* reported the hunting arrangement without editorial comment, but *Jessen's Weekly* described "indignation and dismay…the wave of resentment…astonishment…the strongest disapproval." An editorial the following week condemned the proposal not for the possible reduction in game numbers, but for the utter lack of sportsmanship involved with shooting animals unaccustomed to the threat of men with guns: "killing one of them would be no more difficult than shooting one of Bentley's or Creamer's prize dairy cows."[24] Even patriotic appeal failed to convince Alaskans that soldiers should be allowed to reap a bounty denied others. Buckner's announcement proved wishful thinking and came to naught, due to Newton Drury's effective work in Washington, D.C.[25]

Although many worried about the impact of military sport hunters, others saw opportunities for wolf control by soldiers. Personnel traveling the Alaska Highway had standing orders to fire at will on wolves. A correspondent to the Alaska Game Commission in 1939 suggested enlisting military planes with machine guns in the campaign against wolves since trapping, shooting, and poisoning had proven insufficient to diminish wolf numbers. Most important, soldiers could be used to protect Alaska's "Indian Service Contribution to the War," the reindeer herds. A 1942 Interior Department appropriations bill had contained $91,000 for the operations of the Reindeer Service while providing $40,000 for predator control on reindeer ranges, yet reindeer herd numbers continued their decline. Villagers reported rabies in wolf populations, and the newspaper intoned severely, "When mad wolves attack man and dog teams, the situation demands public attention." The famed arctic explorer Vilhjalmur Stefansson recommended aerial wolf control by soldiers to help the reindeer and improve the men's marksmanship. *The Alaska Sportsman* reported 30,000 dead reindeer killed by wolves in one year—an estimated three million pounds of meat—and in 1943 military personnel took to the air to shoot wolves in the reindeer areas.[26]

The war provided opportunities for Americans to link the enemy abroad to the darkest representations of wolves. Adolf Hitler—Adolf itself being the derivation of a word meaning 'fortunate wolf'—code-named his several fortified headquarters *Werewolf*, *Wolfsschlucht* (Wolf's Gorge) and *Wolfschanze* (Wolf's Lair). The rhetoric of the Third Reich used wolf lore as an analogue of the relationship between the subservient citizenry and the will of the pack leader, Hitler.[27] More real than rhetorical was the U-boat tactic of *Rudeltaktik* (pack attacks) masterminded by Admiral Karl Dönitz, who exhorted his submariners with "U-boats are the wolves of the ocean. Attack! Rend! Destroy! Sink!" Unleashed in the spring of 1940 on the North Atlantic convoys, German commanders rendezvoused at prearranged points in the shipping lanes in order to attack en masse and at night, spreading confusion and destruction. The "Happy Times" enjoyed by the wolf packs in 1940 came close to strangling Britain's supply lines. The malevolence of the Nazi wolf pack came to the doorstep of America in early 1942, as U-boats torpedoed ships within sight of the Atlantic seaboard.[28]

Americans also depicted the enemy with animal imagery in other ways. Weapons manufacturers developed a colorful and patriotic series of advertisements in sporting magazines to keep their name in the public eye, even though their products were unavailable. These often used the American rifleman mythology dating back to routing the redcoats from Lexington and Concord. Ads showed keen-eyed American lads weaned on ducks and deer shooting at new prey; a Winchester ad shouted, "It's *Messerschmidts*, not mallards today, Bill!" More pointed was a Remington ad that discussed "going gunning for varmints." In Alaska, where bounties mattered, readers of *The Alaska Sportsman* could order a "tip-top war-time souvenir," a suitable-for-wall-mounting "Japanese Hunting License" from the "Department of Jap Extermination." The license authorized a bounty payment of "two simoleons" for every "black-livered Japanese." It also indicated the divergent racial animosity held toward the enemies, as "Germans taken incidental to the hunt will be counted two for one in claiming bounty."

Connections between the Axis and wolves were applied even to the McKinley Park situation. A Fish and Wildlife Service biologist took the simile to heart in discussing the park: "Suppose we had let the wolves (Germans and Japanese) just continue their depredations on the sheep (the rest of mankind)."

William Beach, in a letter to a fellow Camp Fire Club member, also made the connection clearly and mocked the Park Service's philosophy of natural balances:

> Unfortunately in this great country of ours there are many people who will cry for leniency when Germany and Japan have been defeated. Certainly in the animal life a wolf is of a similar standard, a killer and destroyer of all that is beautiful inn [sic] the mammals of North America. It would appear to me that if the wolf has a place in the animal kingdom then certainly Hitler, Hirohito, Mussolini and their ilk should be protected, for eventually there would be a balance reached, and by the same line of reasoning we should refrain from the prosecution of murderers, robbers, etc.[29]

These wartime circumstances resulted in a crescendo of negative publicity toward wolves as the war came to an end. A joint memorial of the territorial legislature in February 1945, signed by Governor Gruening and entered into the *Congressional Record*, summarized Alaskan feelings: wolves were responsible for the decrease in reindeer from 641,000 to 90,000 in the past decade, the territory made every effort to kill predators, and the blame lay with the National Park Service, which "is breeding these destructive creatures in great refuges." The memorial sought federal funding for aerial hunters and a removal of wolf hunting restrictions in parks. Acting Superintendent Grant Pearson, sympathetic to Alaskan complaints, admitted having difficulty defending the Park Service against the charges of this memorial. Few efforts to control wolves had been made since Murie's departure in 1941, and the Park Service provided a convenient target for Alaskan frustration.[30]

A spate of articles on wolves appeared in *Jessen's Weekly* during 1945, more than in any other year. Reports blamed wolves for eliminating reindeer on the Alaska Peninsula, and the superintendent of the Alaska Reindeer Service stated that across the territory one million reindeer had been killed by wolves in the past twelve years. One Native group near Bethel reportedly killed their entire reindeer herd in hopes that a lack of prey would cause wolves to hunt elsewhere. The Reindeer Service offered airplane hunters free twelve-gauge ammunition and dressed deer carcasses for wolves killed. Three of the six registered airplane wolf hunters suffered crashes that year, making any financial

The ultimate extrapolation of the bounty mentality in *The Alaska Sportsman* **magazine.**
Alaska Sportsman Magazine collection, box 11. Courtesy Alaska and Polar Regions Archives, Rasmuson Library, University of Alaska Fairbanks

incentives beyond the bounty quite welcome, if not necessary. Miners north of Fairbanks reported a pack of ninety-nine wolves, and wolves were blamed for taking the whole caribou calf crop that year east of Fairbanks. Up north, Brooks Range residents reported that "Big, white wolves have now come out of the Arctic in search of food."[31] That such obvious exaggerations found space in the newspaper reflected the increasingly pessimistic view on the future of Alaska's game as the sourdough era in Alaska's history came to an end.

Adolph, Louise, and the children returned to Wyoming in the autumn of 1941, where a few years earlier they had purchased a house and some land on the south edge of Jackson. There, in his laboratory-study, Adolph continued the analysis of bones brought from Alaska, edited his film footage, and declared his own "blitzkrieg on the wolf report," assisted by Louise, Margaret, and Olaus. After keeping "everlastingly at it," Adolph shipped the report to Victor Cahalane in early 1942, noting that he had not made any policy recommendations on wildlife management in McKinley Park, since he had concluded there existed an adequate number of sheep for tourist satisfaction. Cahalane was pleased with the report, but could not immediately get it published, needing to find supporters within the Interior Department who would supply funding. Ira Gabrielson, director of the Fish and Wildlife Service, quickly recognized the importance of Murie's work and offered to extend "every effort" to achieve prompt publication. Yet wartime prioritization and paper shortages stifled their efforts, and Cahalane decided to delay publication. He wrote to Adolph, "My idea is to line up a definite source of printing funds before publicizing the existence of the completed MMS [manuscript]. If it goes wandering around like an orphan child—shall we say Little Red Riding Hood?—some big bad wolf may start chewing off hunks."[32]

As funding for the National Park Service dwindled, employees like Adolph Murie found themselves wondering about their immediate futures. In April 1942 he received a solicitation from the War Department's Engineer Board, wondering if he would lend his outdoor expertise to the designing of camouflage combat clothing. He declined, though his position was slated for termination in June.[33] In 1943 the Park Service disbanded its Wildlife Division after less than a decade of valuable effort. Adolph found work with the Bureau of Indian Affairs conducting research on cattle and coyote predation on Arizona's San Carlos Indian Reservation. This was far from an ideal assignment, and the family did not enjoy the climate: "Arizona is *too hot*. Can't seem to get adjusted to the summer heat." After fifteen months spent mostly afield Adolph grew ill with pernicious anemia, a chronic condition that resulted in the need for monthly injections of vitamin B-12. The family gratefully moved back to Jackson, where Adolph wrote a report on this research. He exonerated the coyote from blame for the difficulties of raising livestock in the desert, but the bureau promptly filed and forgot the report.[34]

Besides writing the report on McKinley's wolves, Murie had one other situation from that research to resolve: the fate of the wolf pup Wags. Following Murie's departure in 1941 she had lived in the dog kennels at park headquarters, with an uncertain future. Frank Been tried to breed her with a sled dog in order to test the offspring's potential as workers. After Been left, Grant Pearson wanted to kill her. Victor Cahalane suggested she be marked for identification and released back into the park as an experiment. Deprived of her 'pack,' the Murie family, Wags became increasingly restive. Kept on a wire exercise leash, she broke it twice yet caused no harm to the sled dogs. The park staff confined her to a kennel after she slightly wounded a caretaker, and they wondered just what they were to do with her. Murie recommended against releasing her back to the wild, and suggested two options: transport her to a zoo, or shoot her. The Park Service solicited the National Zoological Park in Washington, D.C., for accommodation. The zoo agreed, yet they could not find a freight company willing to take the task. After months of effort between the park staff, Murie, the National Zoological Park, and reluctant shipping companies, the zoo changed its mind. Wags had only one more value to scientist Murie; the park staff shot her and sent him her measurements: 5' 3" long, 2' 7" high, 65 pounds.[35]

Adolph and Louise returned to Wyoming just in time to convince Olaus and Margaret to jointly purchase a dude ranch north of Jackson, near the village of Moose. With three houses and eight cabins on seventy-seven acres, the ranch had plenty of room to absorb all of the clan. On the edge of Grand Teton National Park, they were able to sustain daily contact with the wild animals they all loved. Olaus left government service in 1945 to accept the directorship of The Wilderness Society, a group he had joined eight years earlier. Olaus was unwilling to move to Washington, D.C., for this, so he split the position with Howard Zahniser and retained residence in Jackson Hole, which became the Rocky Mountain center of the wilderness preservation movement.[36]

The year 1944 marked the publication of the most important works on the wolf since Seton's stories in the 1890s. Former wolf hunter Stanley Young's *The Wolves of North America* placed the animal in historical context and, without undue sentimentality, regarded the wolf with a certain respect and desire to see it remain part of North America's fauna. Aldo Leopold penned his short, eloquent confessional essay, "Thinking Like a Mountain," which would become the most-quoted piece on the wolf ever written. And finally, after two years of effort by Park Service staff, Murie's *The Wolves of Mount McKinley*, illustrated by Olaus, emerged from the Government Printing Office as No. 5 of the fauna series, a continuation of the tradition and philosophy started by George Wright and Joseph Dixon. Although both Murie's Yellowstone coyote and McKinley wolf reports received the same drab government printing and noncommercial lack of marketing, the latter received substantially more notice by readers. This may have been a matter of timing, since the coyote report was published just before the nation was consumed by war, while the wolf report came out as the war was ending. The mental image of the wolf likely spurred interest from people who would not buy a book about the less-romantically perceived coyote. Publicity did accrue from print media: sportsmen's magazines had contributed to the wolf-sheep controversy by publishing articles critical of the Park Service, and The Wilderness Society printed excerpts of Murie's report in its magazine. After the war, Superintendent Frank Been at McKinley Park requested boxfuls of the report, since tourists found it inconvenient to write to Washington, D.C., to request it. And the book confirmed Murie's professional reputation and made it a national one: he wrote the first research monograph on wolf ecology, and for most of the rest of his life, the only one available.[37]

Recognition of its influence is still evident. When Durward Allen began his wolf studies on Isle Royale in 1958, Murie's work provided "the most definitive piece of research we could draw upon." David Mech, perhaps the world's most highly respected wolf expert, dedicated his 1970 book *The Wolf* to Adolph Murie. Erich Klinghammer dedicated a 1975 wolf behavior symposium to Murie.[38] With recent increasing popular interest in wolves, the University of Washington Press reprinted Murie's work in 1985, with a third printing in 1992.

The monograph received acclaim in its time as well. Murie's emphasis on the admirable qualities of wolves and wolf society appeared in Victor Cahalane's 1947 book, *Mammals of North America*. Director Drury took time to read Murie's work and thought the research would finally quiet Park Service policy critics. Harold Anthony at the American Museum of Natural History reviewed the work for *Natural History* magazine and called it "a splendid piece of natural history reporting...one of the best statements of its kind that this reviewer has seen." Both Adolph and Olaus kept letters of response they had received, and upon request Adolph sent excerpts to Victor Cahalane at Park Service headquarters. These provide insight on the rigor of Adolph's research and effectiveness of his writing. Praise came from scientific peers at universities and other federal agencies for Murie's science: "your paper on the wolf is very, very good"; "it is the best thing of its kind ever put out"; "one of the very finest jobs anyone has done in...mammalian ecology." Leaders of conservation organizations such as the National Parks Association and Izaak Walton League sent their praise; Richard Pough of the Audubon Society said "an extraordinarily interesting report.... The wolf himself emerges as a remarkably intelligent and likable animal. Don't miss it!" The book reached a broader audience as well, a combination of the subject matter, the price of only forty cents, and Adolph's writing style. A Chicago banker wrote that "It turned out to be far more than a factual report. I found it as engaging as a top-notch novel." A Wisconsin chemist commented that "I think your paper is the smoothest bit of writing I have seen for years." Back in Alaska, a Fairbanks trapper said that "it's written so any guy can understand it," and Ranger John Rumohr of McKinley Park told Adolph that "It is said that the ease with which a book is read is the best proof of its worth. Yours have it. My congratulations."[39]

Over the objection of a friend, who feared it might put him in a bad humor, the Camp Fire Club's William Beach took *The Wolves of Mount McKinley* with him on a trout fishing trip to Canada in May 1944. The Park Service had waited anxiously for publication of Murie's research to vindicate its policies; critics of the Park Service like Beach, with the evidence now in hand, went through the book with the scrutiny of prosecutors. Upon his return from Canada, Beach penned a three-page response to the book and sent copies to Marshall McLean, chair of the Conservation Committee of the Camp Fire Club, Newton Drury at the Park Service, and Governor Gruening. Beach accused Murie and the Park Service of complicity at the outset—"it is quite evident that it was his intention to justify the Park Department in its stand that the wolf should be conserved"; he questioned Murie's research methods, depicted the park as a drain on Alaska's treasury by perpetuating wolves available for bounty, and requested that the Camp Fire Club "exert every effort to have the wolf destroyed to protect our grand game herds."[40]

The conclusions Murie reached provided evidence for advocates on either side of the wolf issue, and one of the ironies of the Camp Fire Club's postwar efforts is its repeated citations of Murie's study to justify its views. The Park Service also cited the study, of course, with both sides taking individual sentences out of the book to support their contentions. Murie wrote to validate the Park Service's philosophy that no native fauna should be exterminated and shaped his conclusions around the premise that park wildlife management should differ from management in other parts of Alaska.[41] The Camp Fire Club disagreed about the park's purpose, holding that it existed to support large game herds, not as an example of a natural world untouched by human interference.

As the war came to a close, questions arose within the Park Service concerning McKinley's wolf policy. Shortly after he assumed the superintendency of the park in 1943, Grant Pearson had requested clarification from Washington, D.C., on wolf policy and was told to terminate any control efforts; the reduced staff had other responsibilities. Subsequent lack of shooting and thousands of friendly soldiers offering sandwiches led to numerous contacts between wolves and people. One wolf approached within twenty feet of a soldier intent on photographing the animal. He was saved—according to the published account—by a companion "brandishing his ski pole in his hand like a bayoneted rifle." Such incidents prompted Victor Cahalane to recommend that rangers fire over the heads of the wolves to "work up a less fraternal spirit in the wolves."[42] Pearson regarded wolves with disfavor and was not pleased that his rangers had to hang up their guns. As an Alaskan trying to maintain his reputation among long-time acquaintances, he made it known that this wolf policy had come from afar. Pearson forwarded an inquiry letter from the Camp Fire Club to his superiors, saying that having "neither the data nor the inclination to answer this letter, and

Grant Pearson
Courtesy of National Park Service, Denali National

feeling that the entire matter is packed with dynamite, I am passing the buck to you." Director Drury wrote the response. Emery Tobin of *The Alaska Sportsman* requested information on park wolf policy, and Pearson again sent the letter to headquarters and told Tobin "I feel this is a subject which should be handled by the Director."[43] Despite his unwillingness to support wolf protection, Pearson remained loyal to the organization. He sent his regional director a report of a conversation held with Governor Gruening and Edwin Arnold from the Division of Territories of the Interior Department in November 1945 indicating the awkward position in which Pearson found himself.

> Governor: Grant, what is your opinion in regard to the wolf situation in the Park? Are they doing any noticeable damage to the Park's wildlife?
>
> Superintendent: We send in our Wildlife Reports to the Director's Office with copies to the Regional Director, and a qualified Biologist makes the decisions and recommendations. I am not qualified along those lines to answer your question.
>
> Governor: That is not answering my question. What is your personal opinion and what would you recommend? This is off the record.
>
> Superintendent: Limited control by Park personnel.
>
> Governor: I would recommend they be exterminated. Do you ever see any wolves around Headquarters?
>
> Superintendent: Occasionally.
>
> Governor: What do you do about it?
>
> Superintendent: We do not molest them.
>
> Governor: I have positive proof that a twelve-year-old boy was killed by wolves at Dillingham. You have a little girl, and if any more wolves come around Headquarters, kill them and I'll back you up.
>
> Mr. Arnold: I'll also back you up.
>
> Superintendent: No comment.[44]

Governor Gruening expressed not merely a personal opinion but that of the Alaska Development Board, a lobbying organization comprised of the territory's most influential politicians and businessmen. Besides accusing the Interior Department of neglect in failing to develop Alaska's national parks more fully, Chairman of the Board Gruening had recently written a letter directly to Secretary Ickes recommending the extermination of wolves in Alaska's national parks and monuments. While sympathizing with a Park Service philosophy of faunal preservation, the board considered it "too costly and destructive."[45]

Park Service sensitivity to Alaskan opinion appeared prominently in correspondence in the mid-1940s. Murie was sure that if the Park Service ceased predator control "Alaskans would howl more than the wolves." Regional Director Tomlinson recommended a harvest of three to five wolves annually, since Alaskans were so adamant against the animal and the wolves seemed plentiful. Reindeer biologist L. J. Palmer of the Indian Service wrote on the subject to Victor Cahalane:

> The control of wolves in McKinley Park would have a good psychological effect on the people, which would probably be of more importance than physical eradication of the predator. The people are now definitely antagonistic to the Park policy of protecting the wolf and are in virtual mutiny against it. It is not favorable to Park administration.[46]

Acting Superintendent Pearson, caught in the middle and protesting continued protection of the wolves to his regional director, regarded Alaskan opinion as the most important factor in the situation. Tired of the "barrage of criticism, ridicule, and sarcasm from the Alaska people," Pearson did not criticize the policies his superiors had ordered, but tried to explain why Alaskans viewed wolves as direct and thus unwanted competitors for food. He ended the letter with either a good prediction or evidence that he was aware of broader action being contemplated against the Park Service: "Nothing short of extreme measures will regain the good will and confidence of Alaskans. Timorous action at this time is certain to bring repercussions the echos [sic] of which may reach as far as the halls of Congress." Feeling preyed upon by encircling critics and recognizing the symbolic value of Park Service actions, Drury penned a note to biologist Cahalane: "Hadn't something better be thrown to the wolves?"[47]

Notes

1   See John C. Paige, *The Civilian Conservation Corps and the National Park Service, 1933–1942: An Administrative History* (Washington, D.C.: GPO, National Park Service, 1985).

2   See Theodore W. Cart, "'New Deal' for Wildlife: A Perspective on Federal Conservation Policy, 1933–40," *Pacific Northwest Quarterly* 63 (July 1972): 113–20; Barry Mackintosh, "Harold L. Ickes and the National Park Service," *Journal of Forest History* 29 (April 1985): 78–84.

3   Donald C. Swain, "The National Park Service and the New Deal, 1933–1940," *Pacific Historical Review* 41 (August 1972): 318.

4   A summary of Drury's life and work is in Waldo Gifford Leland, "Newton Bishop Drury," *National Parks Magazine*, April–June 1951, 42–44, 62–66.

5   Russ Olsen, *Administrative History: Organizational Structures of the National Park Service, 1917–1985* (Washington, D.C.: GPO, National Park Service, 1985), 16; John Ise, *Our National Park Policy: A Critical History* (Baltimore: Johns Hopkins University Press, 1961), 449–53; Ronald A. Foresta, *America's National Parks and Their Keepers* (Washington, D.C.: Resources for the Future, 1984), 48; "Newton Bishop Drury, Parks and Redwoods, 1919–1971": an interview conducted by Amelia Roberts Fry and Susan Schrepfer (Berkeley: Regional Oral History Office, University of California, 1972), vol. 2, 361. See also Newton B. Drury, "The Future of National Forests and National Parks," *The Living Wilderness*, May 1944, 11–15; Richard Sellars, *Preserving Nature in the National Parks: A History* (New Haven: Yale University Press, 1997), 149–55.

6   *Fairbanks Daily News-Miner*, "CCC Activities Central Alaska," "McKinley Park CCC Completes Extensive Work for Season 1938," 3 November 1938; William E. Brown, *A History of the Denali-Mt. McKinley Region, Alaska* (Washington, D.C.: GPO, National Park Service, 1991), 210–12.

7   Grant H. Pearson's *My Life of High Adventure* (Englewood Cliffs, NJ: Prentice-Hall, 1962) is an entertaining account; he details strains with Been on 186–89.

8   Brown, *History of Denali*, 203–5; Superintendent's "Monthly Reports," January–March 1943, DENA; Pearson to regional director, 17 November 1943, File 5968, Box 2, DENA.

9   See chapter nine of Orlando Miller, *The Frontier in Alaska and the Matanuska Colony* (New Haven: Yale University Press, 1975). Although he was Jewish, Alaska's newly-appointed governor, Ernest Gruening, opposed the plan; see Gruening, *Many Battles: The Autobiography of Ernest Gruening* (New York: Liveright, 1973), 268–69.

10   George W. Rogers and Richard A. Cooley, *Alaska's Population and Economy* (College, Alaska: University of Alaska, 1963), Tables P-3 and P-4.

11   Fairbanks *Jessen's Weekly*, "Dogsled Travel Threatened by Motor Toboggan," 6 February 1942.

12 Louis W. Lipscomb, "Procurement of Ammunition for Other Than Military Purposes," in *Transactions of the Eighth North American Wildlife Conference* (Washington, D.C.: Wildlife Management Institute, 1943), 77; *Jessen's Weekly*, "Food Supplies of Natives are Being Replenished," 4 June 43; "Carload of Small Arms Ammunition Coming to Alaska," 17 March 1944.

13 Richard Gerstell, *The Steel Trap in North America* (Harrisburg, PA: Stackpole, 1985), 209; AGC *Annual Reports*, 1940–44.

14 The entire *Transactions of the Eighth North American Wildlife Conference* (Washington, D.C.: Wildlife Management Institute, 1943) is interesting for a look at fish and game concerns during wartime. From this are Elliot S. Barker, "Management for Maximum Production," 122–31; Albert M. Day, "Wartime Uses of Wildlife Products," 45–54; Frederic C. Walcott, "Harvesting Game in Wartime," 19–20.

15 *Exec. Officer's Report to the AGC*, 1943, 2, 6, UAF.

16 *Jessen's Weekly*, "Wednesday Named Meatless Day in Fairbanks," 24 September 1943; "Sheldon Finds Diminishing Wildlife at McKinley," 20 August 1943; "Rabbits Plentiful and Recommended for Meat Supply," 27 August 1943; *Daily News-Miner*, "Control Put On Meat For Alaska," 6 August 1943; "Prunes and Raisins Are Rationed," 2 September 1943; "Hunting At End After Light Kill," 1 October 1943.

17 *Jessen's Weekly*, "Game Eluding Local Sportsman," 8 September 1944; "Hunting Season Opens, 1353 Licenses Issued Locally, Interest High," 1 September 1944.

18 See Morgan Sherwood, *Big Game in Alaska: A History of Wildlife and People* (New Haven: Yale University Press, 1981). This case forms the backbone of Sherwood's excellent book.

19 "Main Trails and Bypaths," *The Alaska Sportsman*, July 1941, 5; AGC *Annual Report*, 1944; *Jessen's Weekly*, "Alaska Invasion Threatens Game, Says Gabrielson," 20 August 1943; Sherwood, *Big Game in Alaska*, 3.

20 *Exec. Officer's Report to the AGC*, 1943, 16, UAF; "Main Trails and Bypaths," *The Alaska Sportsman*, June 1942, 5. The "invasion" was shortlived; resident hunting/ hunting and trapping licenses issued rose to 11,000 in 1943 and topped out at approx. 14,000 before declining in 1947 to 5,000; see *Exec. Officer's Report to the AGC,* 1946, 1948, UAF.

21 Ralph E. Butler, "The Blue Cow," *The Alaska Sportsman*, April 1945, 8; "Main Trails and Bypaths," *The Alaska Sportsman* , August 1948, 4; *Exec. Officer's Report to the AGC*, 1942, 1, UAF; Dave Hall, "Sam O. White: The First Flying Game Warden," *Alaska*, May 1986, 61.

22 M.P. George Black, quoted in Robert McCandless, *Yukon Wildlife: A Social History* (Edmonton: University of Alberta Press, 1985), 74; Lieutenant Colonel J.P. Williams to Governor Gruening, 4 October 1946, RG 101, Box 470, ASA.

23 Buckner to Post Commanders, 2 September 1943, File 5968, Box 2, DENA.

24 Pearson to Drury, 12 January 1944, RG 79, Entry 7, Box 1407, File 208–06, NA; *Daily News-Miner*, "Hunting in McKinley Arranged," 28 September 1943; *Jessen's*

Weekly, "Hunting In Park Arouses Public Condemnation," 1 October 1943; "No Hunting in National Park," 8 October 1943.

25   Brown, *History of Denali*, 204; Olsen, *Administrative History*, 16.

26   "From Ketchikan to Barrow," *The Alaska Sportsman*, May 1943, 18; *Exec. Officer's Report to the AGC*, 1939, 90; *Jessen's Weekly*, "Crazy Fox Attacks Dogs In Nome; Wolves A Menace," 8 May 1942; Richard Olav Stern, "'I Used to Have Lots of Reindeers—The Ethnohistory and Cultural Ecology of Reindeer Herding in Northwest Alaska," (Ph.D. diss., State University of New York Binghamton, 1980), 190; "From Ketchikan to Barrow," *The Alaska Sportsman*, August 1943, 21; "From Ketchikan to Barrow," *The Alaska Sportsman*, December 1943, 23.

27   Erik Zimen, *The Wolf: A Species in Danger* (New York: Delacorte Press, 1981), 4, 307; William L. Shirer, *The Rise and Fall of the Third Reich* (New York: Simon and Schuster, 1960), 849, 1048–54; James Harrington McRandle, *The Track of the Wolf: Essays on National Socialism and its Leader, Adolf Hitler* (Evanston: Northwestern University Press, 1965), 4.

28   Karl Dönitz, *Memoirs: Ten Years and Twenty Days*, trans. R. H. Stevens (Cleveland: World Publishing Company, 1959), 19; Terry Hughes and John Costello, *The Battle of the Atlantic* (New York: Dial Press, 1977), 30, 316; J. P. Mallmann Showell, *U-Boats Under the Swastika* (Annapolis: Naval Institute Press, 1987), 30–34.

29   Dorr Green to FWS Chief of Predator and Rodent Control, 25 April 1945, RG 79, Entry 7, File 715, Box 1414, NA; Beach to Marshall McLean, 5 June 1944, File 5968, Box 1, DENA.

30   Alaska Legislature, *Senate Joint Memorial No. 5*, 17th Session, 1945; Pearson to Regional Director Tomlinson, 26 February 1945; Tomlinson to director, 9 March 1945, RG 79, Entry 7, File 715, Box 1414, NA.

31   *Jessen's Weekly*, " Dillingham Wild Life Agent Here After Juneau Meet," 23 February 1945; "Reindeer Service Head Finds Fairbanks Center of Alaska's Aviation," 2 March 1945; "Eskimos Beat Wolves By Killing Own Reindeer," 30 March 1945; "102 Wolves Killed In Bering Unit During Past Year," 23 February 1945; "Livengood Wolves Drive Caribou Into The Village," 30 March 1945; "Caribou Calf Crop Nil On Salcha Cr. Because Of Wolves," 2 November 1945; "Arctic Wolves Drive Moose Out Of Wild Lake," 23 November 1945; AGC *Annual Report*, 1946, 8.

32   A. Murie to Cahalane, 27 October 1941, A. Murie Collection, Box 3, Folder "Correspondence 1938–1954, Cahalane," AHC; A. Murie, "Quarterly Report," December 1941, DTC; A. Murie to Cahalane, 13 May 1942; Cahalane to A. Murie, 24 October 1942, A. Murie Collection, Box 3, Folder "Correspondence 1938–1954, Cahalane," AHC; Gabrielson to Drury, 29 December 1942, RG 79, Entry 7, File 719, Box 1415, NA.

33   George Nason to A. Murie, 25 April 1942 A. Murie Collection, Box 1, Folder "Correspondence 1934–1966, Letters re: job transfers," AHC; A. Murie to W. B. Bell, 6 March 1942, A. Murie Collection, Box 3, Folder "Correspondence 1934–1966," AHC.

34   A. Murie to Cahalane, 16 July 1944, RG 79, Entry 7, file 715, Box 1414, NA; Louise Murie MacLeod interview. Murie later revised and published this report; Adolph Murie, "Coyote Food Habits on a Southwestern Cattle Range," *Journal of Mammalogy* 32 (August 1951): 291–95.

35   A. Murie, *Wolves of Mount McKinley*, 48–9; A. Murie to Been, 22 September 1941, A. Murie Collection, Box 2, "Correspondence 1939–1949, wolves-McKinley, AHC; Been to Drury, 14 April 1942, A. Murie Collection, Box 4, "Correspondence 1939–1966, McKinley Park," AHC; G.A. Moskey to William Mann, 6 April 1943, File 5968, Box 2, DENA; Cahalane to A. Murie, 3 March 1943, A. Murie Collection, Box 3, "Correspondence 1938–1954, Cahalane," AHC; A. Murie to Cahalane, 8 March 1943, RG 79, Entry 7, File 715, Box 1414, NA. Murie later remembered this situation differently, recounting that he thought Wags should have been freed; interview by Evison, 19.

36   Margaret Murie and Olaus J. Murie, *Wapiti Wilderness* (New York: Alfred A. Knopf, 1966), 266–69.

37   Dorr Yeager to Been, 23 September 1948, File 5986, Box 2, DENA; Adolph Murie, "The Wolves of Mount McKinley," *The Living Wilderness*, February 1945, 9–25.

38   Durward L. Allen, *The Wolves of Minong: Their Vital Role in a Wild Community* (Boston: Houghton Mifflin, 1979), 92; Klinghammer, introduction, in *The Behavior and Ecology of Wolves: Proceedings of the Symposium on the Behavior and Ecology of Wolves Held in Wilmington, N.C., 23–24 May, 1975*, ed. Erich Klinghammer (New York: Garland SPTM Press, 1979).

39   Victor H. Cahalane, *Mammals of North America* (New York: MacMillan, 1947); Drury to A. Murie, 21 October 1944; A. Murie to Cahalane, 20 June 1945, RG 79, Entry 7, File 715, Box 1414, NA; Richard Pough, review of *The Wolves of Mount McKinley*, by Adolph Murie, in *Audubon*, January–February 1945, 58; Harold Anthony, review of *The Wolves of Mount McKinley*, by Adolph Murie, in *Natural History*, January 1945, 46.

40   W.S. Ladd to Drury, 18 May 1944; Beach to McLean 5 June 1944; McLean to Drury 21 June 1944, RG 79, Entry 7, File 715, Box 1414, NA; Beach to Gruening, 22 June 1944, RG 101, Box 470, ASA.

41   A. Murie to Cahalane, 29 March 1943, RG 79, Entry 7, File 715, Box 1414, NA.

42   Pearson to director, 9 March 1943; Tolson to regional director 10 May 1943; Drury to regional director, 10 December 1943, RG 79, Entry 7, File 715, Box 1414, NA; "From Ketchikan to Barrow," *The Alaska Sportsman*, August 1944, 21; Cahalane to Tomlinson, 20 August 1943, File 5968, Box 2, DENA.

43   Adolph Murie's diaries reveal many occasions when Pearson expressed his dislike of wolves and wolf protection. Pearson to regional director, 20 March 1945; Drury to McLean, 31 March 1945; Pearson to Tobin, 22 June 1945 RG 79, Entry 7, File 715, Box 1414, NA.

44   Pearson to regional director, 5 November 1945, RG 79, Entry 7, File 715, Box 1414, NA.

45 *Daily News-Miner*, "Alaska Development Board Reports on Actions Taken During Session At Juneau," 26 September 1945; Gruening to Ickes, 14 September 1945, RG 79, Entry 7, File 715, Box 1414, NA.

46 A. Murie to Cahalane, 13 May 1942, A. Murie Collection, Box 3, Folder "Correspondence 1938–1954, Cahalane," AHC; Tomlinson to director, 21 October 1943, Palmer to Cahalane, 3 May 1945, RG 79, Entry 7, File 715, Box 1414, NA.

47 Pearson to regional director, 11 April 1945, File 5968, Box 2, DENA; marginal note on Drury to Cahalane, 13 March 1945, RG 79, Entry 7, File 715, Box 1415, NA.

*That the wolf problem may be met effectively
in spite of biologists…*
—*Marshal McLean*

7

Taking the Issue
to Congress

William Beach returned to McKinley Park in August 1945. He arrived on the sixteenth, accompanied by his wife and Andy Simons, a hunting guide and Alaska Game Commission member. After driving to Wonder Lake and back, they left the park on the seventeenth. The next week in Fairbanks, with no more evidence than a day's worth of observations, Beach testified on park wildlife policy in Fairbanks before a visiting congressional committee from the Office of Territories. Beach predictably blamed wolves for the disappearance of game and criticized the Park Service for relying too heavily on the advice of men like Adolph Murie and too little on men like Andy Simons. Subsequently, he urged the Alaska congressional committee to force the Interior Department to "correct the evil they have allowed to exist."[1] Notwithstanding Beach's moral fervor, the Camp Fire Club had been receiving disturbing reports for some time on the McKinley park sheep population and encouraged the Park Service to send Adolph Murie back for an inspection.

Murie had recommended follow-up studies in 1941 and Victor Cahalane recommended Murie's return as early as January 1944, but the Park Service could not spare the money on its lean war budget. The Fish and Wildlife Service had Murie on its payroll, conducting rodent studies in the southwest, and parks Director Drury requested Murie's detachment for a McKinley sheep check. Drury had met with Joseph Dixon and Grant Pearson to discuss the wolf-sheep situation, and they agreed that game reports appeared alarming and Murie must visit the park as soon as possible. To soften up Ira Gabrielson and Harold Ickes on his request for Murie's time, Drury went back to the Park Service's old organizational friends, the American Society of Mammalogists. In April 1945 Drury invited the society to analyze his predator policy. On May 12 the mammalogists passed a resolution of full support for Park Service biologists and policies, approving predator control only when "justified by scientific investigation." Ickes and Gabrielson received copies of the mammalogist's resolution on May 17, and by the end of June Murie had funding for a one-month study in McKinley Park. Acting Parks Director Hillory Tolson, while expressing his thanks to the Society of Mammalogists' president, made a further request indicative of the mounting pressure on the Park Service, asking if:

> members of the Society who are in a favorable position could be urged to use any opportunity to publicize, through writings, photographs, or lectures, the facts regarding the place of predators in wild areas. Information of this type is badly needed, especially in sportsmen's magazines, newspapers, and popular periodicals.[2]

Adolph Murie returned to the park shortly after the war's end in August and stayed until September 19, his time afield spent revisiting the peaks and valleys he had come to know so well. He anticipated a delicate mission, in which "the policy on the wolf must be handled in such a way so as not to arouse too much antiwolf emotion." What he found seemed to vindicate Park Service critics. The sheep population had declined to about five hundred since 1941; Murie actually counted only 244 and extrapolated the rest. He guessed the wolf population had also declined, but had too little time in the field to tell. Caribou numbers seemed adequate, judging from reports. Murie admitted that large gaps existed in his knowledge and understanding of wolf-sheep ecology, and that the continued existence of the park's sheep could be in jeopardy. Unlike his prewar research, this time he had to make policy recommendations to Newton Drury. Park Service policy stated that animals could be killed if they threatened the existence of another species. But Murie's ultimate suggestion seemed to contradict his clear affection for wolves, his beliefs on the role of the Park Service, and his notions about noninterference in natural processes. He recommended in his report that as a "precautionary measure" ten to fifteen park wolves be shot or trapped by rangers, with continued control until the sheep population began to increase.[3]

On the face of it, this recommendation followed a linear chain of events: a wildlife problem, addressed through research, followed by subsequent research which modified earlier conclusions, leading to actions within the Park Service's purview. Yet an exchange of letters between Murie and Cahalane indicates they both knew what Murie would recommend *before* he returned to the park. Writing in April, Murie recognized that events of the preceding ten years had not blunted opposition to the Park Service's ideals toward wildlife management: the Camp Fire Club was stubbornly entrenched, service personnel were largely unconvinced of the value of predators, and the taxpaying public remained unenlightened.

> I am wondering if our no control policy of wolves in McKinley may not hurt us. I am wondering if, at this time, such a policy may not be waving a red flag too boldly and arouse too much opposition. May we not be bringing down on the wolf greater hatred, actually increasing the feeling against him.... Possibly some control in McKinley would be, in the end, the best policy for preserving the wolf.

In July, after Cahalane had secured the funding for Murie's one-month return visit, he wrote to Murie recognizing that such a short time would inhibit any substantive research, but the public relations wheels at the Park Service were already turning. "Unfortunately, we have written to the Camp Fire Club that definite plans have been made and have sent copies to the mammal society, the ecological society, and Senator Walcott. Another statement has gone out today to the editor of 'Alaska Sportsman' magazine." Cahalane recognized the fictive elements in Murie's check-up and agreed with Adolph's comment: "Another check should precede any control otherwise we would only be giving in to argument. We should maintain the principle of research first." Murie did not see any alternative in the face of the "psychological intrusion" of Park Service critics, and he knew the best tactic for maintaining wolves in the park was to show skeptics a healthy and numerous Dall sheep population.[4]

Murie's recommendation to kill wolves provided an opportunity for the Park Service to score points on all fronts; Newton Drury wryly noted that critics "seem to have more effect on NPS than on the the wolf. He doesn't

Newton B. Drury, director of the National Park Service from 1940–1951.
Courtesy of National Park Service, Harpers Ferry, West Virginia

read the Alaska press." Antiwolf critics would approve the wolf killings, while the service could emphasize to prowolf critics that they were basing decisions solely on scientific grounds, on the advice of the respected Adolph Murie. Park Service staff sent copies of Murie's 1945 report to the Fish and Wildlife Service, Governor Gruening, the Camp Fire Club, and scientific groups. Aldo Leopold received a copy. He was involved in his own fray over wolf management in Wisconsin, having been both for and against bounties there. He plainly supported Murie: "There are not many people from whom I would accept without question a recommendation for wolf control, but in his case I do accept it." The Park Service prepared a news release outlining service policy and quoting Murie's report; Director Drury explicitly ordered the release sent to the Alaskan news media and the nation's sportsmen magazines. At the park, Grant Pearson received approval on December 6 to begin wolf hunting.[5]

Drury issued a public summary of the situation that sought to justify Park Service actions, and he wrote confidently to Harold Ickes that killing fifteen wolves in McKinley Park would quiet the critics of the wildlife policy.[6] On the contrary: during the war years, the balance of nature had tilted freely in McKinley Park, unobserved and unmanaged; the scientist himself had underestimated the volatility of the animal populations, casting the desired protection of all native fauna into question.

The Camp Fire Club, unsatisfied with the Park Service's response to the reduced sheep population, began another public pressure tactic in 1945. Since the club disagreed with the Park Service on the reason for the park's existence— what exactly did a "game refuge" mean?—they went back to the source for help. Charles Sheldon was dead, as were James Wickersham, George Bird Grinnell, and Steven Mather, who had all testified on behalf of the park's creation in 1916. Belmore Browne was still alive, however, and he had led the Camp Fire Club's efforts for the park from 1912–17, subsequently adding artistic success to his impressive Alaska credentials. From his homes in Banff, Alberta, and Marin County, California, Browne had become a well known landscape and wildlife painter. As an additional specialty, he painted backgrounds for museum exhibits, notably for the Alaska species in the North American Hall of the Museum of Natural History in New York. During the Second World War, Browne served as a consultant for the Air Force Arctic Training School and spent 1942 in Alaska testing cold-weather clothing and combat gear, assessing the effects of cold on machinery and machine operation, as well as teaching survival to airmen. Belmore Browne, thought the

Conservation Committee of the Camp Fire Club, could serve as an impressive advocate for McKinley Park's sheep. Marshall McLean wrote Browne on March 6, 1945, requesting his observations on the wolf and sheep, enclosing *The Wolves of Mount McKinley* for review and an explanatory letter from the Park Service on its wolf policy.[7]

Browne's negative feelings toward wolves were consistent with his time. In his early writings he described wolves as "gaunt murderers" coursing after caribou. Browne was convinced that no wolves existed in the McKinley area prior to the park's creation, and that only after game became protected in the park did the wolves move in for the plentiful prey. Through the summer of 1945 Browne worked on a response to Murie's book in his spare time at the training school, angrily finishing it after Murie's 1945 report became public. The loss of sheep confirmed to Browne the error of Park Service ways: "Murie's report paints in blood and bone what the custodians have done with it [McKinley Park]."[8]

Browne's response, titled *Analysis by Belmore Browne for the Committee on Conservation of the Report of Dr. Adolph Murie's "The Wolves of Mt. McKinley,"* provided the Camp Fire Club a summary document of their arguments against the Park Service, written by a man of "unswerving integrity." It resembled a religious tract more than a factual rebuttal. Browne wrote from a populist stance, casting himself alongside "practical...serious...Northern...outdoor men" supported by "scores of experienced wildlife experts" in a situation that "called for the realistic appraisal of a practical stockman." Opposed to these pragmatic and reasonable men were administrators from the "Department of Parks," desk-bound men "misled" by the theories of biologists, particularly the "scientists laboratory tinged theories" of Adolph Murie.[9] Despite evidence of declining sheep numbers during the 1930s, according to Browne, the Park Service had done nothing until assigning Murie to study the situation, and then let four years pass before admitting the sheep were threatened. Browne called this the "most costly and unnecessary catastrophe in the history of American Governmental game control," a curious statement that ignored the histories of elk in Yellowstone and deer on the Kaibab Plateau.

Browne outlined two central arguments used by the Camp Fire Club. The first discredited the balance of nature concept. He disparaged the Park Service management philosophy, in existence since the early 1930s, of preserving the parks as laboratories for observing natural interactions between the native fauna, calling it a "fallacious doctrine." Browne called Murie's book "An Eulogy to the Wolf," and he accused Murie of commencing his study determined to "prove the wolf a useful citizen on all fronts." As evidence, Browne noted that Murie had stated five times in his book that wolf predation checked game increases, but compared these to the sixty-plus statements by Murie indicating that predation had a negligible or positive effect on the sheep. Browne accused Murie of "a lack of knowledge of the sheep's habits" and of excessive use of qualifying adverbs—probably, likely, appears—in his conclusive statements. Browne caustically hoped that visitors disappointed by the lack of game in the park would "become enthusiastic over their memories of biotic units and natural interrelationships."

While Browne argued as a first-hand expert on sheep, Marshall McLean, a New York attorney since 1898, edited the work and helped craft the second argument: park managers were guilty of ignoring their mission as written in the 1917 enabling legislation that created the park. Section 6 of the McKinley Park bill stated that it was established as a game refuge, and no game could be killed except to "protect or prevent the extermination of other animals or birds."[10] The club felt the presence of predators contradicted the purpose of Section 6. Sheep numbers had clearly declined through the 1930s from previous abundance, and with only five hundred sheep remaining they were apparently headed toward extirpation. What further evidence was needed to declare the Park Service derelict in its mission? Furthermore, although the Park Service had at various times protected wolves as part of the native fauna, they had never been classified as game animals, thereby excluding them from the list of protected animals in McKinley Park, according to the Camp Fire Club. They continued to assert the old reasons for the existence of parks, as places for tourists to see game, as well as to create an overflow of game into surrounding areas for hunters. In all of these, the Park Service had failed. Browne's treatise concluded that the Park Service should take "the necessary steps at once to remove every wolf possible from the Park area."

Marshall McLean told Browne he had done a "splendid job." William Beach liked it so much he agreed to pay the cost of printing Browne's work as a Camp Fire Club pamphlet. McLean also told Browne, in November 1945, that Browne would be "Exhibit A" and receive an expense-paid trip to Washington, D.C., as the club planned to escalate the wolf-sheep controversy by introducing legislation in Congress to force the Park Service to rectify its mistakes in the management of Mount McKinley National Park.[11]

Director Newton Drury received word of the Camp Fire Club's intent just before Christmas 1945. The letter from Marshall McLean discussed the service's "astonishing failure" and requested Drury's cooperation with the legislative amendment. McLean included a copy of the bill that had been introduced in the House of Representatives the previous week by Rep. Homer Angell of Oregon. The bill, H.R. 5004, *To provide for the protection of the Dall sheep, caribou, and other wildlife native to the Mount McKinley National Park area, and for other purposes,* amended Section 6 of the 1917 McKinley Park Act by adding a specific clause concerning wolves:

> Sec. 6. The said park is established as a game refuge, and no person shall kill any game in said park except under order from the Secretary of the Interior for the protection of persons or to protect or prevent the extermination of other animals or birds. The Secretary of the Interior shall take immediate steps to provide for the rigid control of wolves and other predatory animals in Mount McKinley National Park to the end that said refuge be made safe, and so maintained, for the Dall sheep, caribou, and other wildlife native to the area.[12]

Backers modified the bill prior to submittal by the addition of two words: "other wildlife, *except predators*, native to the area [emphasis added]" and relabeled it H.R. 5401. The House referred it to the Committee on Public Lands, and McLean hoped for a March hearing, depending on Belmore Browne's availability. It was a propitious time for such an action, because Republicans had gained a congressional majority in 1946, followed by multiple efforts of westerners to minimize federal controls of public lands.[13]

Drury lost little time in responding. He requested the opinion of the Park Service's chief counsel, who thought that H.R. 5401 could not supersede the National Park Service Act of 1916, which instructed the protection of all animals in parks without preference for game animals. Counsel also suggested that, whatever "game refuge" meant, it could not be construed to specify a management regime in one park different from management purposes in other parks. Drury sent this to McLean on December 29, defending his policy as one based on the best available scientific information.[14] Anticipating the need for public testimony, Drury had his staff compile a list of possible allies and mailed all seventy-nine a copy of Murie's 1945 report and the official service stance on wolf control. The list included scientists—Lee Dice, Charles Adams, Victor Shelford, Tracey Storer, Harold Anthony—as well as conservationists, such as Aldo Leopold of The Wilderness Society, Rosalie Edge of the Emergency

Conservation Committee, Kenneth Reid of the Izaak Walton League, and Devereux Butcher of the National Parks Association. Alaska's Governor Gruening received the information, as did all members of the Camp Fire Club's Conservation Committee. Favorable responses came back; Harold Anthony at the Museum of Natural History specifically commended Drury's tactics and pledged his support. Drury asked Olaus Murie for suggestions on how to deal with the Camp Fire Club, and they agreed that Olaus would narrate Adolph's "Wildlife at Denali" film during the hearings.[15]

The congressional Committee on Public Lands held two brief hearings that spring, and the Park Service barely had a chance to provide testimony, much less enough time to get Adolph or Olaus to Washington, D.C. The first hearing on April 3, 1946, belonged to Marshall McLean, who had impressive witnesses and a friendly audience of western representatives: White of Idaho, Savage of Washington, Lemke of North Dakota, LeCompte of Iowa, Barrett of Wyoming, D'Ewart of Montana, Norblad of Oregon, Rockwell of Colorado, and (nonvoting Delegate) Bartlett of Alaska. McLean began his testimony by filing as evidence a wolf photograph from *The Alaska Sportsman*, the beast supposedly "180 pounds of solid bone and muscle." Belmore Browne presented a synopsis of experiences and perspective as one of the founders of the park. When asked what the Park Service had done about the sheep situation, Browne replied, "They have done nothing," and recommended hiring expert trappers using a new type of poison cartridge to kill off the wolves.[16] Following Browne came a recent recruit to the Camp Fire Club's effort, Bradford Washburn, director of the New England Museum of Natural History. Known as a pioneer in mountaineering, aerial photography, and photogrammetric mapping, Washburn had visited Alaska sixteen times since 1930 and had recently spent time on Mount McKinley leading equipment-testing expeditions for the army. He told the committee that if he wanted to photograph game, the last place he would visit would be McKinley Park, because the wolves had eliminated the game. Dr. James Clark, affiliated with the American Museum of Natural History, came next. An avid world-wide big game hunter, usually for museum specimens, Clark had been a Camp Fire Club member since 1910, and had served as club president in 1929.[17] He based his testimony on a one-week trip to McKinley Park in 1935. Clark strongly disagreed with Park Service management of "holding these wolves as they are to observe the balance of nature and the biology of nature, because they are permitting the wolves to breed as you would foxes in your chicken yard." McLean's final witness hearkened back to the park's founding: Stephen Capps of the Geological Survey,

Victor Cahalane, left, and Lawrence Palmer at caribou corrals, upper Savage River, Mt. McKinley National Park, August 1940.
Courtesy of National Park Service, Harpers Ferry, West Virginia

who had written the 1917 *National Geographic* article which helped convince Congress to create McKinley Park. He too had not visited the park since 1935, and admitted he had never seen a wolf kill a sheep, but guessed that "the average of one sheep or caribou a day per wolf is probably not an exaggeration." Marshall McLean concluded by submitting letters of support for H.R. 5401, including ones from Jack O'Connor and Andy Simons of the Alaska Game Commission, as well as from Horace Albright.

Acting Chairman White admitted the hearing had been arranged on short notice, and that he would have liked the presence of witnesses from the National Park Service. The only Park Service advocate to speak was Devereux Butcher, in attendance as the executive secretary of the National Parks Association, an organization enjoying a record membership of 2,300. Butcher questioned the singular role of the wolf in declining sheep numbers and sought to introduce human hunting pressures on park boundaries into the analysis. White rebuffed these comments, since hunting was not legal within the park, and the hearing ended with committee members well convinced of the Camp Fire Club's arguments. Not only were they unswayed, according to Alaska Delegate Bartlett, but his colleagues voiced desire for even more stringent wolf control.[18]

The Committee on Public Lands met again on May 22, 1946, with the Camp Fire Club introducing the only witness, Brigadier General Dale B. Gaffney of the U.S. Army. Gaffney had been assigned to Alaska in 1940 and specialized in cold weather flying.[19] He based his observations on what he and other military men had seen of game conditions from the air, particularly with caribou and reindeer. Newton Drury attended the hearing and defended the Park Service, noting that the reindeer situation invoked by Gaffney hardly pertained to the park's Dall sheep. Drury also filed documents supporting his case, starting with the recommendation of recently appointed Interior Secretary Julius Krug that H.R. 5401 not be enacted. Other letters of support came from scientists and nature organizations. Since the Park Service had not had a chance to present testimony, the committee tabled the legislation until the following session, giving the Park Service a reprieve.

At stake for the service, and for the Interior Department, was the tradition of the Park Service handling its own affairs without congressional intervention on specific issues. In the first half of the century, agencies had typically operated without detailed oversight by legislators, and the Park Service had successfully cultivated trusting supporters in Congress. Few challenges came from Capitol Hill since legislators lacked expertise when dealing with issues within an agency's purview.[20] Reactions to H.R. 5401 from members of the Committee on Public Lands certainly gave little optimism for letting congressmen decide a matter of wildlife management. Representative Savage wondered if wolves would turn to human prey once they had cleaned out Alaska's game; Barrett asserted the wolves were killing the sheep for enjoyment; White astonishingly claimed there were still plenty of wolves in central Iowa; and Rockwell flatly stated that he was in favor of complete wolf extermination. Bartlett scoffed at the thought of eliminating McKinley's wolves: "I suspect the whole United States army could be turned loose in the Park with instructions to kill wolves and at the end of the year there would be some left." Drury considered this case to have "dangerous implications…. If Congress should pass an act changing the basic policies with respect to a specific national park, this tendency would undoubtedly spread and any special interest group would take advantage of it."[21]

At the hearing Drury had stated for the record his appreciation of the Camp Fire Club's interest in Park Service affairs, yet to Victor Cahalane he wrote "Tell him [McLean] you will follow *truth* wherever it leads. This should be our watchword, together with *tolerance*, even of asininity." Since the early 1930s, the Park Service had formulated wildlife management policies based on science, yet their opponents in the wolf-sheep controversy disagreed more on emotion than facts. Park officials noted that throughout the hearings, Adolph Murie's study had received virtually no mention, despite this being the most factual document available.[22] Olaus Murie attempted to reason with Belmore Browne following a verbal "free-for-all" during a meeting in Washington, D.C., Adolph, said Olaus, had recommended wolf control, and the Park Service proceeded to hunt wolves: "What more does the Campfire Club want?" He urged Browne to let go of the single-minded attack on park wolves and focus the Camp Fire Club on more pressing conservation issues. In the manner which made Olaus such an effective advocate in the political arena, he invited Browne to Jackson Hole "after the smoke clears…to talk about dog mushing and mountain climbing." Newton Drury, in a thoughtful letter to a retired colleague, reflected on the hazards of dealing with strong sentiment:

> I feel that I am on excellent personal terms with Mr. McLean, Senator Wolcott, and many others and have tried not to maneuver them into a position from which they could not with dignity withdraw. I am afraid, however, that Beach, Browne, and others have forced themselves into such a position and perhaps we have been partly responsible for their plight. Pride of opinion, as you know, is the unforgivable sin and causes more sorrow in the world than perhaps any other motive. As a man gets along in years he yearns more and more to be considered an "expert." He wants to be listened to. That, I am sure, is the fix of our friend Mr. Belmore Browne.[23]

The Park Service decision in January 1946 to kill fifteen wolves received favorable publicity back in Alaska. The *Fairbanks Daily News-Miner* credited the new wolf control directive to the "widespread demand from residents of the Territory," and Delegate Bartlett assured constituents of his support for minimizing the park's wolves. The April hearings by the Committee on Public Lands received positive notice in the *Daily News-Miner*. From Ketchikan, *The Alaska Sportsman* reported that rangers had newly given permission to carry rifles in the park for the current wolf hunt. This was, of course, erroneous, as rangers had been shooting at wolves for years. As before, either the Park Service's history of killing wolves had not been effectively communicated to the press, or reporters ignored actual ranger practices in favor of reportage that discredited the federal officials.[24]

The Park Service received an unanticipated result in its 1946 wolf hunt. Rangers covered 125 miles of sheep range in December 1945 and saw only one wolf. In February, they hired an experienced hunter and trapper, John Colvin, who received permission to use snares as well as shooting to achieve the desired quota of wolves. He spent the next two months afield searching for the forty or so wolves presumed to live in the park. To everyone's surprise, he found no wolves, and was relieved of his duties in April. Newton Drury delightedly informed Marshall McLean of this development, assuring him that wolf control would resume if needed. With Grant Pearson absent on a trip to the states, Acting Superintendent Peterson released the news to local papers.[25] Drury prepared a press release in May, but it did not appear in Alaska papers, withheld by the returned Grant Pearson. Always sensitive to local opinion, Pearson reasoned to his superiors that the Park Service would be embarrassed if wolves again appeared with the spring caribou migration, forcing a recantation of the press release. Nevertheless, Drury sent it to his allies, receiving back several comments such as that of Richard Westwood, president of the American Nature Association: "I am delighted to hear that the search for wolves revealed little evidence of these animals and no necessity of any killing of them."[26] It appeared that the Park Service had again appeased both sides of the wolf-sheep argument, first by ordering wolves killed, then by announcing to the prowolf people the failure of its action.

Grant Pearson was right: wolves did return to the park in the summer of 1946, as did William Beach. With the wolf quota still in effect, rangers killed five wolves, yet Beach again made headlines, "wrought up over the destruction of game." An editorial in the *Daily News-Miner* cited Beach as one of an "increasing body of competent authority" questioning the wisdom of Park Service management. For the first time, park rangers had been pursuing wolves with a specific goal, rather than taking the opportunistic shot, yet the *Daily News-Miner* ignored this. The editorial again dredged up the old charge of the wolf-breeding ground, thereby allowing wolves to spread across Alaska, "cutting down and wiping out the animals which have become traditionally identified with our land." With the Camp Fire Club's legislation upcoming in the 1947 Congress, the *Daily News-Miner* urged "every Alaskan to demand passage of this bill." Beach also appeared on the airwaves, gaining an interview on radio station KFAR on August 17. Beach derided Park Service management based on the balance of nature and proposed legislation as the solution. When asked what listeners could do about the park wolf situation, Beach responded, "They can try to force the Department of the Interior to adopt some method of killing wolves and force the Park to kill them."[27]

Adolph Murie arrived at McKinley Park the same day William Beach spoke on the radio. He stayed until September 23, trying to count the sheep and wolf populations and determine the survival of that year's crop of lambs. He still estimated a population of only five hundred sheep, but considered their age class distribution healthier than seven years earlier, and posited that an "equilibrium with the current environment has been reached." Any such balance was tenuous. Murie estimated a wolf population of no more than fifteen and found much less predation on sheep than in his earlier visits, but noted that a single pack entering the park could shift the predator/prey balance overnight. While overnighting at the Sanctuary River ranger cabin, Murie reflected on his dual mission as a biologist and a Park Service advocate. "This is not the critical time for the wolves. That time is coming, when wolves become scarce. Now is the time to build up a generous attitude toward the wolf and the Park Service." Murie refuted Beach's comments by his own appearance on KFAR, a report "worded to favor the park administration." Upon his departure, *Jessen's Weekly* reported that Murie's study confirmed national park policies, "that if undisturbed nature will preserve a balance." Even though wolf predation on sheep was negligible in the fall of 1946, the potential instability between the animal populations coupled with the desire to build positive public attitudes toward the Park Service caused Murie to recommend continued wolf control.[28]

Subsequent Park Service correspondence confirms that wolf control in 1947–48 had less to do with the biological needs of the sheep than with the psychological needs of the public. Victor Cahalane predicted that Murie's statement about a wolf-sheep equilibrium would be "greeted with derision by Beach, Browne, and the rest of the Camp Fire-eaters." In fact, club members held a measure of respect for Adolph; the club reckoned that policies came from administrators in Washington, D.C., not from field biologists, and Murie's boss Cahalane was the obvious target. Cahalane felt wolf control should continue because the chances of taking wolves were slight and continued control would help keep the critics quiet. He also recommended withholding from McLean animal reports from McKinley Park, since "he has chosen to disregard *everything* that emanates from the N.P.S. and to use it, if possible, to the disadvantage of the Service."[29] Newton Drury stated that "Our ideal objective is the removal of artificial management," yet agreed that prudent wolf removal was justified, and tried to convey that message to the Camp Fire Club through the higher offices of Interior Department officials. Adolph Murie justified wolf killing because it would "benefit the wolf most," since "if the public opposition continues, resentment against the wolf and the Service would increase." He advocated a flexible control policy based on the sheep population; with little danger of exterminating the wolf due to its wide-ranging habits, such a plan would minimize "unfavorable public reaction to our conservation efforts without sacrificing anything." To this end, Superintendent Been displayed four wolves killed in March 1948 at park headquarters for public viewing and photography. He wrote that "The observation by people from widely scattered parts of Alaska, including the many who saw the wolves last month will broadcast…that wolves are being controlled in the Park." Been reported these wolf kills in the newspaper as well. As of June 1948, nine wolves of the original 1945 quota of fifteen had been killed and wolves remained scarce in the park. Administrators nevertheless continued the control effort through the summer tourist season in order to portray the Park Service as actively protecting the park's game animals.[30]

Park Service biologist Lowell Sumner, in an appraisal of the wolf-sheep situation, outlined the primary problem facing park administrators:

> I recognize, as do Superintendent Been and Dr. Murie, that we cannot allow nature to take its course at the time because the general public has not yet been educated to a full appreciation of the biological values of our national parks, and the way they function.[31]

This long-term view defined the task of the National Park Service in this issue: effect immediate policies in reaction to current demands, while preserving what the park held unique.

In maneuvering for political support, the Camp Fire Club had a potential ally in the Boone and Crockett Club; membership of the two groups overlapped, and Belmore Browne, James Clark, and Marshall McLean belonged to both. The clubs had mutual interests in wildlife conservation, and had been partners in McKinley Park's creation through the work of Browne and Charles Sheldon. The Boone and Crockett Club had kept an official distance from the wolf-sheep controversy prior to the war. In 1945, however, with the updated sense of endangered sheep and a legislative tactic taking shape, the Camp Fire Club activists sought the backing of their old friends. Rather than visibly pushing their well-known agenda, Browne and McLean recruited the son of Charles Sheldon, William, to lead an initiative with the Boone and Crockett Club. This created all sorts of emotional linkages, from the memory of Charles— esteemed as a hunter, naturalist, and lover of wild sheep—to William, his flesh and blood patrimony, in uniform with five Bronze Stars, a fighter against the Axis. Added to that was William's prewar academic training in biology and interest in making a career in wildlife science. Although he had just returned from military service and understood few details of the McKinley Park situation, William agreed to sponsor a motion at the 1945 Boone and Crockett annual meeting in support of the Camp Fire Club's legislation. Showing respect for the Sheldon name, the club passed William's motion.[32]

In the following year, however, Sheldon read Murie's *The Wolves of Mount McKinley*, learned more about the situation, and changed his mind. At the 1946 Boone and Crockett annual meeting when McLean and Browne attempted to pass another resolution against the Park Service, Sheldon led the successful opposition against "the old die-hards who are making the trouble." To allow for further discussion of the issue, the Boone and Crockett president commissioned a committee to assess the situation, led by Richard Mellon and Dr. Harold Anthony of the Museum of Natural History. The committee met in the museum's Sportsmen's Library on January 23, 1947, with McLean and Browne presenting their views, and with the Park Service represented by its chief naturalist, Carl Russell. The former repeated their legal argument over the definition of McKinley Park as a game refuge, and attempted to discredit Adolph Murie's research. McLean thought that legislation was necessary "in order that the wolf problem may be met effectively in spite of biologists," and Browne asserted that "Dr. Murie is responsible for the National Park Service lethargy."[33]

Carl Russell reported that "McLean's hands shook and Browne leaned over to steady his paper so that the shaking would be less noticeable. They struck me as being two old-timers very upset by the possibility that their baby may be neglected. I feel sorry for them—not sore at them." Russell put forth a spirited defense of Murie and park policy, noting that the situation held such importance that Murie was to take up permanent residence in the park to monitor the situation. As recommended by its wolf committee, the Boone and Crockett Club officially expected the Park Service to ensure a viable sheep population, but would remain neutral on further legislative efforts against the service.[34]

Bradford Washburn, after being "heartily in favor" of the 1946 legislation, continued to be a burr in the side of the Park Service. He spent the summer of 1947 on Mount McKinley filming an ascent for RKO Productions in a project named "Operation White Tower." Upon his return, Washburn submitted statements deploring game conditions to the Park Service and the Camp Fire Club, noting that all of the park rangers he had spoken with agreed that the wolf numbers should be greatly reduced. In a letter to Newton Drury, Washburn accused Adolph Murie of editing research findings to conform to Park Service policy, and ridiculed the opinions of other naturalists. Drury responded coldly: "We desire to follow truth, wherever it leads, in wildlife and all other matters. We cannot, and I believe should not, exterminate the wolf. But short of that I do not believe there is much to argue about." Although a scientist himself, in this instance Washburn preferred public opinion: "I still value the convictions of the vast majority of the local people in the McKinley Park area more highly that those of the biologists...the list of those in opposition to his [Murie's] views seems to me to be a rather distinguished one."[35] Washburn had stated to Drury that this was the only Park Service policy with which he disagreed, yet he pushed for a road extension from Wonder Lake across the tundra to McGonagall Pass, the traditional route to the base of Mount McKinley, "to extend the road right over to the mountain so that he [the tourist] can actually *touch* the peak." (Not quite; this access would have allowed visitors to walk on the surface of the Muldrow Glacier, but the mountain itself is still distant.) Washburn also tried to get permission for the Navy to build a cosmic ray research station on Mount McKinley. Neither of these gained approval. Although Belmore Browne agreed on the wolf policy, he opposed the road idea, preferring that the park retain as much wilderness character as possible. Adolph Murie privately cut Washburn down to size: "actually he is pulling all possible strings to get the projects approved so that he can get lecture material.... We all feel that Washburn, with his commercialization of the Mountain, has already desecrated it enough, enough for one little man."[36]

While the wolf-sheep conflict simmered in Washington, D.C., the battle for public opinion was fought in national magazines. *The Living Wilderness* helped increase awareness of Adolph Murie's research, for example, by publishing long excerpts of his *The Wolves of Mount McKinley*. A January 1946 *Field and Stream* article, "Shall We Protect the Killers?" focused its attention on the National Park Service; calling the wolf a "malignant, malicious beast," author C. Blackburn Miller blamed the Park Service's adherence to balance of nature ideals as pushing the Dall sheep to the brink of extermination, and urged sportsmen to rise up in protest. Though he did not claim Camp Fire Club affiliation in the article, Miller had served on the Conservation Committee alongside William Beach and Marshall McLean.[37]

The Park Service took up the gauntlet. Newton Drury responded with a personal letter to the magazine's publisher objecting to Miller's article. Drury also wrote a published letter to *Field and Stream*, in which he defended the legal basis for their wildlife policy, supported Murie's research, and took pains to note that on the basis of science, rather than hearsay, park rangers were currently in the process of culling wolves from the park. Drury also requested space in *Field and Stream* for a longer rebuttal, which appeared in June. In "Should We Cry Wolf?," Chief Biologist Victor Cahalane defended the wolf as "part of the warp and woof of the pattern of our American wildlife heritage." Appealing to the "well-informed wildlife enthusiasts" rather than the "itinerant wildlife zealots," he derided the "overcrowded pasture of spiritless sheep" that would result in the absence of their natural predator, and assured readers that the Park Service would maintain both species. Another article by Cahalane appeared simultaneously in *The Living Wilderness*. "Shall We Save the Larger Carnivores?" addressed the different readership by urging support for the Park Service against H.R. 5401, since the Park Service stance kept in mind the desires of the nonhunting public: "Perpetuation of the unique values of this area seems to depend on aggressive action by naturalists and sustained interest and support by the nature-loving public." Olaus Murie provided the editorial comment for that issue of the magazine, wondering if Congress would be swayed by a "group of New York people" who would cause McKinley Park to "degenerate into a game refuge." Cahalane continued that theme with an article in *National Parks Magazine*, asking readers if they wanted wild animals in parks with their instincts preserved by the presence of predators, or "apathetic cattle?"[38]

The sportsmen's magazines remained unconvinced. The next month's issue of *Field and Stream* contained an article by an Alaskan trapper, "Arch Villains of the Wilderness," while *Outdoor Life* printed "The Timber Wolf: Scourge of Game and Stock." Although wolves had not preyed on stateside stock in decades, the article declared "the only good wolf is a dead wolf.... Here is an animal for which nobody has a kind word, nor does he deserve one." Alaska hunting guide Russell Annabel resurfaced in the press with several articles. He painted a gloomy picture in a February 1947 *Field and Stream* article, "Wolf Trouble in Alaska." Ignoring that wolves had actually received full protection in McKinley Park for brief periods only, Annabel blamed the "curious official stubbornness" of the Park Service for causing the disappearance of all game in a two-hundred-mile stretch of the Alaska Range. This article appeared as a chapter in Annabel's 1948 book, *Hunting and Fishing in Alaska*, and his charges received coverage in *The Alaska Sportsman* of June 1948. Annabel also sold the issue to the *Saturday Evening Post*, an article that claimed Alaska's caribou had declined to only 100,000. Reasons? Not Annabel's clients, the trophy hunters, but heedless bush Alaskans and, of course, wolves, that had done the "greatest damage." Frank Dufresne, the former head of the Alaska Game Commission, put his considerable credibility into an antiwolf article in *Outdoor Life*, declaring "In man's scheme of things, at least, the wolf has no place." At the least, the wolf held a place as man's enemy, as outlined in another *Outdoor Life* article, "America's Longest War: The Battle With Wolves." Echoing Annabel's broad territorial stroke, *Outdoor Life* also published "Sportsmen: We Must Not Let Alaska's Game Die Out." This article covered wolf predation predictably, but fairly considered the effects on game of Alaska's increased population and the use of airplanes for hunting. While the prewar wolf controversy had been essentially confined to Alaska and the clubrooms of New York City and Washington, D.C., this magazine coverage assured it national prominence.[39]

Additional publicity concerning the wolf-sheep controversy arose from another self-appointed savior of the hoofed animals of the North, a retired evergreen tree grower from Seattle, I. P. Callison.[40] An avid hunter, Callison had traveled throughout the western Canadian provinces and visited Alaska in 1945 in search of big game. He became convinced that the northern game species were rapidly becoming extinct through a combination of advancing civilization and increasing wolf predation. Although he sincerely believed in the validity of his research—which involved talking to wardens, guides, and local residents (and later sending a survey to four hundred guides and trappers)—Callison arrived at some curious conclusions. To explain the supposed increase in predator numbers, he posited a migration of animals northwest, packs of wolves and coyotes driven before the plow and road from the Canadian prairies, who then found the reindeer herds of Alaska and multiplied greatly. The increase in wolves was boosted by the breeding grounds provided by the "balance-of-nature hopheads" of the American and Canadian

Park Services. At age seventy-five, Callison began printing his opinions on the North's game following his Alaskan trip, and gained publication in magazines such as *Game Trails* and *Alaska Life*.[41]

Callison had spent July 1945 in McKinley Park, ostensibly on a photographic mission, and claimed the park's sheep population was only one hundred twenty. He came to the attention of Park Service headquarters after his magazine articles appeared. Victor Cahalane, to his colleagues, dismissed Callison as one of the "amateur doctors of wildlife ills." While Callison may have been an amateur, he was an amateur on a crusade. In July 1948 he privately published a ninety-page pamphlet, *Wolf Predation in the North Country*, and mailed it to his guide and trapper contacts, Alaska politicians, and the Camp Fire Club. Park Service staff requested a copy, and Callison charged them one dollar. They paid.[42]

While Belmore Browne's analysis of Murie's book had been long on rhetoric, short on evidence, and verging on the slanderous, Callison's pamphlet took the wolf-sheep controversy to previously unplumbed depths. Wolves received every vile adjective known and were responsible for all evil in the North, including the killing of a million reindeer. While Callison's informants were all men of vast experience and unshakable integrity, he regarded federal officials as "super-fanatics" who "live in a cloistered vacuum the four walls of which are fashioned out of false theories based on wholly false premises." From this had come a "strange and unrealistic philosophy" which led to a sickness, the "balance-of-nature virus." Although scientists had provided the balance of nature theory, Callison considered its adherents to be involved in a religious deviance to an unproven creed. Conservationists who had given testimony in support of the Park Service at the congressional hearing were "the high priests of the strange cult." In debunking the balance of nature concept, Callison used the same argument that had been used by the Biological Survey in the 1920s: as soon as White men appeared in North America, any preexisting balance disappeared, and Callison rightly pointed out the inroads of civilization and population against the North's game populations.

Adolph Murie, a "poor benighted conservationist," had undertaken a research project unnecessarily, since the evidence against the wolf was obvious to all who lived in Alaska. Nevertheless, he had received a "glorious vacation at the taxpayer's expense," in order to justify the philosophies of Park Service biologists, chiefly the "childish twaddle" of Victor Cahalane. Murie's research report was "a piece of pro-wolf propaganda from start to finish." That notwithstanding, Callison quoted Murie frequently and selectively to emphasize the obvious, that wolves ate sheep. Callison claimed that Park Service employees who disagreed with the theories of top administrators had been "tightly muzzled," and that Murie's research conclusions had been dictated from Washington, D.C., by people whose minds were "utterly impervious to the principles of practical game management." Callison summarized the McKinley Park situation as "the most colossal example of wanton waste in wildlife management ever recorded. The Park was turned over to the Park Service teeming with wild game, a biological spectacle without a rival in all the world." In a reversion to Puritan rhetoric: "In thirty short years it has made of the Park a howling wilderness."

Victor Cahalane understatedly considered *Wolf Predation in the North Country* to be "highly dramatic but unfortunately highly imaginative." Responding to predation inquiries sparked by Callison's work, the Park Service supplied copies of *The Wolves of Mount McKinley* and subsequent reports by Murie, no doubt assuming that objective readers could compare the two authors and draw reasonable conclusions. A Canadian biologist quoted extensively by Callison, C. H. D. Clarke, informed Callison that he objected to Callison's extreme subjectivity, sweeping generalizations, and personal attacks on Adolph Murie. Even Marshall McLean was "bothered about Callison's 'book'—all agree it is very good in spots—but so tied down with extraneous matter—as to lose all point as a weapon of attack."[43]

Olaus Murie, as president of the Jackson chapter of the Izaak Walton League, received a copy of Callison's booklet accompanied by a form letter which urged political lobbying for a predator control program in Alaska. The irony of the situation did not escape Olaus, who politely responded to Callison in defense of brother Adolph and scientific objectivity. Interestingly, Olaus noted that Adolph "thought there was some truth to be found in your bulletin." Callison responded by claiming the "profoundest respect" for Adolph, and considered him to have been censored by the "balance theorists." This was obviously false and yet was a plausible interpretation, given Adolph's careful circumspection in his public writings. But Callison had no intention of backing down from Olaus's "holier-than-thou and wiser-than-thou attitude." Personal correspondence continued between the two men through autumn and then became public, when the Fairbanks *Jessen's Weekly* published a column about Callison's work. The newspaper printed Olaus's lengthy reply to the editor, in which he pointed out some of Callison's fallacious arguments and criticized the "highly denunciatory character of the publication." In his typically conciliatory manner, Murie ended his letter with a rational plea for cooperation. "We say we are a democracy. It might be remembered that all of us like to have the privilege of enjoying our country, each in his own way, and sportsmanship includes tolerance for the other fellow's kind of enjoyment." Olaus wrote this just prior to departing for New Zealand on a wildlife research project sponsored by the Fish and Wildlife Service, using one of the new Fulbright grants. In his absence, Callison retorted in *Jessen's Weekly*, rejecting Olaus's arguments about wolves and attacking him for being on a "Macawber [sic] mission" at taxpayer's expense. Stung by this, Olaus ended the contact in July 1949 after his return, vowing to "forget about our correspondence and assume that we had nothing in common."[44]

Wolf Predation in the North Country, with its combination of fervor and scurrilousness, stands as a singular example of the hostility extant in the late 1940s toward wolves and the National Park Service. In all likelihood, the informants who had sent reports of wolf depredations to Callison found his book consistent with their own beliefs. There was no widespread support for protection of wolves, national park or not. The Park Service still faced a formidable public relations challenge.

In the spring of 1947 the House Committee on Public Lands heard more testimony against the Park Service and its wolf policy, this time during a hearing on statehood for Alaska. When Ralph Rivers, the territory's attorney general, spoke supporting statehood, much of his testimony was a litany of purported federal transgressions against the integrity, sovereignty, and future of Alaska. Had Alaska been a state, asserted Rivers, McKinley Park would not have been allowed to serve as that "breeding ground for hundreds of wolves" despite the protests of residents.[45]

Nevertheless, the legislative reprise in the spring of 1947 became a victory for the Park Service. A bill requiring the immediate reduction of wolves in McKinley Park was again introduced into both houses of Congress and referred to committees.[46] This time the Park Service prepared its defenses adequately. Adolph Murie had published a situation update in the December 1946 *The Living Wilderness*, and the Park Service ordered five hundred copies of the article for distribution to its mailing list. The National Parks Association offered a closely argued statement in support of the service and its predator policies. In anticipation of hearings, potential witnesses submitted their testimony to Park Service headquarters for review by Cahalane and the chief counsel's office. Cahalane distributed lists of congressmen to favorable lobbyists, and urged them also to write directly to the Camp Fire Club outlining their opposition to the legislative tactic.[47] The club was unable to recruit other sportsmen's organizations; the Boone and Crockett Club remained neutral, and in March 1947 the Izaak Walton League passed a resolution at its annual convention opposing the "bad precedent" of game management by politicians and legislators rather than by scientists. The American Society of Mammalogists passed not only a resolution opposing legislation, but a statement directing the Park Service to "pay special attention to the problem of preserving the wolf in Mount McKinley National Park," since the park represented virtually the only sanctuary on the continent for wolves. Frank Been, returned to the superintendent's job from military duty, provided the latest word on conditions in the park: "Fortunately, we can now report that wolves are decreasing and sheep are increasing. The reversal of the situation of the past few years may cool the ardor for enforced control." Interior Secretary Krug registered his opposition to the legislation, concluding it "might well lead to an unhealthy balance of species, with which situation we have had considerable experience on other Federal lands."[48] Opposed by virtually every conservation organization and by the country's leading wildlife biologists, and unwanted by the interior secretary, the Camp Fire Club's bill died quietly. It never gained another hearing.

Notes

1   Superintendent's "Monthly Report," September 1945, DENA; Fairbanks *Jessen's Weekly*, "Easterner Wrought Up Over Wolves In McKinley Park," 24 August 1945; *Anchorage Daily Times*, "Says McKinley Is Breeding Spot For Alaska's Wolves," 25 August 1945; Beach to Alaskan Congressional Committee, 18 October 1945, RG 79, Entry 7, File 715, Box 1414, NA.

2   Cahalane to Drury, 4 January 1944; Drury to McLean, 31 March 1945; Drury to E.R. Hall, April 1945; Hall to Ickes, 17 May 1945; Tomlinson to Drury, 11 May 1945; Tolson to Hall, 17 July 1945, all RG 79, Entry 7, File 715, Box 1414, NA.

3   A. Murie, "A Review of the Mountain Sheep Situation in Mount McKinley National Park, Alaska, 1945," 9 October 1945, manuscript in A. Murie Collection, Box 7, UAF. In fact, judging from his field notes, it appears Murie shaded his public data to make the juvenile sheep cohorts appear healthier than what he observed; A. Murie Collection, Box 14, Folder "Sheep data 1945," UAF.

4   A. Murie to Cahalane, 19 April 1945; Cahalane to A. Murie, 21 July 1945, both A. Murie Collection, Box 5, Folder "Wolf Control McKinley N. P., 1944–1972," AHC; A. Murie to Tolson, 25 May 1945, RG 79, Entry 7, File 715, Box 1414, NA.

5   Drury to staff, 25 October 1945; Leopold to Drury, 6 November 1945; Drury to
      Ickes, 31 October 1945, all RG 79, Entry 7, File 715, Box 1414, NA; Superintendent's
      "Monthly Report," December 1945, DENA. Pearson later took credit for the control
      plan, writing that "We finally prevailed on the Park Service to suspend the hard-and-
      fast rule that nature is its own best regulator"; Grant H. Pearson, *My Life of High
      Adventure* (Englewood Cliffs, NJ: Prentice-Hall, 1962), 102–3.

      On Leopold and Wisconsin's wolves, see Richard P. Thiel, *The Timber Wolf in
      Wisconsin: The Death and Life of a Majestic Predator* (Madison: University of Wisconsin
      Press, 1993), 110–11.

6   Drury to Ickes, 31 October 1945, RG 79, Entry 7, File 715, Box 1414, NA; Drury
      statement, "The Wolf Problem in Mount McKinley National Park," 4 January 1946,
      Stef. Mss., 190–8:88, Dartmouth College Library, hereafter DCL.

7   McLean to Browne, 6 March 1945, Stef. Mss., 190–8:67, DCL.

8   Quotes from Browne, "In the Caribou Country," originally in *Outing* (June 1910),
      reprinted in Robert Bates, *Mountain Man: The Story of Belmore Browne* (Clinton, NJ:
      Amwell Press, 1988). Browne to McLean, 14 and 19 October 1945, Stef. Mss., 190–
      8:67, DCL.

9   Belmore Browne, *Analysis by Belmore Browne for the Committee on Conservation of the
      Report of Dr. Adolph Murie's "The Wolves of Mt. McKinley"* (New York: Camp Fire
      Club, 1946); Browne to McLean, 19 October 1945, Stef. Mss., 190–8:67, DCL.

10   The exception to the ban on hunting allowed this for prospectors until 1928; see
      Theodore Catton, *Inhabited Wilderness: Indians, Eskimos, and National Parks in Alaska*
      (Albuquerque: University of New Mexico Press, 1997), chaps. four and five.

11   McLean to Browne, 8 November 1945; 14 June 1946, Stef. Mss., 190–8:67, DCL.

12   Congress, House, Committee on Public Lands, *To Provide for the Protection of the
      Dall Sheep, Caribou, and Other Wildlife Native to the Mount McKinley National Park
      Area, and for Other Purposes*. 79th Cong., 2nd sess., 1946, H. R. 5004.

13   McLean to Drury, 22 December 1945, RG 79, Entry 7, File 715, Box 1414, NA;
      McLean to Browne, 28 January 1946, copy of H.R. 5004 attached, Stef. Mss., 190–
      8:67, DCL. John C. Miles, *Guardians of the Parks: A History of the National Parks and
      Conservation Association* (Washington, D.C.: Taylor & Francis, 1995), 157.

14   Jackson Price to Drury, 29 December 1945; Drury to McLean, 29 December 1945,
      RG 79, Entry 7, File 715, Box 1414, NA.

15   Drury to mailing list, 11 January 1946; Russell to Drury 13 March 1946; Anthony to
      Drury, 16 January 1946; Drury to O. Murie, 5 January 1946; O. Murie to Drury, 21
      January 1946; Drury to O. Murie, 4 February 1944; all RG 79, Entry 7, File 715, Box
      1414, NA.

16   All quotations, as well as the following statements from May 22, are taken from
      Congress, House, Committee on Public Lands, *Protection of Dall Sheep, Caribou, Etc.,
      Native to Mount McKinley National Park: Hearing before the Committee on Public Lands*,
      79th Cong., 2nd sess., 23 July 1946.

17   James C. Clark, *Good Hunting: Fifty Years of Collecting and Preparing Habitat Groups for the American Museum* (Norman, OK: University of Oklahoma Press, 1966), 125. This autobiography is quite interesting; Clark began as an eighteen year old apprentice taxidermist at the American Museum in 1902, made a career of it, and was responsible for many of the famous habitat displays, including completing the African elephant group following Carl Akeley's death. He became reacquainted with Belmore Browne during WW II while they served as consultants for the War Department—assignments similar to that offered Adolph Murie.

18   Miles, *Guardians of the Parks,*149. Bartlett to harry Cowan, 26 April 1946, Bartlett Collection, Box 1: Interior—NPS, folder 1, UAF.

19   Marshall McLean had written directly to the War Department requesting leave for Gaffney's presence; letter of 19 March 1946, Stef. Mss., 190–8:67, DCL; *Anchorage Daily Times*, "Dale Gaffney Promoted to Full Colonel," 26 January 1942.

20   Ronald A. Foresta, *America's National Parks and Their Keepers* (Washington, D.C.: Resources for the Future, 1984), 74–75. Foresta notes that congressional staff sizes have increased, thus allowing staffers who can take the time to familiarize themselves with the intricacies of issues.

21   *Protection of Dall Sheep, Caribou, Etc.*; Drury to Daniel Beard, 21 November 1946, RG 79, Entry 7, File 715, Box 1414, NA; Bartlett to Harry Cowan, 26 April 1946, Bartlett Collection, Box 1: Interior Dept.— NPS, Folder 1, UAF.

22   Drury to Cahalane, 4 May 1946; Tomlinson to Pearson, 29 May 1946, RG 79, Entry 7, File 715, Box 1414, NA.

23   O. Murie to Browne, 22 April 1946, Stef. Mss., 190–8:67, DCL; Drury to Daniel Beard, 21 November 1946, RG 79, Entry 7, File 715, Box 1414, NA.

24   *Daily News-Miner*, "Washington News-Letter," 18 February 1946; "From Ketchikan to Barrow," *The Alaska Sportsman*, April 1946, 24; *Daily News-Miner,* "McKinley Park Wolf Question Up At Hearing," 4 April 1946; "Washington News-Letter," 5 April 1946.

25   Sumner to regional director, 22 April 1946, RG 79, Entry 7, File 715, Box 1414, NA; Superintendent's "Monthly Reports," February, March, April, 1946, DENA; *Jessen's Weekly*, "McKinley Park Rangers Can't Find Any Wolves," 29 March 1946.

26   Drury to McLean, 6 May 1946, Stef. Mss., 190–8:67, DCL; Pearson to regional director, 16 May 1946; Westwood to Drury, 8 May 1946, RG 79, Entry 7, File 715, Box 1414, NA.

27   *Jessen's Weekly*, "Grant Pearson, McKinley Park Head, In Town," 23 August 1946; "N.Y. Sportsman Here For Game," 16 August 1946; *Daily News-Miner*, "Wolves, Sheep, and Cold Cash," 17 August 1946; Pearson to regional director, 6 September 1946, RG 79, Entry 7, File 715, Box 1414, NA. This latter is a transcript of the radio interview sent to top Park Service administrators.

28   A. Murie, "1946 Alaska Trip," field journal, 15 August, 12 September 1946, A. Murie Collection, Box 12, UAF; A. Murie, "Wolf-Mountain Sheep Relationships in Mount

McKinley National Park, Alaska - 1946," File 5986, Box 3, DENA; Superintendent's "Monthly Report," September 1946, DENA; *Jessen's Weekly*, "Wolves Have Gone, Lambs Are Arriving At McKinley Park," 4 October 1946.

29   Cahalane to Hillory Tolson, 8 January 1947 and 23 April 1948, RG 79, Entry 7, File 715, Box 1415, NA; Arthur Demaray to director, 28 March 1947, in which Demaray quotes Beach as identifying Cahalane as a leading figure who was "completely wrong" about predators; A. Murie Collection, Box 3, Folder "Correspondence 1940–1950, Letters Re: Alaska," AHC.

30   Drury to regional director, 26 February 1948; Drury to regional director, 9 January 1948; Tolson to Doerr and Cahalane, 30 June 1948, RG 79, Entry 7, File 715, Box 1415, NA; A. Murie to Been, 29 January 1948, File 5968, Box 1, DENA; *Jessen's Weekly*, "Park Superintendent Looks For Big Tourist Season in '48," 12 March 1948; Superintendent's "Monthly Report," March 1948, DENA.

31   Sumner to regional director, 6 February 1948, RG 79, Entry 7, File 715, Box 1415, NA.

32   James B. Trefethen, *Crusade for Wildlife: Highlights in Conservation Progress* (Harrisburg, PA: Stackpole, 1961), 301.

33   Sheldon to Cahalane, 17 March 1947; Sheldon to Anthony, 17 March 1947, File 5968, Box 3, DENA; Harold Anthony, "Minutes of the Wolf Committee Meeting of the Boone and Crockett Club," 23 January 1947, RG 79, Entry 7, File 715, Box 1414, NA.

     William Sheldon had been acquainted with the Muries since adolescence. President Coolidge appointed Charles Sheldon to chair an "Elk Commission" to make recommendations on management in the Jackson, Wyoming, area. Fifteen-year-old William spent the summer of 1927 in Jackson Hole as Olaus's field assistant and likely met Adolph then. They kept in touch, as a letter from Adolph dated January 17, 1947, begins "Dear Billy," expresses thanks for helping keep the Boone and Crockett Club neutral, and offers advice on Sheldon's doctoral research at Cornell on foxes; letter in A. Murie Collection, Box 2, Folder "Correspondence 1943–1973," AHC.

34   Russell to Drury, 23 January 1947, RG 79, Entry 19, Box 13, File "Mt. McKinley National Park," NA; Russell to Drury, 27 January 1947; Anthony to Russell, 28 January 1947, RG 79, Entry 7, File 715, Box 1414, NA.

35   Washburn to Bartlett, 7 March 1946, Stef. Mss., 190–8:67, DCL; Washburn to Drury, 14 November 1947; Washburn to McLean, 14 November 1947; Drury to Washburn, 24 December 1947; Washburn to Drury, 2 January 1948, RG 79, Entry 7, File 715, Box 1415, NA.

36   Washburn to Interior Sec. Krug, 2 September 1947, Bartlett Collection, Box 1: Interior—NPS, Folder 1, UAF; Browne to Grant Pearson, 8 December 1949, Stef. Mss., 190–8:69, DCL; A. Murie to Otto Geist, 28 October 1948, Geist Collection, Box 15, UAF. Notwithstanding these issues, Washburn holds great significance in the history of Alaska mountaineering, high latitude and high altitude science, and mountain cartography.

37   Adolph Murie, "The Wolves of Mount McKinley," *The Living Wilderness*, February 1945, 9–25; C. Blackburn Miller, "Shall We Protect the Killers?" *Field and Stream*, January 1946, 96–97. Miller's name appears on a Camp Fire Club membership list in 1939, in RG 79, Entry 7, File 719, Box 1415, NA.

38   Drury to Eltinge F. Warner, 28 January 1946, A. Murie Collection, Box 5, Folder "McKinley Predator Policies, 1936–1957," AHC; Newton Drury, letter to the editor, *Field and Stream*, April 1946, 7–8; Victor H. Cahalane, "Should We Cry Wolf?" *Field and Stream*, June 1946, 103, 107, 37, 104; Victor H. Cahalane, "Shall We Save the Larger Carnivores?" *The Living Wilderness*, June 1946, 22; Olaus Murie, editorial, *The Living Wilderness*, June 1946, 1; Victor H. Cahalane, "Predators and People," *National Parks Magazine*, October–December 1948, 5–12.

39   Chick Ferguson, "Arch Villains of the Wilderness," *Field and Stream,* July 1946, 38, 97–99; P.A. Parsons, "The Timber Wolf: Scourge of Game and Stock," *Outdoor Life,* July 1946, 40; Russell Annabel, "Wolf Trouble in Alaska," *Field and Stream,* February 1947, 74; Annabel, *Hunting and Fishing in Alaska,* 145–57; "From Ketchikan to Barrow," *The Alaska Sportsman,* June 1948, 30; Annabel, "Alaska's Thundering Herds," *Saturday Evening Post,* 27 December 1947, 74; Frank Dufresne, "Ghosts That Kill Game," *Outdoor Life,* April 1948, 37; Fred R. Zepp, "America's Longest War: The Battle with the Wolves," *Outdoor Life,* May 1948, 41, 118; Ben East, "Sportsmen: We Must Not Let Alaska's Game Die Out," *Outdoor Life,* May 1948, 24–25, 116–18.

40   I have not found biographic information on Callison, and cannot explain the coincidence of his crusade and his namesake, Israel Putnam. A major general in the Continental Army, Putnam gained pre-Revolutionary War renown and a place in American wolf history by crawling into a wolf den near his farm in Connecticut and killing the beast who had decimated his livestock the previous night; see Stanley P. Young, *The Wolf in North American History* (Caldwell, ID: Caxton Printers, 1946), 69–72.

41   I. P. Callison, "Wolves and Coyotes, The Major Menace to North American Big Game," *Alaska Life*, June 1946, 10.

42   Superintendent's "Monthly Report," July 1945, DENA; Cahalane to Drury, 29 March 1946, RG 79, Entry 7, File 715, Box 1414, NA; Callison to Gruening, 2 August 1948, RG 101, Box 471, ASA; Cahalane to U.S. Grant, 26 August 1948, File 5968, Box 2, DENA; I.P. Callison, *Wolf Predation in the North Country* (Seattle: By the author, Lloyd Building, 1948); Tomlinson to Callison, 13 August 1948, File 5968, Box 2, DENA.

43   Cahalane to U. S. Grant, 26 August 1948, File 5986, Box 2, DENA; Clarke to Callison, 14 March 1949, File 5986, Box 1, DENA; McLean to Browne, 23 October 1947, Stef. Mss., 190–8:68, DCL.

44   Callison to O. Murie, 2 August 1948; O. Murie to Callison, 1 October 1948; Callison to O. Murie, 8 November 1948; O. Murie to Callison, 25 July 1949, all A. Murie Collection, Box 3, Folder "Correspondence 1930–1967, Wolf Policy - Olaus Murie," AHC; *Jessen's Weekly*, "New Book Out On Wolf Predation In North Country," 24

September 1948; O. Murie, letter to editor, 17 December 1948; Callison, letter to editor, 25 March 1949; *Jessen's Weekly* had previously indicated a positive regard for Olaus with a complimentary editorial on The Wilderness Society, 30 April 1948.

45   Congress, House, Committee on Public Lands, *Statehood for Alaska*, 80th Cong., 1st sess., April 1947, 280.

46   Congress, House, *To Provide for the Protection of the Dall Sheep, Caribou, and Other Wildlife Native to the Mount McKinley National Park Area, and for other purposes*, 80th Cong., 1st sess., 1947, H.R. 2863; Senate, [same title], 80th Cong., 1st sess., 1947, S. 891; copies from File 5968, Box 3, DENA.

47   Adolph Murie, "Another Look at McKinley Park Sheep," *The Living Wilderness,* December 1946, 14–16; Fred Packard, National Parks Association, "Statement on HR 2863 and S. 891," A. Murie Collection, Box 4, Folder "Correspondence 1934–1959; Packard, Fred," AHC; Cammerer to regional director, 31 January 1947; Cahalane to Fred Packard of National Parks Assoc., 13 May 1947, File 5968, Box 3, DENA; Cahalane to Donald Hoffmeister of Soc. of Mammalogists, 17 September 1947, RG 79, Entry 7, File 715, Box 1415, NA.

     Fred Packard had worked with Adolph Murie on a Rocky Mountain National Park bighorn sheep project in 1938; Miles, *Guardians of the Parks,* 161.

48   Robert Beatty, Izaak Walton League, to Marshall McLean, 22 October 1947, A. Murie Collection, Box 4, Folder "Correspondence 1938–1960, General re: McKinley," AHC; Hoffmeister to Drury, 16 September 1947, RG 79, Entry 7, File 715, Box 1415, NA; Been to Drury, RG 79, Entry 7, Box 1405, NA; Krug to Sen. White, Rep. Welch, 22 April 1947, File 5986, Box 3, DENA; Robert Beatty of Izaak Walton League to McLean, 17 November 1947, RG 79, Entry 7, File 715, Box 1415, NA.

     In 1951, Richard Pough, then with the American Museum and the Audubon Society, claimed some influence in channeling organizational sentiment, in a letter to Adolph: "Fortunately, we have been able to keep the Boone and Crockett Club on the right track with reference to such problems as the wolves." 20 November 1951, A. Murie Collection, Box 1, Folder "Correspondence 1939–1966, Wildlife at Denali," AHC.

I hope the sheep will bless you.
—Marshall McLean

8

Sanctuary for Sheep and Wolves

Despite the scientific community's support for Adolph Murie's research and Park Service efforts to generate favorable publicity for its cause, the service still faced criticism from Alaskans, sportsmen's media, and the Camp Fire Club. The club arranged an audience with Assistant Interior Secretary C. Girard Davidson in February 1948 to continue its pressure on the Park Service. The meeting included Director Newton Drury, who felt the club members came "with blood in their eyes." The list of alleged Park Service errors was familiar to Drury, but the club members emphasized an old and unpopular management tool: the use of poison to kill wolves, rather than relying on rifles and snares. Drury adamantly opposed this suggestion. As news of this development spread among Park Service officials, Lowell Sumner commented "it marks a new low in their comprehension of the facts of life as regards conservation and biology." Secretary Davidson promised the Camp Fire Club his support in finding solutions to the problem, without agreeing to the validity of its accusations.[1]

On the same day as Drury and Davidson's meeting with Camp Fire Club representatives, Victor Cahalane made an evening dinner presentation to the club, showing Murie's popular "Wildlife at Denali" film. He despaired at the club's hostility to wolves, noting that he had shown the film to dozens of audiences previously, all of which had been enthusiastic about seeing wild wolves on film, yet that evening, club members "hissed vigorously when the wolves were shown." Their enmity toward the Park Service was equally apparent, as they vehemently rejected the service's data and management rationales. Cahalane wrote to Drury:

> For some time I have felt that it will be impossible to placate this organization. The thinking of the members is so exclusively centered on game, they have so little appreciation of the relationships of living things, and they are so determined to reject any information that does not "jibe" with preconceived ideas, that they are unable to understand our conception of national parks. It is possible that further efforts to pacify the Club will merely encourage further attacks. Certainly the wolf control program at McKinley is being regarded as a confession of past errors and will be used to the utmost against the Service.[2]

Even with the threat of legislation apparently over and indications of an increasing sheep population, the continued pressure forced Park Service officials to seek another way to mollify their critics and validate their management of McKinley Park. Drury decided to revive a previously suggested gambit: to invite an impartial observer respected by both scientists and sportsmen to survey the situation in Alaska and make management recommendations. This had been suggested by administrators two years earlier, when former director Horace Albright had been solicited for suggestions. Opposed to wolf protection, Albright approved the idea yet felt an investigative group should include men "who have not been *too closely tied* to the protection of predators." He proposed Dr. Harold Anthony, among others, and correspondence began between Anthony and the Park Service to arrange a trip to Alaska, culminating in Drury's firm invitation for the summer of 1948.[3]

Harold Anthony seemed an ideal choice. Born in 1890 in Beaverton, Oregon, he had become acquainted with Olaus Murie at Pacific College. Anthony had joined the staff at the Museum of Natural History in 1912, and since 1942 had been chairman of the Department of Mammals. His studies had carried him to distant continents, where he displayed the vigor needed by field biologists of that time. His 1928 *Field Book of North American Mammals* became a standard text. Anthony was well known to the Park Service, serving in 1948 on the Board of Parks, Historic Sites, Buildings, and Monuments. He had long opposed the predator control programs of the Biological Survey, and had previously indicated his support of the Park Service's stance on McKinley's wolves. Anthony's organization memberships indicated his interests: he

Harold Anthony.
*Courtesy of the
Department of Library
Services, American
Museum of Natural
History*

belonged to The Wilderness Society, and in the mid-1930s was president of the American Society of Mammalogists. Furthermore, Anthony enjoyed the prestige of the Boone and Crockett Club. He had been granted full membership in 1929, ensuring that his judgment of Murie's recommendations and park management would be credible to East Coast sportsmen. Funding the McKinley investigation posed a problem; the American Museum was deeply in debt at the time and could not help. The Boone and Crockett Club contributed $500 for Anthony's expenses, and he recruited a New York acquaintance, Ralph Friedman. A businessman, not a scientist, Friedman had hunted extensively and provided museum specimens for Anthony. Friedman offered to defray travel expenses for both of them, and they made plans to arrive at McKinley Park in mid-August.[4]

Marshall McLean got wind of the plan and proposed "with due modesty" that the Camp Fire Club be allowed to send a representative. Newton Drury graciously agreed to "receive any scientist" the club cared to send, and proposed they coordinate with Harold Anthony's plans. The club, though, had made clear they mistrusted biologists, and Anthony, in particular, would "not be acceptable." McLean proceeded to nominate not a scientist, but Belmore Browne, causing some consternation at Park Service headquarters. Lowell Sumner wrote a skeptical memorandum disparaging Browne's "meager understanding of wildlife," and he made two important suggestions: that Browne and the study team agree on their findings before his departure from the park, thereby inhibiting a possibly divergent public statement by the Camp Fire Club, and that Adolph Murie accompany Browne at all times, to make sure Browne saw all of the sheep present in the park. Drury solicited Anthony's reaction to Browne's presence. Anthony thought the club would likely disagree with anything the Park Service could do, yet considered Browne to be a friendly acquaintance and foresaw no personal difficulties. But in view of Browne's history with the wolf controversy, Anthony held "grave doubts that anything short of a miracle will make an impression upon him."[5]

Each man brought to this meeting in 1948 a distinct perspective and role: Ralph Friedman came to see the park, and Harold Anthony carried the burdens of expertise, divided expectations, and presumed impartiality. Their host, Frank Been, unpopular and fighting to keep his post, wanted his visitors and superiors to approve his work. And, curiously, the meeting represented a convergence of the paths of Belmore Browne and Adolph Murie, two men whose reputations were already part of park lore and who personified the opposing camps in the wolf-sheep controversy, yet who had never met. Neither had anticipated, during the preceding years of acrimony, that they would find themselves confronting one another across the space of a canvas tent in the heart of McKinley Park.

Belmore Browne flew to Fairbanks from Calgary via the Alaska Highway air route, and the trip confirmed his presumptions about the state of wildlife in the North. In Fort St. John, British Columbia, he met a mining engineer who spoke bitterly of the dwindling game herds, blaming their demise on biologists and their "equilibrium theories." In Whitehorse, Yukon Territory, Browne spoke with two men who had conducted a wolf poisoning campaign the previous winter, neither of them "believers in the balance of nature theory." He heard tales of the nearby Kluane River area cleaned of caribou by wolves, and of Indians starving due to lack of game animals. A taxi driver in Fairbanks told Browne of the previous season's caribou slaughter by hunters along the Steese Highway, blaming army men.[6] On the train ride from Fairbanks to McKinley Park, Browne noted the "moose country of the best type," and scanned with his binoculars "where moose would have been visible at long distances; no moose or caribou were seen…. An extremely fine moose head on a cabin was a mute reminder of the glory of past days." As the train pulled up the grade from Healy into the foothills of the Alaska Range, Browne remembered his earlier days in the area, before the railroad or park existed. He had returned after an absence of thirty-six years.

> I was struck with the magnificence of these Alaskan grasslands. In my long life as a sheep hunter I have never seen high grass grown mountains that can compare with the N. slopes of the Alaskan Range. I will state without hesitation, that if the white sheep was really protected by good laws and efficient warden service that the number of sheep this range could sustain would be practically limitless. The largest grass lands of the Canadian Rockies pale to insignificance by comparison. Having often seen sheep from the car windows of the C. P. R. [Canadian Pacific Railroad]…I used binoculars continuously from Healy to the Park Station without seeing an animal of any kind.[7]

Harold Anthony and Ralph Friedman had arrived the previous day and driven the park road to Camp Eielson with Adolph Murie, seeing eighty-two sheep. Upon learning of Browne's arrival, they returned to headquarters on the evening of the nineteenth.[8] That evening the men met with Superintendent Been to get acquainted and make plans for their investigation. Browne confessed to some discomfiture "for me in particular, as I, more than any one in the gathering, had been the severest critic of both Murie and the Park administration." But a gentlemanly spirit prevailed, and Murie impressed Browne by his friendliness and overall knowledge, which "convinced me that he knew the McK. Park game situation better than any of us and that he would be a straight shooter during our investigation." Browne perceived Anthony as being "open-minded," although favoring the continued presence of wolves. Friedman was an "amateur…frankly afraid of wolf control." Been struck the veteran Browne as "an energetic Park administrator rather than an experienced outdoorsman." The men agreed to drive to Camp Eielson the following day and use it as a base for exploration.[9]

Cloudy skies prevailed over the Alaska Range that month, gray stratus clouds that grudgingly cleared on only three days to reveal the soaring white peaks punctuating the southern horizon. By midmonth the tundra plants turned their autumnal shades of red and yellow, providing visual relief to the monotony of drizzling skies. August 20 dawned cold and cloudy, yet the party had reasonable visibility for sheep spotting as they drove the park road. Frank Been considered the day a triumph for Murie. Only thirteen sheep were visible with the unaided eye, yet Murie's familiarity with the sheep's haunts enabled the group to see a total of one hundred ten with their binoculars and spotting scopes. Been felt this "illustrates the shallow basis for adverse comment from inexperienced observers," who would have seen only the thirteen sheep. This fell short of the miracle Anthony had hoped for with Browne, who wrote: "Only 110 sheep counted under good visibility in a journey of 66 miles." He compared it to seeing one thousand sheep on a day's foot journey back in 1912, and thought the park should be supporting a sheep population of ten thousand, based on "a cursory glance of the summer grass slopes." Browne lamented for "the great sheep herds that inhabited this area before the wolves began their slaughter," and was shocked at the absence of caribou.[10]

The men set up camp and gathered together in a cook tent for dinner. That evening, as rain drummed against taut canvas, the conversation centered on caribou, typically the most visible large animal in the park. They were scarce that summer. Murie had heard that the main herd was north of the park and in fine shape. Browne, however, insisted their absence from their summer range in the park was due to excessive harassment by park wolves that had driven the caribou from ancestral calving grounds. Browne continued his argument until midnight, and continued talking as the men went into their sleeping tents; somehow, he and Murie shared one. Murie wrote the next day, "He cites endless episodes with game. A single episode proves what he wants to conclude. Browne talks incessantly, poor conversationalist; hard to get an exchange of thoughts on a subject."[11]

The noise of rain on the tents continued into the wee hours, but dwindled as the men fell asleep. When they arose to a silent morning, they opened their tent flaps and found to their surprise that the rain had been replaced by several inches of snow. Browne had brought a travel kit of art supplies and spent the day painting, while the others swapped yarns and played bridge. The following day, August 23, the skies cleared and the party enjoyed the view of Mt. McKinley before driving back to headquarters. They were probably pleased to be active again, for Murie remarked that the superintendent had been a "constant master of ceremonies even during lunch time."[12] The party saw its only wolf that day, along the Teklanika River. "'For gods sake, kill it,' shouted Browne. 'Wait a minute, let me see it,' exclaimed Friedman." The wolf trotted into the brush, and Been noted that it had been "the object of opposing philosophies."[13]

In order to check conditions of the winter sheep pastures in the Outer Range, the party climbed a spur of Sable Mountain the next day. Murie had picked a gentle route up grassy slopes after evaluating the physical ability of the group, but even this proved too ambitious: Friedman quit early because of a bum knee, Browne dropped his pack and stayed at a low elevation, and Anthony turned back shortly afterward. Browne did not seem to understand Murie's intent and evaluated the landscape as evidence of what he sought, writing that "The mountain was smooth, eroded and with no protecting cliffs to offer sanctuary from wolf attacks....Today there is no sheep population. Cause, predation by wolves."[14]

For the next two days, the men took walks in various places near park headquarters and the Savage River. They had been scheduled to take a flight over the sheep ranges, but mechanical problems grounded their plane. According to Murie, Browne spent his days painting rather than investigating game conditions. Browne did not mention painting in his journal, but did reflect on the effects of civilization upon the North, noting that man was responsible for much of the game decrease. Only Browne, of this group, had seen Alaska before the railroad and the towns it produced. He sadly concluded that "The vast wilderness areas of Alaska no longer exist. We are at the threshold of a new era throughout the North."[15]

Murie had accomplished his tasks, which were to help his visitors evaluate the animals and terrain, and convince Browne of his objectivity as a scientist. Frank Been took center stage on the final day of the investigation, introducing with a flourish a joint statement he wished all to sign. "It was pretty awful," according to Adolph. Debate over the message and wording occupied the afternoon, Been regarding the statement as "his baby," while Anthony insisted he couldn't sign anything before filing a report with the Boone and Crockett

Club. The three investigators were due to board the 7:15 PM train to Fairbanks. Been raced from his office to the park depot with a final draft of the statement which the men reluctantly signed, after making still more changes and convincing Been that it was not for public distribution. Murie and Anthony signed the statement because they wanted to make sure Browne also signed it— evidence should Browne return to his club with a different story. Anthony and Friedman considered the whole performance "quite sad." Frank Been, though, was pleased at the "uniformity of thought on a policy" and with the "wholesome tenor of friendliness and respect" that had overlain the ten days.[16]

The one-page statement of understanding represented compromise from both sides. The statement did not blame Park Service mismanagement for reduced sheep numbers, but noted that both natural and artificial factors were involved in fluctuating animal populations. Wolves were considered to be a "large factor" in reducing prey populations, and the agreement dictated that wolves were to be killed for the next five years, or until the sheep population reached 2,500, with authority for this residing in the secretary of the interior. Browne agreed that predator control legislation was a dangerous precedent and should no longer be supported, yet he convinced the others to insert a recommendation that the Park Service purchase telescopic sights for the ranger's rifles to improve their effectiveness in further wolf hunting. The signees urged the continued employment of a biologist to monitor park wildlife, and they recognized the value of education on public opinion: "An enlightened public is also essential in order that there will not exist unfair pressures born of ignorance."[17]

Each of the three park guests submitted lengthy reports to Park Service headquarters, providing individual perspectives. Newton Drury found Ralph Friedman's to be an "unusually keen analysis." Although a newcomer to Alaska, Friedman placed the McKinley Park situation in the larger context of the territory. He blamed the overall decrease of Alaska's game on humans, rather than wolves, and suggested adding twenty-five men to the eight wardens then responsible for the whole of Alaska. With reference to the park, Friedman accepted the concept and desirability of a natural balance existing between predators and prey in the absence of direct hunting pressures. Nevertheless, he agreed with the recommendation to kill more of McKinley's wolves, given the low sheep population, the plentiful numbers of wolves outside the park, and because "the Park Service has been given very bad publicity amongst the 'wolf-conscious' resident Alaskans and it is very desirable from a public relations standpoint that this program we have suggested be instituted." He also recommended that the Park Service widely publicize this renewed control effort.[18]

Belmore Browne's report received mixed reactions from Park Service staff. Frank Been wrote that both Browne and Anthony had "modified their original positions because of their observations here." Lowell Sumner felt the joint investigation had succeeded because Browne's report demonstrated a "noticeable improvement in the attitude of our critics." Adolph Murie, having had those nights of discussion in the tent, felt less positive: "B. Browne's wolf report was at the office today. Bad as I expected....Arguing with Browne is like taking on the Queen of Hearts." While Browne had become convinced of Murie's integrity and agreed not to promote further legislation, his report to the Camp Fire Club (which he copyrighted) ended with an unmodified flourish: "The loss in blood and treasure caused within the boundaries of Mt. McKinley Park by unchecked wolf slaughter transcends anything of a like nature in National Park history."[19]

Browne's frame of reference for the health of the park's animal populations continued to be his previous visit in 1912. He acted as if the park could be frozen in time and impervious to changes in relations between animals and humans—but then, that was the Park Service reference as well. Browne scoffed at the Park Service record in controlling wolves, declaring it should have been easy to kill fifteen wolves in the first year of that effort had competent men been assigned the task. Grant Pearson, for example, was "an excellent man," yet had been kept busy on construction projects rather than wolf hunting. If providing rangers for the task was impossible, Browne shrewdly suggested that one or two aerial hunts could quickly reduce the wolf population and achieve the desired result. Murie escaped Browne's criticism, since he "knows that the wolf is responsible and has so stated in two reports for the Parks Service." At fault, then, were the highest officials in the Park Service, who continued to deny the importance of wolf predation. In a section titled "Can Government Administered Wolf-Control Succeed?," Browne concluded it would not until "the heads of our great wild-life departments have been convinced of the costliness of their errors." Browne wrote his report to validate the almost twenty-year effort by the Camp Fire Club to force park officials to protect sheep to the detriment of wolves. As evidence of their victory, Browne pointed to the joint memorandum signed by the five-man investigative team, which implied admission by the Park Service of previous errors in management, backed by the credibility of Murie and Anthony. Although he had ostensibly conceded the legislative front, Marshall McLean informed the interior

Belmore Browne painting a diorama background for the American Museum of Natural History. The scene is looking up the Muldrow Glacier from the vicinity of McGonagall Pass on Mount McKinley's north side.
Courtesy of the Department of Library Services, American Museum of Natural History

secretary's office that the Camp Fire Club waited willingly to propose further legislation if necessary.[20]

Despite the polemics of Browne's report, the trip had been successful in giving him a better understanding of the situation, even though this did not modify the Camp Fire Club's stance. That autumn he took time to write friendly letters to the Murie brothers. Apparently swayed by his time with Adolph, Browne informed both of them that, prior to the August trip to Alaska, he had been asked by I. P. Callison to write a foreword to his *Wolf Predation in the North Country* pamphlet. Browne was pleased to inform the Muries that he had declined at the time, and was particularly glad of it in retrospect. To Olaus, Browne reported that none of his friends were pleased with Callison's attacks on Adolph. Showing a degree of recognition of his own garrulousness, he continued, "In our (or at least *my*) happy days with Adolph, we never mentioned my analysis of his report. [The 1945 booklet published by the Camp Fire Club.] I have a feeling of deep respect and even affection for that brother of yours." Adolph responded politely to Browne, but steered clear of reference to wolves. In a letter to Victor Cahalane, Adolph did not express any fondness for Browne—"he is hard as granite"—but rather disappointment at Browne's report on the park: "He certainly could have eased off a bit in view of the circumstances." Writing to Lowell Sumner, he speculated that part of Browne's unhappiness with the whole situation in the park included Browne's displeasure with "the omission of his Conquest (?) of Mount McKinley from my discussions."[21]

Belmore Browne returned to his flourishing painting career as part of a group—including Carl Rungius and Sydney Laurence—of artists that dignified the animals and landscapes of the North to critical acclaim. The National Academy of Design displayed his work almost every year, and Camp Fire Club members and Grant Pearson were among those who purchased his canvases. Browne was the only one who profited from the 1948 wolf-sheep investigation. Not only did it afford him the opportunity to return to the scene of his earlier adventures, but while there he began work that resulted in nine paintings, including one purchased by Ralph Friedman.[22]

Harold Anthony purposely did not read Browne's report until Anthony had completed his, and while he anticipated a negative commentary by Browne, he thought that Browne "would have made things darker if he had not been up there and had those long talks with Adolf [sic]." Anthony's report was certainly the one most anticipated by Park Service officials. Anthony had bitterly opposed the predator control programs of the Biological Survey in the 1930s, and had supported the Park Service's stance on McKinley's wolves. He expressed to Newton Drury his displeasure at "being maneuvered into signing that joint statement at Park Headquarters," yet, to the surprise of many, Anthony favored vigorous wolf killing in the park. He confessed that "I went North with the expectation that what I learned would confirm my belief that the wolf-sheep problem was adjusting itself satisfactorily and that all that was needed was the passage of time." He became convinced of the need to shoot wolves because of the low sheep population, but also—echoing Murie's thoughts of early 1945—because of public opinion: "I fear for the *future* of the wolf in the Park unless some concession in the way of active control is made *now*."[23]

While the sheep population was low, its recovery seemed probable; Anthony's primary concern was with preserving a wolf population in the park, against the desires of most people, and the only way to do that was to build up the sheep population immediately and staunch the torrent of criticism toward Park Service policy:

> The announced policy of several years ago, to remove fifteen wolves from the Park has not been implemented in a fashion to impress the Park critics that the Park Service really wants to control the wolves. Partly because of this I believe that the Service should now lean over backward to convince the public that active control is the standing order of the day.
>
> In my opinion, the situation with regard to the wolves in Mount McKinley National Park is a critical one, first with respect to the uncertain future of the Dall Sheep if it must accept any wolf predation at all, and second with regard to the loss of public confidence in the National Park Service as the administrator of the federal wilderness areas.... It is not a theory but a fact that an aggressive segment of the public is inveighing against the Service, the time is too short to attempt to win this fraction over, and the conservationists who oppose this force by generalizations do not gain many converts. This is the time to be realistic and it seems to me that inaugurating rigid wolf control in McKinley Park, as I have suggested, is no great concession to expediency either.[24]

With the reports of the investigative team on his desk, Newton Drury accepted its recommendation and removed any limits to the number of wolves taken and the duration of this effort. Park Service biologists Lowell Sumner and Victor Cahalane warned of the wolf becoming extirpated as a result of this loss of park sanctuary, but Drury had little choice, since Adolph Murie, the avowed expert on McKinley Park wildlife, supported further wolf killing. At the park, Frank Been reported no recent signs of predation, but "rifle bolts are being dried of oil in the hope of cutting more off the quota this winter." Murie began setting snares for wolves around the park's garbage dump, and wrote that ranger John Rumohr "had ordered ammunition and...plans to send the boys out in the park to shoot wolves. He says that the Director wants all wolves killed."[25]

The decision to aggressively hunt an unlimited number of wolves for an indefinite time seemed like sweet vindication of the Camp Fire Club's long effort. Assistant Interior Secretary Davidson informed McLean of the decision to lift the numerical limit on killed wolves and his instructions to pursue them "with all possible vigor." McLean expressed his gratification at this to Newton Drury: "I trust you will feel that we were always motivated by a very honest belief in our case, and an equally honest desire to give constructive help to the wild life of the Park." To Belmore Browne, McLean wrote, "This makes it a clear cut victory—congratulations—I hope the sheep will bless you."[26]

With the new wolf directive in McKinley Park came a change in superintendents. Frank Been had not been particularly missed during his four years of military duty. Acting Superintendent Grant Pearson capably ran the park and in October 1944 added to his personal popularity by heroically leading a mission to a crashed Army plane high in the Alaska Range, for which he received the Medal of Freedom.[27] In April 1946 Pearson received word that Been planned to leave the Army and resume his post as McKinley's superintendent. Pearson expressed his dismay to Alaska Delegate Bob Bartlett. "I can't and will not work under Been…. It looks to me Bob like the Park Service has a lemon and id [sic] trying to keep him in Alaska." Bartlett had already suggested that the Park Service appoint Pearson full superintendent, and in response to this development Bartlett again solicited assistance for Pearson. Newton Drury, however, had a legal obligation to reinstate Been because he would be a discharged veteran. Been returned to McKinley Park in January 1947, and in June Grant Pearson took an arranged transfer to Glacier Bay National Monument.[28]

Frank Been had a rocky time during the next two years. Eight of the ten rangers quit or requested transfers. His relations with Adolph Murie deteriorated, and Murie commented: "our pompous, stuffed shirt irks everyone with every contact." Reports of staff discontent and fiscal improprieties filtered upwards to Been's superiors. Unhappy with his limited leadership abilities and effect on morale, officials made plans for his transfer to Crater Lake National Park. Ironically, Been protested this to Delegate Bartlett, telling him that "The National Park Service is transferring to the States its best trained and experienced man on Alaskan affairs." Bartlett assured Been that he had immediately contacted the highest Park Service officials about this, but Been's fate had been decided; "I regret for your sake that the change will be made." Newton Drury officially informed Been shortly after Christmas 1948, calling the transfer—to assistant superintendent of a very small park—an "advancement in the Service." Been left Alaska a bitter man, convinced that Pearson had brought him down by working behind the scenes. He lasted only a short while in Oregon before abruptly leaving the Park Service. In early 1949 Grant Pearson returned triumphantly to McKinley Park and the wolf campaign.[29]

Although the Park Service had indicated that all of McKinley Park's rangers would be involved in wolf reduction, Adolph Murie controlled the effort. He was then on permanent assignment as the park biologist, a position he had held for two years.[30] Murie was not pleased to be reporting to Pearson, with his clear aversion to wolves, and the two men struggled within their working relationship. Murie wanted a superintendent with "intellectual flexibility," not one interested in "drawing a cult." Pearson wanted all personnel to be armed and ready to shoot wolves whenever and wherever encountered, while Murie wanted to choose his assistants, methods, and locales. That fall and winter Murie focused his efforts on wolves that frequented the park hotel's garbage dump, setting snares and traps and taking one female in November 1948. As had happened in 1946, the announced measures against wolves pleased Park Service critics, yet produced few dead animals. Virtually no wolf sign appeared in the park before the spring of 1949, and that summer only occasional shots rang out. As a means of reducing predators to help the sheep, wolf control was a failure. Month after month, the superintendent reported no wolves killed. The killing of a wolf in December pleased Pearson, who asked Murie whether he should preserve the pelt and skull for a museum exhibit. Murie indicated that museum specimens might well be the only wolves left in the park within a few years. In his diary, at year's end, Murie wrote, "The request for control is not synonymous with the need for control."[31]

Then again, the heart of the wolf-sheep controversy concerned the definition of the need for wolf control, and Belmore Browne, for one, was suspicious about the lack of dead wolves. Writing to Pearson in December 1949, Browne suggested that a "good Alaskan hunter and trapper" would be most effective, and wondered again why aerial shooting had not been tried. He did not accuse Murie of inadequacy, but perhaps he wondered if Murie was putting forth a sincere effort to kill wolves, or merely a convincing performance. A good scientist of his time, Murie did not confuse the fate of individual wolves with the health of their overall population. No trace of

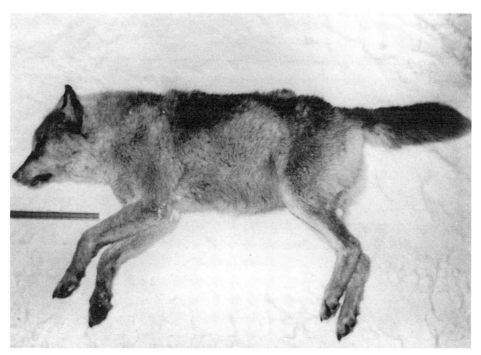

Female wolf snared as part of park control effort, December 12, 1949.
Adolph Murie Collection, temp box 13. Courtesy Alaska and Polar Regions Archives, Rasmuson Library, University of Alaska Fairbanks

remorse enters his writings from this period, be they diary entries or work memoranda; in fact, Murie found the challenge of wolf trapping to be "quite an interesting time." Was he setting snares near park headquarters because it was more convenient than running a trapline by dogsled deep into the park, or more impersonal than finding dens in the spring and waiting nearby with a rifle? It seems clear that Murie's struggle with Pearson (and hence, the rest of the park staff) for control of the wolf program was related to Murie's desire to be selective about which wolves would be sacrificed to the politics of wildlife management. The snares around headquarters were likely to attract lone wolves who lacked pack support for winter hunting, or transient packs that might wander through the Nenana River valley, thus protecting wolves well within the park, such as the East Fork pack Murie had studied during his initial research in 1939–41. An exchange of letters in early 1950 between Murie and Ben Thompson, who had helped Adolph secure his initial Park Service job in 1934, revealed Murie's awkward situation. They had not been in contact for years, and Thompson had serious doubts about the control program. He indicated a willingness to go straight to Director Drury and request revocation of the control orders if Murie concurred, and encouraged Adolph to speak off the record. Murie made clear that he was trying to be selective in the control, but could not admit doing so, since it would "lead to misunderstandings, and the cost would probably not be worth the results." Moreover, Murie admitted his emotional strain from the years of controversy. "The wolf problem has placed me in a difficult position. I have stood in the center, with one side tossing rocks my way, and the other side stretching their patience and good will in my behalf and possibly tending to lose faith in my results, at least in my judgment, which is far worse than the rocks."[32]

In any case, events outside McKinley Park helped minimize the number of wolves within its boundaries, making decisions on selectivity moot. As park wolves moved to the caribou wintering grounds to the north, they were met by lines of poison bait spread by the U.S. Fish and Wildlife Service. This widespread effort to protect caribou and reindeer populations by killing wolves was one factor that ended the wolf-sheep controversy: it clarified the value for wolves of a national park in the middle of Alaska.

Caribou and reindeer numbers had continued to decline after WW II, causing hardship and concern among interior Alaskans accustomed to their bounty. Food shipments to Alaska remained limited in 1946. Basic grocery prices had increased twenty-four percent since 1942, and in Fairbanks bakers quit making cakes and pastries, reserving available flour for bread. The University of Alaska struggled to feed increased numbers of students, many of them veterans. President Charles Bunnell reported in December 1946 that the university had stores only of milk, potatoes, and vegetables, and was awaiting a food order placed in July. The caribou hunting season that fall had again been dismal, and when a herd appeared near the Steese Highway many hunters exceeded their bag limit of two animals.[33]

The decreased caribou numbers likely resulted from a combination of factors, including their own territorial fluctuations, increased hunting pressure, the spread of roads, and availability of aircraft for access into areas not customarily hunted. Yet these latter were all signs of the progressive development desired by Alaskans. Wolves provided an easy scapegoat to explain diminished game numbers. Hunters in the Fairbanks district had poor success in 1947, taking few caribou, twelve moose, and five sheep. Despite the presence of bounty incentives, wolf populations showed no reduction.[34]

The newspaper quoted the head of the Alaska Native Service, who was responsible for the reindeer herds: "the decimation of wild game in Alaska cannot possibly have been caused by the increase in take by man, but in large measure is due to the increase in number of wolves now roving the Territory." The Fish and Wildlife Service had long employed one predator hunter who worked primarily in reindeer regions in cooperation with Native groups. The Alaska Game Commission, in response to the outcry for increased wolf control, supplemented his efforts in 1947 with two agents and an airplane to dispense poison wolf baits. The poison had been developed several years earlier by a Fish and Wildlife Service agent in southeastern Alaska and used there with success, the baits supposedly attracting only wolves and coyotes.[35] The localized poisoning effort continued through 1948. A *Jessen's Weekly* editorial urged vigorous action "if our babies of today are to be able to see caribou, mountain sheep, moose and bear anywhere outside of a zoo or a museum." A member of the Tanana Valley Sportsmen's Association blamed wolves entirely for the decrease in caribou, recommended matching federal funds for bounty moneys, and urged the elimination of all wolves from McKinley Park. The newspaper did, however, report that rangers estimated only fifteen wolves in the park.[36]

In the fall of 1948 Congress granted an appropriation of $104,000 to the Fish and Wildlife Service to fund Alaska's first large-scale federal predator operation, involving trappers, hunters, and pilots, as well as poison. After Christmas, six planes covered areas from Petersburg to Bristol Bay and to the Arctic slope, dispensing strychnine hidden in seal blubber baits and taking aerial shots. Ground agents placed cyanide cartridges—the "Humane Coyote Getter"—during the summer months. A pilot dropped poison on the rivers flowing north from the Alaska Range, including those crossed by the boundary of McKinley Park. The Alaska Game Commission reported "outstanding progress" in the mission, considering predator control to be as important in managing game herds as enforcement of hunting regulations. In areas of concentrated control efforts, the combination of tactics demonstrated that wolves could be effectively eliminated; in the Nelchina Basin area southeast of the park, for example, agents killed over two hundred wolves by the end of 1951.[37]

Most Alaskans welcomed wolf hunting by federal agents. Virtually every sportsmen's group supported the effort, as did the territorial legislature and Governor Gruening. In a letter to Clarence Rhode, Alaska director of the Fish and Wildlife Service, Gruening wrote "the matter of predation is so serious that no aspect of it should be left without action.... [T]he wolf works 365 days in the year." The governor wrote specifically about protection of the reindeer herds. They had continued to decline, which presented humanitarian and economic incentives for killing wolves. Urgent appeals went to Gruening in early 1950, citing the need for immediate dispatch of predator hunters to prevent continued reindeer slaughter.[38] Yet even the federal hunters could not wholly blame the situation along the western coast on wolves. Clarence Rhode himself witnessed hundreds of killed and crippled caribou on the Kobuk River, shot with the rifles and ammunition issued to reservists of the army's Territorial Guard, which consisted of Alaska Natives. A predator agent stationed at Kotzebue reported further inexplicable game killing by Natives: "it looks to be something that I never witnessed before on such a wholesale slaughter.... If I had a movie camera, I could have taken pictures of the damndest thing you ever heard of."[39] In discussing the question of declining caribou herds across Alaska, Rhode did not hesitate to assign blame also to white hunters with better rifles and aircraft access, rather than solely blaming wolf predation—a view shared by many biologists.[40] Questioning the hunting practices of Alaska Natives or the effects of larger numbers of sport hunters was politically volatile, but hardly anyone questioned wolf hunting. Harold Anthony recognized this, in acknowledging the challenge faced by the Park Service in holding onto its wolf population: "The recently announced program for an active campaign against the predators of Alaska is what the community wants, and there will be no mercy shown to wolves anywhere if Alaskans have their way."[41]

Despite this territorial effort to reduce wolves, the federal program did not attempt to extirpate wolves, and it is worth noting that in their best years federal agents took barely half the annual take by resident bounty hunters. The annual average from 1949–57 of slightly over two hundred wolves hardly put a dent in Alaska's total population (see figure, next page). Predator control by the Fish and Wildlife Service remained linked to management of specific game herds, and effects remained localized. When hunters concentrated their efforts, the results could be devastating. In a two-month mission in the spring of 1952, dubbed "Operation Umiat," predator agents flying north of the Brooks Range destroyed 259 wolves. Pilots and gunners covered twenty-five thousand square miles, firing Winchester repeating shotguns with specially-loaded twelve-gauge shells carrying forty-one pieces of #4 shot rather than the standard twenty-eight. Afterwards, the area covered by the Western Arctic caribou herd was "practically devoid of wolves." In the Nelchina basin, the caribou herd

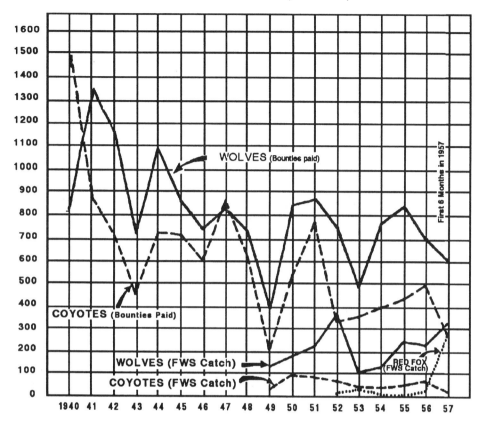

Recorded predator species taken in Alaska, 1940 to 1957.
Alaska Game Commission, 1957

increased from an estimated four thousand in 1948 to near thirteen thousand by 1954, allowing the continuation of a sport hunting season on this caribou herd, the closest to Anchorage. Alaskans, for the most part, heartily approved these results, especially when the federal government paid the price. To achieve even more wolf kills, the territorial legislature approved an appropriation of twenty-five thousand dollars in 1953 for cooperative efforts between the Fish and Wildlife Service and the Alaska Game Commission. Similar predator control projects continued through the 1950s, and the state of Alaska assumed responsibility after 1959. Federal and state control of wolves attracted little criticism until the 1960s, and most of that originated from other states. One of the gunners, Ray Tremblay, wrote that "Preservationists were a relatively small, elite group and any opposition from that quarter had little effect."[42]

Sheer economics dictated the dominance of the sportsmen's views: the National Park Service estimated that sport hunting and fishing revenues in Alaska topped twelve million dollars in 1951–53, while wildlife tourism returned only one and a half million. Alaskans tended to agree with and support the verdict of the Alaska Game Commission: "Thus wolves can destroy caribou and wolf control restore them."[43]

At McKinley Park, the wolf-sheep controversy faded away in quiet fashion. Adolph Murie patrolled the north boundary for evidence of poison baits, but never found dead wolves attributable to them, although he suspected that many of the park's wolves were being killed outside the park. Wolves continued to be scarce in the park, yet Park Service officials agreed that control efforts were desirable "for the benefit of relations between the Service and critical organizations on the outside." Most of the eleven wolves taken in the park between 1949–52 were snared at the garbage dump near the park hotel during the winter; Murie wondered if the availability of garbage near settlements there and elsewhere helped maintain wolf populations through the lean winter months. Grant Pearson kept up the pressure to destroy wolves, since as superintendent he was accountable to his superiors in Washington, D.C. He continued to scoff at suggestions that the park was a place to exhibit the balance of nature. Adolph reported that he was "fed up with the Pearson administration here, which is violently despicable." Since affairs at the park seemed to lack the crisis atmosphere of earlier years, in late 1950 Park Service administrators transferred Murie back to Jackson Hole. He had agreed to a plan where he would provide research assistance to western parks, especially regarding the southern Yellowstone elk herd, while still spending summers at McKinley Park.[44]

Although they thought their battle won, the Camp Fire Club activists maintained pressure on the Park Service to see that wolves remained in check. Marshall McLean was disturbed that "the campaign against the predators does not show more heavy results." Newton Drury continued to supply McLean with wildlife reports from the park, and happily, because the sheep population continued to increase. While this confirmed McLean's cause, he continued to caution Drury to "see that the predator situation is kept under a real control." Drury resigned in the spring of 1951, for reasons unrelated to the wolf-sheep controversy, and McLean graciously offered a letter of regret at the news, although even then he couldn't avoid the subject of wolves. In a postscript, he asked: "Before pulling up your stakes will you be good enough to see that

The Crislers obtained their wolf footage as well as new friends, who provided further evidence of changing times for wolves. Ginny Hill Wood, her husband "Woody" Wood, and Celia Hunter had homesteaded land just beyond the park boundary near Kantishna, where they opened a rustic wilderness lodge, Camp Denali, in 1952. The Park Service welcomed their presence, and the Crislers used the camp between filming trips in the park. The owners of Camp Denali sought to attract the type of tourist who cared little for luxuries, but wished close access to wilderness and wildlife. The possibility of seeing wolves became part of the early sales pitch, demonstrating to the Park Service that wolves had an increasing value in helping attract tourists.[50]

All the factors were headed in the right direction: a reduced wolf population, a rebounding sheep population, imminent film publicity for the park's wolves, and burgeoning recognition by appreciative tourists that McKinley Park was the best place to see wolves. In March 1954, Director Wirth issued a memorandum changing the temporary ban on wolf killing to a permanent one. The times had changed; Wirth wrote:

> The few wolves present will be exposed to control when they wander outside the park. Protection within the park, in our opinion, is amply justified. Therefore, inform…Superintendent Pearson that the control in the park is to be suspended immediately and until change in the relationship of the wolf and its prey species makes resumption of control advisable.[51]

Unlike previous attempts to provide protection for wolves, little public outcry ensued. The Camp Fire Club did not again mobilize against the Park Service. The bounty on wolves had risen to fifty dollars in 1950, keeping their pursuit somewhat lucrative, and the Fish and Wildlife Service control efforts provided evidence that the federal government finally had come to its senses in providing help for Alaska's game herds. Opposition by Alaskans to wolf protection had little subsequent effect on park policy.

Thus came to an end the purposeful killing of wolves by park personnel in Mount McKinley National Park. From 1930 to 1953, at least seventy-six wolves had been taken, a number far smaller than had been anticipated by advocates of control efforts. Twenty years had passed since Horace Albright wrote a wildlife policy advocating protection for all native species within national parks and Arno Cammerer had halted predator control efforts. The situation in Alaska, where the Park Service felt compelled to continue killing wolves, was unique among national parks, and resulted in large part from a vigorous public opinion against protection of wolves by a federal agency. Lowell Sumner, writing in 1949, identified a potential role of the park for wolves:

> The time may come quite soon when wolves will be exterminated in much of Alaska, not because they are doing damage to livestock but through scare publicity based on ignorance and ancient tradition and designed to secure increased appropriations for pest control organizations....When that time comes Mount McKinley National Park will have to be a sanctuary for wolves just as the other parks now are sanctuaries for buffalo, bighorn, grizzlies, wolverines and trumpeter swans in the States.[52]

Sanctuary had become reality, though the wolves could hardly be expected to know that. They went on doing what wolves do, eating and breeding and raising their pups, roaming the wilderness north of the Alaska Range under the soft twilight of summer nights and the brilliant aurora displays of winter. McKinley Park would gain renown for being one of the few places in the world where researchers could study wolf ecology in a setting very nearly approaching Joseph Grinnell's ideal of an undisturbed natural laboratory. The Park Service managed to keep both wolves and sheep in McKinley Park by adhering to its principles, while demonstrating flexibility in the face of widespread criticism. Wolves have not been exterminated in Alaska, though in 1949 Sumner had little reason to think their fate would be different from that of wolves in the western states. Although wolves can be found across Alaska, McKinley Park provides visitors the best opportunity to see what, until recently, they could see nowhere else in the public lands of the United States: a treeless landscape in which wolves, rather than humans, are the active predator.

Notes

1   Drury to S. T. Dana, 19 February 1948; Drury to Davidson, 25 February 1948, RG 79, Entry 7, File 715, Box 1415, NA; Camp Fire Club memo of meeting, 19 February 1948, Stef. Mss., 190–8:77, DCL; Sumner marginal note on Drury to McLean, 17 March 1948, File 5986, Box 2, DENA.

2   Cahalane to Drury, 24 February 1948, A. Murie Collection, Box 1, Folder "Research File 1939–1948, Wolf & Misc.," AHC.

3   Albright to Hillory Tolson, 14 May 1946, RG 79, Entry 7, File 715, Box 1414, NA; Drury to Anthony, 5 May 1947, File 5968, Box 3, DENA.

4   "Comment and News," *Journal of Mammalogy* 8 (August 1927): 267; Harold Anthony, *Field Book of North American Mammals* (New York: G.P. Putnam's Sons, 1928); American Museum of Natural History *Annual Report* (1948). The Boone and Crockett Club's historian, James Trefethen, wrote that the club "dispatched" Anthony to Alaska, ignoring the Park Service involvement, in *Crusade for Wildlife: Highlights in Conservation Progress* (Harrisburg, PA: Stackpole, 1961), 302.

5   McLean to Drury, 26 March 1948; Drury to McLean, 5 April 1948; McLean to Drury, 14 June 1948; Sumner to regional director, 29 June 1948; Drury to Anthony, 22 June 1948; Anthony to Drury, 28 June 1948, all RG 79, Entry 7, File 715, Box 1415, NA; Cahalane to Drury, 24 February 1948, A. Murie Collection, Box 1, Folder "Research File 1939–1948, Wolf & Misc.," AHC.

6   The *Fairbanks Daily News-Miner* called the scene "one of the most degrading examples of human debauchery...a shameful spectacle dominated by the lowest instincts of man, the gory lust to kill, that has no place in civilization." From "Caribou Extermination," 30 October 1947.

7   These are taken from the diary Browne kept of this trip, 17–19 August 1948, Stef. Mss., 190–8:70, DCL.

8   From Adolph Murie's personal diary, "Notes General, 8/14/48 – 12/17/48," A. Murie Collection, Box "Personal Diary," UAF. The following account draws from both men's diaries, as well as Frank Been's Superintendent's "Monthly Report," August 1948, DENA.

9   Browne diary, likely written in retrospect on 27 August 1948.

10   Superintendent's "Monthly Report," August 1948, DENA; Browne diary, 21 August 1948.

11   Browne diary, apparently 22 or 23 August 1948; A. Murie diary, 21 August 1948.

12   A. Murie diary, 22–23 August 1948. The "master of ceremonies" from a different journal, written several days later: A. Murie Collection, Box "Field notes on a variety of species," Folder "Notes on Alaskan vegetation, 1940–1965," UAF.

13   Superintendent's "Monthly Report," August 1948, DENA.

14   A. Murie diary, 24 August 1948; Browne diary, 24 August 1948.

15   A. Murie diary, 25–26 August 1948; Browne diary, 24 or 25 August, 1948. In a memorandum, Been wrote, "An airplane flight to the end of the Muldrow Glacier was made with Dr. Anthony's son, Gilbert, on one of the early days of the investigation." Neither Murie nor Browne included this in their diaries. Been to regional director, 31 August 1948, "Wildlife Reports 1930–50", Box 2, File 5968, DENA.

16   A. Murie diary, 26–27 August 1948; Been to regional director, 31 August 1948, RG 79, Entry 7, File 715, Box 1414, NA. Cahalane agreed with Murie, noting that "the

formulation of any statement was a mistake," in Cahalane to A. Murie, 28 October 1948, A. Murie Collection, Box 3, Folder "Correspondence 1938 – 1954, Cahalane," AHC.

17   "Memorandum on meeting held August 26, 1948, to discuss wolf-sheep relationships," RG 79, Entry 7, File 715, Box 1415, NA. Marginalia by Murie on the copy of this in A. Murie Collection, Box 1, Folder "Research File 1940 – 1957, Wolf Meeting 1948," AHC. A duplicate —sans marginalia— of this copy at the American Heritage Center is found in the National Archives, as well as an earlier draft including this sentence: "Although a national park is sanctuary for all forms of wildlife, including predators, it was considered advisable to recognize the adverse public attitude toward protecting wolves." In RG 79, Entry 7, File 715, Box 1415, NA.

18   Drury to Asst. Interior Sec. Warne, 6 January 1949, RG 79, Entry 7, File 715, Box 1415, NA; Ralph Friedman, "Memorandum for the Interior Department on the Problems of Predation in the Mount McKinley National Park, and Related Wild Life Management Problems in Alaska," copy from D-161, File: Denali, DTC.

19   Been to regional director, 31 August 1948, File 5968, Box 2, DENA; Sumner to regional director, 19 January 1949, File 5968, Box 1, DENA; A. Murie diary, 3 January 1949, A. Murie Collection, Box "Field Notes on Wolves," UAF; Browne, "Report to the Committee of Conservation of Forests and Wild Life of the Campfire Club of America—Subject: Alaskan Game Conditions; Predation and Control of Predators in Mt. McKinley Park, Alaska, August, 1948," RG 79, Entry 7, File 715, Box 1415, NA.

20   Browne, "Report"; McLean to Davidson, 22 November 1948, File 5968, Box 3, DENA.

21   Browne to O. Murie, 7 November 1948, A. Murie Collection, Box 4, Folder "Correspondence 1938 – 1960; General re: McKinley," AHC; Browne to A. Murie, 20 December 1948, A. Murie Collection, Box 2, Folder "Correspondence 1939 – 1949, Wolves-McKinley," AHC; A. Murie to Browne, 19 January 1949, Box 2, Folder "Correspondence 1939 – 1949, Wolves-McKinley," AHC; A. Murie to Cahalane, 10 January 49, A. Murie Collection, Box 2, Folder "Correspondence 1936–1967," AHC; A. Murie to Sumner, 2 March 1949, A. Murie Collection, Box 5, Folder "McKinley Predator Policies, 1936–1957," AHC.

22   Kesler E. Woodward, art professor at the University of Alaska Fairbanks, personal communication, 18 January 1996, and Woodward's "Paintbrush on the Heights: The Alaska and British Columbia Sketchbooks of Belmore Browne in the Stefansson Collection, Dartmouth College" (unpublished manuscript).

23   Anthony to Drury, 29 September, 9 December 1948, RG 79, Entry 7, File 715, Box 1415, NA; Albert Day, USF&WS, to Asst. Interior Sec. Warne, 24 January 1949, File 5968, Box 1, DENA.

24   Harold E. Anthony, "Report on the Status of the Wolf in Mt. McKinley National Park in 1948," copy from D-159, File: Denali, DTC.

25   Drury to regional director, 14 January 1949; Sumner to regional director, 19 January 1949; Been to regional director, 4 November 1948, all File 5986, Box 2, DENA; Tomlinson to Drury, 31 January 1949, RG 79, Entry 7, File 715, Box 1415, NA; A.

Murie diary, 16 January 1949, A. Murie Collection, Box "Field Notes on Wolves," UAF.

26 Davidson to McLean, 31 December 1948, Stef. Mss., 190 – 8:68, DCL; McLean to Davidson, 5 January 1949; McLean to Drury, 5 January 1949, RG 79, Entry 7, File 715, Box 1415, NA; marginal note from McLean to Browne on copy of Davidson's letter.

27 Grant H. Pearson, *My Life of High Adventure* (Englewood Cliffs, NJ: Prentice-Hall, 1962), 190–99.

28 Pearson to Bartlett, 9 April 1946; Bartlett to Tomlinson, 14 February 1946; Drury to Bartlett, 13 March 1946, Bartlett Collection, Interior—NPS, Box 1, Folder 1, UAF; Superintendent's "Monthly Report," June 1947, DENA.

29 Pearson, *My Life*, 212; A. Murie to Cahalane, 10 January 1949, A. Murie Collection, Box 2, Folder "Correspondence 1936 – 1967," AHC; Louise Murie MacLeod interview; Tolson to Rep. Gearhart, 13 August 1948, RG 79, Entry 19, Box 18, File "Personnel - N.P.S.," Records of Newton B. Drury, 1940–51, NA; Been to Bartlett, 1 June 1948; Bartlett to Been, 10 June 1948, Bartlett Collection, Interior: NPS, Box 1, Folder 1, UAF; Drury to Tomlinson, 23 December 1948; Drury to Been 28 December 1948, RG 79, Entry 19, Box 13, File "Mt. McKinley National Park," Records of Newton B. Drury, 1940–51, NA; A. Murie diary, 13 October 1948, A. Murie Collection, Box "Personal Diary," Folder "Notes General 8/14/48–12/17/48," UAF.

30 Murie's 1945 report had recommended a park biologist position to provide consistent year-round monitoring of the wildlife. He was the obvious choice, but he had been on the Fish and Wildlife Service payroll since 1943, and Adolph worried about family housing and schooling for his children at McKinley Park. Cahalane and Drury obtained his release from the F & WS, and Drury personally instructed Grant Pearson to provide acceptable housing for the Murie family. A. Murie to Cahalane, 7 September 1946, A. Murie Collection, Box 3, Folder "Correspondence 1938–1954, Cahalane," AHC; Cahalane to A. Murie, 14 November 1946, A. Murie Collection Box 1, Folder "Correspondence 1934 – 1966, letters re: job transfers," AHC.

31 Louise Murie MacLeod interview; A. Murie, 26 August [no year given, but between '49–'50], A. Murie Collection, Box "Field Notes on Wolves," UAF; A. Murie, "Bimonthly Reports on the Wolf, 1949", DENA. A. Murie diary, 5 December 1949, 30 December 1949, A. Murie Collection, Box "Field Notes on Wolves," UAF.

32 Browne to Pearson, 8 December 1949, Stef. Mss., 190 – 8:69, DCL; A. Murie to Cahalane, 10 January 1949, A. Murie Collection, Box 2, Folder "Correspondence 1936–1967," AHC; A. Murie to Cahalane, 2 March 1949, A. Murie Collection, Box 5, Folder "McKinley Predator Policies, 1936–1957," AHC; Thompson to A. Murie, 17 February 1950, A. Murie to Thompson, 30 March 1950, A. Murie Collection, Box 12, Folder "Wolf 1950," UAF.

33 Fairbanks *Jessen's Weekly*, "Food Dealers Present Local Price Handicaps In Reply To Hilscher," 3 January 1947; "University Struggles," 6 December 1946; "Few Caribou Taken By Game Hunters; Moose Season Opens," 30 August 1946; "Caribou Migration Leads To Slaughter By Highway Hunters," 27 September 1946.

34   *Jessen's Weekly*, "Game is Scarce, Hunters Report," 12 September 1947; "Outdoor Alaska," 5 March 1948.

35   *Jessen's Weekly*, "J. Sidney Rood Takes Up Cudgel To Further Muskoxen Experiments," 3 January 1947; "Game Commission Plans To Destroy Wolves With Poison," 7 March 1947; "Experiments Start in Poisoning Wolves and Also Coyotes," 3 July 1947; "From Ketchikan to Barrow," *The Alaska Sportsman*, June 1947, 24; "From Ketchikan to Barrow," *The Alaska Sportsman*, April 1946, 26.

36   *Jessen's Weekly*, "Later Than We Think," 23 January 1948; "Reed Urges Wolf Elimination Plus Caribou Protection," 13 February 1948; "McKinley Park Tourist Season Officially Opens," 21 May 1948.

37   "Federal Hunters Control Predatory Animals in Alaska," press release from USF & WS, 5 October 1948, RG 126, Entry 1, File 9–1–33, Box 304, NA; *Jessens's Weekly*, "Wildlife Service Predator Control Supervisor Here," 12 November 1948; "Wolf Poisoning Program Under Way," 31 December 1948; "Winter Wolf Control Program Ends April 1," 15 April 1948; AGC *Annual Reports*, 1 July 1948–30 June 1950, 3; Bob L. Burkholder, "Movements and Behavior of a Wolf Pack in Alaska," *Journal of Wildlife Management* 23 (January 1959): 1.

Reports emerged in Alaska of the use of Compound 1080, a new poison developed by the U.S. Army, which was long-lasting and resulted in excessive collateral damage to non-targeted species. Its use by the F & WS was widespread in the western states and Canada. Fairbanksan Harold Herning—one of the park employees Murie did not want involved in wolf control—wrote to Harold Anthony and the Boone and Crockett Club in 1949 protesting the aerial dispersal of 1080. According to the assistant director of the F & WS, 1080 was not used in Alaska. Herning to Anthony, 7 June 1949, Richard Borden to Anthony, 30 June 1949, A. Murie Collection, Box 5, Folder "Conservation Policies Mt. McKinley 1939–1952," AHC. See too Thomas R. Dunlap, "American Wildlife Policy and Environmental Ideology: Poisoning Coyotes, 1939–1972," *Pacific Historical Review* 55 (August 1986): 345–69.

38   AGC *Annual Report*, 1 July 1950 – 30 June 1951, 22; Gruening to Rhode, 11 March 1950, RG 101, Box 470, ASA. This same Box 470 contains whole series of telegrams to Gruening from various people in northwest Alaska about the wolf-reindeer situation.

39   Rhode to Gruening, 10 May 1949, RG 101, Box 471, ASA; Kelly to Rhode, 2 March 1950, RG 101, Box 470, ASA; *Jessen's Weekly*, "Caribou Herds Found Depleted," 20 May 1949; "From Ketchikan to Barrow," *The Alaska Sportsman*, September 1949, 22.

40   See A. W. F. Banfield, "The Present Status of North American Caribou," in *Transactions of the 14th Annual North American Wildlife Conference* (Washington, D.C.: Wildlife Management Institute, 1949): 477–89; see A. Starker Leopold and F. Fraser Darling, *Wildlife in Alaska: An Ecological Reconnaissance* (New York: The Conservation Foundation and Ronald Press Co., 1953) for various speculations on Alaska's game demise.

41   Anthony, "Report on the Status of the Wolf in Mt. McKinley National Park in 1948," copy from D-159, File: Denali, DTC.

42 AGC, *Annual Report,* 1 July 1951–30 June 1952, 15; AGC *Annual Report,* 1 July 1953–30 June 1954, 15; Ray Tremblay, *Trails of an Alaska Game Warden* (Anchorage: Alaska Northwest Publishing, 1985), 99, 101. Jay Hammond, one of the gunners, was elected Alaska's governor in 1974 and 1978.

43 Department of the Interior, *A Recreation Program for Alaska*, vol. 2 (Washington, D.C.: GPO, 1955): 29; AGC *Annual Report,* 1 July 1952 – 30 July 1953, 16.

44 A. Murie diary, 19 March 1949, A. Murie Collection, Box "Field Notes on Wolves," UAF; Herbert Maier to Drury, 28 December 1949, File 5968, Box 1, DENA; Francis J. Singer, *Status and History of Caribou and Wolves in Denali National Park*, Anchorage: National Park Service, 1985), 50; A. Murie diary, 30 December 1949; 9 July 1951, A. Murie Collection, UAF; A. Murie to Cahalane, 12 September 1951, A. Murie Collection, Box 3, Folder "Correspondence 1938 – 1954, Cahalane," AHC; regional director to superintendent, Grand Teton N. P., 2 November 1951, A. Murie Collection, Box 2, Folder "Correspondence 1951 – 1957," AHC.

45 McLean to Demaray, 5 August 1949; McLean to Drury, 7 December 1950, 9 February 1951; McLean to Lee, 21 January 1952, File 5968, Box 1, DENA; obituary, *New York Times*, 7 April 1952. On Drury's resignation, see Richard West Sellars, *Preserving Nature in the National Parks: A History* (New Haven: Yale University Press), 178.

46 A. Murie to Ben Thompson, 22 February 1950, Box 12, Folder "Wolf 1950," A. Murie Collection, UAF.

47 "From Ketchikan to Barrow," *The Alaska Sportsman*, April 1951, 30; A. Murie, "Summary Report on the 1951 Dall Sheep Count in Mount McKinley National Park"; Lowell Sumner, "The 1952 Mount McKinley Sheep Survey"; A. Murie, "Field Studies in Mount McKinley National Park - 1953," File 5968, Box 1, DENA.

48 A. Murie to Wanda Elvin, Walt Disney Productions, 19 December 1945, A. Murie Collection, Box 2, Folder "Correspondence 1943 – 1973," AHC; Bob Thomas, *Walt Disney: An American Original* (New York: Simon and Schuster, 1976), 206–8; Richard Schickel, *The Disney Version: The Life, Times, Art and Commerce of Walt Disney* (New York: Simon and Schuster, 1968), 285–92; "From Ketchikan to Barrow," *The Alaska Sportsman*, June 1952, 36.

49 Lowell Sumner, "The 1952 Mount McKinley Sheep Survey"; Pearson to regional director, 14 January 1953; Wirth to regional director, 24 February 1953, File 5968, Box 1, DENA.

50 Ginny Hill Wood, "Wilderness Camp," *The Alaska Sportsman,* November 1953, 20–24; Celia Hunter, pers. comm., 14 July 1994.

51 Wirth to regional director, 25 March 1954, A. Murie Collection, Box 5, Folder "Wolf Control McKinley N. P., 1944–1972," AHC.

52 Sumner to regional director, 19 January 1949, File 5968, Box 1, DENA.

To change wolf-hatred to a more
generous attitude...
—*Adolph Murie*

9

Evaluation and
Consequence

As a branch of government, the National Park Service has the difficult task of retaining independent authority to manage its affairs, while also responding to the demands of a public constituency. Conflict erupts when these diverge, and wildlife management has often been a contested issue within park management programs. To its credit, the Park Service's treatment of predators preceded public mandates. Its distance from the mainstream of public opinion is evident from the degree of criticism it received during the wolf-sheep controversy. Virtually no one outside of the biologists' associations and a few preservationist groups agreed with the service's stance. Furthermore, within its own institutional habitat—populated by competing organizations—the service had to contend for resources with the U.S. Forest Service and the U.S. Fish and Wildlife Service, which offered greater popular appeal to westerners and Alaskans. A comment written in 1945 by a Fish and Wildlife Service predator control specialist typified this difference:

> [T]he Park Service finds itself in the inescapable and often uncomfortable position of a protagonist for the advanced ideas of a very small percentage of the population—a crusader, if you please, for the ultimate in a scientifically impregnable wilderness philosophy. Whether or not this is a proper function of a government agency is a question open to debate...[1]

The Park Service sustained its ideals because, despite internal differences, key administrators in Washington, D.C., believed that predators had a place in parks. In the 1930s, Assistant Director Harold Bryant convinced directors Arno Cammerer and Arthur Demaray of the ecological and philosophical value of predator inclusion. Bryant's role as lead wolf advocate was then taken by Victor Cahalane, who became chief of the Wildlife Division in 1939 and served as chief biologist from 1944–55. The wolf issue certainly complemented Newton Drury's preservationist leanings. The directors received support from the Interior Department secretaries during the affair—Harold Ickes, Julius Krug, and Oscar Chapman—but their support likely had less to do with positive regard for wolves than with desires to avoid any rifts that could be exploited by hostile congressmen.

Nevertheless, substantial disagreement persisted within the organization over the place of predators in parks. Had Horace Albright remained director past 1933, predator protection would have likely been delayed beyond Cammerer's 1934 instructions to halt control efforts. Park superintendents varied in their support for changing views on wildlife management. Adolph Murie often commented in his diary on the difficulties of promoting positive attitudes toward an ideal that included predators. In a report written well after the wolf-sheep controversy, Murie warned against the Park Service taking too much credit for success in maintaining wolves, since they had survived in spite of a recent antiwolf superintendent at McKinley Park.[2] This could have been none other than Grant Pearson, who was never convinced of the desirability of wolves in the park. Despite its minority stance, the Park Service became the first public agency in the United States, and perhaps the world, to change tracks and offer protection to wolves. However, to laud the service for halting predator control in the 1930s, as other authors have done, ignores the subsequent twenty years of wolf killing in McKinley Park. While the Park Service apparently made decisions based on science, the record shows a willingness to eliminate a few wolves in order to reduce criticism of park policies. While it was not obvious at the time, this tactic would become essential in helping gain local acceptance of wolves in other parts of the country; a few wolves killed for agreed-upon reasons is the price demanded for the lives of others.[3]

In many respects, the resolution of the wolf-sheep controversy reflected not a triumph of fact over fable, or reason over irrationality, but a changing of generations. The activists of the Camp Fire Club functioned within lingering nineteenth-century concepts of relations among animals, and of human relations to those animals. These men were products of a time when the actions of the industrial complex produced widespread changes across the continent, when trains allowed the transport of game and fowl to urban markets, and when the science of ballistics yielded new weapons that enhanced the killing power of hunters at the expense of older skills such as close stalking and deception. The passenger pigeons were gone, the bison barely saved, and deer populations reached all-time lows. Sportsmen reacted to these developments by finding reasons to establish game refuges, codify hunting regulations that favored recreation over consumption, and justify these with social rationales. They cared deeply that game animals survived and saw no contradiction between this affection and the pleasures derived from hunting. To them, wolves were another threat to be countered by human actions, and parks were refuges for the threatened. William Greeley, William Beach, Marshall McLean, and Belmore Browne, all sportsmen of that ilk, helped create McKinley Park and felt a sense of ownership toward it. They took a personal interest in the campaign for the refuge, doggedly confronting a succession of Park Service administrators, equating the temporary decline of the Dall sheep to the slaughter of the buffalo herds and unrestricted felling of the nation's forests, even though the comparison was flawed.[4] The lack of support for the Camp Fire Club by similar national organizations, such as the Izaak Walton League and the Boone and Crockett Club, indicated that the fervor of the Camp Fire Club leaders was more personal than persuasive. Although sincerely motivated, their concept of conservation remained fixed in a simplistic fashion, unalloyed by the new research on predators and prey. Olaus Murie recognized this difference, writing favorably to Belmore Browne of the "earnest young fellows" hard at work bringing new information to bear on old problems.[5] They were old men fighting an old battle, but as they entered their final years of life they had the satisfaction of having achieved their victory, as after 1948 the Park Service continued to kill wolves on behalf of the sheep. The controversy ended as sheep populations rebounded, but it also ended because the men died and no one took their place: McLean passed on in 1952, Browne in 1954, Beach and Greeley in 1955.

Generational differences appeared in the Park Service as well. Horace Albright, Harry Liek, and Grant Pearson represented the old guard, while George Wright, Adolph Murie, and Victor Cahalane the new, men who broadened the scope of wildife preservation in parks. When Harold Bryant made his marginal notation that the "N. P. S. is the only bureau that can," he meant that within the Wildlife Division were men with the idealism and scientific background to overthrow attitudes based on ignorance and fear. They represented new voices in the Park Service and were able to modulate their own opinions toward predators with the mental flexibility associated with youth. George Wright himself made the comparison as he referred to predator opponents as the products of a different era, when "one spoke of campaigning against the carnivores as though they were something devilish, just as one did of Huns in the World War and with as little reason." As the editor of the *Journal of Wildlife Management* wrote to Adolph Murie, "People in this field are writing for the next generation, I guess." Recent research indicates that value changes toward the environment are associated with generational changes, and the wolf-sheep controversy fits into this pattern.[6]

The National Park Service walked a fine line during those years, as it received criticism from game advocates for being overprotective of predators and from biologists for not doing enough to protect them. Invoking the authority of science was a preferred way to respond to external critics, as doing so buttressed the service's stance without impugning the intelligence or motivation of critics. Harold Byrant's views on park management came out of his background in and affiliation with science, against Horace Albright's concerns about making the parks a public success by promoting visitation. Arno Cammerer answered the furor over predator protection by insisting that research precede decisions, thus giving Adolph Murie his most important assignments. Murie's wolf research provided justification for both sides of the argument. He couched his 1945 recommendation to resume wolf control in the rhetoric of research, allowing the Park Service to accept this policy with a justification that preserved the service's integrity, rather than appearing reactive to public pressure. The pattern continued with the invitation to Harold Anthony in 1948, as the Park Service could demonstrate its adherence to the recommendations of an esteemed biologist rather than admitting that keeping critics appeased was most easily done by continuing wolf control policies. The argument was less over whose scientists were correct than one over values and opinions.

Yet the situation involved important scientific concepts, and underlying the details was the notion of the balance of nature. Preserving all fauna supported the centuries-old theological idea of "nature's economy," that all animals played a role in God's creation. Preservation also agreed with the theories of the early ecologists, from the notions of "communities of interest" between predator and prey through the work of Joseph Grinnell. He urged preservation in parks to provide biologists with examples of natural systems, in comparison to areas affected by human activities. As noted earlier, and by other scholars, Grinnell's students played important roles in promulgating these ideas within the National Park Service. The wildlife recommendations of George Wright, Joseph Dixon, and Ben Thompson, recorded in their Fauna Series Nos. 1, 2, and 3, sound remarkably familiar to the modern reader, as their emphasis on preservation, minimal human intervention, and inclusion of predators became the models for park management. Interestingly, Grinnell's legacy extends through the wolf-sheep controversy clear to today's arguments over wolves, as illustrated in the chart on the next page.

Historians of the biological sciences differ on the extent to which the balance of nature concept affected the development of ecological theory,[7] but the concept certainly mattered in the evolution of wildlife management in the national parks. Park Service biologists recognized that a presumptive balance of nature did not preclude changes in animal populations, but they posited an achievable long-term equilibrium. As Victor Cahalane stated, "'Nature's balance,' that much-derided term, is never static, but always in motion on its own fulcrum." The search for empirically demonstrated examples of equilibria appeared in much of Adolph Murie's research. Trying to manage national parks on the basis of an abstract goal far different from the models provided by European game parks provided seemingly intractable challenges: How to reduce interventions and manage for process, not product? How to modify visitor expectations and educate them that changes were inevitable and desirable? How to modify theory and practice to be able to adjust to changing definitions of "natural," the most obvious example being attitudes toward wildfires? These were all complicated by the service's assumption that one of its missions was to preserve primitive parks as they were at the time of Euroamerican contact, a goal stated in the 1930s and affirmed in the 1960s, with the other often contradictory mission of creating access for visitors.[8]

The situation in Isle Royale National Park confirmed for the Park Service the direction it established in McKinley Park. In the 1930s Adolph Murie recognized the need for fewer moose there; ten years later, without intervention, wolves crossed winter ice to the island and gave the Park Service another site in which wolves and prey coexisted. Isle Royale was an even better place to watch for the intricate balance of nature, without the artificial boundary lines of other parks and with fewer external influences. While for decades its wolf-

Wolves, Sheep, and the Academic
Lineage of Joseph Grinnell

Joseph Grinnell
(1877–39)
• Ph.D. Stanford, 1913
• Director, Museum of Vertebrate Zoology,
  U.C.-Berkeley, 1908–39

STUDIED OR WORKED WITH GRINNELL

Joseph Dixon
(1884–1952)
• Ph.D. 1910, Stanford
• Museum of Vertebrate
  Zoology, 1910–31
• NPS Field Naturalist
  1931–46
• coauthor NPS Fauna
  Surveys, 1927–33

George M. Wright
(1904–1936)
• M.F., 1927
• NPS Fauna
  Surveys,
  1927–33
• Chief, Wildlife
  Div.,1933–36

E. Lowell Sumner
(1907–1989)
• M.A., 1933
• NPS biologist,
  1935–67
• Desert Bighorn
  Council,
  1967–1986

PH.D.s SUPERVISED BY GRINNELL

Harold C. Bryant
(1886–1968)
• Ph.D., 1910
• NPS Nature
  Education,
  1920–29
• NPS Ass't Director,
  1930–38
• Superintendent,
  Grand Canyon,
  1939–54

Lee R. Dice
(1887–1977)
• Ph.D., 1915
• Faculty, Univ.
  of Michigan,
  1919–57

Ian McTaggart Cowan
(1910–)
• Ph.D., 1935
• Faculty, Univ. of
  British Columbia,
  1940–75
• Wolf research in
  Canadian parks

STUDENTS OF COWAN

Valerius Geist
(1938–)
• Ph.D., 1967
• Publications,
  *Mountain Sheep:
  A Study in Behavior
  and Evolution* (1971);
  and *Mountain Sheep
  and Man in the
  Northern Wilds* (1975)

Gordon Haber
(1942–)
• Ph.D., 1977
• Dissertation on
  McKinley's wolves
• Independent wolf
  research and critic
  of Alaska wildlife
  management

Paul Joslin
(1940–)
• B.Sc., 1963 with Cowan
• Ph.D. 1973
• Wolf research in Canada
• Director, Alaska Wildlife
  Alliance, 1998–

STUDENTS OF DICE

Olaus Murie
(1889–1963)
• M.S., 1927
• U.S. Biological
  Survey, 1920–45
• Director, Wilderness
  Society, 1945–1962

Adolph Murie
(1899–1974)
• Ph.D., 1929
• NPS and Biological
  Survey, 1934–64

Carl Russell
(1894–1967)
• Ph.D., 1932
• Naturalist,
  Yosemite,
  1923–36
• Chief, NPS Wildlife
  Div., 1936–39
• Superintendent,
  Yosemite,
  1947–52

Victor Cahalane
(1910–1993)
• M.F., Yale;
  postgraduate
  work at Michigan
  1927–29
• NPS Wildlife Div.,
  1934–55
• President, Nat'l Parks
  Assoc., 1959–60
• President, Defenders
  of Wildlife,
  1962–71

moose interactions reinforced prevailing notions of predator-prey interactions, in the 1980s the wolf population sharply declined for unknown reasons, producing a dilemma in management: let nature take its course, or intervene to preserve the famous wolf packs?[9]

This has been an important, if not the central, question throughout the history of managing nature in national parks. Early assumptions seem quaintly archaic now: the desire to freeze a balance as it was in some Edenic precontact past, the dismissal of Native American influences, the quixotic attempts to counter the political realities of visitor desires with research studies on faunal needs. During the wolf-sheep controversy, the Camp Fire Club continually challenged the Park Service's adherence to the concept of natural balance with the argument that any such balance had been upset by the migration of Europeans to the New World, and claimed it was silly to ignore this on the basis of a shaky principle. Since then, as biologists question equilibrium theories and recognize the problems of preserving areas limited by artificial boundaries, the club's stance seems increasingly apt. Whatever we are preserving in parks is the product of our current values and actions.

As mentioned at the beginning of this book, those involved in the wolf-sheep controversy were the harbingers of the third shift in our relations with wolves. The question for recent years, of course, is why respect and affection for the wolf became more widespread. Obviously wolves held some sort of symbolic importance connected to wildness, and our times changed so that this became attractive to many people. No doubt increased knowledge about wolves helped with this shift, modifying the lurid folktales, but it also appears that science had less to do with the change than did emotional appeal. The scientific work of Sigurd Olson, Aldo Leopold, and Olaus and Adolph Murie all gained significance and posterity because they dispersed their knowledge of wolves beyond government reports and professional journals into writings that reached the public.[10]

Sigurd Olson's 1938 wolf study promoted wolves as a healthy force for deer, but few read *Scientific Monthly*. Olson became the voice of preservation for the lake country of the upper Midwest and its wolves through his many subsequent essays, books, and efforts with The Wilderness Society. Aldo

Leopold converted from wolf hunter to wolf advocate during these years, after seeing the effects of deer overpopulation on vegetation in western ranges and Wisconsin. *A Sand County Almanac*, published posthumously in 1949, changed more reader's minds about wolves than anything else he wrote. The Muries, through their coyote studies, concluded by the 1930s that old myths about canid predators did not match their field observations. But like Olson, Olaus Murie found his enduring role confirmed in public work and writings on behalf of wilderness and its denizens. And certainly Adolph's *The Wolves of Mount McKinley* informed and educated the public in ways that surpassed its origins as a research monograph.

The release of the Disney True-Life Adventure *White Wilderness* in 1958, which brought to the public the wolf films of Herb and Lois Crisler, accelerated public perception of wolves as interesting animals. Adolph Murie's wildlife films had long been a staple for visitors at the McKinley Park hotel, but a Disney production—this the fifth True-Life film, indicating the success of the series—meant nationwide distribution at thousands of Saturday matinees. *White Wilderness* followed typical fauna through the seasons of the year, including walrus, polar bear, lemmings, wolverine, and wolves. The film offered, for the most part, comfortable stereotypes: snow and glaciers, the wolverine as ruthless killer, bear cubs as playful, lemmings as driven to periodic mass suicide, their actions set to mood-enhancing music and narration. The Crisler's footage of wolves hunting caribou and feeding at carcasses was offset by scenes of endearing pups, tenderness, and family bonds. While foisted upon the public as "True-Life," much of the film had been contrived, although this was probably not obvious to audiences unfamiliar with the new genre of wildlife documentaries. Adolph Murie wrote a blistering unpublished review of the film with speculations about how certain images had been captured: he assumed a scene of polar bear cubs nuzzling their supposedly sleeping mother in a den had used a dead adult, that trapped lemmings had forcibly been driven over a confined slope, and that the wolverine and wolves were confined rather than free-roaming. This latter was certainly true, as much of the intimate footage of wolves had been filmed at a location in the Canadian Rockies. Another wildlife photographer, Warren Garst, had seen this taking place and, in a prescient suggestion, wrote to Adolph that he would see if the wolves could be released in Yellowstone after their film career ended. Murie was clearly piqued at the film—"cheapened nature"—but perhaps this included resentment that his own less contrived films had been viewed but unused by the Disney studios.[11] Nevertheless, the Disney version of the big bad wolf established a new standard:

the *New York Times* reviewer wrote "Surprisingly, the most domestic family portrait is that of the wolf (not, we learn, the legendary professional killer)."[12] *White Wilderness* brought Alaska's wildlife to viewers in a new light, in which the animals were charming, cuddly, and romantic rather than threatening, replacing Jack London's North with an image tamed for juvenile mass consumption.[13] *White Wilderness* took the 1958 Oscar for feature documentaries in a decade in which that genre shifted from one centered on the winning of WW II toward nature appreciation. The Disney films changed American perceptions of animals in much the same way as the development of coffee-table photography books from the Sierra Club enhanced appreciation for the untrammeled American landscape.[14]

The following year brought a new book on the wolf. *Arctic Wild*, by Lois Crisler, documented the months spent filming *White Wilderness*.[15] Readers learned how to raise wolf pups, how to howl and communicate with wolves, how to hunt and play with and, ultimately, love wolves. Predation by wolves was only positive to the caribou, as the crippled and sick were killed; the Crislers claimed a wolf could not kill a healthy caribou. At the end of the book one of their wolves fell to a bounty-hunter's poison, a tragic event far different than the triumphant wolf killings on the pages of *The Alaska Sportsman*. Crisler told the story with sympathy and awe for nature, and the photos of their life with wolves caused a sensation worldwide, as the book was quickly translated into other languages. *White Wilderness* and *Arctic Wild* provided significant boosts in rehabilitating the wolf, the most important vehicles for change since Murie's *The Wolves of Mount McKinley*.

Adolph continued various research projects in national parks, but increasingly wrote for the public rather than for his peers. This reflected not only an outreach to a wider audience but changes within American society that produced a modern market for nature writings.[16] The Murie articles told interesting stories about the lives of their subjects, based on his accumulation of field notes, conveying the verities of northern ecology in unassuming yet attractive prose.[17] Adolph was a careful writer through habit borne of countless hours of field observation. Son Jan noted that Adolph had saved a quote by Margary Allingham on the craft of writing: "I write every paragraph four times: once to get my meaning down, once to put in everything I left out, once to take out everything that seems unnecessary, and once to make the whole thing sound as if I had only just thought of it."[18]

The culmination of this phase of Adolph's career came in the 1961 publication of *A Naturalist in Alaska*. He and Olaus had been talking about such a compilation for at least a decade, although Adolph thought a book blending information about animals from a scientist, combined with personal philosophical reflections, was "rather unorthodox." Adolph combined the best of his research findings with the wealth of animal 'stories' recorded over the years in his field notebooks, accompanied by photographs and Olaus's sketches. Published by the Devin-Adair Company as part of their American Naturalists Series, his book let Adolph join the select company of Burroughs, Seton, Roosevelt, and Bartam. Reviewers acclaimed *A Naturalist in Alaska*; Sigurd Olson called it "the sort of book that never dies," and it received a third printing within two years. The book also won the John Burroughs award for nature writing. At the award banquet, publisher Devin Garrity lauded Murie's integrity, esthetic appreciation, and willingness to write for the general public. Adolph's quarter-century of writings played a significant role in the broad shift toward a more positive view of predators.[19]

Farley Mowat's *Never Cry Wolf*, published in 1963, is deservedly recognized as an important step in changing attitudes, but it did not burst upon an unprepared public. He received inspiration from Murie and, eventually, a gentle rebuff. In 1948, a youthful Mowat was on a two-year caribou study in the Northwest Territories, when he contacted Adolph for advice. Mowat had been watching wolves. He wrote that he had "for the hundredth time glanced through *The Wolves of Mount McKinley* to see how your observations coincide with my own." Mowat had found a wolf den in the spring and watched the family behavior, much as Murie had done, and asked for advice on "the mechanics of observing" and for suggestions on research questions. Adolph's reply is unknown, but judging from comments in later letters the men did not correspond further.[20]

In May 1963 the Atlantic Monthly Press contacted Murie, requesting his review of Mowat's manuscript so that "if there is an outcry, we can say the foremost wolf experts have read the book and pronounce it reliable," and for a "blurb" about the book. Murie declined, citing his busy research schedule, and suggested the publisher read *The Wolves of Mount McKinley* for comparison. Privately, Murie admitted that he did not want to "get mixed up with anything," because he was aware of the controversy surrounding Mowat's earlier book on the Inuit, *The People of the Deer*, which had come under heavy fire from Canadians. *Never Cry Wolf* provoked a similar outcry, receiving scathing reviews by biologists, most famously for Mowat's claim that rodents composed an important part of the wolf's diet.[21] Numerous people contacted Murie for a reaction, but he kept it private. He did write back to the publisher, applauding

Mowat's general view on wolves: " I think the book should be helpful in many quarters.… [B]ut as I read it seemed that the book must have been greatly fictionalized." Mowat had claimed to rely on *The Wolves of Mount McKinley*, but Adolph asked, "How could he write about the mouse mystery and much else in the book in the way he does if he was reading about McKinley wolves?" Murie concluded, "in the long run books such as his may do more harm than good."[22] The publisher passed on this letter to Mowat, who defended his book to Murie. Rather than letting the truth be obscured by "too much data," Mowat admitted taking "considerable liberties with time and place," though he did not modify his claims about the mouse diet. He was, after all, "attempting to do my best for the wolves."[23]

In this, Farley Mowat was doing the same thing as Adolph Murie had long done, although Murie did not receive the same kind of criticism. Murie was as good and careful in his research as anyone of his time, yet he was motivated to do more than merely file his scientific reports because of a desire to change attitudes toward animals, a mission admitted only privately. The appeal to readers of *The Wolves of Mount McKinley* lay largely in Murie's description of attractive wolf behavior. As he commenced writing the monograph, Murie confessed that his emphasis in describing the wolf's home life resulted from a desire "to change wolf-hatred to a more generous attitude," since the gamboling of wolf pups had little to do with the sheep population. In a 1947 letter to William Sheldon, Adolph said, "We must get the facts and then try to use them to create a wholesome attitude towards a situation. In the case of some of the predators one must arouse sympathy for the esthetics so that the question is not judged entirely on an economic basis." As he started on *A Naturalist in Alaska*, Murie repeated that he intended to create in the reader "a wholesome attitude toward wildlife." To fellow biologist Lowell Sumner, Murie wrote that for this book he planned to "bring in esthetics, feelings—our stock in trade." In questioning someone else's research proposal on bears in McKinley Park, Adolph wrote, "What we do need…is more esthetic writing about grizzlies in wilderness environment[s] in order to create more sentiment for saving them."[24] As the popularity of writings by Leopold, Mowat, and Murie show, it was emotion rather than research that changed people's minds. These men could communicate effectively with biologists and with the general public, getting respect from one group and emotional response from the other. For the wolf, the latter was essential.

Murie was an idealist, and although his actions during the wolf-sheep controversy indicated a willingness to compromise certain ideals in the face of political realities, he maintained high standards in his expectation of the role of national parks. He tirelessly campaigned for wilderness preservation in the parks. While for many this was synonymous with setting aside areas of outstanding scenery, or areas where people could go to experience a place unaltered by human activities, Adolph campaigned instead for wilderness on behalf of its animals. He was fond of the rejoinder by a frequent McKinley Park visitor, a retired logger, to the tourist question, "'Where are all the animals? 'This ain't no zoo, lady.'"[25]

The National Park Service itself had continued to evolve through and beyond the years of the wolf-sheep controversy, and not usually for the benefit of wildlife. In 1951 Conrad Wirth succeeded Newton Drury as director and immediately brought new priorities to the service, emphasizing visitation and facilities improvements. Several years later Wirth unveiled Mission 66, an ambitious ten-year project to bring the parks into the automobile age, which Congress quickly approved. The new priorities disappointed Park Service biologists; Victor Cahalane was the highest ranking one to quit in protest.[26]

Throughout Adolph Murie's career he had sounded off on a good many policies, but he was becoming increasingly critical of the Park Service as the years passed. Murie disapproved of the increased emphasis on parks as "recreation areas," and rebelled against what he considered to be misguided priorities.[27] Mission 66 included plans to improve the quality of the road in McKinley Park, which for decades had been little more than a passable track. Murie thought the new road resembled a speedway and criticized the engineers for ignoring the subtleties of the landscape.[28] He also objected to plans for a series of interpretive signs along the park road, claiming they would stifle curiosity and self-discovery. "There is the stark label—one might think he were looking at a museum showcase. The opportunity to discover the trails for oneself, to wonder about them—what animal made them, and why and where he was going—has been taken away."[29] Unavoidable changes were coming to Alaska and McKinley Park, changes that grieved Adolph. His objections could be seen as those of an older man fixated on the landscape of his former years, as Belmore Browne had been. There may have been elements of that, but Adolph was careful to articulate his concerns on behalf of the wildlife and what he considered to be the end purpose of national parks, especially McKinley: an essential purity of wilderness values.[30] In the end, his vision for the Park Service could not be attained by a public agency.

By the twilight of his career, Murie's role in the Park Service did not match his reputation. In later years a bit of petulance crept into his writings, as he voiced objections to what others were doing in his park. In 1963 administrators turned down his summer research proposal, prompting a defensive rebuttal from him. He objected to others deciding on research priorities for McKinley Park: "the author is best qualified to know what further field work is desirable...in years when I have not been able to return, something was always lost." Adolph rather plaintively noted that he had been assigned for long-term research in 1947, and "What seemed true in 1947 seems true in 1963." He pointed out some of the misjudgments rendered in recent years by other biologists who lacked his familiarity with the park: an inaccurate caribou census by a wildlife management professor, another university professor wrongly assuming a failed blueberry crop and predicting starvation for the grizzlies, a third miscalculating the grazing impact of Dall sheep.[31] No one could match his experience, to be sure, but with the wolf-sheep controversy ended, other research priorities—and researchers—encroached on Murie's domain.

This new generation of biologists had new research tools to use, but Adolph's idealism made him skeptical of those as well. Researchers had worked out the details of radio telemetry on the bears in Yellowstone, using tranquilizing drugs to allow attachment of transmitters for remote sensing. Murie objected to this in McKinley Park. He thought that "the significant information could be secured without tagging," presumably through walking and watching, which Adolph was then doing for his planned grizzly monograph. He also objected on esthetic grounds to the visible collars that held the transmitters. Although used in Yellowstone, Murie thought its bears were "already contaminated" by virtue of the park's garbage dumps. Because of the field techniques, and their popularity in television wildlife shows, "when we think of Yellowstone grizzlies we do not think of wilderness animals, but rather of radios, anesthetized bears, and general manhandling." Murie thought that visitors to McKinley had a right to see wild bears, and that tagging them was "destroying the very essence of the poetry of wilderness." He also opposed radio researchers using airplanes for tracking purposes and even plane use by rangers for taking animal counts, feeling that airplanes destroyed the wilderness setting.[32]

Although friends urged him to leave the Park Service and by doing so gain the ability to speak out with greater vigor, Adolph Murie remained in government service.[33] He did what he could internally, functioning as a voice of conscience in the National Park Service, encouraging it to act wisely, cautiously, and with deference to faunal needs. He understood the educational role available to those wearing Park Service uniforms, and worked to influence attitudes within the organization. He sought increased sensibilities "not only in the public but among Service employees. Here esthetics are involved, a 'reverence for life,' and the fundamentals of the park philosophy." A McKinley Park ranger of the next generation said that Murie, "more than any other individual, changed the way park managers perceived wolves and other predators."[34]

Perhaps Adolph remained in federal service because Olaus had not. The brothers had shared much and accomplished much since those early years in Minnesota. According to Louise, Adolph continually provided ideas and information that Olaus in turn acted upon as president of The Wilderness Society. Adolph was the introvert, Olaus the extrovert; Adolph preferred time afoot, binoculars and journal in hand, while Olaus had a deft touch with people and chose to make his second career effecting political and social change. As a result, Olaus received virtually every national conservation award available. One Jackson Hole friend reported that Adolph was proud of the work his brother did, while not wishing any of it for himself.[35] Given the number of Adolph's books and articles that Olaus illustrated, it seems likely that Olaus was equally proud of Adolph's work. If Adolph had pursued political activism we would celebrate him as one of the prophets of the environmental movement, as we do Olaus. Adolph was "devastated" upon Olaus's death from cancer on October 21, 1963. He wrote to The Wilderness Society's Howard Zahniser: "I still feel his kindly sympathy and understanding which always came from the depths of his being…. As always, I wanted to discuss…events with Olaus, and how poignantly I realized that I could not, not ever."[36]

Adolph retired the following year, after thirty years of federal service. To his surprise, in 1965 the Department of the Interior gave him its Distinguished Service Award. He accepted the gold medal in a ceremony at Camp Denali with the Alaska Range as a backdrop. Adolph continued work on his grizzly monograph during Alaska's short summers, with winters at the family place in Jackson Hole. He remained politically aware; in a 1966 letter to his congressman Murie opposed the "inhumane, stupid" war in Vietnam, favored voting by eighteen year olds, supported inclusion of communist China in the United Nations, and, biologist that he was, favored curbs on global human population rather than encouraging increased food production. Not surprisingly, he supported a ten-year delay for studies prior to the construction of the trans-Alaska oil pipeline.[37]

Murie's close friend Victor Cahalane helped sustain recognition of Adolph's work. Cahalane, after quitting the Park Service in 1955, served as

Olaus and Adolph Murie on Cathedral Mountain, McKinley Park, 1961.
Adolph Murie Collection, temp box 13. Courtesy Alaska and Polar Regions Archives, Rasmuson Library, University of Alaska Fairbanks

president of the National Parks Association for one year, and then in 1962 assumed presidency of Defenders of Wildlife, which emerged as a vigorous and important lobby against federal predator control. Increased public awareness about predators brought requests to the government for Murie's monographs, which were hard to obtain. With the help of Cahalane, Murie had the satisfaction of seeing *Ecology of the Coyote in Yellowstone* and *The Wolves of Mount McKinley* reprinted by the Government Printing Office in 1972.[38]

Adolph died at home on August 15, 1974, of complications related to epilepsy that had developed during his later years. If he could visit McKinley Park today, he would not be pleased with the way it has matured: more layers of bureaucracy and regulations, a haphazard collection of tourist facilities near the park's entrance, and visitors measured in the hundreds of thousands, many on packaged tours devoid of intimate encounters with the park's landscape and life. Murie died before seeing the results of his campaign to enlarge the park's boundaries. He had long recognized the importance for caribou and wolves of the lowland spruce forests north of the original boundary. Increased control efforts in the 1950s outside that line, and its permeability to wolf poachers, made park expansion even more important. In 1965 Murie submitted a formal proposal suggesting new boundaries. It gained the endorsements of National Park Service Director George Hartzog and Interior Secretary Stewart Udall. They put it on President Johnson's desk just before he left office, but Johnson refused to sign it. Finally in 1980, the Alaska National Interest Lands Conservation Act expanded the park by four million acres and renamed it Denali National Park and Preserve. Park Service historian William Brown calls Adolph Murie "the single most influential person in shaping the geography and the wildlife-wilderness policies of the modern park." In recognition of his life's work, the Park Service named the vista beneath Polychrome Pass, on the park road, the Plains of Murie.[39]

The two-tier designation of additional park lands did not provide total protection for the wolves; in the new preserves the Park Service allowed a season on wolves (and other animals) by subsistence hunters and trappers. This was a compromise implemented in Alaska parks, resulting from recognition of Alaska Native claims for traditional subsistence activities, although eligibility for subsistence use was not restricted racially. At the time, this compromise received support from the major conservation groups. Since then, however, wolf advocates have harshly criticized the National Park Service for this infringement of complete federal protection.[40]

The National Park Service, by adding an ecological purpose to the park rationales of scenery, game refuges, and recreation areas, introduced a land use concept that did not make intuitive sense to people who perceived themselves as still wresting a living from the raw frontier. The situation caught the Park Service between its intention to preserve all native fauna and its desire for good local relations. One analyst of national parks outlined two methods by which an agency can gain public support: portraying a favorable image by convincing the public that the agency supports popular values, and demonstrating tangible benefits to the public of the agency's presence or actions.[41] In Alaska the Park Service had a difficult time with the former, since wolf protection held little popular appeal until after the wolf-sheep controversy ended. The service focused on the latter method, but had to convince Alaskans that it could sustain the favored wildlife and retain a few wolves. Public relations consumed much of McKinley Park's staff and was as important in the superintendent's monthly reports as the animal counts. The park staff made vigorous efforts to bring Alaskans to the park, to show them what the park was about and why it mattered. By the mid-1930s Alaskans recognized the importance of McKinley Park to the tourist economy. Alaskan merchants supposed that a herd of sheep was of far greater interest to the tourists than a wolf, but visitation to the park after the war increased steadily regardless of the decline of game animal populations. Belmore Browne may have been disappointed to see only a hundred sheep in a day, but most visitors expressed delight at seeing such numbers.

Alaskans' criticism of McKinley Park's management was vigorous and consensual, from poor trappers to the territory's governor and congressional delegates. Adolph Murie assembled considerable evidence showing that weather conditions and disease played major roles in determining sheep numbers, yet Alaskans preferred prejudice to evidence. The Park Service never successfully refuted the popular conception of the park as a protected wolf breeding ground. Time and again the service pointed out that the several dozen wolves of McKinley Park could not possibly contribute in a significant way to the wolf populations that continued to exist in interior Alaska despite decades of trapping pressure and bounty incentives.[42] The decline of Alaska's reindeer and caribou herds had nothing to do with McKinley Park, but it kept Alaskans howling for more wolf carcasses and affronted by distant administrators who seemed to prefer wolves to live meat.

Broader tensions between the Alaska territory and the federal government helped produce opposition to the National Park Service. Conventional local wisdom of the time held that Alaska's economic development had been inhibited because of federal neglect. Governor Gruening spoke of Alaska as being in a legislative straitjacket imposed by Congress.[43] Alaskans sorely felt the lack of local control over resources, resenting the distant landlords in Washington, D.C., and the political appointees who held territorial offices. The secretary of the interior, particularly, held considerable power vested in the numerous agencies critically important to Alaskans: the Office of the Territories, the Office of Indian Affairs, the General Land Office (now Bureau of Land Management), the Fish and Wildlife Service, the Geological Survey, the Alaska Road Commission, the Alaska Railroad, and the National Park Service. Alaskans saw wolf protection as another example of ill-advised federal control over an essentially local issue.

Statehood arrived in 1959, and with it came local control over wildlife (except for national parks and refuges) and some changed policies toward wolves, including a ban on the use of poisons for predator control. The U.S. Fish and Wildlife Service restricted its control efforts to the western reindeer ranges. In 1963 the legislature redefined wolves, changing their status from vermin to big game and furbearers, thus requiring licenses for wolf hunters and trappers. Hunters could still take wolves from the air, but few people objected. In 1968 the state finally ceased offering bounties on wolves in most areas, with all bounties ended in 1972. The decade was a relatively quiet time as far as wolf controversies went, an interlude between the wolf-sheep argument and the conflicts that subsequently emerged from an American public sensitized in new ways to the value of wolves.

It turned out that statehood did not increase Alaska's abilities to manage its animals without external influences. The changing nature of *The Alaska Sportsman* during this time shows the trends that would diminish the possibility of autonomy. Through the 1950s the magazine showed continuity in its sentiment toward wolves. It praised federal control efforts and ran numerous articles by private aerial wolf gunners who sought to maintain a place in the sporting tradition by emphasizing their own skill and daring, while regarding wolf killing as a public good. A two-page editorial in the November 1956 issue questioned the application of the balance of nature argument against predator control: "the balancing of Nature was all left with man when God said, 'Let man have dominion over all.'"

Emory Tobin remained editor until March 1958, when the magazine changed ownership and came under the editorial control of Alaska journalists Robert Henning and Robert DeArmond. In 1961 the editors offered an opinion on the future of Alaska's economic development that foresaw not fish, fur, oil, timber, nor defense expenditures as critical, but claimed "the great Alaskan wilderness itself is our dominant resource." This was prescient, as the 1964 Wilderness Act, the back-to-nature movement, and Earth Day all lay in the future. Henning and DeArmond offered no spiritual rationale for this, but rather an economic one about the future of tourism, concluding, "A wilderness-first policy isn't just 'park stuff.' It's the method a hard-headed merchant must recognize as the way to ring the cash register."[44]

The magazine slowly began to reflect new attitudes toward wolves. An October 1960 issue carried the first neutral article about wolves and coyotes, informative without questioning predator control. Entertaining articles about wolf killing became infrequent in following years; the last one appeared in June 1967, except for some sourdough memoirs published later. The July 1967 issue offered an article that clarified the increasing ambivalence toward wolves. Titled "Big Bad Wolf," the biologist authors proposed that it was the wolf's turn to find advocates among conservationists. In December 1968 Henning offered an editorial in favor of wolves. Sparked by an encounter with a wolf that left him feeling "privileged," Henning took a modest stance against wolf control programs. The cover photo for the April 1969 issue showed a nonthreatening wolf, and subsequent years saw good coverage of the growing disagreements over game management.[45]

These changes did not necessarily reflect the sentiment of residents, as Alaska readership diminished in importance to the magazine. A survey in 1968 showed that only forty percent of subscribers lived on the West Coast, including Alaska. Over half the non-Alaskans wanted to visit, and, tellingly, the majority of respondents liked the magazine because it was about Alaska, not because it was about fishing and hunting. This brought a shift in focus for *The Alaska Sportsman*, visible in 1969 as the editors tinkered with the magazine's cover. From July to September, "Alaska" gained visual prominence, while "Sportsman" diminished; the new look and title *Alaska* was complete in October. "The Alaska Sportsman" became a small section on fishing and hunting within the magazine, as Henning explained to readers that he was "just giving the magazine a title all Alaskans can be proud of without feeling they have to be the outdoors type to join the family." Quite likely most Alaskan residents did not care, as the magazine had moved away from being a source of useful information and became a vehicle for the tourist industry, which over the years came to rank second only to oil in the economy.

A number of factors coincided to lay the foundation for the wolf controversies of the 1970s, years that Richard Nixon proclaimed would be the "environmental decade." Increasing tourist visitation made Alaska tangible for thousands, and certainly some percentage of visitors retained an interest in Alaska affairs. The part of the environmental movement concerned with wilderness preservation had enough influence to help enact the 1964 Wilderness Act, which highlighted how few untrammeled areas remained in the contiguous states and how much of Alaska still had de facto wilderness status. The discovery of the Prudhoe Bay oil fields in 1968, and the resulting discussion over how to develop them, heightened preservationist concerns about threats to Alaska's wild lands. In 1966 Congress passed the first act for protection of endangered species, and wolves were quickly listed as one of these.[46] Awareness of a variety of environmental issues led to increased membership in established organizations—Sierra Club, Audubon Society—as well as new groups, many devoted to wildlife concerns. These helped disseminate information about the activities of the U.S. Fish and Wildlife Service's Division of Predator and Rodent Control, which had come to increasingly rely on chemical means to kill unwanted animals: Compound 1080 for coyotes and strychnine for rodents. Questions about the efficacy of these became increasingly conflated with ethical concerns, and by 1971 citizen groups were filing lawsuits against these government activities.[47] This ethical questioning of humanity's technocratic domination and manipulation of wildlife also apppeared in an increasing hostility toward sport hunting and a continuing decrease in the percentage of Americans who hunted. The 1960s and 1970s were also a time of enhanced interest in Native American history and spirituality. The Puritans had once regarded Indians and wolves as malevolent forces. The two combined anew in popular culture, but this time as coequal victims of oppression, reminders of the stains of guilt underlying our history, and symbols of a time when natural harmony prevailed.

Thus, in 1975, when Alaska's Board of Fish and Game approved a plan to hire aerial gunners to cull the wolf population near Fairbanks for the sake of improved hunting possibilities, there was no chance of this being only a local matter. Caribou and moose populations had been high during the 1960s but then declined for no obvious reasons. This coincided with two other developments related to the oil boom: Alaska's population expanded, with an increase of sport hunters, and Alaska Natives pressed their claims on land and resources into the courts and Congress, resulting in formal recognition of the need to sustain subsistence wildlife harvests. Alaska's wildlife managers regarded wolves as direct competitors and were confident that wolf reduction would increase game for humans, but found themselves the target of nationwide criticism. Any honeymoon period of local control enjoyed after statehood was over; Alaska's animals were no longer solely the state's to manipulate for the sake of hunting harvests.

Since then Alaska has been embroiled in a number of conflicts over wolf management.[48] Public opinion plays a larger role in Alaska's wolf politics than ever before, as evidenced by Alaska's 1992 wolf controversy. The dispute flared after the Board of Game approved a plan to kill half the wolves, about three hundred, in three game management units near Fairbanks, and then to continue culling wolves in these areas over the next few years. Three consecutive winters of deep snow had depressed caribou and moose populations. State biologists were confident that reducing predation would help the ungulate populations rebound more quickly, a view heartily endorsed by subsistence and sport hunters who did not want to see the game harvest decreased. This specific program emerged within the context of a statewide wolf management plan that had been agreed upon earlier by a citizen committee consisting of a cross section of interests, which itself was a precedent for the state. The control program targeted areas comprising less than four percent of Alaska's land area and involved five to seven percent of the state's nonendangered wolf population. Wolf advocates, in Alaska and nationally, erupted and brought enough pressure to cause the state to revise its plans in the face of withering hostility from the public and threats of tourist boycotts. Arguments over Alaska's wolves have grown louder and more complicated. In comparison with the wolf-sheep controversy, today's conflicts show that the questions are more complex, public interest is broader, Alaskans' opinion has diversified, and new perspectives have been added.

The issue in McKinley Park involved less confusion over the ends and means of wolf control. Once the Park Service had decided that it would keep the wolves, the question revolved around the number of wolves killed to allay critics and reduce pressure on the sheep. The desired sheep population was one that was healthily reproducing and provided enough sightings to please tourists, not one that would allow for a human harvest. Wolves and people were not competitors. The means of wolf control provoked little comment, other than the Park Service declining to use aerial hunting, although, as Belmore Browne pointed out, it was easily the most effective way to kill wolves.

Alaska's wolf arguments have since been about animals outside national parks, with the exception of the recent preserve areas. But whose wolves are they? How should claims on animals from different groups—protectionists, subsistence users, sport hunters—be mediated? What should be the role of nonresident opinion in deciding these? If biologists decide that wolf control is justified, how should it be done? Lost in the rhetorical fray over the issue of aerial hunting was that trappers before and since legally take about one thousand wolves annually, yet this has occasioned far less comment than aerial hunts to curb specific wolf populations for the sake of specific game herds. As with most wildlife management arguments, attempts to create and validate plans by scientific rationales foundered under the sentiment generated by a public more interested in discussing values than mortality ratios and carrying capacities. Ultimately, the questions boil down to the rights of animals. Notions about the balance of nature affect all of these, from whether human hunting is natural to whether our knowledge is sufficient to presume we know the reasons for animal population fluctuations and ways to modify those. As the 1997 study on Alaska's wildlife management by the National Research Council concluded, it would be foolish to think we fully understand the cycles of life in the North.[49]

The degree of public awareness and involvement has also changed considerably from midcentury. Sportsmen's groups and magazines made the wolf-sheep controversy a national one, yet it did not engage widespread attention. McKinley Park simply was not well known or visited by large numbers of people, and wolves were literally a dead issue for most Americans. Increased membership in environmental groups and related wolf awareness gave subsequent controversies far greater public prominence, as did the visual media and eyewitness reportage. Some three thousand letters arrived in Alaska state offices in early 1976 protesting planned wolf control; in 1992, some 180,000 calls and letters opposing the control plan deluged state officials.[50] This most recent wolf controversy stands on a continuum of increasing public involvement with Alaska's wolves, which began during the wolf-sheep controversy.

The increased involvement of nonresidents in local affairs caused much frustration among Alaskans. Environmental groups whose memberships were greater than Alaska's population could rally sympathy, support and legal funds from their mailing lists. In 1992–93, some groups urged a tourist boycott aimed at that billion-dollar sector of Alaska's economy. This provoked much resentment among residents, who regarded this as economic extortion. The Alaskan Independence Party, under whose banner then-governor Walter Hickel had been elected, warned that

> OUTSIDE MANIPULATORS are turning Alaska into a park for tourists. Government Bureaucrats and Big Business Power Brokers, and 'environmental' groups are reducing our land to the level of a simplistic *National Geographics* video showing cute little wolf pups froliking *[sic]* in the snow.

While this was the sentiment of a group fond of polemics and lacking significant political power—Hickel's affiliation was largely convenient, as he had lost the Republican primary—many Alaskans who opposed state wolf control found the boycott potential threatening. The situation emphasized the degree to which Alaska's economic health remains contingent on forces far beyond Alaska's control.

While Outsiders found it easy to disparage Alaskans over state wolf issues, a consensus among residents is harder to find now than it was at midcentury. Disagreement among Alaskans about wolves in the 1950s were largely about control techniques—opposition to poisoning and aerial hunts—rather than on control per se. This had changed by the 1970s as local groups in Anchorage and Fairbanks began questioning the single-minded game harvest rationales of the state wildlife managers. Stephen Kellert's late 1970s national research found that of all the demographic groups he isolated—by age, locale, education, and income—the category of Alaskans had greater knowledge about and positive regard for wolves. Alaskans also differ with respect to hunting, as harvesting wild foods continues to matter economically, dietarily, and spiritually. A greater percentage of residents hunt, and fewer object to hunting, than in most other states. But within these generalizations demographic categories matter, with substantial differences of opinion on hunting and wildlife management among Alaskans based on rural or urban residence, age, gender, and level of education. During the 1992 debate, a poll found that seventy-four percent of residents disapproved of aerial culling by state personnel.[51] While images of cretinous armed woodsmen or uniformed state hunters slaughtering Alaska wolves made for powerful appeals to the prowolf constituencies in the Lower 48, the diversity of opinion among Alaskans belies such caricaturization.

In January 1993 sportsmen formed a new group to support state wolf control, with the deliberately ambiguous title of the Alaska Wildlife Conservation Association. They published a newspaper ad with the bold headline "It's *not* about wolves...." Indeed not, as wolves once again became symbolic pawns in gambits played for the sake of sociopolitical positions. Resentful Alaskans arrayed their defensive ranks around issues of states' rights and self-determination against the threats brought by outside interference. The two main perceived threats were gun control and animal rights, which included curtailment of hunting and trapping and abolishment of sled dog breeding and racing. The whole of it looked to many Alaskans like a tyranny of the majority wrapped with bleeding-heart liberalism. As a correspondent to the Fairbanks newspaper wrote, "It's time to quit talking and start shooting. Alaskans have two options, either pursue predators or hang up your guns." Anticontrol advocates explored different rhetorical frontiers. Priscilla Feral of the Connecticut-based Friends of Animals declared, "Right now you've got an animal more persecuted in Alaska than blacks during slavery." Renee Askins of the Wolf Fund, who conducted her activism from the Murie country of Moose, Wyoming, equated Alaska's wolf control plan to the Holocaust, claiming "little difference in causation." Greenpeace's Cindy Lowry said, "Fortunately, most human beings have evolved and no longer fear wolves."[52] Broad public support was not likely to accrue to either extremity of opinion, but these examples emphasize one trend within wolf politics, that of increasing polarization. Both sides have entrenched interests: in Alaska, these include people who make a living from consumptive wildlife usage and the state game bureaucracy supporting them, while those who make a living organizing environmental groups depend on member recruitment and endless fundraising. Wolves are no longer anyone's enemy. The stakes are social, moral, and financial, and the enemies are those who hold different opinions.

Attitudes towards animals have undergone many shifts in the past, and our current regard for the wolf marks a notable change. But this history of changing attitudes implies that what now holds sway may not endure. A recent generation of Americans found new values in wolves, but what of the next generation? The cultural rehabilitation of wolves occurred within the overlaps between sport hunting, animal rights, conservation, and environmentalism, these all products of the dominant White American culture. But if, as demographers predict, ethnic and cultural pluralism continue to modify American society, what changes lie in our future attitudes toward animals, and wolves in particular? Do the sentiments of Aldo Leopold have the same appeal to recent non-Anglo immigrants, or with others for whom the concept of wilderness holds little appeal, whatever their background? Stephen Kellert's research on American attitudes toward animals suggests that positive regard for wolves has established only shallow roots across the populace. Kellert finds that generally positive attitudes are just about balanced by negative feelings, that youth correlates with positive regard, as does educational attainment and participation in birdwatching and backpacking. Respondents who live nearer wolves—Alaska, the North Central states, and in the West—have more positive feelings toward wolves than residents in the Northeast and South.[53] If wolf reintroduction efforts in the Carolinas, Texas, and the Adirondacks continue, this proximity may result in more positive regional feelings, at least until wolves begin killing dogs and livestock. The wolf's future lies in demarcated refuges; this is better than life in zoos, but support for wolves will exist only if their social and economic cost is low. As advocates across the range of environmental concerns warn, implicit suggestions of misanthropy from animal rights proponents deter collaboration from people focused on worker health, the spread of industrial toxins, and social justice. The wolf is now a romantic symbol for many, but that role may have its own limits of time and place.

By the time the wolf-sheep controversy ended, there were those who felt the sheep had survived in spite of the National Park Service, while others concluded that the wolves had been saved in spite of Alaskans. The controversy confirmed the close relationship between wilderness and wolves and the mutuality of interests between proponents of either. It helped the Park Service distinguish itself from other federal land agencies in ways the early service administrators had not anticipated. Keeping wolves in McKinley Park gave rise to a perceived natural connection between wolves and parks, reinforced for baby boomers by the wolf packs on Isle Royale and emphasized recently in Yellowstone. Only in retrospect was it obvious that the Park Service had won the argument over wildlife in McKinley Park. The service held its ground as the years passed, the Dall sheep population rebounded, and the era changed. For the first time, Americans had found a place for wolves. People who found satisfaction in that could begin to think toward further opportunities to expand our acquaintance with them.

Notes

1   Clifford Presnall to chief of Wildlife Research, F & WS, 21 April 1945, RG 79, Entry 7, File 715, Box 1414, NA.

2   Murie recorded that at least one ranger did not report all the wolves he killed because of the resultant paperwork; from an undated page, A. Murie Collection, Box "Field Notes on a Variety of Species," Folder "Denali Mammals 1947–53," UAF. Superintendent comment from A. Murie, "Some Policies and Problems Related to McKinley Park Wildlife," n.d., unpublished report, Pamphlet 591, DENA. This was probably written between 1961–65.

3   James B. Trefethen, in writing about wolf protection in Minnesota in the early '70s, quotes Craig Rupp of the U.S. Forest Service, who could have borrowed this comment directly from the wolf-sheep controversy: "Complete protection of a predator which had an unjustified but nonetheless bad reputation could result in a social-political situation that would force actions and cause reactions detrimental to the wolf." In *An American Crusade for Wildlife* (New York: Winchester Press, and the Boone and Crockett Club, 1975), 293. In a similar vein, commenting on the efforts to reintroduce wolves to stateside areas, David Mech says, "If we have learned anything from this ordeal, it is that the best way to ensure continued wolf survival is, ironically enough, not to protect wolves completely. If we carefully regulate wolf populations instead of overprotecting them, we can prevent a second wave of wolf hysteria, a backlash that could lead once again to persecution." In Mech's "Foreword" to Hank Fischer, *Wolf Wars: The Remarkable Inside Story of the Restoration of Wolves to Yellowstone* (Helena, MT: Falcon Press, 1995), vii.

4   McLean, "Memorandum filed on behalf of the Camp Fire Club of America through its Committee on Conservation in the above matter," 28 November 1947, RG 79, Entry 7, File 715, Box 1415, NA.

5   O. Murie to Browne, 22 April 1946, Stef. Mss., 190–8:67, DCL.

6   George M. Wright and Ben H. Thompson, *Fauna of the National Parks of the United States: Wildlife Management in the National Parks*, Fauna Series No. 2 (Washington, D.C.: GPO, National Park Service, 1934), 15; Harlow Mills to A. Murie, 31 March 1949, A. Murie Collection, Box 1, Folder "Correspondence 1935–1974," AHC; Samuel P. Hays, *Beauty, Health, and Permanence: Environmental Politics in the United States, 1955–1985* (Cambridge: Cambridge University Press, 1987), 33.

7   See Donald Worster, *Nature's Economy: A History of Ecological Ideas* (Cambridge: Cambridge University Press, 1977. Daniel Botkin considers that equilibrium theories impeded clear understandings of natural systems in *Discordant Harmonies: A New Ecology for the Twenty-First Century* (New York: Oxford University Press, 1990). Joel Hagen challenges Botkin's interpretation in *An Entangled Bank: The Origins of Ecosystem Ecology* (New Brunswick, NJ: Rutgers University Press, 1992).

8   Victor Cahalane, "Wildlife and the National Park Land-Use Concept," in *Transactions of the 12th North American Wildlife Conference* (Washington, D.C.: Wildlife Management Institute, 1947), 434. George Wright's notion of preserving parks as they were at the time of contact was repeated in the important review by A. Starker Leopold, et. al., "Study of Wildlife Problems in National Parks," in *Transactions of the 28th North American Wildlife and Natural Resources Conference*, (Washington, D.C.: Wildlife Management Institute, 1963), 43. See Sellars, *Preserving Nature*, 214–17, for a discussion of this report.

A useful discussion of management metaphors is found in chapter six, "Ecological Terms and Concepts that Influence Policy Directions," in Frederic H. Wagner, et. al., *Wildlife Policies in the U.S. National Parks* (Washington, D.C.: Island Press, 1995). A pertinent example of how wildlife biologists are now considering the balance of nature is chapter eight, "The Denali Wolf-Prey System," in L. David Mech, et al., *The Wolves of Denali* (Minneapolis: University of Minnesota Press, 1998).

9   I don't know the extent to which wolf policies on Isle Royale were influenced by what had happened in McKinley Park, but connections are plausible. See L. David Mech, *The Wolves of Isle Royale*, Fauna Series No. 7 (Washington, D.C.: GPO, National Park Service, 1966); Rolf O. Peterson, *The Wolves of Isle Royale: A Broken Balance* (Minocqua, WI: Willow Creek Press, 1995); Botkin, *Discordant Harmonies*, 27–49.

10   This point is also made by Erich Klinghammer, but, like many, he identifies only Farley Mowat in this; see "The Wolf: Fact and Fiction," in *Perceptions of Animals in American Culture*, ed. R. J. Hoage (Washington, D.C.: Smithsonian Institution Press, 1989), 85.

11   Adolph Murie, manuscript titled "White Wilderness," 20 January 1959, apparently unpublished, A. Murie Collection, Box 1, Folder "Correspondence 1939–1966, Adolph Murie Movie," AHC; Warren Garst to A. Murie, 18 September 1959, A. Murie Collection, Box 1, Folder "Correspondence 1937–1970, misc. letters," AHC.

A letter from Erwin L. Verity, Walt Disney Productions, to A. Murie, 25 November 1952, indicated that Disney was interested in buying the rights to some of Murie's films (A. Murie Collection, Box 1, Folder "Correspondence 1939–1966, wildlife at Denali," AHC), but Murie is not listed in the credits for *White Wilderness*; Leonard Maltin, *The Disney Films* (New York: Crown Publishers, 1973), 148.

12   Howard Thompson, review of *White Wilderness*, *New York Times*, 13 August 1958.

13   For more on Disney's impact on animal attitudes, see Matt Cartmill, *A View Toward a Death in the Morning: Hunting and Nature Through History* (Cambridge: Harvard University Press, 1993), for a chapter specifically on the influence of the film *Bambi*, as well as the fourth chapter in Alexander Wilson, *The Culture of Nature: North American Landscape from Disney to the Exxon Valdez* (Toronto: Between the Lines, 1991).

14   Hays, *Beauty, Health, and Permanence*, 37. Hollywood awarded Oscars for two documentary categories, short and feature films; of the decade's twenty possible documentary Oscars, nature films won nine, five from the Disney studios.

15   Lois Crisler, *Arctic Wild* (London: Secker and Warburg, 1959).

16   See, for example, David Peterson del Mar, "'Our Animal Friends:' Depictions of Animals in *Reader's Digest* During the 1950s," *Environmental History* 3 (January 1998): 25–44.

17   These include "The Mysterious Mouse," *Audubon*, July–August 1948, 202–10; "Wolverine Trails at Denali," *The Living Wilderness*, Winter 1951–52, 13–20; "Grizzly Mothers in the Alaska Range," *The Living Wilderness*, Autumn 1952, 15–21; "Gulls and Mice in McKinley Park," *The Living Wilderness*, Spring 1957, 17–19; "Why Teen-Age Grizzlies Leave Home," *National Parks*, June 1959, 8–10; "Birds and Beasts in the Far North Wilderness," *Westways*, April 1960, 28–29.

18   Adolph Murie, *The Grizzlies of Mount McKinley*, with a preface by Jan O. Murie; Scientific Monograph Series No. 14 (Washington, D. C.: GPO, National Park Service, 1981), xi. Adolph's final monograph was completed posthumously by Jan, now a professor emeritus in biology at the University of Alberta.

19   A. Murie to Lawrence Merriam, 2 April 1951, A. Murie Collection, Box 2, Folder "Correspondence 1951–1965 re: articles and pamphlets," AHC; compilation of reviewers' comments from Devin-Adair Company, A. Murie Collection, Box 1, Folder "Correspondence 1935–1974; letter, re-publications, and honors," AHC; Garrity remarks, n.d., A. Murie Collection, Box 1, Folder "Correspondence 1957–1965," AHC.

20   Mowat to A. Murie, 28 June 1948, A. Murie Collection, Box 4, Folder "Correspondence 1948–1970, *Never Cry Wolf*," AHC.

21   See A. W. F. Banfield, "Review of F. Mowat's *Never Cry Wolf*," *Canadian Field Naturalist* 78 (1964): 52–54; D. H. Pimlott, "Review of F. Mowat's *Never Cry Wolf*," *Journal of Wildlife Management* 30 (1966): 236–37; Jim Rearden, "Fairy Tales and Wolves," *Alaska*, January 1985, 27, 74–75.

22   Peter Davison to A. Murie, 17 May 1963; A. Murie to Davison, 5 June 1963; A. Murie to Dev Butcher, n.d., probably late 1963; A. Murie to Davison, 6 November 1963, all A. Murie Collection, Box 4, Folder "Correspondence 1948–1970, *Never Cry Wolf*," AHC. Murie reiterated his reasons for avoiding association with Mowat's book in a letter to Francois Leydet, 13 March 1965, A. Murie Collection, Box 2, Folder "Correspondence 1943–1973," AHC.

23   Mowat to A. Murie, 25 November 1963, A. Murie Collection, Box 4, Folder "Correspondence 1948–1970, *Never Cry Wolf*," AHC. See too Peter Steinhart, *The Company of Wolves* (New York: Alfred A. Knopf, 1995), 58–61, and Thomas R. Dunlap, *Saving America's Wildlife* (Princeton: Princeton University Press, 1988), 106–8.

24   A. Murie to regional director, 7 March 1963, A. Murie Collection, Box "Correspondence," UAF; A. Murie to William Sheldon, 17 January 1947, A. Murie Collection, Box 2, Folder "Correspondence 1943–1973," AHC; A. Murie to Lawrence Merriam, 2 April 1951, A. Murie Collection, Box 2, Folder "Correspondence 1951–1965 re: articles and pamphlets," AHC; A. Murie to Sumner, 9 January 1951, A. Murie Collection, Box 1, folder "Correspondence 1951–1963," AHC; A. Murie to

regional chief of interpretation, 5 March 1962, A. Murie Collection, Box "Correspondence," UAF.

25 I have seen this in three sources: Murie's "A Plea for Idealism in National Parks" and *The Grizzlies of Mount McKinley*, 239–40; and Louise Murie MacLeod, "Denali Wilderness," *National Parks*, January 1978, 7.

26 R. Gerald Wright, *Wildlife Research and Management in the National Parks* (Urbana: University of Illinois Press, 1992), 23.

27 A. Murie diary, 24 June 1957, A. Murie Collection, Box "Personal Diary," UAF.

28 A. Murie interview by Evison, 7–8. The road improvements were not quite completed as planned. The first twelve miles from park headquarters are broad and paved; the next thirty miles are improved gravel, along the obtrusive route to which Adolph objected, and the remaining thirty-five miles are not for the faint of heart or those in a hurry. Travel by private auto has been restricted since 1972 beyond the paved section, with visitors transported by buses.

29 A. Murie, "Field Studies in Mount McKinley National Park, 1953," reprint, DTC.

30 Quoted in William E. Brown, *A History of the Denali-Mt. McKinley Region, Alaska* (Washington, D.C.: GPO, National Park Service), 220; he quotes extensively a critique of Mission 66 plans written by Murie in 1956.

31 A. Murie to regional director, 7 March 1963, A. Murie Collection, Box "Correspondence," UAF.

32 A. Murie to regional chief of interpretation, 5 March 1962, A. Murie Collection, Box "Correspondence," UAF; A. Murie to Tilden, 1 January 1965, A. Murie Collection, Box 2, Folder "Correspondence 1943–1973," AHC.

33 Among those friends was Devereaux Butcher, an ally from the 1940s; Butcher to A. Murie, 16 February 1962, A. Murie Collection, Box 8, Folder "Subject File—Adolph and Olaus Murie," AHC; Butcher to A. Murie, 16 May 1965, Box 1, Folder "Correspondence 1945–1965; tagging grizzlies," AHC.

34 A. Murie to regional director, 7 March 1963, A. Murie Collection, Box "Correspondence," UAF; Rick McIntyre, *A Society of Wolves: National Parks and the Battle Over the Wolf* (Stillwater, MN: Voyageur Press, 1993), 90.

35 Pete Sinclair, *We Aspired: The Last Innocent Americans* (Logan: Utah State University Press, 1993), 209.

36 Louise Murie Macleod interview; A. Murie to Zahniser, 11 November 1963, A. Murie Collection, Box 2, Folder "Subject File —1948–1964," AHC.

37 *Jackson Hole Guide*, "Adolph Murie Received Citation from Udall," 15 July 1965; *Fairbanks Daily News-Miner*, "Murie Gets Interior's Gold Medal," 6 August 1965; A. Murie to Teno Roncalio, 27 April 1966, A. Murie Collection, Box 2, Folder "Correspondence 1940–1972," AHC; A. Murie to Boyd Rasmussen, 13 February 1971, A. Murie Collection, Box 1, Folder "Correspondence 1933–1974, Adolph, personal-misc.," AHC. This letter was entered into the congressional hearings on the pipeline.

38   There are various letters in the Murie collections written over the years by people from around the world requesting copies of Murie's monographs. To cite two of these, Mr. and Mrs. Gilbert Staender of Sisters, Oregon (20 February 1972), wrote to Oregon Congressmen Hatfield, Packwood, and Nelson requesting their influence to see a reprint of the coyote study, comparing Murie to Rachel Carson. Stewart Brandborg, executive director of The Wilderness Society, lobbied the Interior Department for reprints of both; reply from [signature unclear], Asst. Secretary of the Interior, 25 April 1972; both in A. Murie Collection, Box 1, AHC.

39   Murie began agitating for expansion in 1953, and Victor Cahalane made a formal study of the issue on behalf of the Park Service the following year, agreeing that expansion was necessary; A. Murie, "Field Studies, 1953"; Victor H. Cahalane, "A Boundary Study of Mount McKinley National Park," unpublished report, National Park Service, 30 December 1954, reprint from DTC. Murie repeated his plea in 1959, warning that if wolves were eliminated "the park ecology will be thrown violently askew. Activities north of the park have developed which some of us failed to anticipate a few years ago." In Adolph Murie, "Biological Studies at Mount McKinley National Park - 1959," unpublished report, National Park Service, 22 October 1959, reprint from DTC. Gordon Haber, through his ten-year wolf study, had ample opportunity to find evidence of poachers; he recounted some of this in a letter to Robert Weeden, n.d., but apparently 1967, A. Murie Collection, Box 2, Folder "Subject File, 1966–1972," AHC. See too Brown, *History of Denali*, 219–21, 239–41, 161.

40   *Fairbanks Daily News-Miner*, "NPS Dismisses Ad Campaign," 25 July 1995; Theodore Catton, *Inhabited Wilderness: Indians, Eskimos, and National Parks in Alaska* (Albuquerque: University of New Mexico Press, 1997), chapter eight, "We Eskimos Would Like to Join the Sierra Club."

41   Ronald A. Foresta, *America's National Parks and Their Keepers* (Washington, D.C.: Resources for the Future, 1984), 25.

42   David Mech's recent Denali wolf project has provided data on wolf dispersal from the park. From 1986–94, fifty-six wolves left the park's packs to join other packs or establish new ones. The farthest-traveled wolf ended up north of the Brooks Range, a straight line distance of 435 miles; see Mech et. al., *The Wolves of Denali*, 47–49. This indicates some truth to objections to the park as a breeding ground, yet if this rate of dispersal represents any kind of average through this century, the number of wolves leaving the park could not have exerted the effects claimed by critics.

43   Ernest Gruening, "The Political Ecology of Alaska," in *Proceedings of the 2nd Annual Alaskan Science Conference*, 1951, 13.

44   This three-part editorial appeared in the June, July, and August issues.

45   Maurice W. Kelly, "The Wolf—and the Coyote," *The Alaska Sportsman*, October 1960, 36–38; Robert Rausch and Alan Courtright, "Big Bad Wolf?," *The Alaska Sportsman*, June 1967, 6–9, 59–60; "Main Trails and Bypaths," *The Alaska Sportsman*, December 1968, 3.

46   This was the Endangered Species Preservation Act of 1966, expanded in 1973 with the prevailing Endangered Species Act which justifies current wolf reintroduction efforts. For details on these, see Michael J. Bean and Melanie J. Rowland, *The Evolution of National Wildlife Law*, 3rd ed. (Westport, CT: Praeger, 1997), Chapter 7, "Endangered Species." Protection under this act was only for wolves in the contiguous states, as wolf populations in Alaska have not been endangered.

47   See the second half of Dunlap's *Saving America's Wildlife* on opposition to federal control programs; also useful is Frederic H. Wagner, *Predator Control and the Sheep Industry: The Role of Science in Policy Formation* (Claremont, CA: Regina Books, 1988).

48   Chapter 11, "Hunting the Hunters," in Bruce Hampton's *The Great American Wolf* (New York: Henry Holt, 1997), provides a good chronology of Alaska's recent wolf controversies.

49   National Research Council, *Wolves, Bears, and Their Prey in Alaska: Biological and Social Challenges in Wildlife Management* (Washington, D.C.: National Academy Press, 1997), 182–88.

50   Hampton, *Great American Wolf*, 232, 242.

51   Stephen R. Kellert, "Public Perceptions of Predators, Particularly the Wolf and Coyote," *Biological Conservation* 31 (1985):182; *Wolves, Bears, and Their Prey*, 138–40; Hampton, *Great American Wolf*, 243.

52   *Fairbanks Daily News-Miner*, 8–9 January 1993; *Daily News-Miner*, letter to editor, 26 March 1993; Feral quote in *Anchorage Daily News*, "We Alaskans" section M-7, 17 October 1993; Askins and Lowry quotes from my notes at the Alaska Wolf Summit, 16 January 1993, Fairbanks. This three-day event, bringing together biologists, state officials, representatives from interested groups, and the public, was a result of the controversy raised by the state control plans and recognition by the state government of the power and threat of the opposing groups.

53   Stephen R. Kellert, "Perceptions of Animals in America," in *Perceptions of Animals in American Culture*, ed. R. J. Hoage, 5–24 (Washington, D.C.: Smithsonian Institution Press, 1989); Kellert, "Public Perceptions of Predators," 167–89; Kellert et al., "Human Culture and Large Carnivore Conservation in North America," *Conservation Biology* 10 (August 1996): 977–90.

Bibliography

Archival Materials

Alaska and Polar Regions Department, Rasmuson Library, University of Alaska Fairbanks (UAF):
- Alaska Game Commission (AGC)
- E. L. "Bob" Bartlett Collection
- Lee R. Dice Collection
- Otto Geist Collection
- Adolph Murie Collection
- Olaus Murie Collection
- L. G. Palmer Collection
- Charles Sheldon Collection

Alaska State Archives (ASA), Juneau
- Record Group 101, File 25, 470–75: Office of the Territorial Governor, Alaska Game Commission, Predator Control, 1933–1953

Alaska State Historical Library (ASHL), Juneau

American Heritage Center (AHC), University of Wyoming
- Adolph Murie Collection, #8004
- Arthur Demaray Collection, #4031
- Paul Goodwin Redington Collection, # 7321

Dartmouth College Library (DCL):
- Belmore Browne Collection, part of the Vilhjalmur Stefansson Collection

Denali National Park and Preserve Library and Files (DENA):
   Superintendent's "Annual Reports," 1925–1955
   Superintendent's "Monthly Reports," 1925–1955
   "Wildlife Reports," 1930–1955
   File 5968, materials related to the wolf-sheep controversy copied from
      National Archives, Washington, D.C., and San Bruno, California

Denver Technical Center (DTC), National Park Service

National Archives, Washington, D.C. (NA):
   Record Group 79, Entry 7, File 715 and 719, Boxes 1413, 1414, 1415:
      National Park Service, Mt. McKinley National Park, Wildlife/Predators
   Record Group 79, Entry 7, Boxes 1405, 1406, 1407: National Park Service
   Record Group 79, Entry 19, Box 13: National Park Service, Records of
      Newton P. Drury 1933–49
   Record Group 126, File 9-1-33: Office of the Territories, Alaska, Game

Newspapers and Magazine

Fairbanks Daily News-Miner, 1925–1960
Jessen's Weekly, Fairbanks, 1942–1955
Anchorage Daily Times, 1930–1955
The Alaska Sportsman, Editorials "Main Trails and Bypaths," and notes "From
   Ketchikan to Barrow," 1935–1960

Interviews

"Newton Bishop Drury, Parks and Redwoods, 1919–1971." Interview by Amelia
   Roberts Fry and Susan Schrepfer. Berkeley: Regional Oral History Office,
   University of California, 1972.

Celia Hunter, Fairbanks conservationist, interview by author, 14 July 1994.

Adolph Murie. Interview by Herbert Evison, 19 October 1962. Transcript,
   Adolph Murie Collection, Western History Department, Denver Public
   Library.

Louise Murie MacLeod, interview by author, 21 June 1997.

Published Materials

Adams, Charles C. "The Conservation of Predatory Mammals." *Journal of Mammalogy* 6 (February 1925): 83–96.

———. "Rational Predatory Animal Control." *Journal of Mammalogy* 11 (August 1930): 353–62.

Aikio, Pekka. "The Changing Role of Reindeer in the Life of the Sámi." In *The Walking Larder: Patterns of Domestication, Pastoralism, and Predation*, ed. Juliet Clutton-Brock, 169–84. London: Unwin Hyman, 1989.

Alaska. Alaska Game Commission. *Annual Report of the Alaska Game Commission to the Secretary of the Interior.* 1932–1958.

———. Alaska Game Commission. *Annual Report of the Executive Officer to the Alaska Game Commission.* 1932–1948.

———. Legislature. *House Joint Memorial No. 10.* 11th Legislature. 1933.

———. Legislature. *Senate Joint Memorial No. 8.* 11th Legislature. 1933.

———. Legislature. *House Joint Memorial No. 7.* 13th Legislature. 1935.

———. Legislature. *Committee Substitute for Senate Joint Memorial No. 2.* 14th Legislature. 1939.

———. Legislature. *Senate Joint Memorial No. 16.* 14th Legislature. 1939.

———. Legislature. *Senate Joint Memorial No. 5.* 17th Legislature. 1945.

———. Legislature. An *Act to Preserve the Food Supply of Alaska, Placing a Bounty on Certain Wild Animals and Providing for the Payment of Same.* 2nd session, 1959. S.B. 11.

"The Alaska Sportsmen's Association." *The Alaska Sportsman,* January 1935, 20.

"The Alaska Sportsmen's Association." *The Alaska Sportsman,* February 1935, 18, 28.

"Alaskans' Per Capita Harvests of Wild Foods." *Alaska Fish & Game*, November-December 1989, 14–15.

Albright, Horace. "Our National Parks as Wild Life Sanctuaries." *American Forests* 35 (August 1929): 505–7, 536.

———. "The National Park Service's Policy on Predatory Animals." *Journal of Mammalogy* 12 (May 1931): 185–86.

———. *The Birth of the National Park Service: The Founding Years, 1913–33.* Salt Lake City: Howe Brothers, 1985.

Allen, Durward L. *Our Wildlife Legacy.* New York: Funk & Wagnalls, 1962.

———. *The Wolves of Minong: Isle Royale's Wild Community.* Ann Arbor: University of Michigan Press, 1993. (reprint, first paper edition.)

Annabel, Russell. "Wolves Look Better Dead." *Field and Stream*, September 1941, 38–40, 68–70.

———. "Flying in for the Big Ones." *Field and Stream*, January 1942, 16–18, 57, 68–69.

———. "Wolf Trouble in Alaska." *Field and Stream,* February 1947, 19–21, 73–75.

———. "Alaska's Thundering Herds." *Saturday Evening Post*, 27 December 1947, 19, 73–74.

———. *Hunting and Fishing in Alaska.* New York: Alfred A. Knopf, 1948.

Anthony, Harold. *Field Book of North American Mammals.* New York: G. P. Putnam's Sons, 1928.

———. Review of *The Wolves of Mount McKinley*, by Adolph Murie. In *Natural History,* January 1945, 46.

Bailey, Vernon. *Wolves in Relation to Stock, Game, and the National Forest Reserves.* Forest Service Bulletin No. 72. Washington, D.C.: GPO, Department of Agriculture, 1907.

Banfield, A. W. F. "The Present Status of North American Caribou." In *Transactions of the Fourteenth North American Wildlife Conference*, 477–89. Washington, D.C.: Wildlife Management Institute, 1949.

———. "Review of F. Mowat's *Never Cry Wolf.*" *Canadian Field Naturalist* 78 (1964): 52–54.

Barker, Elliot S. "Management for Maximum Production." In *Transactions of the Eighth North American Wildlife Conference*, 122–31. Washington, D.C.: Wildlife Management Institute, 1943.

Bass, Rick. *The Ninemile Wolves.* Livingston, MT: Clark City Press, 1992.

Bates, Robert. *Mountain Man: The Story of Belmore Browne.* Clinton, NJ: Amwell Press, 1988.

Bauer, Erwin A. *Wild Dogs: The Wolves, Coyotes, and Foxes of North America.* San Francisco: Chronicle Books, 1994.

Beach, Hugh. "Comparative Systems of Reindeer Herding." In *The World of Pastoralism: Herding Systems in Comparative Perspective*, eds. John G. Galaty and Douglas L. Johnson, 255–98. New York: The Guilford Press, 1990.

Beach, William N. *In the Shadow of Mt. McKinley.* New York: Derrydale Press, 1931.

———. "Game Marches On." *The Backlog,* February 1938, 2–4.

Bean, Michael J., and Melanie J. Rowland. *The Evolution of National Wildlife Law.* 3rd ed. Westport, CT: Praeger, 1997.

Bekoff, Marc, ed. *Coyotes: Biology, Behavior, and Management.* New York: Academic Press, 1978.

Bergerud, Arthur T. "Decline of Caribou in North America Following Settlement." *Journal of Wildlife Management* 38 (October 1974): 757–70.

———. "Caribou." In *Big Game of North America: Ecology and Management*, ed. John L. Schmidt and Douglas L. Gilbert, 83–101. Harrisburg, PA: Stackpole Books, for the Wildlife Management Institute, 1978.

Botkin, Daniel. *Discordant Harmonies: A New Ecology for the Twenty-First Century.* New York: Oxford University Press, 1992.

Brandenburg, Jim. *Brother Wolf.* Minocqua, WI: NorthWord Press, 1993.

Brickey, James and Catherine. "Reindeer, Cattle of the Arctic." *Alaska Journal,* Winter 1975, 16–24.

Brockman, C. Frank. "Park Naturalists and the Evolution of National Park Service Interpretation Through World War II." *Journal of Forest History* 22 (January 1978): 24–43.

Brooks, Alfred H. *An Exploration to Mount McKinley, America's Highest Mountain.* Washington, D.C.: GPO, 1904.

Brooks, Paul. *Speaking for Nature: How Literary Naturalists from Henry Thoreau to Rachel Carson Have Shaped America.* Boston: Houghton Mifflin Company, 1980.

Brown, David E., ed. *The Wolf in the Southwest: The Making of an Endangered Species.* Tucson: University of Arizona Press, 1983.

———. "Rambo: The Desert Bighorn Sheep as a Masculine Totem." In *Counting Sheep: Twenty Ways of Seeing Desert Bighorn,* ed. Gary Paul Nabhan, 188–200. Tucson: University of Arizona Press, 1993.

Brown, William E. *A History of the Denali-Mt. McKinley Region, Alaska.* Washington, D.C.: GPO, National Park Service, 1991.

Browne, Belmore. *The Conquest of Mount McKinley.* New York: G. P. Putnam's Sons, 1913.
———. *Analysis by Belmore Browne for the Committee on Conservation of the Report of Dr. Adolph Murie's "The Wolves of Mt. McKinley."* New York: Camp Fire Club of America, 1946.

Bryant, Harold C. "Nature Lore for Park Visitors." *American Forests* 35 (August 1929): 501–4, 540.

———. "George M. Wright, 1904–1936." *Bird-Lore,* March-April 1936, 137.

———. "Obituary Notices: George Melendez Wright." *Journal of Mammalogy* 17 (May 1936): 191–92.

————. "Predators Necessary to Wild Life." *Bird-Lore* (November-December 1936): 448–50.

Bryant, Harold C., and Wallace W. Atwood, Jr. *Research and Education in the National Parks.* Washington, D.C.: GPO, National Park Service, 1932.

Budiansky, Stephen. *The Covenant of the Wild: Why Animals Chose Domestication.* New York: William Morrow and Company, 1992.

Burbank, James C. *Vanishing Lobo: The Mexican Wolf and the Southwest.* Boulder, CO: Johnson Books, 1990.

Burch, E. S., Jr. "The Caribou/Wild Reindeer as a Human Resource." *American Antiquity* 37 (July 1972): 339–68.

————. *The Iñupiaq Eskimo Nations of Northwest Alaska.* Fairbanks: University of Alaska Press, 1998.

Burgess, Robert L. "The Ecological Society of America." In *History of American Ecology,* ed. Frank N. Egerton. New York: Arno Press, 1977.

Burkholder, Bob L. "Movements and Behavior of a Wolf Pack in Alaska." *Journal of Wildlife Management* 23 (January 1959): 1–11.

Busch, Robert H., ed. *Wolf Songs: The Classic Collection of Writing about Wolves.* San Francisco: Sierra Club Books, 1994.

Busch, Robert H. *The Wolf Almanac: A Celebration of Wolves and Their World.* New York: Lyons & Burford, 1995.

Butler, Ralph E. "The Blue Cow." *The Alaska Sportsman,* April 1945, 8–10.

Cahalane, Victor H. "The Evolution of Predator Control Policy in the National Parks." *Journal of Wildlife Management* 3 (July 1939): 229–37.

————. "Shall We Save the Larger Carnivores?" *The Living Wilderness,* June 1946, 17–22.

————. "Should We Cry Wolf?" *Field and Stream,* June 1946, 37, 103–7.

———. *Mammals of North America.* New York: MacMillan, 1947.

———. "Wildlife and the National Park Land-Use Concept." In *Transactions of the 12th North American Wildlife Conference,* 431–36. Washington, D.C.: Wildlife Management Institute, 1947.

———. "Predators and People." *National Parks Magazine,* October-December 1948: 5–12.

Callen, Bob. "The Lomens of Nome." *Alaska Life,* March 1946, 8–10, 35–37.

Callison, Israel Putnam. "Wolves and Coyotes, the Major Menace to North American Big Game." *Alaska Life,* June 1946, 10.

———. *Wolf Predation in the North Country.* Seattle: privately printed, 1948.

Cameron, Jenks. *The National Park Service: Its History, Activities, and Organization.* Washington, D.C.: GPO, 1922; reprint New York: AMS Press, 1974.

———. *The Bureau of Biological Survey.* Washington, D.C.: GPO, 1929; reprint, New York: Arno Press, 1974.

Camp Fire Club of America. "National Park Standards, as Defined by the Camp Fire Club of America." *American Forests* 35 (August 1929): 476.

Capps, Stephen R. "A Game Country Without Rival in America." *National Geographic,* January 1917, 69–84.

Carroll, Peter N. *Puritanism and the Wilderness.* New York: Columbia University Press, 1969.

Cart, Theodore W. "'New Deal' for Wildlife: A Perspective on Federal Conservation Policy, 1933–40." *Pacific Northwest Quarterly* 63 (July 1972): 113–20.

Cartmill, Matt. *A View Toward a Death in the Morning: Hunting and Nature Through History.* Cambridge: Harvard University Press, 1993.

Catton, Theodore. *Inhabited Wilderness: Indians, Eskimos, and National Parks In Alaska.* Albuquerque: University of New Mexico Press, 1997.

Caughley, Graeme. "Eruption of Ungulate Populations, with Emphasis on Himalayan Thar in New Zealand." *Ecology* 51 (Winter 1970): 53–72.

Chase, Alston. *Playing God in Yellowstone: The Destruction of America's First National Park.* New York: Harcourt Brace Jovanovich, 1987.

Clark, James L. *The Great Arc of the Wild Sheep.* Norman: University of Oklahoma Press, 1964.

———.*Good Hunting: Fifty Years of Collecting and Preparing Habitat Groups for the American Museum.* Norman: University of Oklahoma Press, 1966.

Clarke, Jeanne N., and Daniel McCool. *Staking Out the Terrain: Power Differentials Among Natural Resource Management Agencies.* Albany: State University of New York Press, 1985.

Clutton-Brock, Juliet. *Domesticated Animals From Early Times.* Austin: University of Texas Press, 1981.

Cole, Terrence, ed. *The Sourdough Expedition.* Anchorage: Alaska Northwest Publishing, 1985.

"Comment and News." *Journal of Mammalogy* 6 (August 1927): 267.

———. *Journal of Mammalogy* 10 (February 1929): 95.

Connery, Robert H. *Governmental Problems in Wildlife Conservation.* New York: Columbia University Press, 1935; reprint New York: AMS Press, 1968.

Cook, Frederick. "Round Mount McKinley." *Bulletin of the American Geographical Society* 36 (1904).

———. *To the Top of the Continent.* New York: Doubleday, 1908.

Crisler, Lois. *Arctic Wild.* London: Secker and Warburg, 1959.

Curry, Peggy Simson. "Portrait of a Naturalist." *The Living Wilderness,* Summer-Fall 1963, 15–21.

Darling, F. Fraser, and Noel D. Eichhorn. *Man & Nature in the National Parks: Reflections on Policy.* Washington, D.C.: The Conservation Foundation, 2nd ed., 1969.

Dassow, Ethel. "The Voice of the Last Frontier." *Alaska,* October 1984, 15–21, 85–89, 92–93.

Day, Albert M. "Wartime Uses of Wildlife Products." In *Transactions of the Eighth North American Wildlife Conference,* 45–54. Washington, D.C.: Wildlife Management Institute, 1943.

Diamond, Jared. *Guns, Germs, and Steel: The Fates of Human Societies.* New York: W. W. Norton & Co., 1997.

Dice, Lee R. "Notes on the Mammals of Interior Alaska." *Journal of Mammalogy* 2 (February 1921): 21.

———. "The Scientific Value of Predatory Mammals." *Journal of Mammalogy* 6 (February 1925): 25–27.

Dixon, Joseph. "General Notes: A Coyote from Mount McKinley, Alaska." *Journal of Mammalogy* 9 (February 1928): 64.

———. *Fauna of the National Parks of the United States: Birds and Mammals of Mount McKinley National Park, Alaska.* Fauna Series No. 3. Washington, D.C.: GPO, National Park Service, 1938.

Dobie, J. Frank. *The Voice of the Coyote.* Boston: Little, Brown and Co., 1949.

Dönitz, Karl. *Memoirs: Ten Years and Twenty Days.* Translated by R. H. Stevens. Cleveland: World Publishing Company, 1959.

Drury, Newton B. "The Future of National Forests and National Parks." *The Living Wilderness,* May 1944, 11–15.

———. Letter to Editor. *Field and Stream,* April 1946, 7–8.

Dufresne, Frank. "What of Tomorrow?" *The Alaska Sportsman,* April 1937, 9.

———. "The Game and Fur Belong to All the People." *The Alaska Sportsman,* April 1944, 16–18, 21.

———. *Alaska's Animals and Fishes.* New York: A. S. Barnes and Company, 1946.

———. "Ghosts that Kill Game." *Outdoor Life*, April 1948, 36–37.

Dunlap, Thomas R. "Values for Varmints: Predator Control and Environmental Ideas, 1920–1939." *Pacific Historical Review* 53 (May 1984): 141–61.

———. "American Wildlife Policy and Environmental Ideology: Poisoning Coyotes, 1939–1972." *Pacific Historical Review* 55 (August 1986): 345–69.

———. "Sport Hunting and Conservation, 1880–1920." *Environmental Review* 12 (Spring 1988): 51–60.

———. "That Kaibab Myth." *Journal of Forest History* 32 (April 1988): 60–68.

———. *Saving America's Wildlife.* Princeton: Princeton University Press, 1988.

———. "Wildlife, Science, and the National Parks, 1920–1940." *Pacific Historical Review* 59 (May 1990): 187–202.

———. "The Realistic Animal Story: Ernest Thompson Seton, Charles Roberts, and Darwinism." *Forest & Conservation History* 36 (April 1992): 56–62.

Dupree, A. Hunter. *Science in the Federal Government: A History of Policies and Activities to 1940.* New York: Harper & Row, 1957.

East, Ben. "Sportsmen: We Must Not Let Alaska's Game Die Out." *Outdoor Life,* May 1948, 24–25, 116–18.

Egerton, Frank N. "Changing Concepts of the Balance of Nature." *The Quarterly Review of Biology* 48 (June 1973): 322–50.

———. "Ecological Studies and Observations Before 1900." In *History of American Ecology*, ed. Frank N. Egerton. New York: Arno Press, 1977.

Elhard, Jay Robert. *Wolf Tourist: One Summer in the West.* Logan, UT: Utah State University Press, 1996.

Elton, Charles. *Animal Ecology*. London: Sidgwick & Jackson, Ltd., 1927; London: Methuen, 1966.

————. *Animal Ecology and Evolution*. Oxford: Clarendon Press, 1930.

Errington, Paul L. "Feathered vs. Human Predators," *Bird-Lore*, March-April 1935, 122–26.

————. *Of Predation and Life*. Ames, IA: Iowa State University Press, 1967.

————. *A Question of Values*. Ed. Carolyn Errington. Ames, IA: University of Iowa Press, 1987.

Evans, Francis C. "Lee Raymond Dice (1887–1977)." *Journal of Mammalogy* 59 (August 1978): 635–44.

Evans, Gail E. H. "From Myth to Reality: Travel Experiences and Landscape Perceptions in the Shadow of Mount McKinley, Alaska, 1876–1938." M.A. Thesis, University of California Santa Barbara, 1987.

Everhart, William C. *The National Park Service*. Boulder, CO: Westview Press, 1983.

Fabich, Henry J. "Poaching for Profit." In *Proceedings of the 60th Annual Conference of the Western Association of Fish and Wildlife Agencies*, July 13–17, 1980, Kalispell, MT, 181–86.

Ferguson, Chick. "Arch Villains of the Wilderness." *Field and Stream,* July 1946, 38, 97–99.

Fischer, Hank. *Wolf Wars: The Remarkable Inside Story of the Restoration of Wolves to Yellowstone*. Helena, MT: Falcon Press, 1995.

Flader, Susan. *Thinking Like a Mountain: Aldo Leopold and the Evolution of an Ecological Attitude toward Deer, Wolves, and Forests*. Lincoln: University of Nebraska Press, 1974.

Foresta, Ronald A. *America's National Parks and Their Keepers*. Washington, D.C.: Resources for the Future, 1984.

Fox, M.W., ed. *The Wild Canids: Their Systematics, Behavioral Ecology, and Evolution.* New York: Van Nostrand Reinhold, 1975.

Freemuth, John C. *Islands Under Siege: National Parks and the Politics of External Threats.* Lawrence: University of Kansas Press, 1991.

Fuch, Victor R. *The Economics of the Fur Trade Industry.* New York: Columbia Studies in the Social Sciences #593, Columbia University Press, 1957.

Gabler, F. W. "The Wolf Pack." *The Alaska Sportsman,* January 1935, 16–17, 21, 27.

Gier, H. T. "Ecology and Behavior of the Coyote (*Canis latrans*)." In *The Wild Canids: Their Systematics, Behavioral Ecology, and Evolution*, ed. M. W. Fox, 247–62. New York: Van Nostrand Reinhold, 1975.

Geist, Valerius. *Mountain Sheep: A Study in Behavior and Evolution.* Chicago: University of Chicago Press, 1971.

————. *Mountain Sheep and Man in the Northern Wilds.* Ithaca, NY: Cornell University Press, 1975.

————. "Did Large Predators Keep Humans Out of North America?" In *The Walking Larder: Patterns of Domestication, Pastoralism, and Predation*, ed. J. Clutton-Brock, 282–94. London: Unwin Hyman, 1989.

"General Notes," *Journal of Mammalogy* 16 (August 1935): 239.

Gerstell, Richard. *The Steel Trap in North America.* Harrisburg, PA: Stackpole, 1985.

Glacken, Clarence J. *Traces on the Rhodian Shore: Nature and Culture in Western Thought from Ancient Times to the End of the Eighteenth Century.* Berkeley: University of California Press, 1967.

Glover, James M. "Thinking Like a Wolverine: The Ecological Evolution of Olaus Murie." *Environmental Review* 13 (Fall/Winter 1989): 29–45.

————. "Sweet Days of a Naturalist: Olaus Murie in Alaska, 1920–26." *Forest & Conservation History* 36 (July 1992): 132–40.

Goldman, E.A. "The Predatory Mammal Problem and the Balance of Nature." *Journal of Mammalogy* 5 (August 1925): 28–33.

———. "The Coyote—Archpredator." *Journal of Mammalogy* 11 (August 1930): 325–35.

Grant, Campbell. "The Desert Bighorn and Aboriginal Man." In *The Desert Bighorn: Its Life History, Ecology, and Management,* eds. Gale Monson and Lowell Sumner, 7–39. Tucson: University of Arizona Press, 1980.

Grant, Madison. "Brief History of the Boone and Crockett Club." In *Hunting at High Altitudes,* ed. George Bird Grinnell, 435–91. New York: Harper & Bros., 1913.

———. "The Establishment of Mt. McKinley National Park." In *Hunting and Conservation: The Book of the Boone and Crockett Club,* ed. George Bird Grinnell, 438–45. New Haven: Yale University Press, 1925.

Grinnell, Hilda Wood. "Joseph Grinnell: 1877–1939." *The Condor* 42 (January–February 1940): 3–34.

Grinnell, Joseph. *Birds of the Kotzebue Sound Region,.* Santa Clara: Cooper Ornithological Club, 1900.

———. "The Niche-Relationship of the California Thrasher." *The Auk* 34 (1917): 427–33.

Grinnell, Joseph, and Tracy Storer. "Animal Life as an Asset of National Parks." *Science* 44 (15 September 1916): 375–80.

Grooms, Steve. *The Return of the Wolf.* Minocqua, WI: NorthWord Press, 1993.

Gruening, Ernest. "The Political Ecology of Alaska." In *Proceedings of the 2d Annual Alaskan Science Conference,* 1951.

———. *Many Battles: The Autobiography of Ernest Gruening.* New York: Liveright, 1973.

Haber, Gordon C. "Socio-Ecological Dynamics of Wolves and Prey in a Subarctic Ecosystem." Ph.D. dissertation, University of British Columbia, 1977.

Hadwen, Seymour, and Lawrence J. Palmer. *Reindeer in Alaska.* Bulletin No. 1089. Washington, D.C.: GPO, Department of Agriculture, 1922.

Hagen, Joel B. *An Entangled Bank: The Origins of Ecosystem Ecology.* New Brunswick, NJ: Rutgers University Press, 1992.

Haines, Aubrey. *The Yellowstone Story: A History of Our First National Park.* Two volumes. Yellowstone Library and Museum Association, in cooperation with Colorado Associated University Press, 1977.

Hall Dave. "Sam O. White: The First Flying Game Warden." *Alaska,* May 1986, 14–17, 59–62.

Hall, Roberta L., and Henry S. Sharp, eds. *Wolf and Man: Evolution in Parallel.* New York: Academic Press, 1978.

Hampton, Bruce. *The Great American Wolf.* New York: Henry Holt, 1997.

Hays, Samuel P. *Conservation and the Gospel of Efficiency: The Progressive Conservation Movement, 1890–1920.* Cambridge: Harvard University Press, 1959.

———. *Beauty, Health, and Permanence: Environmental Politics in the United States, 1955–1985.* Cambridge: Cambridge University Press, 1987.

Herman, Steven G. *The Naturalist's Field Journal: A Manual of Instruction Based on a System Established by Joseph Grinnell.* Vermillion, SD: Buteo Books, 1986.

Hornaday, William T. *Our Vanishing Wildlife: Its Extermination and Preservation.* New York: New York Zoological Society, 1913.

———. *A New Game Act for Alaska for the Better Protection and More Rational Utilization of Alaska's Game Animals.* New York Zoological Park: Permanent Wildlife Protection Fund. Bulletin No. 6, February 1920.

———. *The Minds and Manners of Wild Animals.* New York: Charles Scribner's Sons, 1927.

Howell, A. Brazier. "At the Crossroads." *Journal of Mammalogy* 11 (August 1930): 377–89.

Hughes, Terry, and John Costello. *The Battle of the Atlantic*. New York: Dial Press, 1977.

Huntington, Sidney. "Koyukuk and Yukon Valley Wildlife, Yesterday and Today." *Alaska,* January 1985, 60–62.

Huth, Hans. *Nature and the American: Three Centuries of Changing Attitudes.* 2nd ed. Lincoln: University of Nebraska Press, 1990.

Irwin, R. W. "I Stalk Villains of Wildlife." *The Alaska Sportsman* , March 1943, 14–16, 19–20.

Ise, John. *Our National Park Policy: A Critical History.* Baltimore: Johns Hopkins Press, 1961.

Jenkins, Ken L. *Wolf Reflections*. Merrillville, IN: ICS Books, 1996.

Kaufman, Polly Welts. "Challenging Tradition: Pioneer Women Naturalists in the National Park Service." *Forest and Conservation History* 34 (January 1990): 4–16.

———. *National Parks and the Woman's Voice: A History*. Albuquerque: University of New Mexico Press, 1996.

Keim, Charles J. *Aghvook, White Eskimo: Otto Geist and Alaska Archaeology*. Fairbanks: University of Alaska Press, 1969.

Keller, Betty. *Black Wolf: The Life of Ernest Thompson Seton*. Vancouver: Douglas & McIntyre, 1984.

Kellert, Stephen R. "Public Perceptions of Predators, Particularly the Wolf and Coyote." *Biological Conservation* 31 (1985): 167–89.

———. "Perceptions of Animals in America." In *Perceptions of Animals in American Culture*, ed. R. J. Hoage, 5–24. Washington, DC: Smithsonian Institution Press, 1989.

Kellert, Stephen R., et. al. "Human Culture and Large Carnivore Conservation in North America." *Conservation Biology* 10 (August 1996): 977–90.

Kelly, Maurice W. "The Wolf—and the Coyote," *The Alaska Sportsman*, October 1960, 36–38.

Kendrick, Gregory D. "An Environmental Spokesman: Olaus J. Murie and a Democratic Defense of Wilderness." *Annals of Wyoming* 50 (Fall 1978): 213–302.

Kennedy, Michael S. "Belmore Brown and Alaska." *Alaska Journal*, Spring 1973, 96–104.

Kimball, David, and Jim Kimball. *The Market Hunter*. Minneapolis: Dillon Press, 1969.

Kingsland, Sharon. *Modeling Nature: Episodes in the History of Population Ecology*. Chicago: University of Chicago Press, 1985.

Klinghammer, Erich. "Introduction." In *The Behavior and Ecology of Wolves: Proceedings of the Symposium on the Behavior and Ecology of Wolves Held in Wilmington, N. C., 23–24 May, 1975*, edited by Erich Klinghammer. New York: Garland STPM Press, 1979.

————. "The Wolf: Fact and Fiction." In *Perceptions of Animals in American Culture*, ed. R. J. Hoage, 77–91. Washington, DC: Smithsonian Institution Press, 1989.

Klinghammer, Erich, Monty Sloan, and De Wayne R. Klein. *Wolf Literature References: Scientific and General Books and Articles Listed Alphabetically by Author*. Battle Ground, IN: North American Wildlife Park Foundation, Inc., 1990.

Lantis, Margaret. "The Reindeer Industry in Alaska." *Arctic* 3 (April 1950): 27–44.

————. "Edward William Nelson." *Anthropological Papers of the University of Alaska* 3 (December 1954): 5–15.

Lawrence, R. D. *Secret Go the Wolves*. New York: Holt, Rinehart, and Winston, 1980.

————. *In Praise of Wolves*. New York: Henry Holt, 1986.

————. *Trail of the Wolf*. Buffalo, NY: Firefly Books, 1997.

Legge, Tony. "The Beginning of Caprine Domestication in Southwest Asia." In *The Origins and Spread of Agriculture and Pastoralism in Eurasia,* ed. David R. Harris, 238–62. Washington, D.C.: Smithsonian Institution Press, 1996.

Leland, Waldo Gifford. "Newton Bishop Drury." *National Parks Magazine*, April-June 1951, 42–44, 62–66.

Leopold, Aldo. "The Wilderness and its Place in Forest Recreational Policy." *Journal of Forestry* 19 (November 1921): 718–21.

———. *Game Management.* New York: Charles Scribner's Sons, 1933.

———. "Naturshutz in Germany." *Bird-Lore*, March-April 1936, 102–11.

———. *A Sand County Almanac.* New York: Oxford University Press, 1949; reprint New York: Ballantine Books, 1966.

Leopold, A. Starker. "Study of Wildlife Problems in National Parks." In *Transactions of the 28th North American Wildlife and Natural Resources Conference*, 28–45. Washington, D.C.: Wildlife Management Institute, 1963.

Leopold, A. Starker, and F. Fraser Darling. *Wildlife in Alaska: An Ecological Reconnaissance.* New York: The Conservation Foundation and Ronald Press Company, 1953.

Lester, Joseph. "Come and Get 'Em." *The Alaska Sportsman*, April 1940, 8–9, 24–25.

Link, Mike, ed. *The Collected Works of Sigurd F. Olson: The Early Writings: 1921–1934.* Stillwater, MN: Voyageur Press, 1988.

———. *The Collected Works of Sigurd F. Olson: The College Years: 1935–1944.* Stillwater, MN: Voyageur Press, 1990.

Link, Mike, and Kate Crowley. *Following the Pack: The World of Wolf Research.* Stillwater, MN: Voyageur Press, 1994.

Lipscomb, Louis W. "Procurement of Ammunition for Other Than Military Purposes." In *Transactions of the Eighth North American Wildlife Conference*, 73–77. Washington, D.C.: Wildlife Management Institute, 1943.

Little, John. "Adolph Murie and the Wilderness Ideal for Isle Royale National Park." In *The American West: Essays in Honor of W. Eugene Hollon*, ed. Ronald Lora, 97–114. Toledo, OH: University of Toledo, 1980.

Loftus, Audrey. "Tom Gibson—Meat Hunter." *The Alaska Sportsman* , August 1967, 20–22.

Lomen, Carl J. *Fifty Years in Alaska*. New York: David McKay Company, Inc., 1954.

Lopez, Barry Holstun. *Of Wolves and Men*. New York: Charles Scribner's Sons, 1978.

Luick, Jack R. "The Cantwell Reindeer Industry 1921–1928." *Alaska Journal*, Spring 1973, 107–13.

Lutts, Ralph H. *The Nature Fakers: Wildlife, Science, & Sentiment*. Golden, CO: Fulcrum Publishing, 1990.

Lutz, H. J. *History of the Early Occurrence of Moose on the Kenai Peninsula and in Other Sections of Alaska*. Juneau: U.S. Department of Agriculture, Alaska Forest Research Center, 1960.

Mackintosh, Barry. "Harold L. Ickes and the National Park Service." *Journal of Forest History* 29 (April 1985): 78–84.

Main Trails and Bypaths, *The Alaska Sportsman*, December 1968, 3.

Maltin, Leonard. *The Disney Films*. New York: Crown Publishers, 1973.

Marsh, George Perkins. *Man and Nature*. New York: Charles Scribner's Sons, 1865; reprint, Cambridge: Harvard University Press, 1965.

Martin Paul S., and Richard G. Klein, eds., *Quaternary Extinctions: A Prehistoric Revolution*. Tucson: University of Arizona Press, 1984.

McCandless, Robert G. *Yukon Wildlife: A Social History*. Edmonton: University of Alberta Press, 1985.

McGuire, J. A. *In the Alaska-Yukon Gamelands*. Cincinnati: Stewart Kidd Company, 1921.

McIntyre, Rick. *A Society of Wolves: National Parks and the Battle Over the Wolf.* Stillwater, MN.: Voyageur Press, 1993.

McIntyre, Rick, ed. *War Against the Wolf: America's Campaign to Exterminate the Wolf.* Stillwater, MN: Voyageur Press, 1995.

McNamee, Thomas. *The Return of the Wolf to Yellowstone.* New York: Henry Holt, 1997.

McNight, Donald E. "The History of Predator Control in Alaska." Internal report, Alaska Department of Fish and Game, 1970.

McRandle, James Harrington. *The Track of the Wolf: Essays on National Socialism and its Leader, Adolf Hitler.* Evanston: Northwestern University Press, 1965.

Mech, L. David. *The Wolf: The Ecology and Behavior of an Endangered Species.* 2nd ed. Minneapolis: University of Minnesota Press, 1981.

————. *The Way of the Wolf.* Stillwater, MN: Voyageur Press, 1991.

————. *Wolves of the High Arctic.* Stillwater, MN: Voyageur Press, 1992.

————. *The Arctic Wolf: Ten Years with the Pack.* Stillwater, MN: Voyageur Press, 1997, rev. ed.

Mech, L. David, Layne G. Adams,Thomas J. Meier, John W. Burch, and Bruce W. Dale. *The Wolves of Denali.* Minneapolis: University of Minnesota Press, 1998.

Meine, Curt. *Aldo Leopold: His Life and Work.* Madison: University of Wisconsin Press, 1988.

Mighetto, Lisa. "Wolves I Have Known: Naturalist Ernest Thompson Seton in the Arctic." *Alaska Journal,* Winter 1985, 55–59.

————. *Wild Animals and American Environmental Ethics.* Tucson: University of Arizona Press, 1991.

Miles, John C. "Charting the Course." *National Parks,* November-December 1993, 40.

———. *Guardians of the Parks: A History of the National Parks and Conservation Association.* Washington, D.C.: Taylor & Francis, 1995.

Miller, C. Blackburn. "Shall We Protect the Killers?" *Field and Stream,* January 1946, 40–41, 96–97.

Miller, Orlando. *The Frontier in Alaska and the Matanuska Colony.* New Haven: Yale University Press, 1973.

Moore, Terris. *Mount McKinley: The Pioneer Climbs.* Fairbanks: University of Alaska Press, 1967.

Mowat, Farley. *Never Cry Wolf.* New York: Dell Publishing, 1963.

Murie, Adolph. *The Moose of Isle Royale,* University of Michigan Museum of Zoology, Miscellaneous Publications No. 25. Ann Arbor: University of Michigan Press, 1934.

———. *Mammals From Guatemala and British Honduras.* University of Michigan Museum of Zoology Miscellaneous Publications No. 26. Ann Arbor: University of Michigan Press, 1935.

———. *Following Fox Trails.* University of Michigan Museum of Zoology Miscellaneous Publications No. 32. Ann Arbor: University of Michigan Press, 1936.

———. "Some Food Habits of the Black Bear." *Journal of Mammalogy* 18 (May 1937): 238–40.

———. *Ecology of the Coyote in Yellowstone.* Fauna Series No. 4. Washington, D.C.: GPO, National Park Service, 1940.

———. *The Wolves of Mount McKinley.* Washington, D.C.: GPO, National Park Service, 1944; reprint, Seattle: University of Washington Press, 1985.

———. "The Wolves of Mount McKinley." *The Living Wilderness,* February 1945, 9–25.

———. "Another Look at McKinley Park Sheep." *The Living Wilderness,* December 1946, 14–16.

———. "The Mysterious Mouse." *Audubon,* July-August 1948, 202–10.

———. "Coyote Food Habits on a Southwestern Cattle Range." *Journal of Mammalogy* 32 (August 1951): 291–95.

———. "Grizzly Mothers in the Alaska Range." *Living Wilderness,* Autumn 1952, 15–21.

———. *A Naturalist in Alaska.* New York: Devin-Adair Company, 1961.

———. *The Grizzlies of Mount McKinley.* Scientific Monograph Series Number 14. Washington, D.C.: GPO, National Park Service, 1981.

Murie, Louise. "Denali Wilderness." *National Parks and Conservation Magazine,* January 1978, 4–8.

Murie, Margaret. *Two in the Far North.* 2nd edition. Seattle: Alaska Northwest Publishing, 1983.

Murie, Margaret, and Olaus J. Murie. *Wapiti Wilderness.* New York: Alfred A. Knopf, 1966.

Murie, Olaus J. *Alaska-Yukon Caribou.* North American Fauna Series Number 54. Washington, D.C.: GPO, Bureau of Biological Survey, 1935.

———. *Food Habits of the Coyote in Jackson Hole, Wyoming.* Washington, D.C.: GPO, Dept. of Agriculture Circular No. 362, 1935.

———. "Editorial." *The Living Wilderness,* June 1946, 1.

———. *The Elk of North America.* Harrisburg, PA: Stackpole Company, 1951.

———. "Wolf." *Audubon,* September-October 1957, 218–21.

———. *Journeys to the Far North.* Palo Alto: American West Publishing, 1973.

Olaus J. Murie and Adolph Murie. "Travels of *Peromyscus.*" *Journal of Mammalogy* 12 (August 1931): 200–9.

————. "Further Notes on Travels of *Peromyscus*." *Journal of Mammalogy* 13 (February 1932): 78–79.

Murray, John A., ed. *Out Among the Wolves: Contemporary Writings on the Wolf.* Anchorage: Alaska Northwest Books, 1993.

Nash, Roderick. *Wilderness and the American Mind.* 2nd ed. New Haven: Yale University Press, 1973.

National Research Council. *Wolves, Bears, and Their Prey in Alaska: Biological and Social Challenges in Wildlife Management.* Washington, D.C.: National Academy Press, 1997.

Nelson, Edward W. *The Eskimo About Bering Strait.* Washington, D.C.: GPO, 1899; reprint, Washington, D.C.: Smithsonian Institution Press, 1983.

Newhouse, Sewell. *The Trapper's Guide.*, 6th ed. New York: Oakley, Mason, & Co., 1874.

Norris, Frank. "A Lone Voice in the Wilderness: The National Park Service in Alaska, 1917–1969." *Environmental History* 1 (October 1996): 66–76.

North, Frank. "Wilderness Opportunities." *The Alaska Sportsman,* July 1940, 18–20, 22–23.

Olsen, Russ. *Administrative History: Organizational Structures of the National Park Service, 1917–1985.* Washington, D.C.: GPO, National Park Service, 1985.

Osborne, Henry Fairfield. "Preservation of the Wild Animals of North America." In *American Big Game and its Haunts,* George Bird Grinnell, ed. New York: Forest and Stream Publishing, 1904.

Osgood, Wilfred H. *Results of a Biological Reconnaissance of the Yukon River Region.* North America Fauna No. 19. Washington, D.C.: GPO, Biological Survey, 1900.

————. *Biological Investigations in Alaska and Yukon Territory.* North American Fauna No. 30. Washington, D.C.: GPO, Biological Survey, 1909.

Paige, John C. *The Civilian Conservation Corps and the National Park Service, 1933–1942: An Administrative History.* Washington, D.C.: GPO, National Park Service, 1985.

Palmer, Lawrence J. *Raising Reindeer in Alaska.* Washington, D.C.: GPO, Department of Agriculture, 1934.

Palmer, T. S. *Progress of Reindeer Grazing Investigations in Alaska.* Department Bulletin No. 1423. Washington, D.C.: GPO, Department of Agriculture, 1926.

Park, Barry C. "Problems from Creation of Refuges for Big Game." In *Transactions of the Eighth North American Wildlife Conference*, 339–46. Washington, D.C.: Wildlife Management Institute, 1943.

Parsons, P.A. "The Timber Wolf: Scourge of Game and Stock." *Outdoor Life*, July 1946, 40.

Pearson, Grant H. *The Seventy Mile Kid.* Los Altos, California: By the author, 1957.

———. *My Life of High Adventure.* Englewood Cliffs, New Jersey: Prentice-Hall, 1962.

Perkins, Elmer. "Bounty Hunter." *The Alaska Sportsman,* May 1938, 10–11, 22.

Peters, Roger. *The Dance of the Wolves.* New York: McGraw-Hill, 1985.

Peterson, Rolf O. *The Wolves of Isle Royale: A Broken Balance.* Minocqua, WI: Willow Creek Press, 1995.

Peterson del Mar, David. "'Our Animal Friends': Depictions of Animals in *Reader's Digest* During the 1950s." *Environmental History* 3 (January 1998): 25–44.

Phillips, Michael K., and Douglas H. Smith. *The Wolves of Yellowstone.* Stillwater, MN: Voyageur Press, 1996.

Pimlott, D. H. "Review of F. Mowat's Never Cry Wolf." *Journal of Wildlife Management* 30 (1966): 236–37.

"Poisoning Campaigns." *Bird-Lore,* May-June 1932, 235–39.

Pough, Richard. Review of *The Wolves of Mount McKinley*, by Adolph Murie. In *Audubon*, January-February 1945, 58.

Postell, Alice. *Where Did the Reindeer Come From? Alaska Experience, the First Fifty Years*. Portland, Oregon: Amaknak Press, 1990.

"Predators Necessary to Wild Life." *Bird-Lore,* November-December 1936, 448–50.

Putvin, William. "Wolves, Eagles, and Seals." *The Alaska Sportsman,* January 1940, 12–13, 23–25.

Rausch, Robert and Alan Courtright, "Big Bad Wolf?," *The Alaska Sportsman*, June 1967, 6–9, 59–60.

Ray, Dorothy Jean. *The Eskimos of Bering Strait 1650–1898*. Seattle: University of Washington Press, 1975.

Rearden, Jim. "Fairy Tales and Wolves." *Alaska*, January 1985, 27, 74–75.

Redington, Paul G. "The United States Bureau of Biological Survey." *The Scientific Monthly* 37 (October 1933): 289–306.

Reed, Nathaniel P. and Dennis Drabelle. *The United States Fish and Wildlife Service*. Boulder, CO: Westview Press, 1984.

Reiger, George. "The Salvation of Wild Rivers." *Field & Stream*, July 1993, 12, 14.

———. "Golden Oldies." *Field & Stream*, October 1993, 18–20.

Reiger, John F. *American Sportsmen and the Origin of Conservation,* 2nd ed. Norman, Oklahoma: University of Oklahoma Press, 1986.

Roberts, Brian. "The Reindeer Industry in Alaska." *Polar Record* 3 (January 1942): 568–72.

Rogers, George W., and Richard A. Cooley. *Alaska's Population and Economy.* College, Alaska: University of Alaska, 1963.

Roosevelt, Theodore. *The Wilderness Hunter*. New York: G. P. Putnam's Sons, 1893.

Rowland, Beryl. *Animals with Human Faces: A Guide to Animal Symbolism.* Knoxville: University of Tennessee Press, 1973.

Runte, Alfred. *Trains of Discovery: Western Railroads and the National Parks.* Flagstaff, AZ: Northland Press, 1984.

———.*National Parks: The American Experience. 2nd Ed.* Lincoln: University of Nebraska Press, 2nd ed., 1987.

———. *Yosemite: The Embattled Wilderness.* Lincoln: University of Nebraska Press, 1990.

———. "Joseph Grinnell and Yosemite: Rediscovering the Legacy of a California Conservationist." In *Yosemite and Sequoia: A Century of California National Parks,* eds. Richard J. Orsi, Alfred Runte, and Marlene Smith-Baranzini, 84–95. Berkeley: University of California Press, 1993.

Russo, John P. *The Kaibab Deer Herd: Its History, Problems, and Management.* Phoenix, AZ: State of Arizona Game and Fish Department. Wildlife Bulletin No. 7, Federal Aid in Wildlife Restoration Act, Project W-53-R, 1964.

Sancrant, D. L. "The Life that Never Knows Harness." *The Alaska Sportsman,* May 1941, 12–13, 24–26.

Savage, Candace. *Wolves.* San Francisco: Sierra Club Books, 1988.

Schaller, George B. *Mountain Monarchs: Wild Sheep and Goats of the Himalaya.* Chicago: University of Chicago Press, 1977.

Schickel, Richard. *The Disney Version: The Life, Times, Art and Commerce of Walt Disney.* New York: Simon and Schuster, 1968.

Schueneman, Albert. "I Match Wits With Wolves." *The Alaska Sportsman,* April 1941, 18–20.

Schwartz, Marion. *A History of Dogs in the Early Americas.* New Haven: Yale University Press, 1997.

Scott, Robert F. "Wildlife in the Economy of Alaska Natives." In *Transactions of the Sixteenth North American Wildlife Conference*. Washington, D.C.: Wildlife Management Institute, 1951.

Sellars, Richard West. *Preserving Nature in the National Parks: A History*. New Haven: Yale University Press, 1997.

Shankland, Robert. *Steve Mather of the National Parks*. 2nd ed. New York: Alfred A. Knopf, 1970.

Sheldon, Charles. *The Wilderness of the Upper Yukon*. New York: Charles Scribner's Sons, 1911.

———. *The Wilderness of Denali: Explorations of a Hunter-Naturalist in Northern Alaska*. New York: Charles Scribner's Sons, 1930.

———. *The Wilderness of the Southwest: Charles Sheldon's Quest for Desert Bighorn Sheep and Adventures with the Havasupai and Seri Indians*, eds. Neil B. Carmony and David E. Brown. Salt Lake City: University of Utah Press, 1993.

Sheldon, Jennifer W. *Wild Dogs: The Natural History of the Nondomestic Canidae*. San Diego: Academic Press, 1992.

Shelford, Victor. *Animal Communities in Temperate America, as Illustrated in the Chicago Area: A Study in Animal Ecology*. Chicago: University of Chicago Press, 1913.

Sherwood, Morgan B. *Exploration of Alaska, 1865–1900*. New Haven: Yale University Press, 1965.

———. *Big Game in Alaska: A History of Wildlife and People*. New Haven: Yale University Press, 1981.

Shirer, William L. *The Rise and Fall of the Third Reich*. New York: Simon and Schuster, 1960.

Showell, J. P. Mallmann. *U-Boats Under the Swastika*. Annapolis: Naval Institute Press, 1987.

Sinclair, Pete. *We Aspired: The Last Innocent Americans.* Logan: Utah State University Press, 1993.

Singer, Francis J. *Status and History of Caribou and Wolves in Denali National Park.* Anchorage: National Park Service, 1985.

"Sixth Annual Meeting of the American Society of Mammalogists." *Journal of Mammalogy* 5 (August 1924): 218–21.

Skoog, Ronald O. "Range, Movements, Population, and Food Habits of the Steese-Fortymile Caribou Herd." M.S. thesis, University of Alaska Fairbanks, 1956.

———. "Ecology of the Caribou in Alaska." Ph.D. dissertation, University of California Berkeley, 1968.

Smith, Bernard L. "The Status and Management of the Wolf in the Yukon Territory." In *Wolves in Canada and Alaska,* Ludwig N. Carbyn, ed., 48–50. Edmonton: Canadian Wildlife Service Report Series Number 45, 1983.

Snow, C. R. "The Trap Line." *The Alaska Sportsman,* March 1935, 20, 30.

———. "The Trap Line." *The Alaska Sportsman,* December 1935, 20–21.

Snyder, Harold. "Adventurous Life." *The Alaska Sportsman,* October 1940, 10–11, 31–33.

Steinhart, Peter. *The Company of Wolves.* New York: Alfred A. Knopf, 1995.

Stephenson, Robert O., and Robert T. Ahgook. "The Eskimo Hunter's View of Wolf Ecology and Behavior." In *The Wild Canids: Their Systematics, Behavioral Ecology, and Evolution,* ed. M. W. Fox, 286–91. New York: Van Nostrand Reinhold, 1975.

Sterling, Keir B. *Last of the Naturalists: The Career of C. Hart Merriam.* New York: Arno Press, 1977.

———. "Builders of the U.S. Biological Survey, 1885–1930." *Journal of Forest History* 33 (October 1989): 180–87.

Stern, Richard Olav. "'I Used to Have Lots of Reindeers'—The Ethnohistory and Cultural Ecology of Reindeer Herding in Northwest Alaska." Ph.D. dissertation, State University of New York at Binghamton, 1980.

———. *A Selected Annotated Bibliography of Sources on Reindeer Herding in Alaska.* Occasional Papers on Northern Life, No. 2. Fairbanks, Alaska: Institute of Arctic Biology, University of Alaska Fairbanks, n.d.

Stevenson, Marc. "Dire Wolf Systematics and Behavior." In *Wolf and Man: Evolution in Parallel*, eds. Roberta L. Hall and Henry S. Sharp, 179–96. New York: Academic Press, 1978.

Stiles, Henry R., ed. *The History of Ancient Wethersfield, Connecticut.* Volume I. New York: Grafton Press, 1904.

Stuck, Hudson. *The Ascent of Denali, (Mount McKinley), A Narrative of the First Complete Ascent of the Highest Peak in North America.* New York: Charles Scribner's Sons, 1914; reprinted as *The Ascent of Denali*, Seattle: The Mountaineers, 1977.

Sutton, Ann, and Myron Sutton. "The Man From Yosemite." *National Parks Magazine*, July-September 1954, 102–5, 131–32, 140.

Swain, Donald C. *Federal Conservation Policy 1921–1933.* Berkeley: University of California Press, 1963.

———. "The Passage of the National Park Service Act of 1916." *Wisconsin Magazine of History* 50 (Autumn 1966): 4–17.

———. *Wilderness Defender: Horace M. Albright and Conservation.* Chicago: University of Chicago Press, 1970.

———. "The National Park Service and the New Deal, 1933–1940." *Pacific Historical Review* 41 (August 1972): 312–32.

Thiel, Richard P. *The Timber Wolf in Wisconsin: The Death and Life of a Majestic Predator.* Madison: University of Wisconsin Press, 1993.

Thomas, Bob. *Walt Disney: An American Original.* New York: Simon and Schuster, 1976.

Thompson, Howard. Review of *White Wilderness. New York Times*, 3 August 1958.

Thorson, Robert M., et al. *Interior Alaska: A Journey Through Time.* Anchorage: Alaska Geographic Society, 1986.

Tober, James A. *Who Owns the Wildlife? The Political Economy of Conservation in Nineteenth-Century America.* Westport, CT: Greenwood Press, 1981.

Trefethen, James B. *Crusade for Wildlife: Highlights in Conservation Progress.* Harrisburg, PA: Stackpole, and the Boone and Crockett Club, 1961.

————. *An American Crusade for Wildlife.* New York: Winchester Press, and the Boone and Crockett Club, 1975.

Tremblay, Ray. *Trails of an Alaska Game Warden.* Anchorage: Alaska Northwest Publishing Company, 1985.

Uerpmann, Hans-Peter. "Animal Exploitation and the Phasing of the Transition from the Paleolithic to the Neolithic." In *The Walking Larder: Patterns of Domestication, Pastoralism, and Predation,* ed. J. Clutton-Brock, 91–96. London: Unwin Hyman, 1989.

————. "Animal Domestication—Accident or Intention?" In *The Origins and Spread of Agriculture and Pastoralism in Eurasia,* ed. David R. Harris, 227–37. Washington, D.C.: Smithsonian Institution Press, 1996.

U.S. Congress. House. Committee on Public Lands. *Protection of Dall Sheep, Caribou, Etc., Native to Mount McKinley National Park: Hearing before the Committee on Public Lands.* 79th Congress, 2nd session., H. R. 5004.

————. House. Committee on Public Lands. To *Provide for the Protection of the Dall Sheep, Caribou, and Other Wildlife Native to the Mount McKinley National Park Area, and for Other Purposes.* 80th Congress, 1st session, 1947, H.R. 2863.

————. House. Committee on Public Lands. *Hearings on Statehood for Alaska.* 80th Congress, 1st session, 16–24 April 1947.

————. Senate. Subcommittee of Committee on Territories. *Hearings on Conditions in Alaska.* 58th Congress, 2nd session, 22 July 1903.

————. Senate. Committee on Territories. *Hearing on A Bill to Establish the Mount McKinley National Park.* 64th Congress, 2nd Session, 5 May 1916.

————. Senate. *To Provide for the Protection of the Dall Sheep, Caribou, and Other Wildlife Native to the Mount McKinley National Park Area, and for Other Purposes.* 80th Congress, 1st session, 1947, S.B. 891.

U.S. Department of Agriculture. *Annual Report of the Alaska Game Commission to the Secretary of Agriculture.* Washington, D.C., 1928–1939.

———. *Annual Report of the Chief of the Bureau of Biological Survey.* Washington, D.C., 1936.

U.S. Department of the Interior. *Annual Report of the Alaska Game Commission.* Washington, D.C., 1940–1958.

———. *Annual Report of the Director of the National Park Service to the Secretary of the Interior.* Washington, D.C., 1930, 1931.

———. *Annual Report of the Governor of Alaska on the Alaska Game Law.* Washington, D.C., 1919.

———. *Annual Report of the Governor of Alaska to the Secretary of the Interior.* Washington, D.C., 1916–1931.

———. *Hearings Before the Reindeer Committee in Washington, D.C.* February-March, 1931.

———. *A Recreation Program for Alaska.* Vol. 2. Washington, D.C.: GPO, 1955.

Vogel, Oscar H. "My Years with the Wolves." *Alaska,* May 1972, 10–12, 56–58.

Wagner, Frederic H., et. al. *Wildlife Policies in the U.S. National Parks.* Washington, D.C.: Island Press, 1995.

Walcott, Frederic C. "Harvesting Game in Wartime." In *Transactions of the Eighth North American Wildlife Conference,* 12–20. Washington, D.C.: Wildlife Management Institute, 1943.

Warren, Louis S. *The Hunter's Game: Poachers and Conservationists in Twentieth-Century America.* New Haven: Yale University Press, 1997.

Washburn, Bradford, H. Adams Carter, and Ann Carter. "Dr. Cook and Mount McKinley." *American Alpine Club Journal* (1958): 1–30.

Weaver, John. *The Wolves of Yellowstone: History, Ecology, and Status.* National Park Service. Natural Resources Report No. 14, 1978.

Wickersham, James. *Old Yukon: Tales, Trails, Trials.* Washington, D.C.: Washington Law Book Company, 1938.

"Wild Life in National Parks." *Bird-Lore,* January-February 1931, 100–1.

Wilson, Alexander. *The Culture of Nature: North American Landscapes frm Disney to the Exxon Valdez.* Toronto: Between the Lines, 1991.

Wilson, William H. "Railroad and Reindeer." *Alaska Journal,* Winter 1980, 56–61.

Wing, Leonard. "Predation is Not What it Seems." *Bird-Lore,* November-December 1936, 401–5.

Wishart, William. "Bighorn Sheep." In *Big Game of North America: Ecology and Management,* eds. John L. Schmidt and Douglas L. Gilbert, 161–71. Harrisburg, PA: Stackpole, 1980.

Wister, Owen. "The Mountain Sheep: His Ways." In *Musk-Ox, Bison, Sheep and Goat,* eds. Caspar Whitney, George Bird Grinnell, and Owen Wister, 167–226. New York: Macmillan, 1904.

Wolfe, Art. *In the Presence of Wolves.* New York: Crown, 1995.

Wolfe, R. J., and R. J. Walker. "Subsistence Economies in Alaska: Productivity, Geography, and Development Impacts." *Arctic Anthropology* 2 (1987): 56–81.

"Wolves." *National Geographic,* February 1907, 145–47.

Wood, Ginny Hill. "Wilderness Camp." *The Alaska Sportsman,* November 1953, 20–24.

Worster, Donald. *Nature's Economy: A History of Ecological Ideas.* Cambridge: Cambridge University Press, 1977.

Wright, George M., Joseph S. Dixon, and Ben H. Thompson. *Fauna of the National Parks of the United States: A Preliminary Survey of Faunal Relations in National Parks.* Fauna Series No. 1. Washington, D.C.: GPO, National Park Service, 1930.

Wright, George M. and Ben H. Thompson. *Fauna of the National Parks of the United States: Wildlife Management in the National Parks.* Fauna Series No. 2. Washington, D.C.: GPO, National Park Service, 1934.

Wright, R. Gerald. *Wildlife Research and Management in the National Parks.* Urbana: University of Illinois Press, 1992.

Young, Stanley P. *The Wolf in North American History.* Caldwell, ID: Caxton Printers, 1946.

Young, Stanley P., and Edward A. Goldman. *The Wolves of North America.* Washington, D.C.: The American Wildlife Institute, 1944.

Young, Stanley P., and Hartley H. T. Jackson. *The Clever Coyote.* Harrisburg, PA: Stackpole, 1951.

Zepp, Fred R. "America's Longest War: The Battle with the Wolves." *Outdoor Life*, May 1948, 40–41, 118–20.

Zimen, Erik. *The Wolf: A Species in Danger.* Translated by Eric Mosbacher. New York: Delacorte Press, 1981; Munich: Meyster Verlag GmbH, 1978.

Index

Timothy Rawson is a member of the teaching faculty at Alaska Pacific University. He has had articles published in *Alaska History, International Educator, The Northern Review* and has presented papers at numerous history conferences in the United States and Canada. Rawson's research interests include twentieth century social history, environmental history, and the history of the American West, and of Latin America. As a field instructor for the National Outdoor Leadership School for nearly ten years, Rawson traveled extensively through North and South America, fostering a love of adventure and for the natural beauty of the Americas.